THE RETURN OF NAT TURNER

THE RETURN OF Nat Turner

HISTORY, LITERATURE, AND CULTURAL POLITICS IN SIXTIES AMERICA

ALBERT E. STONE

The University of Georgia Press

Athens & London

© 1992 by the University of
Georgia Press
Athens, Georgia 30602

All rights reserved

Designed by Richard Hendel
Set in Century Expanded

The paper in this book meets
the guidelines for permanence
and durability of the Committee
on Production Guidelines for
Book Longevity of the Council
on Library Resources.

Printed in the United States of America
96 95 94 93 92
5 4 3 2 1

Library of Congress Cataloging in
Publication Data
Stone, Albert E.
 The return of Nat Turner : history,
literature, and cultural politics in sixties
America / Albert E. Stone.
 Includes bibliographical references
and index.
 ISBN 0-8203-1363-7 (alk. paper)
 1. United States—Civilization—1945–
2. United States—Civilization—Afro-
American influences.   3. United States—
History—1961–1963—Historiography.
4. United States—History—1963–1969—
Historiography.   5. Turner, Nat, 1800?–
1831, in fiction, drama, poetry, etc.
I. Title.
E169.12.S84   1992
973.923'072—dc20   90-28346
                          CIP

British Library Cataloging in Publication
Data available

For

David M. Potter,

friend and premiere historian,

for

Arthur Burr Darling,

who first opened the doors,

and for

Jonathan Walton,

colleague extraordinaire

Cultures are dramatic conversations about things which matter to their participants.

—Habits of the Heart

Contents

Preface / xiii

Acknowledgments / xvii

Chapter 1
The Return of Nat Turner in Sixties America / 1

Chapter 2
William Styron's Meditation on History / 38

Chapter 3
The Public Controversy:
Before and After *Ten Black Writers Respond* / 101

Chapter 4
Other Images, Other Imaginations / 177

Chapter 5
New Historical Explanations:
Paradigms and Popularizers / 246

Chapter 6
Newer Historical Explanations:
Culture as Resistance / 299

Chapter 7
Echoes in the Eighties / 330

Notes / 387

Appendix / 405

Index / 431

Nineteenth-century engraving of Nat Turner and his five original followers planning their revolt (Courtesy of the Library of Congress).

Nat Turner in the Clearing

Ashes, Lord—
But warm still from the fire that cheered us,
Lighted us in this clearing where it seems
Scarcely an hour ago we feasted on
Burnt pig from our tormentor's unwilling
Bounty and charted the high purpose your
Word had launched us on. And now, my comrades
Dead, or taken; your servant, pressed by the
Blood-drenched yelps of hounds, forsaken, save for
The stillness of the word that persists quivering
And breath-moist on his tongue; and these faint coals
Soon to be rushed to dying glow by the
Indifferent winds of miscarriage—What now,
My Lord? A priestess once, they say, could write
On leaves, unlock the time-bound spell of deeds
Undone. I let fall upon these pale remains
Your breath-moist word, preempt the winds, and give
Them now their one last glow, that some dark child
In time to come might pass this way and, in
This clearing, read and know.

—Alvin Aubert

Preface

Though this history of a recent cultural controversy aims to define that debate in more socially inclusive terms than theirs, previous scholars in American studies early placed me in their debt and these influences should be acknowledged. Basic arguments and assumptions in my examinations of the Nat Turner controversy—as it came to be called by journalists, academics, artists, political activists, and general readers—arise from Henry Nash Smith's *Virgin Land*, R. W. B. Lewis's *The American Adam*, and William R. Taylor's *Cavalier and Yankee*. But these fifties classics have in certain theoretical and ideological ways come under searching critique in the intervening decades. Reevaluation began during the period between 1965 and 1975, the very time William Styron's novel *The Confessions of Nat Turner* was provoking deep questions about history, literary tradition, and the nature of American culture and character.

My own involvement in these debates both within and beyond the campus began at this time. Having come to the South, my mother's native region, from New England, the land of my father's birth and education, I began teaching courses in literature and history at predominantly white Emory University and, somewhat later and more occasionally, at predominantly black Atlanta University. The excitement, confusion, and the ideological and interracial conflicts of those early seventies classroom experiences are indelibly fixed in my memory, as perhaps they are in some of my readers'. They have been revived and revised by reading Taylor Branch's *Parting the Waters: America in the King Years, 1954–1963*. Branch's magisterial grasp of detail and panorama, of character and cultural conflict, has become for me a model of historiography. The range, variety, and emotional intensity of American cultural politics as Branch recaptures them will not—cannot—be matched in this more circumscribed account of the return of Nat Turner, so that for an adequate evocation of the mood and tempo of the sixties social scene—and, especially, of later events—I must, therefore, rely upon my readers' personal recollections. The larger picture is, of course, one of confrontation. Sixties cultural politics were everywhere in portentous and often bitter ferment. At campus demonstrations and teach-ins, on marches, and in the pages of Norman Mailer's *The Armies of the Night*, in musical performances such as Jimi Hendrix's at Woodstock or Janis Ian's "Society's Child," in poetry readings, KKK parades, and countless renditions of "The Battle Hymn of the Republic" and "We Shall Overcome," Americans, black and white, young and old, articulated and acted out their passionate beliefs about war and violence, justice and order, art and politics. For younger readers, conjuring the cultural landscape around and within the Nat Turner controversy may be a more difficult task. Television documentaries such as *Eyes on the Prize*, books such as *Parting the Waters*, and movies such as *Born on the Fourth of July* and *Ashes and Embers* (to date the only black-directed film to depict the Vietnam War) can begin to shorten distances and broaden horizons.

Readers of all ages, of course, combine personal experience with ongoing education, and in this process Branch has taught me lessons about cultural history that Smith, Lewis, and Taylor could not. American historical experience must be grounded in a larger vision of culture than has been assumed or articulated by many white writers and scholars. By focusing on politics, religion, and biography, Branch demonstrates convincingly that the King years constituted an *American* cultural epoch in which white culture and black culture were equal partners but often unequal antagonists. Although issues of hegemony, domination, oppression, and prejudice inevitably appear, recent history is misunderstood unless both scholars and citizens recognize that at least two distinct cultures—ways of life, modes of belief and behavior, language and custom, politics and personality—exist in the United States and have for centuries. In particular, concepts like "subculture" obscure the force of this insight. (I do not recall Branch ever using the term. His implicit hypothesis is rather of an inclusive American culture.) Anthropologists have characterized culture as the organization of diversity rather than the replication of uniformity. Within this larger system Martin Luther King, Jr., Rosa Parks, Robert F. Kennedy, and Stanley Levinson are members, allies, and antagonists.

Such an assumption, perhaps somewhat more theoretically articulated than Branch's, lies behind the present work. Furthermore, Taylor Branch has clarified another of this book's problematic foundations. If American cultural history can be based on the belief in a single yet conflicted culture, to which and within which white culture and black culture are additions rather than superordinate or subordinate entities, a white critic like myself is able to interpret black texts and behavior as well as white experience and expression. Partiality, ignorance, and prejudice will still appear—black readers of *Parting the Waters* have doubtless detected these shortcomings in Branch—but it is my hope that the dismissive charge that I am still another white scholar tinkering with black American literature and history can be defused if I can show that, unlike William Styron or Thomas R. Gray, I am not speaking to white readers on behalf of Nat Turner or Sherley Anne Williams. Nor do I intend to speak to black readers on behalf of Styron, Eugene Genovese, or Robert Lowell. Readers of both races—as well as Americans of other cultural backgrounds and foreign readers—may judge the plausibility of this aim and the adequacy of its realization.

Acknowledgments

Particular intellectual debts and inspiration must be recognized here. I have learned much from my own contemporaries and juniors, most especially Alan Trachtenberg, John Blassingame, Janice Radway, Tony Bennett, and the late Gene Wise. Heartfelt personal as well as professional thanks go to former Emory colleagues James Harvey Young, John Juricek, Robert H. L. Wheeler, and Peter Dowell, and to others from the Atlanta years: Richard Lowitt, Roseann P. Bell, Michael Lomax, and Vincent Harding. Over the past decade here at the University of Iowa I have benefited immeasurably from the encouragement and criticism of many, including Richard P. Horwitz, John Raeburn, the late Jonathan Walton, Thomas Lutz, Kathleen Diffley, James C. Hall, Peter Thornton, Dale Rigby, Dolly McPherson, and Kesho Scott. Invaluable expert assistance has been generously forthcoming from JoAnn Castagna, Nicholas Natanson, John Groch, Alison Kibler, and, most particularly at the project's end, Sharon E. Wood and Catron Grieves. These names must stand for the many students at Emory, Atlanta University, Iowa, and Université Paul Valéry who helped clarify my responses to Nat Turner and his legacy, as did lecture audiences at Iowa, the Midwestern American Studies Association, and Lafayette College.

Institutional support has been equally steady and generous. The University of Iowa awarded me a senior faculty fellowship in the Humanities in 1983–84 and a developmental assignment in 1987. University House and its director, Jay Semel, provided a haven of seclusion and support. Libraries and librarians from the following institutions have proved unfailingly obliging: the University of Iowa, the Library of Congress, the Schomberg Collection of the New York Public Library, Yale University, Southern Connecticut State University, and Bowdoin College.

A section of chapter 4 was first published, in different form, as "A New Version of American Innocence: Robert Lowell's *Benito Cereno*," *New England Quarterly* 45 (December 1972): 467–83. Part of chapter 1 was first published as "Literature, History, and American Culture: The *Nat Turner* Controversy Re-examined," *Crisis in the Humanities: Interdisciplinary Responses*, edited by Sara Putzell-Korab and Robert

Detweiler (Potomac, Maryland: Studia Humanitatis, 1983): 31–46. An earlier version of chapter 1 was published in *Prospects: An Annual of American Cultural Studies* 12 (New York: Cambridge University Press, 1987): 223–53.

Finally, though the three men to whom this book is dedicated have influenced me deeply in the past, they neither challenge nor replace my chief inspiration and beloved friend, Grace Woodbury Stone.

Alvin Aubert's "Nat Turner in the Clearing" is reprinted, by permission, from *South Louisiana and Selected Poems* (Grosse Pointe Farms, Mich.: Lunchroom Press, 1985). I have corrected one erratum, line 12, at the author's suggestion.

The entry on Nat Turner from the *Dictionary of American Biography*, vol. 19, is reprinted by permission of the American Council of Learned Societies.

The lines from "The Ballad of Nat Turner" are reprinted from *Angle of Ascent: New and Selected Poems*, by Robert Hayden, by permission of Liveright Publishing Corporation. Copyright 1975, 1972, 1970, 1966 by Robert Hayden.

Daniel Panger and John F. Blair, Publisher, have given permission to quote from *Ol' Prophet Nat* (1967). I am also indebted to Mr. Panger for the biographical data summarized on p. 179.

Quotations from Charles E. Silberman, *Crisis in Black and White*, copyright 1964, are reprinted by permission of Random House, Inc.

Quotations from "The Uses of History in Fiction," *Southern Literary Journal*, vol. 1 (Spring 1969), are reprinted with the permission of the editors.

Permission to reprint passages from William Styron, *The Confessions of Nat Turner*, copyright 1966, 1967 has been granted by Random House, Inc.

Permission to reprint passages from William Styron, *This Quiet Dust & Other Writings*, copyright 1953, 1961, 1962, 1963, 1964, 1965, 1968, 1972, 1974, 1975, 1976, 1977, 1980, 1981, 1982 has been granted by Random House, Inc.

1

The Return of Nat Turner in Sixties America

One of the less publicized public events of that annus mirabilis 1968 was the annual meeting of a venerable academic institution, the Southern Historical Association. Convened in New Orleans was a group of intellectuals knit together by a common preoccupation with the southern past. Prominent among these were C. Vann Woodward, arguably America's most eminent historian of the South, and three famous novelists, Robert Penn Warren, Ralph Ellison, and William Styron. All southerners (if Oklahoma City, Ellison's birthplace, qualifies as a southern city), they were there as participants in a panel, chaired by Woodward, on "The Uses of History in Fiction." The session took place on November 6, the day after the election of Richard Nixon and seven months after the assassination of Martin Luther King, Jr. It was probably the liveliest, best-attended event of an otherwise staid meeting of professors. The topic and the distinguished panelists generated much of the interest, but a cluster of young blacks in the audience added additional electricity. As passionately interested in the subject as those on the platform, they came chiefly to challenge Styron. It was *his* use of history in fiction upon which much of the evening's discussion devolved.

At that moment the white Virginian's name was as familiar to the public and to this audience as his older fellows', the authors of *All the King's Men* and *Invisible Man*. Just thirteen months earlier, Random House had published Styron's fourth novel, *The Confessions of Nat Turner*. In the interval, this fictional version of an 1831 slave revolt in southeastern Virginia had become a popular hit and the storm center of controversy predicted by many early reviewers. A Book-of-the-Month Club selection, *The Confessions of Nat Turner* within six months appeared in a paperback edition whose cover boasted "Pulitzer Prize Winner of the Year" and "An All-Time Best Seller." A full orchestration of ads, reviews, interviews, and feature stories spurred sales. "Major advertising . . . 75,000 first printing," *Publisher's Weekly* reported, adding as encouragement to booksellers that this "long-awaited new novel . . . is a historical novel but viewed in the context of today's headlines it seems only too contemporary."[1] On the cover of *Newsweek* and in newspapers from Boston and Charleston to Indianapolis and Fresno, Styron was hailed for his bold attempt to retell in a first-person narrative the story of a black figure and a bloody event from history.[2] He thereby raised a number of touchy social and ideological questions about American culture, past and present. Although these questions center, naturally enough, on slavery and racism, violence and revolution, they also involve converging—and diverging—assumptions about religion, sex, personal identity, and heroism. Scarcely less controversial, as subsequent events proved, are some usually more academic issues he revived: what fictional and historical narratives have in common and how they differ; what "truths" each story aims at and how these are related to "facts"; what the fiction writer's privileges and responsibilities are with respect to historical subjects including, more particularly, the past experiences of members of another race. In 1967 Styron with the help of Nat Turner—or, conversely, Nat Turner through William Styron and others—brought home anew to hundreds of thousands of Americans, white and black, the social uses—and, some would say, misuses—of history and historical fiction.

Because Styron's articulation of these often emotionally charged questions seemed imaginative, audacious, and successful, his novel was praised by *Time* magazine as "a new peak in the literature of the South."[3] Woodward himself, reviewing *The Confessions of Nat Turner* in the *New Republic*, flatly declared: "this is the most profound fictional treatment of slavery in our literature."[4] Had everyone agreed with Woodward, the noted author of *The Strange Career of Jim Crow* and *The Burden of Southern History* might not have found himself in the chair of the SHA section. For the planners of the program were well aware of different and no less vigorous reactions to Styron's book. In fact, from the first there ran through the communications network, which on one level *is* American culture, an undercurrent of strong disagreement over Styron's assumptions, aims, and achievements. This opposition initially surfaced in such disparate places as the *New York Times* (in a review by Wilfred Sheed), the *New Leader* (in a review by

Albert Murray, the black novelist), then later abroad and anonymously, in *Blackwood's*.[5]

But the most vehement and comprehensive attack upon Styron and the white cultural institutions heaping him with plaudits and profits came in the spring of 1968. Fresh in the minds of many in the SHA audience was the recent publication of John H. Clarke's *William Styron's Nat Turner: Ten Black Writers Respond*.[6] The contributors to this collection were less well known than James Baldwin, John Hope Franklin, and Saunders Redding, all well-known black intellectuals who joined in the early favorable reception of Styron's story. The ten black writers were a diverse group, generally younger, angrier, and more militant. They included novelists, journalists, editors, librarians, literary critics, and historians, as well as one political scientist and a psychiatrist—a broad representation indeed of a new black intelligentsia. Because their various disagreements with Styron's version and vision of history were sharp and often couched intemperately, they were at first dismissed by some (mostly white) readers as extremist black power ideologues, to be lumped with Stokely Carmichael, Rap Brown, and Eldridge Cleaver as racists and supporters of the current politics of "burn, baby, burn." Hence when certain questioners from the audience invoked the ten black writers, it was scarcely surprising Styron stoutly repudiated their assertions.

What happened in New Orleans mirrored, therefore, other confrontations occurring in cities and political meetings as well as in classrooms, libraries, and the press. In returning Nat Turner to wide public consciousness, Styron resurrected an actual and symbolic presence whose historical power persisted. It is understandable that *The Confessions of Nat Turner* was the center of attention at the historians' session. It had already become the most talked-about book of the past season. In longer perspective, too, Styron's book was the most controversial novel of its tempestuous decade. To map this history of reception will be one aim of this book. More important a task, however, will be to explore the broader cultural terrain—literary, social, historical, and ideological—surrounding and informing Styron's story. To study this complex interplay between texts and contexts, between authors and their diverse audiences, and thus to connect the elite disciplines of history and literature to more popular social activities, inevitably leads back into nineteenth-century America as well as forward into the 1970s and to our own day. For only by locating the charged figure of the rebellious slave in previous and subsequent imaginations can we identify the continuities and changes in the consciousness and cultural values that characterized sixties Americans as they confronted this portion of their pasts.

The SHA as Social Occasion and Cultural Confrontation

Woodward did not open the evening by directly mentioning these extramural aspects of the academic occasion. Instead, he precipitated discussion at the level of what Styron called "very intelligent abstractions." He reminded the audience, first, of the ancestry history and fiction share. As "historical siblings" born together in the eighteenth century, both modes of narrative "sprang from a common parentage of story tellers. Both grew up together in an environment permeated with the growing historical consciousness of western man."[7] Though twentieth-century historians have frequently repudiated this belletristic heritage by claiming kinship with social scientists, they have never developed, Woodward claimed, the specialized vocabulary or distinctive concepts and methodologies characteristic of a science. Properly speaking, history is a mixture of art and human science. This means that "if the historian feels free to borrow concepts and insights from the psychologist, the analyst, the sociologist in his efforts to explain human motivation and behavior, the novelist is equally free to use the same resources in doing much the same thing" (59). Furthermore, another basic characteristic unites novelist and historian:

> An historian stands in no less need of imagination than the novelist . . . if anything, he needs rather more. There are firm rules, of course, about what his discipline permits and forbids him to do with his imagination. He cannot, for example, as the novelist can, invent characters, invent motives for his characters. I certainly have no wish to relax those rules or to confuse or blur the distinction between the historian and the novelist. But over the years . . . I have learned to appreciate more and more how much we have in common in our uses of the past, our interest in it, our concerns with it. (59)

Awareness of these distinctions and convergences, Woodward continued, has been especially keen among modern southern writers. Thus William Styron, the youngest present in a distinguished artistic line of descent, quite naturally made his new novel both a fictionalized reimagining of the life and death of Nat Turner and itself a "meditation on history," a phrase Woodward quoted from the "Author's Note" prefacing *The Confessions of Nat Turner*. The presence of an explicit authorial announcement underlines Styron's serious historicist intentions. In exploring the antebellum history of his native state, Woodward added, Styron comes "very close indeed, given the license of the novelist, to doing what the historian does in reconstructing the past" (59). Characteristically southern in another respect, too, is Styron's distrust of abstractions. This outlook he shares with Warren and Ellison. Out of devotion to the particular human experience as well as to larger "myths, both Southern and Northern," Styron and Ellison find a common theme in "the memory of slavery and the hope of emancipation" (60).

Woodward's embrace of fiction as history's time-honored partner and his flattering references to Styron were themes picked up by the three novelists in their own opening remarks. As the first to speak, Robert Penn Warren insisted upon the separateness and, for many humane purposes, the superiority of his art over its historical sibling. He assimilated history and fiction by pointing out that the historian as the maker of narratives constructs an imagined world of words just as the novelist does. However, the historian creates only within limits, for the knowledge generated about the past results from uncovering external facts about and behind that world. The novelist, on the other hand, lays "claim to *know* the *inside* of his world for better or for worse. He mostly fails, but he claims to know the inside of his characters, the undocumentable inside" (61). As artificer of moral and psychological reality, therefore, the novelist reimagines a personal past, whereas the historian, confined by the documentary imperative to the outside of experience, has as his proper territory "the racial past, the national past, the sectional past, all kinds of the past" (60–61). Warren underlined his preference for the novelist's narrow but bottomless domain by quoting an artistic credo: "Either art is a pure irreducible activity, one that provides its own peculiar content, its own morality—it includes itself in its own meaning; or art is, on the other hand, a pleasanter form of presenting facts, meanings and truths pertaining to other realms of reality like history, sociology, morality, where they exist in purer and fuller form" (61). Although the materials of fiction frequently derive from history, Warren added, "their factuality gives them no special privilege, as contrasted with imagined materials" (61–62). Nevertheless, historical materials often possess great social potency, for they enter the novel bearing "all the recalcitrances and the weights and the passions of the real world" (62). Hence it sometimes happens that history as the subject of art overwhelms its medium. "There is," he warned, "always a point where the exigencies and the pains of the materials of fiction or drama or poetry are too great to be absorbed. This recalcitrancy, which is the basis of contention between the form and the content of literature, can become too great" (62). Thus tensions between documentary history and fictional art arise that involve not simply intransigent material but the author's and reader's "practical commitment in relation to it" (62). In making this point Warren aptly described, without directly saying so, the situation already engulfing his fellow novelist.

Ellison, too, aimed his opening observations in the direction of the white Virginian seated beside him. Taking a different tack from Warren's, he pointed out that "lies" rather than "truths" are what history and fiction really have in common. Both activities owe much not just to eighteenth-century Europe but to early nineteenth-century America and its tradition of the tall tale. "I would suggest that historians are responsible liars. Liars are not bad people; I am by profession a liar" (62). History, however, lies *officially*. So as a cultural activity it is more powerful and dangerous than fiction.

> I can't, here in New Orleans, fail to point out that so much of American history has turned upon the racial situation in the country. . . . Our written history has been as "official" as any produced in any communist country—only in a democratic way: individuals write it instead of committees. Written history is to social conduct and social arrangements in this country very much like the relationship between myth and ritual. And myth justifies and "explains" facts. . . . But too often history has been an official statement, and it has danced attendance to political arrangements. (63)

Because, socially speaking, the novel is a less sacred form of "lying," the novelist is freer to manipulate reality in ways that oppose official history "by re-arranging experience . . . to tell us in small ways the symbolic significance of what actually happened" (64). But this strategy succeeds, Ellison asserted, only if the novelist takes pains never to confuse his role with the historian's.

> The moment you say something explicit about history in a novel, everybody's going to rise up and knock the Hell out of you, because they suspect that you are trying to take advantage of a form of authority which is sacred. History is sacred, you see, and no matter how false to actual events it might be. But fiction is anything but sacred. By fact and by convention fiction is a projection from one man's mind, of one man's imagination . . . And through that imaginative integration he attempts to seize the abiding circumstances, the abiding problems, the abiding and time-tested forms of humanity—heroism, truth and failure and love and death—all of the ramifications of those experiences which make us human. (64)

Ellison concluded with another observation aimed apparently at Styron. Referring to *All the King's Men* and its central character, Willie Stark (who in some but not all respects bears a striking resemblance to Huey Long), Ellison noted that Warren "wrote about a great American politician who governed his state and refused to intrude into the area of the historian . . . because he was canny enough to realize that he could never get *that* particular man into fiction. And yet, I believe that he did use that man to bring into focus within his own mind many, many important facts about power, politics and class and loyalty. So today we possess an essence of that man presented in a highly imaginative, moving and enduring way, without the novelist having taken anything away from the man" (64–65).

Styron, of course, had deliberately elected not to imitate *All the King's Men*. His protagonist from history is explicitly named Nat Turner. Most of his other characters, too, have historical prototypes. Nevertheless, when it came his turn to speak, he avoided responding directly to his colleagues' comments. Instead, he addressed what he took to be the basic issue of the meeting—"the freedom of movement and choice any good novelist must exercise when writing historical fiction" (65). If the present-day American writer is to be successful in rescuing historical fiction from its discredited status as mere titillation for female readers, Styron said, he must neither evade controversial historical subjects nor tie himself slavishly to the specific data found in historical documents. Like Warren, Styron offered the audience a model for his own brand of creative historicism. In *The Historical Novel*, he pointed out, Georg Lukács, the great Hungarian Marxist critic, treats Sir Walter Scott as *the* exemplary historian-novelist. By a careful choice of theme, characters, and setting, Scott was able to move around freely yet responsibly inside a host of complex historical subjects. His steady aim in every instance was "to reproduce the spirit of an age faithfully and authentically" (66). But emulating Scott today is no simple matter. In fact, "it would require a particularly happy accident for all the well-known and attested actions of a familiar historical figure to correspond to the purposes of literature" (66–67). Hence careful selections must always be made. In doing so responsibly, the historical novelist must be granted great latitude. "What matters in the novel," he quoted Lukács as saying,

> is fidelity in the reproduction of the material foundations of the life of a given period, its manners and the feelings and thoughts derived from these. This means . . . that the novel is much more closely bound to the specifically historical, individual moments of a period than is drama. But this never means being tied to any particular historical facts. On the contrary, the novelist must be at liberty to treat these as he likes . . . if he is to reproduce the much more complex and ramifying totality with historical faithfulness. From the standpoint of the historical novel, too, it is always a matter of chance whether an actual historical fact, character or story will lend itself to the particular method by which a great novelist conveys his historical faithfulness. (67)

If by invoking the impressive name of Lukács Styron hoped to fend off attacks from the assembled listeners, his strategy was only partly successful. Yet he was able to stake out a position already endorsed by Warren and Woodward: "a writer's responsibility is not to the dead baggage of facts, but to the unfettered and replenishing power of his own imagination" (67). In subsequently defending this conviction and his own practice of historical fiction, Styron returned repeatedly to this point, not only in New Orleans but in other arenas as well: "It's simply to say that with a certain absolute boldness, a novelist dealing with history has to be able to say that such and such a fact is totally irrelevant, and to Hell with the person who insists that it has any real, utmost relevance" (75).

Though Styron's statement had the ring of truth to some listeners, it did not go unchallenged in this den of historians. Yet neither Woodward nor his fellow scholars raised the sharpest questions. Rather it was Ellison who, in a manner at once conciliatory and probing, led the attack. Conceding freely (and perhaps disingenuously) that he had not read *The Confessions of Nat Turner*, though he had read *Ten Black Writers Respond*, Ellison confessed also that his own lack of militancy disqualified him from speaking for other blacks. "I don't cuss out white folks enough," he noted wryly, though "I cuss them out in my own ways" (74). Nonetheless, he reiterated his conviction that "facts are a tyranny for the novelist," since "you don't have the freedom to snatch any and everybody, and completely recreate them. This is why you must lie and disguise a historical figure" (74). Addressing the specific instance of *The Confessions of Nat Turner*, Ellison turned to his neighbor: "Bill, I would suggest that whether you like the dissonance you've picked up, you've written a very powerful novel, and it's very self-evident. . . . Just leave history alone" (74).

Styron was in no mood to "leave history alone." After the floor was opened for discussion the first question gave him his opportunity. "I'd like to know about the fact that Nat Turner was married—didn't that fit into your novel?" (78). Styron's reply was instantaneous and categorical: "in the evidence which was available to me when some years ago I began to collect the few basic materials to write this book, there was no evidence which told me he had such a wife" (78). This failed to satisfy or deter his questioner: "Didn't Thomas Gray's *Confessions* say that?" (78). "No," Styron shot back, "if you read the *Confessions* yourself . . . this is one of the amazing things about it. He mentions all the rest of his family, but mentions no wife" (78–79). Then modifying the artistic credo just voiced, Styron asserted: "if I had been given any kind of substantial evidence that he had a wife, then as a novelist I would have felt compelled to create a wife for him" (79).

There were, then, limits to this novelist's "absolute boldness" in disregarding specific data, which he likened derisively to "the fuzz that collects in the tops of dirty closets" (75). Certain facts do constitute compelling historical *and* artistic evidence when derived from what the writer himself deems a reliable documentary source. In welcoming

Thomas R. Gray's *The Confessions of Nat Turner* to his aid, Styron surprised no one present. After all, his novel's title was borrowed from Gray's twenty-one-page pamphlet, which purports to be a faithful record of Nat Turner's confessions as taken down in Jerusalem jail by a white Virginia lawyer.[8] Furthermore, the opening pages of Styron's story consisted of selected passages from Gray, who is himself an actor in the opening and closing scenes. In addition, many in this audience would doubtless recall from Styron's author's note his reference to "the single significant contemporary document concerning this insurrection"—clearly Gray. Though in the ensuing debate this claim would prove exaggerated, Styron had indeed rescued Gray along with Nat Turner from popular, if not scholarly, oblivion. In November 1831, when the original *Confessions* appeared, shortly after Turner's execution, as many as fifty thousand copies were sold, thus spreading early word of the revolt across the South and nation. Now, after 136 years of neglect, reprints of Gray were, thanks to Styron, once again figuring prominently in the historical career of Nat Turner.

Nonetheless, it was curious that the first questioner, like others among Styron's antagonists, so zealously invoked Gray's authority. One of the controversy's cruxes was the moral status and historical standing of a white writer speaking for as well as about a dead black figure from the past. Both Gray in 1831 and Styron in 1967 occupied that position and asserted that right. Both thereby reaped profits, and both exerted ideological influence over the minds of their respective American publics. Yet Gray's authority as a historical source went unimpeached that evening. Not until several years later in *The Southampton Slave Revolt of 1831* did the historian Henry I. Tragle carefully examine Gray's account in light of other contemporary sources and, in the process, criticize Styron for not having bothered to do the same.[9]

Meanwhile, Gray and the nagging matter of Nat Turner's wife returned in a second attack by Styron's interrogator. Referring to Styron's Nat Turner, he asked, "Is Margaret Whitehead, in the evidence, completely obsessed in his mind?" (79). Though clumsily phrased, this loaded question was one of several that mixed issues of historical fact, authorial fancy, and ideological interpretation. Simply as fact, Margaret Whitehead, as any reader of Styron or Gray would recall, was an actual person who lived on a farm near Turner's master, Joseph Travis. All sources agree in identifying her as the sole person Nat

Turner himself killed among the fifty-seven whites murdered in the three-day revolt. Though Gray neither mentions nor implies any other connection between Turner and the seventeen-year-old white woman, the situation's psychological and sexual possibilities are richly exploited in Styron's novel, which explains the novelist's bold reply: "Margaret Whitehead is part of my fictional imagination. I have no apologies for her" (79). Having once admitted translating an actual historical figure into a full-blown fictional character, Styron felt no need to discuss the question of Nat Turner being "completely obsessed" with her. Yet many of the audience grasped the black questioner's point: had not Styron created in Margaret Whitehead a literary, psychosexual, and cultural characterization directly counter to the historical evidence?

A notable aspect of the Southampton slave revolt is that, although women and children were the principal victims of black vengeance, not one act of sexual violence against white women was reported. Nor did Nat Turner confess to the court or imply to Gray any sexual motive behind his or his followers' deeds. Indeed, the court records indicate that the white judges and lawyers never even hinted at such motivations. Thus there appears to the questioner a striking—and suspicious— divergence between fictional and historical motivations. Yet when challenged on this point, Styron was unwilling to identify any larger historical truth that, in line with Lukács, might justify such treatment. When pressed by the first questioner to state "the reason for being for *The Confessions of Nat Turner*," Styron, sensing the hostility, evaded the whole issue: "It's so majestic a question that I don't think I'm able to answer it" (79).

Pointed exchanges like these disclosed diametrically different definitions and explanations of the violent historical event and its chief actors. Styron's right to respect, alter, or ignore documentary evidence, in line with his announced artistic creed, was challenged by several blacks in the audience. These questioners, acting perhaps as spokesmen for other black readers, historians, and literary critics, were clearly eager to defend (or redefine) Nat Turner in terms of "what he actually represents to black people" (80). They believed this southern novelist had appropriated Nat Turner and his revolt, reconceiving the man and rewriting the event strictly in white terms. For them, the central question was the propriety and legitimacy of Styron's decision to assume Nat Turner's own voice and point of view.

In debating particular facts and broader dimensions of the past, both Styron and his questioners treated women as both a specific and symbolic issue. For Styron, Margaret Whitehead easily shed her minor but distinct historical role as victim to assume a larger symbolic place in the "undocumentable inside" of a slave's reimagined consciousness. This translation apparently necessitated Styron's denying either fictional or historical status to the black slave's alleged wife. Her absence, it seemed, became necessary in order for certain moral, sexual, and spiritual dimensions of Turner's experience to be fictionally presented as if historically true. That at least was the way it appeared to Styron's black antagonists. For them, Margaret Whitehead's name became shorthand for a cluster of nonhistorical, private, sexual, and probably racist preoccupations in Styron and many of his white readers. Whitehead is one of several white women about whom Styron's protagonist (again, with no historical justification) has masturbatory fantasies. To further complicate the sexual-racial theme bothering Styron's questioners, the fictional Nat Turner's past also contains one homosexual encounter but no heterosexual experiences in the slave community. These are, it was pointed out, the wholly imaginary activities ascribed to an ascetic Baptist preacher known to his contemporaries and to posterity as Ol' Prophet Nat. Hence the second questioner's bitter remark: "I heard Warren say a few minutes ago that fact can destroy, that fact can be deadly. I contend that imagination and lying can also be deadly and can also destroy" (80).

It soon turned out that this second questioner and Styron had already met at a similar symposium at Harvard Summer School. Styron suddenly recognized him and addressed him (in questionable taste) as "my bête noir." What exasperated Styron was the young man's accusation that he had deliberately catered to white fantasies and phobias in order to sell his book: "whites *wanted* to read that Nat Turner was not a strong, black revolutionary figure, but that he had certain sexual drives that drove him on" (81). The second questioner did acknowledge that Styron's Nat Turner, in line with Gray's history, "was probably a preacher or something, who had some vision about killing white folk" (80). But he also recalled what he had inferred from Styron's earlier remarks at Cambridge, "that the white woman was a higher symbol or goal for the black man or the black slave" (80). This he refused to see as anything but a white lie against history.

In leveling these charges the questioner invoked the ten black writers. In rebuttal, Styron countered by citing Eugene Genovese, a prominent white historian (and a Marxist) who had already endorsed Styron's depiction of the black rebel in *The Confessions of Nat Turner:*

> I think he pointed out, at least to my satisfaction, that if you will read the evidence—if you read the crude evidence of Nat Turner and his insurrection, and you can read it in twenty minutes—you will get the impression, and any rational person will get the impression, when he is finished, of a ruthless and perhaps psychotic fanatic, a religious fanatic who, lacking any plan or purpose—admittedly, because it is in the testimony, lacking any plan or purpose—takes five or six rather bedraggled followers and goes off on a ruthless, directionless, aimless forty-eight-hour rampage of total destruction, in which the victims are, by a large majority, women and little children. (82)

"But *white*," the young black rejoined. At that the exchange, heated by Styron's derogatory characterization of Gray's Nat Turner, grew angry and pointed.

STYRON: No. Wait a minute. This is the crude evidence; this is what Lukács would say. These are facts. Deal with them. [. . .] this is the impression you would get. A deranged—[. . .]

SECOND QUESTIONER: It may be a white impression. [. . .]

STYRON: I don't think so. What Genovese was generous enough to grant me, in my dealings with this man, was that I supplied him with the motivation. I gave him a rationale. I gave him all of the confusions and desperations, troubles, worries. [. . .]

SECOND QUESTIONER: He was a slave, and that gave him enough reason. [. . .]

STYRON: All right.

SECOND QUESTIONER: You didn't have to create anything for him. He saw brothers and sisters killed all around him. He saw families being broken up.

STYRON: The evidence . . .

SECOND QUESTIONER: I notice your other point, that these were kind slavemasters. It doesn't matter how kind they were; they were slavemasters. [. . .]

STYRON: Well, then, we're at an impasse, my friend, because you say it's one way, and I say it's another.
SECOND QUESTIONER: Yes, but every time we meet, you always jibe and say that I miss your point. You ought to stop lying.
WOODWARD: Are there other people who want to ask questions?
(83–84)

Though other questions were asked and answered, discussion never quite reached the same pitch of simplifying, clarifying acrimony. Once, for example, Styron sharply disagreed with two other questioners about another southern historical fiction and Pulitzer Prize winner. *Gone with the Wind*, he declared, is "a remarkable novel, precisely because this little woman from Atlanta has a fire of an imagination, which captured her and somehow allowed her to breathe some kind of miraculous spirit through and around the rather threadbare facts about antebellum Georgia" (84). This praise brought another ironic rejoinder from an older black man: "as long as we call ourselves black and white, then even if we gain black power, unless we censor that movie I'm sure all the white folks will go to it. They love that myth" (85).

These words were soon to prove prophetic. Early in 1969, movie censorship became more than a vague threat in Styron's case. Shortly after his novel became a bestseller, the author was offered a contract by Twentieth-Century Fox for a film adaptation of *The Confessions of Nat Turner*. Plans had been advanced so far as to involve mention of Ossie Davis and Ruby Dee in leading roles when news of the project became known. A storm of surprising virulence ensued. The prospect of a black boycott with pickets and demonstrations became—at least in Styron's mind—prime reasons for the project's cancellation, although rising costs and persistent questions about historical inaccuracies in Styron's account of the past were also mentioned.[10] If "they love that myth" indeed describes the appeal of *Gone with the Wind* to white readers and moviegoers, it seems equally plausible that the altered atmosphere of 1969 produced quite another set of expectations and responses from a new generation of readers and potential moviegoers of both races.

What disturbed black readers here in New Orleans and elsewhere was not simply the prospect of Hollywood giving worldwide currency to what was for blacks an inaccurate and demeaning picture of a slave hero from history, but more broadly, the whole system of commercial manipulation of racial myths and stereotypes embedded in historical events and lives. Ellison was quick to point out this power of popular myths. When asked about his own oblique reference to Marcus Garvey in the character of Ras the Destroyer in *Invisible Man*, he replied, "I wouldn't dare to tell the truth about him because it would destroy the same myth, and this myth is a valuable myth" (88). The implication was clear: myths are essential ingredients in the creation of both literary and political heroes.

Implications and Assumptions

Formulations like Ellison's and the older black questioner's take for granted firm boundaries between fact and fiction. Such assumptions were not necessarily shared by other speakers, however. Perhaps because of such fundamental differences, no clear consensus emerged at the end of this lively exchange among historians, novelists, and representatives of the reading public. Though some may have wanted or expected it, no final summary was offered by Woodward or by one of the other panelists. In hindsight, however, several social and cultural issues emerged with clarity from this vigorous scholarly exchange. More than two decades later, these issues call, with still potent urgency, for further analysis.

It is impossible to overlook the mixture of genuine intellectual concern and strong emotional involvement displayed by many at this meeting. Even the silent majority of convening historians appeared deeply interested in the wide-ranging and at times heated dialogue. Immediate social relevance was clearly attributed to fictional narratives like Styron's, which treat familiar yet frequently undiscussed experiences such as slavery and slave revolts, and which thereby articulate deeply shared but also deeply divided belief systems. The year 1968—its spring violence, summer riots, and autumn marches—and the urban southern setting doubtless had much to do with these recognitions. So, too, did the presence of articulate artists, a noted scholar, and an audience of responsive readers and questioners. Whatever the causes, further explorations of the return of Nat Turner must model themselves on this occasion of cultural dialogue in which relatively esoteric ideas were passionately debated by both academic and nonacademic persons.

Another dimension of this debate relevant to larger cultural issues is the oddly divided allegiances and attachments shown to the institutions of history and fiction. Some in the room, including the blacks, seemed fearful of the social influence and cultural status of literature. These individuals appeared to trust history, even though, like Ellison, they acknowledge its dangerous powers. Others, including perhaps many historians, seemed awed by elite literature's prestige and power. By their silence as well as through Woodward's remarks, some historians at least appeared willing to grant historical novelists the freedom and authority so confidently claimed by Warren, Styron, and (to a lesser degree) Ellison. To these professional historians, literature (even in the fictional mode most closely linked to their own field) merited the "sacred" status that Ellison accorded history. If other evidence corroborates these impressions, what do they reveal about the ways common cultural attitudes are acquired (or repudiated) by different subcultural groups? Are, for example, schoolteachers and librarians likely to support these respectful historians?

To be sure, these speculations rest, in part, on the shaky ground of silence. Besides the usual considerations of afterdinner lethargy and unfamiliarity with specific texts, many in the audience were probably silenced by the unaccustomed and unsettling presence of the vociferous amateurs in their midst. Enlarging the social arena in which previously esoteric subjects are discussed brings into public awareness new faces, voices, and points of view. A crucial question to be investigated further is, therefore, the cogency and scope of Ellison's concluding observation: "What I am suggesting is that *everybody* reads now. *Everybody* is American whether they call themselves separatists, black separatists, secessionists or what not. And everybody is saying: Damn it, tell it like *I* think it is. [A]nd this is a real problem for the novelist" (90).

As the discussion wore down, the ramifications of Ellison's remark became clearer, not only for novelists like Styron but also for historians of slavery. As the historians sat largely quiet, Styron found himself driven by hostile questioners to revise his previous statements about historicism and historical fiction. In the process of defending himself against a new and critical readership of blacks, he seemed to distance himself from history itself and take refuge in the citadel of art. In fact, he ended by making even more sweeping claims than Warren or Woodward for the transcendent status of works of literature. Without specifically including his own novel in this company, he declared of great historical fictions: "there are works . . . which do exist outside of history, which gain their power from history, to be sure, which are fed by a passionate comprehension of what history does to people and to things, but which have to have other levels of understanding, and have to be judged by other levels of understanding. It may be that in our history, which can be so valuable, we lost sight of the ineffable othernesses which go to make a work of art" (72).

This represents a significant limitation on the loyalty to historical sources voiced in the Author's Note to *The Confessions of Nat Turner*. It suggests the need to examine other *obiter dicta* made by Styron on different occasions and in various contexts, and to juxtapose them against his own novel as an extended statement about history and "ineffable othernesses." Without according this author or his bestseller a more privileged status in the unfolding discussion of slave revolts than various publics did at the time, we must consider carefully both the rhetoric and the content of Styron's historicism as deployed in fictional contexts and before various audiences.

One perspective from which to assess Styron's dual role as author and public polemicist is Ralph Ellison's. Speaking more for himself than for fellow blacks, Ellison questioned Styron's recourse to "ineffable othernesses." Instead, he proposed that historical novelists take a new step deeper into, not away from, history. Americans of all races and regions, he observed, "have reached a great crisis in American history, and we are now going to have a full American history. . . . We're beginning to go back and to evaluate those realities of American historical experience which were ruled out officially" (68). Then he sketched the shape of a new American history as it might be re-created in fictional forms responsive to black experiences and consciousness. "Part of this is legend. Part of this is myth. But so much of it . . . is what actually happened, happened to them. And if official history, if conscious historians do not take cognizance of this experience, then what a critic like Lukács says has very little validity." Then he continued:

> Much of it is not in the history textbooks. . . . But somehow, through our Negro American oral tradition and through the

names given to children and to public institutions . . . these reminders of the past as *Negroes* recalled it found existence and were passed along. Historical figures continued to live in stories of and theories about the human and social dynamics of slavery. . . . Assertions of freedom and revolts were recalled along with triumphs of labor in the fields and on the dance floor; feats of eating and drinking and of fornication, of religious conversion and physical endurance, and of artistic and athletic achievements. . . . This record exists in oral form and it constitutes the internal history of values by which my people lived even as they were being forced to accommodate themselves to those forces and arrangements of society that were sanctioned by official history. (68–69)

Fiction, Ellison concluded, is, has been, and must continue to be "involved with serious historical and personal matters" (70). In this ongoing enterprise, William Faulkner, despite his limitations, provides a model for such involvements. Through characters like Sam Fathers and Lucas Beauchamp the great Mississippi novelist "was mainly involved in those things which historians would not talk about, and this is one of the important roles which fiction has played, especially the fiction of southern writers: it has tried to tell that part of the human truth which we could not accept or face up to in much historical writing because of social, racial, and political considerations" (70).

In their summations, then, Styron and Ellison exhibit more differences than Woodward originally attributed to them. Styron's engagement with both friendly fellow panelists and hostile interrogators suggests an increasingly uneasy relationship with the documentary conventions of historical discourse and the changing writer-reader relationships emerging in sixties America. His historicism, as expressed on this occasion at least, is shaped by an artist's defensive sense of autonomy and authority; it finally draws a sharp line between history as documented description of concrete past experiences and history as the vision of a "complex and ramifying totality" of truth behind concrete data. By turns cavalier and defensive toward black critics of his bold story about the black slave experience, Styron seems also unresponsive to Ellison's appeal to merge official and folk history.

To the black novelist, on the other hand, popular and textbook history really matter. No matter how false to the everyday experiences and emotions of oppressed persons like black Americans, official history is constrained by the documentary imperative that it exploits. "Facts" can be made to confirm the status quo; they may also be manipulated to expose previous lies and silences. Novelists who recognize and would use history's power must devise new tactics in the battle to make fictional "truth" an instrument of both social and artistic power. If they wish to participate in the contemporary political struggle to liberate the oppressed (a motive Ellison assumes Styron shares), fiction writers must deploy their "lying" (that is, their symbolizing) imaginations upon new historical subjects. By all sorts of devices—including legends and myths, displacements and condensations, jokes and tall tales—they must invite into their narratives the disguised figures from official history, as they must also recapture forgotten or unknown people from the past. Thereby they can challenge official explanations and silences. Ironic and conciliatory toward both his white co-panelists and the black members of his audience, Ellison stressed these same qualities in his historicism. Lies, masks, and symbols are this historical novelist's weapons for simultaneously exploding and confirming the sanctity of history in a multiracial culture.

Toward a Transactional Theory of Texts and Other Occasions

This account of a not-so-ordinary academic evening in New Orleans offers a suggestive introduction not only to the return of Nat Turner in 1967–68 but perhaps also to what his revolt represents in other situations and imaginations. The value of the SHA begins with its being an actual event. Despite its formalized, brief, and inconclusive nature, the meeting dramatically enacted certain attitudes toward the past in terms that underline and often transcend the particular moment. Furthermore, the actors were socially if not always individually identifiable; they included the well known and the unknown. In contrast to a representative group of American historians in their annual professional ritual, the three noted novelists were unusual and atypical. They appeared under the dual guise of outsider and honored guest. The anonymous and largely passive audience—predominantly white and male—was somewhat unusual for 1968 in containing a small and vociferous group of blacks whose professional or amateur standing was not clearly established. Five or ten years earlier, these blacks, even if they had been historians teaching at Ellison's alma mater Tuskegee, would probably not have been present. Custom, if not law, had to some extent been broken.

The episode, however, is not simply a sixties scene and context. As a dramatic display of contemporary American attitudes about literature, history, and the southern past, the session can be read itself as a text. This is possible—indeed, necessary—on two levels. First, "The Uses of History in Fiction" is preserved—and thus enlarged in social significance—as an actual text, published in *Southern Literary Journal* in the spring of 1969. Like other historical documents, this text is not without its ambiguities. Four of the speakers are identified though the four questioners from the audience are not. Was this usual procedure when sessions of this professional group were recorded for publication? In a concluding postscript, Woodward and the three novelists, together with the executive secretary of the Southern Historical Association, are thanked "for permission to record and transcribe the foregoing." The "we" who thank them are not named though presumably they are editors of the journal. Here the phrase "record and transcribe" is unclear. Questions arise about other speakers who, or additional remarks that, may have been edited out. Readers who wonder if this thirty-two-page record contains everything said during more than two hours of debate may question the text's ellipses. Are these merely signs of speakers' pauses, interruptions by the next speaker, or something else? Such uncertainties point to a process of production that is only partly specified. Taken together, they underscore the need for imaginative interpretation of a journal article that, neither interview nor signed essay, is a complex verbal artifact—at once historical document, dramatic script, and ideological statement.

On another level, too, the SHA session invites treatment as text. Following Clifford Geertz, Erving Goffman, and other students of social behavior, we can take the words and gestures of these eight men before the Jung Hotel audience to be symbolic acts, components of a microsocial interaction. If we do so, it becomes possible to unravel and reconstruct their actions linguistically.[11] To consider social actions as language analogous to written account is more than a rhetorical ploy;

it is a method of recognizing that, as Kenneth Burke has long argued, all human communications are metaphoric, dramatic actions.[12] Communication from this perspective is always socially contextual, culturally determined, and linguistically constituted. The action-language of the SHA session exhibits this constitution through its verbal spontaneity, display of emotions, and distance from formal written discourse as well as through certain carefully articulated statements of the participants. Treating everything that transpired there as elements in an overdetermined text (overdetermined in the psychoanalytic sense of multiple causation) allows us to read the event rhetorically as part of a wider social, historical, and literary continuum. This in turn makes the actors more than individuals. As Richard H. Brown has written: "once social phenomena are envisaged as texts, it becomes possible to say not only that people speak through language, but also that language—the collective culture and consciousness—speaks through people. . . . Not merely the stylistic aspects of texts, or their specific contexts, but all human communication is fit subject for literary analysis, including such apparently concrete structures of communication as political parties, institutions, social classes, and events themselves. All are forms of symbolic communication."[13]

This textual/contextual approach to social behavior has particular utility for a cultural history such as the present project. It permits easy movement from the written texts where the controversy over Nat Turner has been inscribed ever since 1831 to actual social episodes linked to these texts such as the SHA session, the 1968 Pulitzer Prize award to *The Confessions of Nat Turner*, or the threatened boycott of a projected film version of Styron's novel. All such associated activities transmit information, feelings, and ideological appeals over the culture network operating at a given moment. Through such text-acts cultural values are simultaneously constituted, transmitted, and criticized. Each to some degree is a metaphoric utterance—whether as word, gesture, or act—expressing or implying a relationship between this message and other social and mental realities, present or past. Each is the expression not only of the individuals who act but also of the cultural institutions and subgroups that speak through these persons. Hence to treat writing and reading as social actions and social actions as texts to be interpreted is to recognize and use language as the necessary link between the structures within which we function in everyday life and the attitudes, values, and concepts by which we identify ourselves as members of a culture and its subgroups.

A second advantage derives from this employment of symbolic linguistic analysis. It avoids the kind of privileging of written documents and elite subgroups that has characterized, for example, past cultural critiques in the myth-symbol tradition—works such as R. W. B. Lewis's *The American Adam* and William R. Taylor's *Cavalier and Yankee*. As the behavior of the black questioners and Ellison's commentary both indicate, the SHA session displays and dramatizes a breaching—in fact, a double breaching—of convention and social usage.

On one hand, the black questioners mount a challenge to the traditional hegemony of white, male, literate, middle-class artists and professionals. This dominant group, as the panelists on the dais show, contains many influential southern writers and intellectuals who have long been active in the production, dissemination, and preservation of books and historical explanations that have helped define the American past.[14] Confrontation between the two groups was one of many changes taking place in sixties America. As Ellison trenchantly observed, "now you have more literate Negroes, and they are questioning themselves and . . . everything which has occurred and been written in this country" (89). These newcomers are not only questioning and denouncing but are also demanding admission to the social process of production. They are, moreover, pointing to the existence of an alternative historical and literary tradition and social process often ignored by the dominant culture.

On the other hand, William Styron too has made a breach of social convention. He has precipitated this conflict in cultural values by writing a long fictional autobiography of Nat Turner, thus interjecting his voice and imagination into territory about which the black American intellectual community feels proprietary. His first-person narrative and "meditation on history" challenges, indeed often affronts, many convictions held by black intellectuals—convictions about the nature of North American chattel slavery as well as slave resistance to it; about Nat Turner as man, myth, and martyr; about the kind of stories that can or ought to be told about such past black figures and experiences. That the intruder is a respected member of the white intelligentsia as well as an outspoken southern white liberal merely sharpens the situation's complexities and ironies.

We can imagine, through Ellison's agency and a heightened sense of historical horizons, other blacks drawn into the controversy, who find that they, too, have or had a stake in the return of Nat Turner. These often will be less educated persons, living perhaps in the rural Southeast, who along with some of their white neighbors find that family stories and songs about Ol' Prophet Nat have suddenly become a part of a wider network in the wake of Styron's success. As Ellison again points out, "there is, certainly in the Negro part of the country and in the Southern part of the country, a stream of history which is still as tightly connected with folklore and the oral tradition as official history is connected with the tall tale" (68).

Thus by identifying and interpreting the various texts and text-acts produced by or pointed to at the Southern Historical Association meeting we can begin to recover—or reconstruct—a historical domain and cultural tradition around the figure of Nat Turner. Some of the sometimes shadowy occupants of this domain are readily recognizable. On the far historical horizon are specific individuals like Nat Turner himself and his small band of co-conspirators. Others from the Virginia context of 1831 were less powerful of voice yet still possessed of public identities: the fifty-seven white victims, the rebels' captors, and the court that condemned or pardoned them. Their visibility then and today is due to the activity of frontline historians including court recorders, newspaper correspondents from Richmond, and local opportunists like Thomas R. Gray.

Then, still back in the past of the 1830s, there are other participants or bystanders whose voices are waiting to be heard. Among these are slaves who did not join Nat Turner, slaves who reportedly sided with their masters against the rebels, and the more than one hundred blacks massacred in the Revolt's aftermath. Present, too, though often impotent and unheard, are white farmers and their families terrified by reports of the sudden outbreak. Along with the citizenry of nearby counties and cities, these Virginians and North Carolinians sometimes preserve vivid memories and even memorabilia of Nat Turner. Occasionally these came to the attention of journalists and historians and so passed from the porches and firesides of the Chowan Valley into the pages of the *Atlantic Monthly*, county histories, and scholarly monographs, to be eventually distilled into history textbooks like the one Styron recalled reading as a schoolboy in Newport News. These accounts, oral and written, have in turn stimulated (and been stimulated by) the imaginations of a number of literary artists: nineteenth-century novelists like Harriet Beecher Stowe, G. P. R. James, and Mary Johnston, modern novelists like Arna Bontemps and Daniel Panger, the poets Robert Hayden and Sterling Brown, playwrights Randolph Edmonds and Paul Peters. Through these channels the name and history of Ol' Prophet Nat has been variously defined and preserved. In 1968 relatively few Americans—including Tidewater Virginians and professional historians—were familiar with these several strands of historical, literary, and folk tradition.

Though it came late in a surprisingly rich record, Styron's version of *The Confessions of Nat Turner* succeeded in stirring the consciousness of Americans, creating fresh interest in a remarkable man and event. How much of the book's reception was a reawakening of forgotten facts and how much a first encounter will remain an open question. A larger, more problematic issue is to establish, if possible, the full reach and impact of Nat Turner's return in the 1960s. Who, in fact, became aware of this slave's existence and found what significance in his life and death? By what means, through what networks of communication and criticism, and for what motives, did interest spread from the relatively circumscribed readership of the Book-of-the-Month Club to professional meetings and symposia, newspaper columns or editorials, radio or television interviews, talk shows and college syllabi? How did participants in this ramifying network eventually succeed—if they did—in arousing popular interest not only in the often-neglected subject of slave revolts but in earlier returns of Nat Turner during the decades between the 1830s and the 1960s?

As catalyst and proximate cause, Styron's *The Confessions of Nat Turner* holds, then, a plausible claim to first attention. To begin with the novelist's imaginative vision of Nat Turner is not, however, to assume the superiority of fictional over nonfictional narrative or to accord unique value to this novel within the whole imaginative literature on slavery and slave revolts. The same caveat must be repeated with respect to Thomas Gray's *Confessions*. Neither book should be taken as a measuring stick for competing fictional or historical representations of Nat Turner. Neither is a fixed pole of reference, setting terms for critical discourse and settling questions of historical fact or interpretation. As even the relatively brief exchanges at the SHA suggest, there simply are no texts or historical records of this event whose authority remains unquestioned. This interpretation is, to be sure, by no means universally accepted. We have already heard Styron saying of Gray's *Confessions*, "These are the facts. . . . Deal with them." Similarly, we will encounter a number of readers—including well-known reviewers and critics as well as esteemed historians, white and black—who approach Styron's first-person fictional narrative and Gray's impersonation of Turner's voice in jail assuming that both texts contain accurate statements of historical fact. Nevertheless, the dangers of endowing either literary or historical works with fixed or authoritative meanings have been emphasized by many contemporary critics of narrative.

Two present-day narratologists particularly alert to the social and ideological implications of doing this are Tony Bennett and Barbara Herrnstein Smith. Together, they offer some useful generalizations to guide the cultural historian through the various texts—written and oral, inscribed and performed—composing the Nat Turner phenomenon. Bennett's 1983 essay "Texts, Readers, Reading Formations" can help us formulate—or at least to imagine—the return of Nat Turner in terms of its popular as well as elite reception. He examines from a broadly Marxist perspective "the determinations that organize the social relations of popular reading," and concludes "that the text that critics have on the desk before them may not be the same as the text that is culturally active in the relations of popular reading."[15] This finding is supported, I believe, in some of the exchanges between Ellison and Styron and, even more clearly, in those among Styron and his four questioners. Further evidence is to be found in other records of Nat Turner. Indeed, this controversy is paradigmatic precisely because it is a struggle over meaning—of texts, of a life, of an event, of an institution—that takes place in language as a consequence of conflicting social interests within a diverse culture. Styron's text, Bennett would argue, should not be construed "as existing in some pure and limiting condition of 'in-itselfness' that is independent from the reading relationships that regulate its productive activation in different moments of its history" (10). This condition of in-itselfness, he contends, is not *of* the text, but rather an assertion *about* it, like Styron's plea for the "ineffable othernesses" of great novels. To make claims for any text as autonomous object or structure, separate from its social production and reading formations, is implicitly to privilege certain interpretations—usually, in American culture, those authorized by the cultivated codes of the author and his or her contemporary academic critics. We need to pay attention to such conventional strategies and avenues of interpretation, of course, since they are preserved and discussed and become influential among a certain—perhaps growing—class of sixties readers. But Bennett bids us also consider other interactions between culturally activated texts and various culturally activated readers, and to recognize that all such interactions are "structured by the material, social, ideological and institutional relationships in which *both* text and readers are inescapably inscribed" (12).

When it comes to the knotty problem of actually tracing the generation of popular reader acts, Bennett is well aware of the difficulties. Ordinary readers, though they may buy, read, and discuss a book that interests and moves them, do not commonly preserve records of that response. Some indication of the popularity of Styron's novel or of *Ten Black Writers Respond*, for example, can be found in the distribution figures of the Book-of-the-Month Club or the paperback sales records of New American Library and Beacon Press. But answers to specific questions about actual reading experiences are far harder to come by. Bennett therefore suggests paying special attention to the forms and institutional processes by which popular readings are superintended. He cites, as an analogy, the operation of the star system in a mass culture, by which heroes are produced and audiences primed to consume stories about them. This process incorporates such familiar nonacademic functions as interviews and public appearances, fan magazines, and advertising. Setting aside the question of whether Nat Turner or William Styron were sixties heroes produced in this way, we may profitably borrow Bennett's concept that any popular reading formation is superintended and limited by various hermeneutic systems operative within its cultural ambience. Though we may with difficulty discover actual sixties readers who recall in detail their first encounter with Nat Turner, we can work toward describing the conditions within which such experiences may have actually taken place. Pertinent to such an analysis will be the whole range of communications media in which news of *The Confessions of Nat Turner* was disseminated. When we find, for example, Robert Penn Warren's interview/profile of Styron in *Book-of-the-Month Club News* we can read it not simply as an early critical exercise but as a "trigger" or activator of popular readings of the club's current selection.[16] The same approach can be taken to column-reviews in leading black publications such as the *Amsterdam News*, *Ebony*, or *Black World*, to radio interviews and television talk shows, and to letters to the editor of the *Chicago Tribune Book World* from readers in Washington, D.C., and Bridgman, Michigan. Though all these messages reflect personal responses, they also invite other readers to respond in specific ways to Styron's story.

Yet to challenge the facticity of "the text itself" and to urge greater attention to ordinary readers' superintended responses does not mean arguing for an infinite series of popular—or for that matter, elite—readings. Rather, Bennett's concern with "the social destinies" (17) of a text encourages sharper attention not simply to "untutored" readings—too often dismissed as misunderstandings or distortions—but to the specific histories of all sorts of productive activations. In abandoning the illusory or tendentious belief in the authority of "the text itself," we adopt a more flexible but still principled position, namely that all texts contain embedded meanings within a particular discursive formation. These meanings, however, are constantly being disembedded and reembedded in other discursive formations in the activity of reading. Bennett urges that we understand readings in their own terms by taking seriously this " 'living life' of written texts" (16).

Barbara Herrnstein Smith develops these theoretical assumptions and analytic guidelines in at least two fruitful directions. In "Narrative Versions, Narrative Theories," she discusses an issue central to any consideration of the return of Nat Turner: the retelling of prior narrative accounts. The history of the Southampton slave revolt is the history of various versions of a bygone event, beginning with the first shouted warnings and questions echoing in the early morning darkness of August 22, 1831. Frequently, narratologists will refer to such a history as retellings of a basic story, one which (if the critic happens to be a structuralist) exhibits a deep-plot structure. A two-level conceptualizing results, leading to the identification of *"the* story" and its various alternatives. This kind of thinking derives from, and in turn lends weight to, commonly expressed assertions (by historians or by William Styron) that "these are the facts." What actually occurs in this process, Herrnstein Smith asserts, is not that the true account has been identified but rather that someone has abstracted or summarized the plot of a story from its multiple versions. Because readers and writers of both fictional and historical narratives are commonly taught to perform these acts of summarizing and abstracting in very much the same way, such operations seem natural. "The inclination and ability to perform precisely those operations are, however, by no means innate; they must be learned, and they may be learned differently—or not at all—and therefore performed differently, or not at all."[17] She concludes, therefore, "that what narratologists refer to as the basic stories or deep-plot structures of narratives are often not abstract, disembodied, or subsumed entities but quite manifest, material, and particular retellings—and thus versions—of those narratives, constructed, as *all* versions are, by someone in particular, on some occasion, for some purpose, and in accord with some relevant set of principles" (214).

Instead of a dualistic model of narrative discourse, therefore, Herrnstein Smith offers this alternative:

> one in which narratives [are] regarded not only as *structures* but also as *acts*, the features of which . . . are functions of the variable sets of conditions in response to which they are performed. Accordingly, we might conceive of narrative discourse most minimally and most generally as verbal acts consisting of *someone telling someone else that something happened*. Among the advantages of such a conception is that it makes explicit the relation of narrative discourse to other forms of discourse and, thereby, to verbal, symbolic, and social behavior generally. (227–28)

Another—and for our purposes equally promising—advantage follows from viewing texts as social transactions. New and perhaps unexpected dimensions of narrative may emerge when they are approached with the hypothesis "that every telling is produced and experienced under certain social conditions and constraints and that it always involves two parties, an audience as well as a narrator" (229). Furthermore, it alerts us to the fact that all parties to a transaction are variously motivated to participate: "in other words . . . each party must have some *interest* in telling or listening to that narrative" (229). These considerations provide the cultural historian with grounds for determining "the necessarily contingent *value* of a narrative in terms of how successfully it accommodates the interests of the parties involved in any of the particular transactions in which, at any time, it figures" (230).

The second direction in which Herrnstein Smith extends Bennett's concept of reading formation is, then, historical. Because she makes no distinction between genres, her approach applies equally to different kinds of stories and storytelling situations. Thus comparisons between fictional and historical narratives can more responsibly be drawn when both are conceived as dynamic transactions involving "the *particular* motives and interests of narrators and audiences and to the *particular* social and circumstantial conditions that elicit and constrain the behavior of each of them" (229). To be sure, human motives and interests, always unpredictable, are more difficult to reconstruct or reimagine when embedded in a bygone situation; moreover, "individual narrators may vary greatly in their ability to gauge accurately their audience's interests and in their sensitivity and responsiveness to feedback" (230). Nevertheless, the actual variety of narrative transactions made available and comparable under this rubric encourages critics "to acknowledge and explore the *multiplicity* of functions that may be performed by narratives generally and by any narrative in particular. We would, accordingly, be less likely to expect to find (or claim to have identified) any single fundamental political purpose or psychological (or transcendental) effect of narratives, whether it be to reflect reality or to supplement it, to reinforce ruling ideologies or to subvert them, to console us for our mortality or to give us intimations of our immortality" (231). Since all of these functions have been imputed to the texts of the Nat Turner revolt by interested retellers or readers, this is a useful admonition to the cultural critic of this conflicted event.

Bennett and Herrnstein Smith, then, provide not only a set of principles and arguments for a transactional critique of the return of Nat Turner but also underscore specific dangers in clinging to narrowly conventional versions of literary-historical analysis. They deter us from positing any single author or narrative version as definitive. We should be warned not to consider any of the surviving records of Nat Turner as reproducing what actually happened in 1831—much less telling us why. In other words, we must not grant history priority over literature—or vice versa. To be sure, Nat Turner and the Southampton slave revolt are temporal phenomena; they are prior parts of subsequent reality or necessity, as Fredric Jameson would say, whether one recognizes it or not. In *The Political Unconscious* Jameson reminds us that although history as the past is not a text, in fact "history is inaccessible to us except in textual form"; hence "it can be approached only by way of prior (re)textualization."[18] Conflict and ambiguity are, therefore, unavoidable. Since we can no longer keep narrative history and literature in separate pigeonholes, we are denied recourse to traditional procedures: seeing what the literary text *says*, seeing what the historical record *contains*, then relying on literary critics to resolve textual problems and on historians to settle questions about priorities among surviving records. Having surrendered such consoling simplifications, we must be prepared—at least in theory—to take seriously *all* retextualizations. As Jameson asserts, "no interpretation can be effectively disqualified on its own terms by a simple enumeration of inaccuracies or omissions, or by a list of unanswered questions. Interpretation is not an isolated act, but takes place within a Homeric battlefield, on which a host of interpretive options are either openly or implicitly in conflict" (13). All texts are indeed complex symbolic acts and artifacts. Part of this complexity derives from readers' historical and social location in each reading formation. As Jameson also points out, "we never really confront a text immediately, in all its freshness as a thing-in-itself. Rather, texts come before us as the always-already-read; we apprehend them through sedimented layers of previous interpretations, or—if the text is brand-new—through the sedimented reading habits and categories developed by those inherited interpretive traditions" (9).

A Cultural History: Its Shape and Sequences

Armed with these preliminary principles and procedures for evaluating the significance of symbolic American text-acts, we can now outline more specifically the shape of an appropriate cultural history of Nat Turner's return. In terms of our transactional model, the first task is to identify those intersections among individuals, texts, occasions, and institutions that compose the networks over which historical images and data were—and are—transmitted and by which cultural attitudes and communities were—and continue to be—created, challenged, and changed. We may typify this process by tracing the telling and retelling of narratives emanating from this black slave's life and death. Since Bennett is persuasive in urging concreteness in accounting for "such *real* variations in the social destinies of texts as *have actually* taken place"[19] we would do well to concentrate attention upon a number of key—or at least representative—texts and their contexts. Though these are or become sixties transactions, they are also historical texts and so point backward in American experience. Therefore Nat Turner's most recent return leads necessarily to certain comparisons with his original inscribed appearance on the stage of history. Moreover, some attention must be paid intervening returns as retextualizations so as to specify continuities as well as shifts in the embedded and reembedded meanings for various Americans of the cultural image of the rebellious slave.

Because it so thickly exhibits the multiple functions of Nat Turner as individual story and cultural narrative, Styron's novel is an appropriate text-act to be activated first. What are the imaginative features of this retelling that help account for the initial controversy attending the reappearance of Ol' Prophet Nat? In thus digging deeper into the issues and interactions displayed at the Southern Historical Association session, we begin by taking Styron as a model of the literary artist as historian *and* representative southern white liberal. These were, after all, roles cast for him by both admirers and antagonists. Similarly, we shall treat *The Confessions of Nat Turner* as most readers did in 1967 and 1968: as a verbal artifact simultaneously constituting the "undocumentable inside" of Styron's black protagonist and reconstituting the historical world of antebellum Virginia. This entails, on one level, examining the wellsprings of the author's imagination and historical consciousness as displayed in the artistic choices and formal qualities of a long introspective narrative. From both internal textual evidence and authorial statements before and after publication we must seek to reconstruct Styron's forays into history and so account for the "meditation on history" announced in the author's note and defended elsewhere.

A cultural reactivation of the Nat Turner controversy can never, of course, emerge from one writer's early life, literary and political career, or his aesthetic and historicist assumptions and strategies. Locating Styron's *Confessions* in an appropriate cultural field means that we must also investigate the author's implicit claim made at New Orleans that, like all great works of historical fiction, his novel tries to transport its readers beyond time and social circumstance, beyond even the language of action, description, and meditation, into the transcendental realm of the unconscious and the ineffable. Tracing the spiritual trajectory of *this* Nat Turner's reimagined fate leads through and beyond Old Testament retribution, African portents, and New Testament love, just as it incorporates and also transcends the psychological mechanisms of puritanical repression or latent homosexuality. This plunge within the psyche and beyond time is dramatized in the opening pages of the first-person narrative where Nat Turner recalls his recurrent dream. Yet such flights of imagination, as interpreted by critics as acute as Stanley Kauffmann, must be qualified by other readings, themselves culturally conditioned, by ordinary as well as expert members of Styron's diverse audiences.[20]

Making the necessary move of simultaneously sympathizing with and unmasking Styron involves, therefore, juxtaposing textual evidence of authorial intentions against various culturally significant reading formations. This brings to the fore the second central text—Clarke's *William Styron's Nat Turner: Ten Black Writers Respond*. Because the range and intensity of opinion in this topical anthology is remarkably inclusive, and because the responses to it were so varied, vehement, and socially revealing, this text affords immediate access to several compartments of this controversy. In the "Homeric battlefield" of sixties criticism, *Ten Black Writers Respond* represents a highly visible rallying point. Despite differences among the ten critics, several common arguments are reiterated. We may preliminarily summarize these as follows: Whether knowingly or unconsciously, Styron has written a story the tone and explicit content of which have the side effect of degrading and emasculating Nat Turner and casting doubts upon the moral legitimacy of the revolt he led; the novel represents a serious misreading of history and folklore, which has occurred under pressure from persistent (if not always recognized) white myths and stereotypes; finally, the book's popular and critical success confirms the deepest of divisions within American society—the chasm between the black and white cultures. Why these accusations and responses should have surprised Styron and shocked some of his admiring readership of prominent historians and influential literary critics and reviewers is an issue with several social implications.

A second typical response to *Ten Black Writers Respond* is also to be noted. Many readers of Clarke's collection (including Styron himself) sought to refute its arguments by excluding all but a few contributions. By ignoring several admittedly intemperate essays and authorizing engagement only with a select few as worthy of "serious consideration," these contestants in effect limited, redefined, and misrepresented the blacks and their agenda. Thus in reinterpreting Clarke as well as other responses and retextualizations, one should remember Jameson's *caveat:* "no interpretation can be effectively disqualified on its own terms." Deciding what these terms are should not be an a priori procedure.

From the vantage point of *Ten Black Writers Respond* two paths of inquiry lead deeper into the near past of the sixties and ultimately back into the remoter world of the 1830s. Though the ten black writers are not unanimous in asserting that only a black artist could do justice to Nat Turner's life and character, there is agreement that black writers have, in fact, produced more accurate fictional narratives of slave revolts than Styron. One title mentioned as a model to measure *The Confessions of Nat Turner* by is Arna Bontemps's *Black Thunder*. Originally published in 1936, this novel about Gabriel Prosser's abortive revolt of 1800, which took place in Henrico County, Virginia, was reissued in 1968, another by-product of the Nat Turner controversy.[21] To select this historical fiction as a third locus of literary and ideological forces is not to ignore such other literary parallels, antecedents, or direct influences as have been suggested by Marc Ratner.[22] Several of these had already been named at New Orleans. Others include Styron's own earlier novels as well as the French existentialist fiction represented by Albert Camus's *The Stranger*. But foregrounding *Black Thunder* allows a more direct American historicist discussion that also embraces other literary retellings and reflections. Bontemps also affords an opportunity to note the significance of paperback reprints as popular, often influential retextualizations and assertions of altered meaning. Bontemps's new introduction to the 1968 edition of *Black Thunder*, for instance, uncovers the personal and historical contexts connecting and separating the 1930s and the 1960s. Other thirties artists, including the playwright Randolph Edmonds and poet Sterling Brown, also wrote about Nat Turner, though their contexts and occasions differed from Bontemps's.

The contrasts between Styron's meditation on history and Bontemps's more conventional historical novel must, therefore, be set within a cadre of often less well-known writers impelled to recreate Nat Turner or other slave rebels. The works of these artists, obscure and famous, of the mid-twentieth century and after, are, I submit, more immediately present in sixties consciousness than the slavery stories of Stowe, James, Wells Brown, or Melville. The little-noted novel by Daniel Panger, *Ol' Prophet Nat*, like the plays of Edmonds and Peters and the amateur poetry of Ophelia Robinson, illustrate (sometimes with fervor and subtlety) the surprising range of social contexts and occasions in which knowledge of Nat Turner was preserved, disseminated, redefined and revalued. These writers and their interpretations need to be juxtaposed against more famous representations of the violent slave by Robert Lowell, Martin Duberman, and Robert Hayden. All of these occasions and texts coexist with and challenge the Pulitzer Prize–winning novel of 1968 as imaginative histories of slavery, and their presence qualifies the claims of Styron and his supporters that his novel in effect caused the return.

Because these artists were also historians, Styron, Bontemps, and their contemporaries perforce led readers back into the early nineteenth century. In virtually every case, the return to the original scene reactivates the single most powerful narrative circulating in Nat Turner's own day and aftermath. Thomas R. Gray's *The Confessions of Nat Turner* occupies, as we have noted, a unique place in both historical and imaginative literature. For it is at once a firsthand account, a polemical argument, and a mythic portrait. Gray was, in a sense, a New Journalist writing a century and a half before, but on the same theme as, Norman Mailer's *The Executioner's Song*. The white lawyer's transparent aim was to defuse Nat Turner's revolt as a condemnation of slavery by inscribing the event as the misguided action of a religious fanatic. (We have already seen Styron, in the exchange with the second questioner, accepting, or at least using, this argument.) Gray does so, however, in language which, though clearly a white translation of slave speech, evokes, by often vivid imagery, the awesome simplicities of an Old Testament prophet. Gray's retelling, therefore, possesses wide appeal for later historians and artists, white and black, southern and northern, amateur and professional.

But as indicated by Henry Tragle's 434-page collection of historical sources for the Southampton slave revolt as cultural history, Gray's *Confessions* has always been but one document in a richer contemporary record. Especially is this caveat necessary when my attention turns below to the outpouring of explanations of slavery and slave revolts in the last few decades. This is indeed a remarkable and influential literature that succeeded in revolutionizing American thinking (popular *and* academic) about the antebellum South and its core institution. In the aftermath of *Brown vs. Board of Education* and concurrently with civil rights demonstrations, American historians began a basic and thoroughgoing revision of Ulrich B. Phillips's long-established proslaveowner paradigm. In the process, historicists' horizons widened beyond Nat Turner and Southampton County. New narratives and analyses embraced other insurrections and their leaders, in North America as well as in the Caribbean, Latin America, and, indeed, post-Revolutionary France and Europe. This enlargement of events, issues, and ideologies often contrasts sharply with the continued focus by novelists, poets, and playwrights on Nat Turner himself or similarly circumscribed subjects. The contrast between historians' penchant for inclusive comparisons and artists' preference for probing individuals illustrates a generalization floated in 1970 by Fred Chappell: "Individuation is obviously a function of both of these intellectual endeavors but while history strives to individuate between several events, fiction must individuate inside single events."[23] This book's argument, I hope, will provide both support and qualification to this bold hypothesis.

In doing so, it may first be pointed out that historians' reinterpretations and debates from the mid-fifties to the mid-seventies fit a familiar pattern. There initially appeared new and suddenly more persuasive explanations of slavery and violent resistance—explanations often built upon new sources by slaves and southern women as well as plantation owners and travelers northern and foreign. These reformulations were stimulated by political events (often verging on the violent) demonstrating the active roles oppressed people can actually play in social change. These circumstances made blacks—and in hindsight, slaves—more equal partners in both maintaining and disrupting the American status quo. Moreover, seeing the slave plantation and southern society generally as interacting groups and interracial transactions led historians to explore with fresh zeal and imagination black slave culture itself as the context and crucible for various kinds of resistance and accommodation. In the process, the Nat Turners of the past tended to be reseen as somewhat less unique yet (even more unequivocally) as full participants in the ordinary cultural life of the slave quarters. This radical shift is first glimpsed in the work of four post-1954 historians—Herbert Aptheker, John Hope Franklin, Kenneth Stampp, and Stanley Elkins. From their influential books, new data and new arguments spread to other professionals (white and black), who seized particular provinces of the freshly revealed terrain for intensive mapping. Soon popularizers and textbook writers began to play their social role of transmitting innovative explanations to wider audiences. Often these included children, the general public and others unfamiliar with or excluded from traditional historical networks. Still other Americans became involved as creators, stimulators, and intermediaries in the wider network. Such participants included members of school boards and citizen action groups, teachers and librarians, authors and illustrators, makers of television documentaries and educational filmstrips. The result, by the close of the seventies, was far broader awareness of Nat Turner by Americans of different classes and generations, the historical events associated with his name, and the cultural matrix (black and white) within which his life and fate could or should be set. Furthermore, this historical knowledge was, in virtually every case, linked to recent events and individuals seen as modern parallels and descendants.

William Styron, the ten black writers, Arna Bontemps, Thomas R. Gray, sixties and seventies historians and their audiences of schoolchildren, readers, moviegoers, and television watchers compose diverse yet interconnected speakers and listeners in a changing social dialogue. Surveying the issues contained in these new stories and the insights they suggested, we should no longer be surprised by the emotional and ideological intensity of the Nat Turner controversy of 1967–68 and after. Rather, the continuing returns of Nat Turner—and particularly his most recent appearances in works of history and fiction, which form the content of the final chapter of this study—should remind our citizenry how prone Americans have often been to withhold attention from and then suddenly to become aware of the most pernicious institution in our common past and the chief source of our society's chronic infection. Neither past myopia nor present willingness to look has uniformly characterized all sectors of contemporary society. Thus Styron is not the only participant to assert (too quickly, many would say) that in the early sixties blacks were as ignorant as whites of the presence of a succession of Nat Turners in their past. During the tumultuous decade 1965–1975, many minds were enlightened or reminded of different features of past reality. In the often traumatic process, dark corners and old wounds were disclosed. By the mid-seventies, popular and professional awareness of history's (*and* historical literature's) power to affect, unite, and divide American society had—at least for the moment—grown dramatically.

In exploring this overdetermined phenomenon, my initial premise is that William Styron's fictional "meditation on history" played an initiating, influential, but never decisive role in redirecting attention to the actual (i.e., the ideological) and symbolic (i.e., the mythic) functions of history in our multicultural society. His retelling of a never-totally-forgotten tale of oppression and resistance touched many nerves and fired many imaginations. The novel appealed widely and variously to readers sensitized by civil rights, the Vietnam War, and black power struggles. Especially perhaps for the young and for blacks, those events created new opportunities for principled rebellion against official power and violence. Such opposition constituted a challenge to conventional spiritual as well as social horizons. Because in these wider arenas social commitment frequently coexisted with indifference or contempt for the past, Styron's novel and the controversy it provoked also aroused interest in history, thus reopening another battle sector for contemporary politics. In his latest and most popular return as a white man's fiction or impressionistic history, this archetypal rebel once again challenged American consciences, triggered rationalizations, and confounded popular assumptions. In reactivating *The Confessions of Nat Turner* as fiction, history, and double personal confession, Styron became locked in an ambiguous mortal combat with his black protagonist, just as the white man and the slave once struggled in the pages and on the fields and country roads of the past.

2 William Styron's Meditation on History

> *Nat Turner, reports Clifton Fadiman, "was one of the most remarkable, appalling and tragic figures in the entire chronology of the American Negro." Born into slavery in Virginia, he led an uprising of a handful of slaves against their white masters in 1831. Although the insurrection was speedily suppressed, it frightened the white South into freezing the rigid caste system then prevailing. Nat Turner was swiftly hanged, but not before his extraordinary "confessions" were recorded by a white lawyer. Upon this curious 136-year-old document William Styron has constructed "a narrative at once somber and exciting," as Mr. Fadiman puts it, one that cannot fail to throw light on the bleak dilemmas of our own anguished era. . . . Advance orders in the book trade already indicate that this book is certain to be a best seller in the United States and throughout the world.*
> —Book-of-the-Month Club News, *October 1967*

In assessing William Styron's fictional historicism as effective cultural communication, our initial task is to reconstruct the social and commercial networks within which *The Confessions of Nat Turner* was conceived and made ready for Clifton Fadiman's endorsement. How might Americans of Styron's generation, whites and blacks in the second quarter of this century living either in the South or North, have learned about slave revolts generally and Nat Turner in particular? As a Virginian, who in the late forties conceived a plan to write a novel about Nat Turner, Styron possessed personal experiences and particular historical insights not shared by most fellow Americans. At the same time, common funds and avenues of information were available, so that when the public controversy erupted in 1967–68 Styron's readers—supporters and detractors alike—had different but overlapping grounds for responding to his reinvention of the man and the event. How widely Styron and his several publics shared the same information and assumptions became issues in the ensuing debate. An appropriate starting point is with textbooks of American history. These are, after all, primary social instruments of interpretation of the past to which the young are routinely and by law exposed. As Frances FitzGerald argues in *America Revised*, history textbooks are slow-working but always revealing barometers of an era's ideological climate. Like other historical accounts, they show as much about current attitudes as they do about the past—their ostensible subject. That the schoolroom study of history is a political and ideological instrument in the socialization of American children is a truism explaining the existence and power of state and local boards that scrutinize and select textbooks. Only those topics and treatments that have become safe for the young to learn are allowed, and these decisions will be made on grounds in Texas different from Detroit. In the process of textbooks' creation and production, silences often speak as eloquently as elaborate explanations or detailed descriptions in revealing shared or conflicted values. As Ellison pointed out at the SHA, this has been especially true for treatments of black experience. A signal instance of such deafness is David S. Muzzey's *American History*. For half a century after 1911 this was the most widely taught text to American schoolchildren. For much of this span Muzzey's book contained but a single black American's name—Dred Scott. "Not until the 1961 edition," FitzGerald reports, "did the book suggest that blacks might be numbered among the 'Southern People.'"[1] Even then, Nat Turner never appeared in the New Englander's narrative.

As a Virginian, however, Styron's experience was different.

> When I was learning my lessons on the banks of the James River, one of the required texts was a history of Virginia—a book I can recall far more vividly than any history of the United States or of Europe I studied at a later time. It was in this work that I first encountered the name Nat Turner. The references to Nat were brief; as a matter of fact, I do not think it unlikely that it was the very brevity of the allusion—amounting almost to a quality of haste—which captured my attention and stung my curiosity. I can no longer quote the passage exactly, but I remember that it

went something like this: 'In 1831, a fanatical Negro slave named Nat Turner led a terrible insurrection in Southampton County, murdering many white people. The insurrection was immediately put down, and for their cruel deeds Nat Turner and most of the other Negroes involved in the rebellion were hanged.' Give or take a few harsh adjectives, this was all the information on Nat Turner supplied by that forgotten historian, who hustled on to matters of greater consequence.[2]

Had the young Styron or others less well served by their schoolbooks sought further enlightenment on what was clearly a touchy topic, a logical place to visit would have been the public library (where, in many parts of the country before World War II, a black reader—Richard Wright in Memphis, for example, or Arna Bontemps in Alabama—would have been turned away). Once inside, though, one could have after 1936 consulted the *Dictionary of American Biography*, which reference work contained the following entry:

> TURNER, NAT (Oct. 2, 1800–Nov. 11, 1831), leader of slave insurrection, the son of Nancy, a slave woman and native of Africa, was born on the plantation of her owner, Benjamin Turner, in Southampton County, Va. He successively became the property of Samuel Turner, Thomas Moore, and Putnam Moore, and in 1830 he was hired to Joseph Travis, whom Mrs. Thomas Moore had married. His mother was little removed from savagery at the time of his birth, and his father, whose name has not survived, ran away while Nat was a child. Nat, who was precocious, was given the rudiments of an education by one of his master's sons, and, early developing a religious fanaticism, under his mother's encouragement came to believe himself inspired. A fiery preacher, he soon acquired leadership among the negroes on the plantation and in the neighborhood. According to his sworn confession, he deliberately set about convincing them of his divine inspiration, and presently believed himself chosen to lead them from bondage. He began to see signs in the heavens and on the leaves, and to hear voices directing him. An eclipse of the sun in 1831 convinced him that the time was near and caused him to enlist four other slaves, to whom he communicated his plans. They plotted an uprising for July 4, but abandoned it. After a new sign

was seen in a peculiar solar phenomenon on Aug. 13, they settled upon Aug. 21 as the day of deliverance.

With seven others Nat attacked the Travis family and murdered them all. Securing arms and horses, and enlisting other slaves, they ravaged the neighborhood. In one day and one night they butchered horribly and mangled the bodies of fifty-one white persons—thirteen men, eighteen women, and twenty-four children. With the blood of the victims Nat sprinkled his followers. At the first armed resistance the revolt collapsed and on Aug. 25 Nat went into hiding in a dugout, less than two miles from the Travis farm, where he remained, successfully concealed in the daytime, for six weeks. Discovered by accident, he was at once tried, and after conviction was hanged at Jerusalem, the county seat. He faced his fate with calmness. Thomas R. Gray, who was assigned to defend him, said: "He is a complete fanatic, or plays his part most admirably" (Gray, *Post*, p. 19). Of his sixty or seventy followers, twenty-eight were convicted and condemned; sixteen, including the one woman involved, were executed, and twelve were transported. The number that were killed in the suppression has never been ascertained.

The revolt, following closely upon slave insurrections in Martinique, Antigua, Santiago, Caracas, and the Tortugas, caused a profound shock in the slaveholding states. Exaggeration magnified both the real and the false, and for weeks there was widespread terror. As a result almost every Southern state enacted new laws which greatly increased the severity of the slave codes, though, after a brief time, most of them were more honored in the breach than in the observance. The insurrection dealt a death blow to the manumission societies which had flourished in the South, and put an end there to the organized emancipation movement. Further, the blame for the uprising was placed upon the Garrisonian abolitionists, though not a scintilla of evidence ever connected them with it, and intensified the detestation and dread with which the South regarded them. Perhaps the most important result of all was that never again was the slaveholding South free from the fear, lurking most of the time, of a wholesale and successful slave uprising, a fact potent in the history of the republic during the next thirty years.[3]

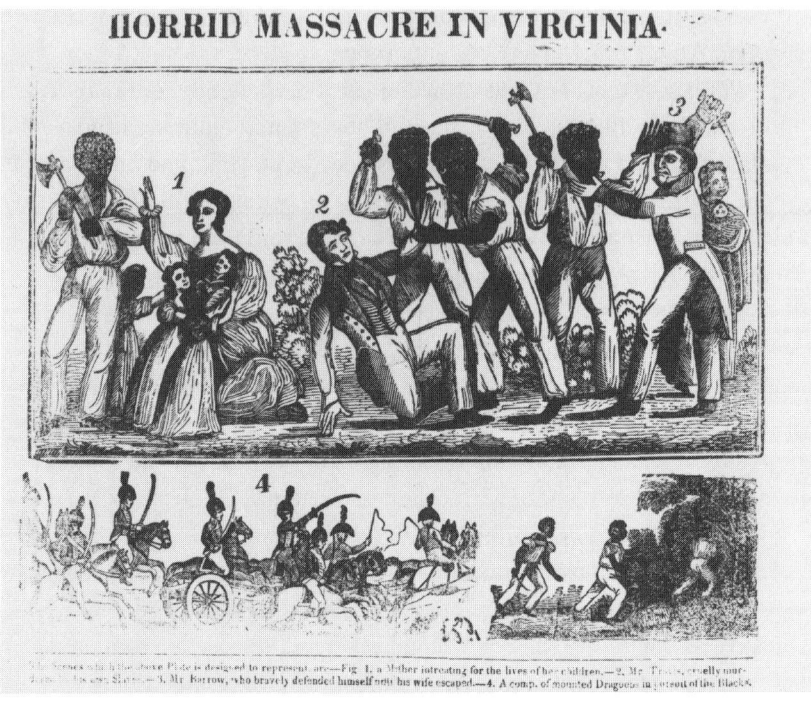

Magazine illustration depicting Turner's revolt (Courtesy of the Library of Congress).

The *DAB*'s first editor was the eminent southern historian and future biographer of Jefferson, Dumas Malone. The author of this entry, also a southerner, was James G. deR. Hamilton, editor of the letters of the firebrand secessionist Thomas Ruffin. That his account is a retelling is amply evidenced by Hamilton's bibliography. Of its six items (all written by white southerners), Gray's *Confessions* is the only one quoted, suggesting that Hamilton considered Gray his most reliable source. Even clearer are the author's ideological allegiances, signaled by such phrases as "little removed from savagery," "butchered horribly and mangled," "rudiments of an education," "religious fanaticism," "with the blood of the victims Nat sprinkled his followers." This language explicitly sets the primitive Africans off as the Other from both southern and northern whites, the civilized. This separation is underlined by the emphatic assertion that not a "scintilla of evidence" linked abolitionists to the revolt.

Further, a later reader consulting the *DAB* after having learned about Nat Turner from Styron and Gray would be struck by another of Hamilton's data. The woman rebel executed along with Nat Turner might catch a novelist's eye, providing a potential love interest for a historical plot. This possibility, refused by Styron in favor of Margaret Whitehead, was taken up by Arna Bontemps, in whose *Black Thunder* (also published in 1936) the hero has a beautiful black woman as co-conspirator at his side.

In subsequent chapters we shall note several repetitions of Hamilton's sources and how other readers of Gray's *Confessions* exploit this and different documents for a variety of purposes. Here it should simply be pointed out that library reference works, though often considered "sacred" sources of historical data, are tailored to certain audiences' belief systems. This cultural function would have perhaps been clearer to black readers than to white readers during Styron's youth, yet it should be apparent that Hamilton was not addressing black readers.

However, other libraries in pre-sixties America held, in addition to the *DAB*, books and magazines not generally found in public libraries serving white readers, including the pioneer writings of black historians such as William Wells Brown, George Washington Williams, W. E. B. Du Bois, and Carter G. Woodson, founder in 1919 of the *Journal of Negro History*.[4] Even though these works contained sometimes lengthy accounts of the Southampton slave revolt, they were not deemed worthy of citation by Hamilton. Nor did Styron later give evidence of having consulted any of these narratives. Yet as Ellison asserted in New Orleans, pioneer black historians, along with storytellers in the black folk tradition, long served the black community's readers, listeners, and fellow storytellers. Through such institutional channels as segregated schools, black colleges, fraternal lodges, and service clubs the presence and significance of the rebellious slave in antebellum America was preserved. In addition to Negro history weeks and black history months, these reactivations often occurred informally, never getting into libraries or onto the printed page. Because of the color line, the nature and extent of this network is difficult to establish, though we shall later suggest some direct and indirect evidence.

If often short on works written by black pioneer historians, public libraries in the forties and fifties did contain shelves of books by white writers on the broader topics of the American South and its peculiar institution. Some few of these proved of direct assistance to the youthful Styron who, in the spring of 1952, was living in Paris. "I've pretty much decided what to write next," the author of *Lie Down in Darkness* wrote his father on May 1, "—a novel based on Nat Turner's rebellion. The subject fascinates me, and I think I could make a real character out of old Nat. It'll probably take a bit of research, though, and I've written to people in the U.S.—among them Professor Saunders Redding (whom I saw Christmas, you remember) of Hampton Institute—asking them to pass on any reference material they might have. Perhaps you know of a book or something on Nat Turner and would be willing to get it sent to me somehow."[5] Styron's residence abroad only partly explains this letter's breezy assumptions about researching a historical novel. As later comments amply confirm, he never took the task as seriously as some readers of *The Confessions of Nat Turner* considered necessary. Nevertheless, several books sent him by Redding were available to American readers of the day—at least in Virginia libraries or in college or university collections. Three of these, as Arthur D. Casciato and James L. W. West have documented, were of specific value to the self-confessed amateur historian. In addition to Gray's *Confessions* (a work not easy to find outside of rare book rooms in fifties America), Styron read and relied heavily on William S. Drewry's *The Southampton Slave Insurrection*, a 1900 volume not widely available outside Tidewater libraries or historical societies. A more familiar source of general historical usefulness was Frederick Law Olmsted's classic nineteenth-century travel narrative, *A Journey in the Seaboard Slave States.*[6]

Easier to get at (at that time and even subsequently) are other, less arcane or segregated media through which Americans acquire historical lore. In the era of the automobile, one of these is the highway historical marker. Visible to passing motorists and pedestrians in present-day Virginia, for instance, is the Virginia Conservation and Development Marker U-115 alongside Highway 58, three miles west of Courtland (called Jerusalem in Nat Turner's day). This sign defines publicly one important spot in the Southampton slave revolt: "BUCKHORN QUARTERS. One mile west was the estate of Major Thomas Ridley. In the servile insurrection of 1831, the houses were fortified by faithful slaves and made a place of refuge for fugitive whites. In this vicinity Nat

Turner, the leader of the insurrection, spent the night after his defeat near Courtland, August 23, 1831."[7]

On his visit to Courtland in 1964, Styron apparently stopped and inspected this sign. In the opinion of Henry Tragle, the novelist may well have been inspired or confirmed by this message (which contains a factual error in the date August 23) to relocate the Blount fight at Major Ridley's and to make it the military climax of his narrative. In any case, Styron reiterates the notion of faithful slaves actively defending their masters' families against the rebels featured in the commonwealth's highway marker version of the Revolt.[8]

Advance Publicity and Piecemeal Retellings

"This Quiet Dust," the *Harper's* essay of April 1965 that records Styron's visit to Southampton, illustrates still other avenues Americans possess to (re)acquaint themselves with this event. Since schoolbooks, encyclopedias, and highway markers afford at best sketchy information, and if black histories are frequently ignored by readers, white and black, the persistent inquirer may, like Styron, actually visit the scene and inspect the cultural geography and surviving architecture. One might also talk to those who, if certainly not survivors of the revolt, presently live amid its history and may carry records of it in their heads. The *Harper's* piece presents the novelist-historian in this act of confronting, collecting, and meditating. As an early announcement to prospective readers (though a brief dialogue between Styron and James Jones had appeared in the July 1963 *Esquire*),[9] "This Quiet Dust" deserves careful attention. It exhibits an expatriate Virginian home on a visit from Roxbury, Connecticut. He is briefly trying on the role of amateur fieldworker and oral historian. Though casual, even ironic, about the need of such a performance for a novelist like himself, Styron candidly reveals his methods and motives for probing this corner of the past.

Another reason for the magazine article is clearly commercial. In addition to its larger purposes to inform and predispose, "This Quiet Dust" paves the way for Random House and *Harper's* (which in September 1967 would run a long excerpt) to attract a readership for the forthcoming book. Thus the magazine piece represents a means for readers to learn more about this historical episode, a device for superintending the process, and a commercial commodity.

Even more explicitly, "This Quiet Dust" is an autobiographical message about the private memories of a white boy growing up in Newport News, Virginia, before World War II and linking these to *The Confessions of Nat Turner*. Though his boyhood was distinctly southern and specifically Virginian, the writer represents it as in certain key respects indistinguishable from northern and suburban boyhoods. Newport News, "a small seaside city about equally divided between black and white" (136), lay on the upper edge of the Black Belt. Yet this native son recalls none of that casual social familiarity with blacks, which readers assume or know was the common heritage of other southern writers like Carson McCullers or Flannery O'Connor. By contrast, Styron explains that his childhood

> was the typically ambivalent one of most native Southerners, for whom the Negro is simultaneously taken for granted and as an object of unending concern. . . . Unnoticed by white people, the Negroes blend with the land and somehow melt and fade into it, so that only when one reflects on their possible absence, some magical disappearance, does one realize how unimaginable this absence would be: it would be easier to visualize a South without trees, without *any* people, without life at all. Thus at the same time ignored by white people, Negroes impinge upon their collective subconscious to such a degree that it may be rightly said that they become the focus of an incessant preoccupation, somewhat like a monstrous recurring dream populated by identical faces wearing expressions of inquietude and vague reproach. (136)

As if to underline his perspective on the matter, Styron quotes Ralph Ellison's terse description of the same social relation: "Southern whites cannot walk, talk, sing, conceive of laws or justice, think of sex, love, the family or freedom without responding to the presence of Negroes" (136). But Styron reiterates his own separation and isolation: "Surrounded by a sea of Negroes, I cannot recall more than once—and then briefly, when I was five or six—ever having played with a Negro child, or even having spoken to the Negro, except in trifling talk with the cook, or in some forlorn and crippled conversation with a dotty old grandfather angling for hardshell crabs on a lonesome Sunday afternoon many years ago" (136). *Harper's* readers from Hartford or Cleveland, say, would be surprised and perhaps comforted to learn how little different Styron's experience was from their own: "Whatever knowledge I gained in my youth about Negroes I gained from a distance, as if I had been watching actors in an all-black puppet show," he observes. "I have come to understand at least as much about the Negro after having lived in the North" (136). Understandable, therefore, but also disturbing is his confession that a principal motive for writing *The Confessions of Nat Turner* was to penetrate a southern slave's mind in order to achieve interior consciousness about a rural Virginia past once intimately shared by whites and blacks.

What is striking about Styron's remarks is the way his metaphoric language prefigures the forthcoming novel. Absence as a condition reinforcing presence, metaphoric associations of blacks with puppets, dreams, and lifeless landscapes, together with memories of "forlorn," "crippled," and "lonesome" confrontations, all emphasize the present autobiographer's moods and motives. Many readers of the later novel would note there a similar pattern linking whites and the introspective black protagonist: physical proximity to but social isolation from the racial Other.

Distance and displacement are repeated themes elsewhere in Styron's essay. Though he records the day's activities as interviewer and tourist, he is more preoccupied with his own thoughts and projections onto the Southampton scene. Out of this meditative mood emerges another motive for going in search of the historical Nat Turner. Lacking rich personal memories and associations, he is determined to fill the gaps by imagination. Penetrating such barriers will also help the writer discharge a pressing public duty: "the Negro may feel that it is too late to be known," he admits, "and that the desire to know him reeks of outrageous condescension. But to break down the old law, to come to *know* the Negro, has become the moral imperative of every white Southerner" (138). Here Styron explicitly links artistic and historical concerns to his duties as citizen and white Southern liberal.

It is clear that the road to racial reconciliation proceeds from understanding the past rather than the tempestuous present, and so it is as amateur historian that Styron presents himself most fully to his *Harper's* audience. Yet in this activity what is immediately apparent is the curious mixture of enthusiastic interest in and insouciance about the past. "What research it was possible to do on the event I had long since done," he observes breezily. "The Southampton court records, I had already been reliably informed, would prove unrewarding. It was not a question, then, of digging up more facts, but simply a matter of wanting to savor the mood and atmosphere of a landscape I had not seen for quite a few years" (141). Struck by many signs of change since his youth, Styron and his father (a retired naval engineer) are driven around the county in the sheriff's car, "with its huge star emblazoned on the doors, and its radio blatting out hoarse intermittent messages, and its riot gun protectively nuzzling the back of our necks" (44–45). Thus sponsored, he visits surviving sites and old landmarks. He also asks questions about Nat Turner. He wants to see if, and how strongly, old memories survive in the very neighborhoods where the black slave once lived and died. Driving along dusty roads and inquiring at crossroads stores and filling stations, he discovers few whites or blacks who know anything at all definite about Nat Turner: "most of them confused him, I think, with something spectral, mythic, a black Paul Bunyan who had perpetrated mysterious and nameless deeds in millenia past. They were neither facetious nor evasive, simply unaware. Others confounded him with the Civil War—a Negro general. One young field hand, lounging at an Esso station, figured he was a white man. A white man, heavy-lidded, and paunchy, slow-witted, an idler at a rickety store, thought him an illustrious race horse of bygone days" (145).

The day's foray, then, distilled one ineluctable truth: a century and a third later and in his native region, Nat Turner is a forgotten figure; "not one of these back-country people could offer the faintest hint or clue" (145). Styron questions neither the superficiality of a one-day visit nor the effects on its results of the patrol car and its riot gun. Instead, he is confirmed in his belief that the dead rebel is more real in his own imagination—where "he had acquired larger spirit and flesh than most of the living people I encountered day in and day out" (145)—than in the collective folk memory of Southampton County.

This claim to superior imaginative possession of the past may not have convinced all readers in 1965 (it certainly did not do so later). One dissenter, though not addressing this particular essay, was Roy Parker, Jr., who reviewed *The Confessions of Nat Turner* upon its appearance in October 1967, for the *News and Observer* in Raleigh,

North Carolina. Parker was raised in Hartford County, North Carolina, further down the Chowan Valley from Southampton County. "As a native and sometime weekly newspaper editor there," he wrote, "it seems I can hardly remember a day in my life when Nat Turner did not intrude. . . . Nearly everyone had a family story about the insurrection. Any written account of local history almost always had had its Nat Turner passages." Then Parker pointed to another place where readers far beyond the region could learn about Nat Turner: "Today, few in the Chowan Valley would begrudge Nat Turner his place in history. A cursory check [reveals that] Nat Turner is the only Chowan Valley native save one to hold a place in the Encyclopedia Britannica. The other invented the machine gun."[10] Even more skeptical of Styron's assertions about folk memories was historian Henry Tragle who, several years later, also visited Southampton County. There he met and interviewed Percy Claud, a seventy-year-old black resident of Boykin, Virginia. Claud's memories of family tales about Nat Turner corroborate the testimony of Roy Parker. Though often mixed with superstitions and other fancies, his remarks suggest that a white interlocutor from the North could elicit a different and livelier folk history than Styron was able or willing to discover.

More significant, both to the writer himself and to his *Harper's* readers, than these rather airy assumptions about the presence or absence of memory are Styron's private ruminations. These take place most prominently on the porch of an abandoned farmhouse Styron believes from his map was the original Whitehead place. On the very spot, as he thinks, where Nat Turner slew Margaret Whitehead he recalls Gray's terse account. Again, he senses

> something baffling, secret, irrational about Nat's own participation in the violent uprising. The leader was unable to kill. Time and time again in his confession one discovers him saying (in an off-hand tone; one must dig for the implications): 'I could not give the death blow, the hatchet glanced from his head' or 'I struck her several blows over the head, but I was unable to kill her, as the sword was dull. . . .' It is too much to believe, over and over again: the glancing hatchet, the dull sword. It smacks rather, as in Hamlet, of rationalization, ghastly fear, an access of guilt, a shrinking from violence, and fatal irresolution. . . . What happened to Nat

in this place? Did he discover his humanity here, or did he lose it? (146)

Standing on the broken-down steps, he reimagines the bloody scene of long ago. "For an instant, in the silence, I thought I could hear a mad rustle of taffeta, and rushing feet, and a shrill girlish piping of terror; then that day and this day seemed to meet and melt together, becoming almost one, and for a long moment indistinguishable" (146).

Styron's language here as elsewhere evokes *Gone with the Wind* more than it does the Emily Dickinson poem that provides the essay's title. In other passages, however, Styron's mood and rhetoric are markedly less melodramatic. "This Quiet Dust" is not merely a somewhat self-indulgent advertisement, ostensibly recording a casual day in the southern countryside. His cavalier behavior as fieldworker must be seen in light of previous reading about slavery and the revolt, for he wishes his readers to accept him as a sincere, if unprofessional, historian. He therefore gives a relatively detailed account, running more than five pages, of Nat Turner's history. As capsule narrative, this section constitutes a skillful plea for the historical validity of the forthcoming novel.

Styron's search for the historical Nat Turner had taught him two basic truths about American chattel slavery. First, it was "singularly free of organized uprisings, plots, and rebellions" (138). To this generalization there were but three exceptions, all from the nineteenth century: the conspiracies led by Gabriel Prosser, Denmark Vesey, and Nat Turner. Moreover, this scanty record of actual armed resistance is satisfactorily explained in two works, Frank Tannenbaum's *Slave and Citizen* and Stanley Elkins's *Slavery: A Problem in American Institutional and Intellectual Life*. (Both books, as we shall later note, were reviewed by Styron in the *New York Review of Books* in 1963.)[11] "American Negro slavery, unique in its psychological oppressiveness—the worst the world has ever known—was simply so despotic and emasculating as to render organized revolt next to impossible" (138). In history's annals, Nat Turner alone "achieved a kind of triumph" (138). Yet this feat, he adds, has gone largely unnoticed not only because its memory disturbs many regional notions about the relative mildness of slavery in Virginia as compared with the Deep South, but also by the scarcity and inaccessibility of surviving records. But two works, Gray's *Confessions* and Drewry's *The Southampton Insurrection*, a proslavery treatise written in 1900 at the height of Jim Crow segregation, are the sources Styron says he had to rely on. Other earlier and even later documents are noted only to be dismissed. For instance, the few newspaper accounts of the revolt are, he writes, "sketchy, remote, filled with conjecture, and are thus virtually worthless" (138). Existing court records, too, are little better; they constitute "mere dull lists, a dry catalogue of names in fading ink" (138).

Far from a problem, this dearth of reliable and useful information is exactly what this novelist needs in order to speculate and reimagine. This artistic right Styron insists on and freely exercises in "This Quiet Dust." But gaps in information also invite the historian in Styron. Thus he advances historical hypotheses to explain "this extraordinary black man . . . out of those early mists of our history" (139). One comes from the new field of psychohistory, in particular from Erik Erikson's *Young Man Luther*. Because Nat Turner at thirty-one was "exactly the same age as many revolutionaries at the decisive moment of the insurgency" (139), he invites comparison with Luther, Robespierre, Danton, and Fidel Castro. "Although it is best to be wary of heavy psychoanalytical emphasis," he observes, "one cannot help believing that Nat Turner's relationship with his father (or his surrogate father, his master) was tormented and complicated, like Luther's" (139). No evidence for this assertion is adduced. Nevertheless, signs of precocity are not lacking: these include learning very young to read and write and an interest in two symbolic manufacturing processes—the making of paper and gunpowder. Styron remarks that this last item mentioned by Gray "is almost too odd to be true" but cannot bring himself to doubt it, inasmuch as Gray, "in all major respects . . . seems completely honest and reliable" (139).

The parallel between Turner and Luther appears especially pertinent to Styron. In a thoroughly Christian time and place as he assumes Southampton County was in the 1820s and 1830s, it was religious belief and not scientific know-how that gained Ol' Prophet Nat the respect and power he enjoyed among blacks and even among some whites. He became a Baptist preacher known around the countryside for preaching and prophesying. In his late twenties, he withdrew socially from the slave community in order to fast, pray, and entertain visions. Styron cites a graphic passage from Gray in which the captive rebel recalls seeing heavenly battles between black and white spirits, with drops of blood on the corn like heavenly dew. He heard a voice telling him to fight the Serpent. Under such inspiration he concocted a plan for the annihilation "of every white man, woman, and child on the ten-mile route to Jerusalem" (140), to be followed by seizure of the town's weapons and ammunition and then escape to the nearby Great Dismal Swamp. "It was a scheme so wild and daring," Styron concludes, "that it could only have been the product of the most wretched desperation and frustrate misery of the soul; and of course it was doomed to catastrophe not only for whites but for Negroes—and for black men in ways from which the vantage point of history now seem almost unthinkable" (140). Few readers in 1965 would miss the contemporary implication of the shift in Styron's final sentence from "Negroes" to "black men."

After the biographical beginning, the remainder of Styron's retelling of the uprising is surprisingly unsensational and brief. Though the band of slaves killed nearly sixty whites "with merciless and methodical determination," they did no sexual violence to their female victims, an "interesting" detail Styron attributes to the leader's "Christian and high-minded" view of sex. He notes, too, that several homes of poor whites were bypassed with motives "perhaps obscurely pre-Marxist" (140). But the revolt's momentum crested swiftly. Disorder and plentiful apple brandy combined with white resistance on the second day soon precipitated the band into panic and flight. Turner hid from the avenging whites for two months but was eventually captured, tried, condemned, and hanged. "He went to his death with great dignity and courage," Styron concludes and quotes without comment Drewry's report that Nat Turner's body was delivered to the doctors, who skinned it and made grease of the flesh (141).

"The killing of so many white people was itself an act of futility," the writer observes. For one thing, as many as two hundred blacks (many of them free) may have been murdered in retaliation. "News of the revolt spread among the Southern whites with great speed: the impossible, the unspeakable had at last taken place after two hundred years of the ministrations of sweet old mammies and softly murmured 'Yassuhs' and docile compliance" (141). The wider reverberations were equally ironic and tragic. This "bold and desperate bid for liberty" (141) produced a backlash of repressive legislation and restraints "which persisted throughout the slave-holding states until the Civil War. Virginia had been edging toward emancipation," he added, "and it seems reasonable to believe that the example of Nat's rebellion stampeded many moderates in the legislature into a conviction that the Negroes could not be safely freed, was a decisive factor in the ultimate victory of the pro-slavery forces" (141). He concludes that "Nat brought cold, paralyzing fear to the South, a fear that never departed. If white men had sown the wind with chattel slavery, in Nat Turner they had reaped the whirlwind for white and black alike" (141).

As these generalizations suggest, "This Quiet Dust" is an ambitious and complex cultural message. Simultaneously historical, autobiographical, and politically topical, it advances Styron's claim to speak for himself, his region, his race, and his generation on a subject reverberating with contemporary relevance. In the process, he glosses his own fictional narrative while it is being written and thus begins to superintend its future reception by an audience like the *Harper's* readership. There are, therefore, clear links between the essay's *raison d'être* and the author's postpublication performances such as the SHA session three years later.

After this preliminary public, Styron and the book industry next went after a broader audience. During 1965 and 1966, as racial unrest and violence escalated in the North and South, the fears of many Americans, especially middle-class whites and blacks, were fed by newspapers and television. Sensing the potential appeal of Styron's story, New American Library bought for $100,000 the paperback rights to the still-unfinished novel. When news of this deal broke, the author faced accusations of deliberately exploiting the current situation. He vigorously defended himself in an interview in *Per/Se*, an obscure literary magazine: "Anyone who wished to have an *a priori* disapproval of the book and its themes might possibly say that, but it wouldn't be worth the time it would take to convince them that I'd been interested in this since I was fifteen years old, before the last war."[12] This reply downplays the prepublication campaign already underway.

Of the advance notices for *The Confessions of Nat Turner*, two especially addressed distinct middle-class groups. The first came in early September 1967 and indicates that the publisher and at least one black newspaper had black readers as well as white in their sights. In the New York *Amsterdam News* for September 2, 1967, appeared a prepublication announcement that *Harper's* was soon to publish a fifty-four-page excerpt from William Styron's forthcoming novel, which would later be distributed by the Book-of-the-Month Club: "This extraordinary novel, Styron's fourth, is based on the only effective sustained revolt in the annals of American Negro slavery." Then followed a summary of the story that nevertheless resembled the blurbs circulating in the predominantly white press:

> Nat Turner, the leader of the revolt, was a thirty-year-old educated slave who felt himself divinely ordained to annihilate all the white people in the region and, together with his followers, to escape to the Dismal Swamp nearby, to set up an empire of fugitive black men.
>
> On August 21, 1831, heading in the direction of Jerusalem, the county seat, Nat Turner set forth with a small nucleus of disciples and began to wreak upon the white inhabitants death and devastation such as had never been seen in the South before.
>
> During the three-day uprising sixty white people were killed and every dwelling on the thirty-five mile path was plundered or destroyed. The insurrection was put down by white landowners and units of the Virginia militia, and close to two hundred Negroes, slave and free, were killed in retaliation. Nat Turner, along with seventeen others, was hanged.[13]

Certain features of this brief notice accrue additional cultural weight in light of subsequent developments. Immediately obvious is the favorable term "extraordinary" used to characterize Styron's novel. The *Amsterdam News* would reflect changing opinions about the white novelist's bestseller after it was published, as we shall see. At this point it is clear that, as a black superintendence of reader responses, the language of the *Amsterdam News* reflects the newspaper's dual function as a channel for mainstream white culture and a voice of black middle-class concerns. Less guardedly than the *DAB* or *Harper's*, the *Amsterdam News* expresses its attitude toward Nat Turner through references to the rebels' plan to "set up an empire of fugitive black men" and the characterization of his followers as "disciples." If the phrase "death and devastation such as had never been seen in the South before" echoes Styron's own language or that of Random House blurbs, it does not explain the enthusiastic description of the rebels' plundering "every dwelling on the thirty-five mile path." Also revealing is the newspaper's replacement of religious fanaticism as the prime motivation for the revolt by the phrase "felt himself divinely ordained." Although similar prepublication notices did not appear in other leading black newspapers like the Chicago *Defender*, the Pittsburgh *Courier*, or the Washington *Afro-American*, these organs were later drawn into the controversy over Styron's retelling of Nat Turner's story as black middle-class readers, initially impressed, lined up in condemnation and protest.

Compared to this modest but significant indication of sympathetic responses from one American audience, the *Harper's* issue of September 1967 represents much more unequivocally the way mainstream readers of books and magazines were urged to welcome *The Confessions of Nat Turner*. Never in its history had *Harper's* paid $7,500 for a single article; seldom had *Harper's* gone to such lengths to endorse in advance a work of historical fiction.[14] The excerpt from Styron's long novel was itself lengthy, running to more than fifty pages and taking up most of the issue. In other ways, too, the editors aggrandized Styron's achievement—on the cover, in a laudatory foreword and biographical afterword, and with eleven sepia-and-black illustrations by artist Robert White. The cover blurb hailed the "book-length section, complete in itself": "the year's most awaited and important novel by the author of *Lie Down in Darkness*. This extraordinary new book is based on the single effective slave revolt in American history. The insurrection, led by Nat Turner, took place in Virginia in 1831. This long excerpt is a moving narrative of Nat Turner's early life and of the white world in which he lived."[15]

As several of these phrases suggest, the editors lifted Styron's own words from his author's note to underscore the novel's literary importance and historical authority. This common publishing practice continued in the foreword. "Little is known about Nat's early life and the motivations for the revolt," they informed expectant readers, "and the meagre details of the rebellion itself are contained in a slim volume entitled 'The Confessions of Nat Turner,' which was taken down from Nat's lips as he awaited trial by a lawyer named Thomas Gray. Gray—a racist like most white men of his time—was nonetheless so impressed by Nat as to say of him that 'for natural intelligence and quickness of apprehension he is surpassed by few men I have ever seen.'" Echoing Styron's assertions in "This Quiet Dust" or the as-yet-unpublished author's note, the editors contrasted the ironic consequences of the revolt—"the establishment of patrols, further restrictions upon movement, education, and assembly" and "other severe and crippling restraints"—with the rebel's own hopes for his "desperate bid for liberty." However, the editors added that Nat Turner's revolt did have far-reaching effects: "a shock wave of panic ran thoughout the entire South and the realization that their black servitors were, after all, capable of violent retribution continued to haunt white men throughout the following decades" (52).

After pointing readers in the directions Styron desired, the editors then endorsed his credentials as a historian with further borrowings from the writer's own assertions:

> In his re-creation of this catastrophic event, William Styron had adhered to the known facts of the revolt wherever possible. In those areas, however, where little is known of Nat's early life and the germination of the revolt (and this is most of the time) the author has allowed himself the utmost liberty of imagination in reconstructing that distant yet close antebellum world, attempting to create what, in his own words, is "less an historical novel in conventional terms than a meditation on history." The entire novel is narrated from the point of view of Nat Turner himself. The following excerpt, which comprises the central portion of the book, is a long reverie that takes place in Nat's mind as he lingers in jail through the cold, autumnal days before his execution. (52)

The narrative that follows clearly presents Styron the creative artist more than the circumstantial historian. Scattered through the pages of *Harper's* are specific details about the past, like the allusion to the recently invented Carey plough "of stout cast iron," and chronological benchmarks such as "On February 21, 1822, in the village of Sussex Courthouse, Virginia, the Reverend Eppes sold me into bondage for $460" (55, 99). In the main, however, Styron freely dramatizes key moments, experiences, and relationships in Turner's shadowy past. Readers are led to assume that these inventions help explain the revolt, which is, in fact, scarcely mentioned. Nor does this "central portion of the book" contain the jailhouse interaction between Thomas Gray and Nat Turner, which provides both the historical and dramatic framework of the published novel's part 1. Instead, by presenting the novel's part 2 as a self-contained story (later entitled "Old Times Past—Voices,

Dreams, Recollections"), Styron and the editors invite readers into a peaceful if not serene Virginia of the 1820s. As some readers would later point out, certain highlighted themes and moods contradict the historical source that readers are promised has been followed faithfully.

Seen in this dual perspective of part and whole, part before the whole, this preview is notable, first, for locating Nat Turner himself firmly in command of the story through a distinctive voice, language, and point of view. The small slave boy who swims into the captive's memory is trapped—or, rather, happily if precariously suspended—between the social universes of the slaves and the Big House. There at the master's, his mother is cook to Samuel Turner, the beneficent lord of Turner's Mill. There, too, Nat is a house servant. The opening scene reveals the future rebel circling the dinner table, pouring cider for his master's family and guest. In the soft spring twilight he gazes out from the bastion of white civility onto a pastoral scene peopled by trees, animals, and his less fortunate fellow slaves:

> Past them, far down the slope where a log road separates the lawn and looming forest, I can see an empty cart drawn by two flop-eared mules, making its last trip of the day from the store house to the mill. On the seat of the cart sits a Negro man, a yellow straw hat raked down upon his head. As I watch, I see that the man is trying to scratch his back, first his left arm snaking up from his waist, then his right arm arching down over his shoulder as the black fingers grope in vain for the source of some intolerable itch. Finally, as the mules plod steadily down the slope and the cart ponderously rocks and veers, the man stands up with a lurching motion and scrapes his back cowlike up and down against the side post of the cart. (53)

Nat's early distancing of himself from the animal-like existence of the Turner field hands is underlined throughout part 2. Also emphasized, though more obliquely, is this typical slave's nonviolent way of dealing with the "intolerable itch" of his bondage. The boy's preference for white ways and his contempt for all slaves except his mother follow in part from his favored status as the "little black jewel of Turner's Mill" (71) who is taught by white ladies to spell and read. The reminiscing rebel recalls with irony but surprisingly little bitterness Marse Samuel's idealistic experiment in thus encouraging his precocious young slave. The master, he observes, "could not have realized, in his innocence and decency, in his awesome goodness and softness of heart, what sorrow he was guilty of creating by feeding me that half-loaf of learning: far more bearable no loaf at all" (66). Yet in jail Nat expresses no yearning for the no-loaf life of the slave quarters. Learning to read has opened doors to the Bible and to other books with prophetic titles like Bunyan's *Life and Death of Mr. Badman.* The religious sensibility thus developed differs from both his Episcopalian and Methodist masters' and the slaves' mindless imitation thereof. It is a fervent spirituality tinged with rebelliousness and suffused with sexual longings running counter to both black and white beliefs. Styron's interlacing of social, spiritual, and psychological threads in his protagonist's memory is complex and ambiguous. For those *Harper's* readers given to thinking of historical fiction in terms of Margaret Mitchell or Frank Yerby, the effect of this prose must have at once dazzled and puzzled. Its virtuoso effects often divert attention away from the historical setting and certain gritty realities of Virginia slave plantations toward Nat Turner's pseudo-autobiographical consciousness.

That landscape of memory and dream is a baffling mixture of mists and vividly lit scenes, recaptured in the bookish rhetoric that is Styron's slave's prime characteristic. Words are first and last; they are what set Nat Turner apart. The early recognition of the gulf between his playmate Wash and himself is one of language. Wash, he realizes,

> has almost no words to speak at all. So near to the white people, I absorb their language daily. I am a tireless eavesdropper, and their talk and comment, even their style of laughter, vibrates endlessly in my imagination. . . . Wash is molded by different sounds—even now I am aware of this—nigger voices striving clumsily to grapple with a language never taught, never really learned, still alien and unknown. With such a poor crippled tongue, Wash's way of speaking comes to seem to me a hopeless garble, his mind a tangle of baby-thoughts; so gradually that I barely know it, this playmate floats away out of my consciousness, dwarfish and forgotten, as I settle deep into my own silent, ceaselessly vigilant, racking solitude. (61)

Readers who remembered "This Quiet Dust" of two years earlier, with its revelation that Styron failed to remember any meaningful childhood conversations with blacks, would not be surprised by the congruity of Styron's and Turner's voices.

Nat's precocious appropriation of the dominant culture's language, his location at the edges of that culture, and his training as "tireless eavesdropper" fuel a succession of powerful memories of white plantation life at Turner's Mill. They also affect recollections of his own family—mother, father, and grandmother. While the dominant overlay is the white culture of formal language, books, Christianity, paternalistic racism, and slaveholding, his own family provides an even deeper imprinting, grounded as it is in the mother's presence and the father's absence. As Nat has (or desires) few playmates, his mother is his constant companion. She tells him about his proud father who, once slapped by his master, turned on his heel and, that same night, ran away from slavery. "Said he couldn' stand to be hit in de face by nobody. Not *nobody*! Oh yes, dat black man had pride, awright, warn't many black mens aroun' like him" (58). Presumably, too, the mother tells Nat about his African grandmother. "I never laid eyes on my grandmother," he recalls. Nevertheless he is able to imagine vividly the wild Coromantee girl fresh off the slave ship who, after giving birth to Nat's mother, "had been driven crazy by her baffling captivity . . . was sent into a frenzy, and when presented with the babe, tried to tear it to pieces" (57).

Despite the African heritage of resistance, Nat's mother openly encourages her son's identification with white culture. Lou Ann views the other slaves at Turner's Mill much as her grown son is to do; she complains bitterly about having to share the privy with these dirty slaves whom she encourages her son to think of "as a lower order of people— a ragtag mob, coarse, raucous, clownish, uncouth" (59). The ten-hole privy, he recollects, was the one place where the black worlds of Big House, mill, and field met. Partly for this reason, but more importantly influenced by close ties to his mother, the youthful Nat is unable to behave—or, indeed, even to fantasize—sexually toward black women.

The social and emotional chasm thus established is widened by Nat's eavesdropping discoveries about sex in the white world. These experiences constitute the most sensational sections of the *Harper's* excerpt. The most disturbing of Nat's memories in this vein is the earliest: his mother's rape by the Irish overseer. The little boy's blind rush away from the pantry on whose table he had glimpsed the black woman and the drunken white man brutally intertwined is prophetic, for it symbolizes the future rebel's violent revulsion against both cultures and the sexual basis on which they often conflict and relate. "I am bound for the ends of the earth" (63), Nat observes of his traumatized younger self running down the road, and these words are echoed in the captive's consciousness as he awaits death in Jerusalem jail. His entrapment in the world and the flesh is more painful as the boy, a few minutes later, hiding miserably beneath the kitchen floor with Bunyan's book clutched to his chest, listens to his mother singing a spiritual, "her voice again, gentle, lonesome, unperturbed, and serene as before" (64). Her apparent acquiescence to white sexual violence is of a piece with the "docile equanimity and good cheer" with which, he later recalls, the slaves responded when sold away from Turner's Mill.

That *Harper's* readers of this separate segment could catch all the overdeterminations of Nat Turner's early psychosocial imprinting is unlikely; only the novel itself could weave together all threads of part 2. Nonetheless, the oedipal pattern in the larger tapestry can already be traced. One seemingly minor moment comes more clearly into focus only after the rape scene. Once, as the child lay on his straw bed "at the drowsy edge of sleep," his tired mother came to their bed from the kitchen. "Almost at once she is fast asleep," he recalls, "breathing in a gentle rhythm, and I reach out and lightly touch the rough cotton shift above her ribs, to make certain that she is there. Then at last the spring night enfolds me . . . and dimly I hear a whippoorwill call through the dark, the word *columbine* still on my lips as I sink away into some strange dream filled with inchoate promise and a voiceless, hovering joy" (56).

This memory of lying at the mother's side is followed immediately by a more vivid vision. The dream that will appear at the outset of Nat's reminiscences in part 1 of the novel is described here and will be again at the novel's end. In *Harper's*, the dream-vision's importance is underlined by Robert White's illustration of the adult Nat Turner peacefully asleep in the stylized bow of a drifting boat, his head resting on a pillow. In the dream's second return—the first for these readers—Nat remembers his

> spirit filled with a familiar yet mysterious peace as I drifted through the afternoon quiet of some wide and sunlit river toward the sea. In the distance I hear the ocean booming with the sound

of mighty unseen breakers crashing on the shore. [Far above me on its promontory stood the white temple, as ever serene and solitary and majestic, the sunlight bathing it as if with the glow of some great mystery as I moved on downriver past it, without fear, to the sandy cape and the tumultuous groaning sea.] . . . Then this vision glimmered out and I awoke, raging with fever, and I fell asleep again. . . . And so in this way, between waking and oblivion, with these reveries, voices, recollections, I passed the days and nights before the day of my execution. (56)

Along with its two other settings, Nat's dream-vision accumulates complexities. The bracketed sentence is printed here from the published novel (page 179) as one significant addition that underlines, through the mysterious white temple on the promontory, the sexual as well as spiritual, political, and racial meanings of Nat's psychic history.

As elements in this emerging oedipal pattern the maturing boy learns some disturbing facts about the white women at Turner's Mill. Miss Emmaline, Marse Samuel's youngest daughter, becomes his chief—and safely unattainable—infatuation. While Samuel Turner is worshipped as the divine father of the boy's universe, Miss Emmaline at first occupies an analogous eminence in his innocent heart; she is "an immaculate effulgence of purity and perfection" (74). Her taffeta gown does not remain unsullied, however. During a summer house party for the neighboring gentry, Nat, ever the sensitive eavesdropper, overhears Emmaline and her cousin Lewis making love in the garden "in the moonless and murky dark." What most deeply shocks the boy is the blasphemous language in Emmaline's mouth: "I remained half paralyzed, fascinated yet suddenly sick near unto death at the sound of the Saviour's name spoken thus, as if He had been stripped shamelessly naked by the hot urgency of her lips. 'Wait, wait!' she again implored, and a gentle sigh came from the man's throat, and once more she continued her rhythmic whispering: 'Oh mercy . . . mercy . . . wait now, slowly! . . . Oh Jesus . . . oh Christ'" (76).

Even more shattering are the young white woman's postcoital curses. "Oh God, how I hate this place. Oh God, how I hate life. Oh God, how I hate God!" Henceforth the beautiful blasphemer becomes a compelling enigma to the black boy. Fallen from her sacred niche in the temple of his imagination, she replaces the previously nameless white girl "with the golden curls" as the object of Nat's adolescent masturbatory fantasies. Now "it was Miss Emmaline whose bare white full round hips and belly responded to all my lust and who, sobbing 'mercy, mercy, mercy' against my ear, allowed me to partake of the wicked and godless yet unutterable joys of defilement" (77).

Sexual experience of a different yet clearly related kind soon follows for Styron's now eighteen-year-old protagonist. Blocked by heterosexual inhibitions, Nat befriends Willis, a slim, gentle slave his own age. Though Willis's "talk was childish and guileless and obscene" (84), he stands out from the other field slaves as one "blessed with an unencumbered, happy spirit" like an "eager, fluttering young bird who might soar away if only one were able to uncage him." Nat, already renowned in the slave quarters for precocity and piety, gains power over Willis and tries to bring him "out of ignorance and superstition and into the truth of Christian belief." But before a baptism takes place in the fishing hole the two boys become lovers: "I reached up to wipe away the blood from his lips, pulling him near with the feel of his shoulders slippery beneath my hand, and then we somehow fell on each other, very close, soft and comfortable in a sprawl like babies; . . . and I heard him sigh in a faraway voice, and then for a long moment as if set free into another land we did with our hands together what, before, I had done alone. Never had I known that human flesh could be so sweet" (85). Leaving the creek with Willis chattering happily at his side, Nat "knew that I must consecrate myself to the Lord's service from this point on, as I had promised Him, avoiding at all costs such pleasures of the flesh as I had experienced that morning" (86).

Willis is entwined with Nat's reminiscences by two subsequent threads. One bitter memory is driving his friend and several other slaves to a nighttime rendezvous with slave traders, a transaction Marse Samuel, increasingly unsuccessful as a businessman, misrepresents to his adoring apprentice, whom he had promised to train and eventually set free. Instead of manumission, Nat's fate, after the Turners' removal to Alabama, is to be left behind in the empty plantation house, where he is picked up by Reverend Eppes. Ostensibly on loan to the frosty-faced old pederast, Nat is worked hard and then sold to even more brutal masters. Eppes's fumbling advances, couched in clumsy Old Testament rhetoric, confirm Nat's repulsion to and attraction toward sexuality as it is inextricably identified in his early experience with slavery and religion.

When Nat leaves Turner's Mill to serve these lower class masters, he exchanges a patrician's paradise for what he later knows was "the true world, in which a Negro moves and breathes. It was like being plunged into freezing water" (97). Riding home with the illiterate Moores, he is forcefully reminded of the dubious legacy Samuel Turner has bequeathed him. When Nat reveals his ability to read signs, he is brutally lashed by the humiliated whites. This is his first beating. Consciousness of being a slave had already struck Nat, but under the relatively benign circumstance of a porch conversation between Samuel Turner and two visiting (and effeminate) clergymen. In this muted realization scene Styron diverges from most previous novelists and autobiographers, for whom typically the slave first knows he is one upon seeing a loved one beaten or sold down the river. Thomas Moore's whip "sending me afloat outside myself on a reddish cloud of pain" (102) is the first dramatic sign of Nat's condition.

This turning point in the rebel's life is, however, not the final point in Styron's re-creation of Turner as a young slave. As the whipping reverberates in his memory, he recalls his answer to a question Gray asked about divine inspiration. God, he recalls explaining to Gray, had spoken many times to him but never in complicated or lengthy messages. Most often God's presence was signaled by silence. On this occasion, however, as he crouched in Moore's wagon wiping the blood from his neck, God answered his servant:

A cold winter wind breathed suddenly across the roof of the woods.
"Lord," I whispered, raising my eyes. "Lord?"
Then high at the top of the icy forest I heard a tremendous cracking and breaking sound, and that voice booming in the trees:
I abide. (102)

Styron's imagined epiphany for his future rebel does not quite conclude the *Harper's* account of Nat Turner's past, for the editors append an epilogue containing a biographical sketch. Therein they approvingly repeat the novelist's belief that it is the moral imperative of every white southerner to "know the Negro." The excerpt is, therefore, offered on

Styron's terms: "my own private attempt as a novelist to re-create and bring alive that dim and prodigious black man" as "at least a partial fulfillment of this mandate" (102).

In the mid-sixties campaign to sell American readers on *The Confessions of Nat Turner*, this long section appearing in advance of publication played a significant role. Yet *Harper's*, though an influential journal with a long history, had in 1967 a circulation of only 278,957.[16] Its readership was chiefly middle class, educated, and white, though of course *Harper's* was available in libraries and thus reached a wider audience. Nevertheless, *Harper's* remained the organ of a limited group of Americans. A far larger potential readership, one differently constituted in socioeconomic terms, was the target of the next phase of Nat Turner publicity when, on October 13, 1967, *Life* carried both an excerpt from the just-published book and an article on its author. Even more strenuously than *Harper's*, *Life* played up Styron himself, giving him more space and illustrations than it did Nat Turner. The novelist was photographed in front of the Capron, Virginia, farmhouse "said to be the one where the Turner revolt began with the murder of its occupants."[17] In another photograph he crouched in a swamp near Courtland where "local legend has it that the runaway slave Nat Turner was apprehended . . . after whites put down the rebellion. He was hanged and his body skinned" (54). Another caption reiterated Styron's attitude toward historical records: "You can do all the Nat Turner research in a day because there's not very much to read" (54). In sharp contrast with *Harper's*, *Life* informed its readers that its excerpt constituted the "crucial episode" in Styron's "brutally vivid account of Turner's three-day rebellion" (54). The title *Life* gave the eight or so pages from the new novel was "Novel's Climax: Night of the Honed Axes." In it, Nat's recollections begin not with childhood but with the killing of the Travis family, his present owners. Abject fear figures so prominently in Nat's memories that *Life* readers must have wondered how Nat Turner and his lieutenants—Nelson, Hark, Will, and the others—could possibly be considered heroes. Nat Turner's Old Testament rhetoric, far from invoking God's righteous punishment on slaveowners like Travis, dramatizes feelings that all but immobilize him: "I wondered suddenly if the Lord had also permitted Saul and Gideon and David to endure this fear before their day of warfare: did they too know this demoralizing terror, this tremor in the bones, this whiff of imminent, hovering death? . . .

For an instant panic seized me. I arose as if to flee headlong through the pines, to find some refuge in the distant woods where I would be hid forever beyond the affairs of God and men. *Cease the war, cease the war*, my heart howled."[18] By contrast with his followers' savagery and their victim Travis's bravery, Nat's trepidation seems stronger than momentary panic. "Whatever else he was, he was a man," Nat observes of the white farmer who in the very moment of death Nat admits was a "forebearing and lenient master" (386). Goaded by his fellows to strike the revolt's first blow, Nat hits

> not Travis's skull but the headboard between him and his wife.
> ... In this way I inaugurated my great mission—*Ah Lord!*—I
> who was to strike the first blow. It seemed as if all strength had
> left me, my limbs were like jelly, and for the life of me I could not
> pry the blade of the broad-ax from the imprisoning timber. . . .
> "Shit!" I heard Sam say behind me. . . . Half deafened by Miss
> Sarah's screams, I reached to retrieve the ax; as I bent down
> I saw that Travis, regaining charge of his senses, had wheeled
> about and clutched a pewter vase in hand, prepared to defend
> himself. His gaunt work-worn face was the hue of his white night-
> shirt—but at last how brave he was! Ready for anything, he had
> joined the battle. . . . "Kill; him!" I heard Sam roar behind me.
> But *I* was not ready. (388–89)

In this relived moment of paralysis Nat stands in vivid contrast to Will, whose hatchet is "honed to an exquisite edge" and whose lust for vengeance and rape "was so voracious as to be past all fathoming" (390). Astride Miss Sarah "this scarred, tortured little black man was consummating at least ten thousand old swollen moments of frantic and unappeasable desire. Between Miss Sarah's thrashing, naked thighs he lay in still elongate quest like a lover . . . even as the hatchet went up again and down, and chopped off her scream. Then unimaginable blood spewed forth and I heard the inhabiting spirit leave her body; it flew past my ear like a moth" (390–91).

The counterpointing of external event and inner consciousness here creates a succession of powerful but confusing effects. The casual *Life* reader who misses the oblique reference here to Coleridge's ancient mariner might just as easily misread Nat's irony as he reconstructs Joseph Travis's "sleep-drowned" thoughts just before death.

For surely in the watches of the night, like all white men, he must from time to time have flopped over with a sick groan, thinking of those docile laughing creatures down at the rim of the woods, wondering in a flash of mad and terrible illumination what might happen if—if like gentle pets turning into rampaging beasts they should take it into their hearts to destroy him. . . . If by some legerdemain those comical simpleheads known for their childish devotion—so affecting along with their cunning faults and failings—but never known for their manhood or their will or their nerve, should overnight be transformed into something else. . . . Just as surely as his pathetic faith in history had at last erased these frights and apprehensions from his head, allowing him more often sweet composure and pleasant dreams—for was it not true that such a cataclysm had never happened? Was it not fact, known even to the humblest yeoman farmer and white-trash squatter and vagabond, that there was something stupidly inert about these people, something abject and sluggish and emasculate that would forever prevent them from so dangerous, so bold and intrepid a course, as it had kept them in meek submission for two centuries and more? (386–87)

Other chances, too, abound of misinterpreting the black narrator's irony. Particularly for those unfamiliar with history but susceptible to current fears of ghetto violence, Styron's use of historical myths and racial stereotypes in the ironic act of disrupting them might puzzle many. Given editorial and authorial assertions of this famous writer's trustworthiness as historian and literary artist, many *Life* readers must have found it as difficult to evaluate parts of this brief narrative as others had the longer *Harper's* excerpt.

Readers of both magazine pieces might register two strikingly different impressions of the forthcoming novel. Whereas *Harper's* and Styron divert attention away from the bloody rebellion, dramatizing instead its personal sources in the leader's past, *Life* (again with Styron's consent or insistence) declares the "crucial section" of *The Confessions of Nat Turner* to be the event's violent beginning and its leader's fears and failures. The imbalance between reminiscence and violent action—fifty-four pages of one to eight pages of the other—is, moreover, reflected in the complete novel. Both magazines—*Life* perhaps more aggressively than *Harper's*—engaged in commercial marketing, selling not just fiction but this writer of fiction. While no Beatle or Norman Mailer, Styron bears many of the marks of a "star" with these periodicals serving as his publicity agents.

Styron and His Readerships

After October 1967, the avenues of information, commercial exploitation, and superintendence here briefly identified were by no means preempted by Random House's publication of William Styron's *The Confessions of Nat Turner*. But so loud was the salvo of publicity and praise attending the event, so newsworthy the book's distribution by the Book-of-the-Month Club and its Pulitzer Prize, so impressive its sales figures during the following months (especially after New American Library brought out the paperback edition) that Styron's book could, by the spring of 1968, plausibly be called the immediate cause of the dramatic rise in public consciousness of Nat Turner and slave revolts. A large audience, some already familiar with previous retellings but many encountering Nat Turner for the first time, were assembled in the space of less than a year. They were brought together by the cultural-commercial network eventually defined by *Harper's*, Random House, New American Library, the *New York Times*, *The New York Review of Books*, and the Book-of-the-Month Club. This newly activated group began, in various ways and with varying degrees of explicit ideological awareness, to re-embed Styron's version of the Southampton slave revolt in new and different mental and discursive formations. A majority of such reactivations were private and cannot easily (if at all) be recovered by the cultural historian. They consist of cognitive and emotional responses, which, if articulated, were communicated orally to others in the family or within an immediate social circle.

But in between private reading acts and the institutional networks of the communication culture lay a large sector of the American literate public. Its various members' encounters with Styron's book may be inferred from imprecise data such as sales figures, anecdotes, and other ephemeral sources. Tony Bennett and others emphasize problems in evaluating all private reader expectations and responses, especially toward the mass-market/paperback end of the spectrum. Nonetheless, some tentative speculations can be advanced to support the claims that Styron and the communication industry were successful in attracting at least three distinct readerships for *The Confessions of Nat Turner*.

The joint effort commenced some time in the early sixties. At that point, the author, a notoriously slow writer, was still in mid-manuscript. In point of visibility, familiarity, and influence, Styron's first target was his previous readers and admirers. Members of the culturally dominant white community of educated and expert novel-readers, this community now expanded to include historians, amateur and professional. Supervisors of this canonically or classically minded audience consisted of academics, literary critics, book reviewers in leading elite periodicals, and fellow novelists. We have already encountered one subset of this inner ring at the SHA. Other transactions were interviews on the pages of literary magazines such as the *Paris Review* and *Per/Se*. Styron's second circle of anticipated customers was larger, more diverse, yet easily influenced by the first group. Though activated by a different (and somewhat overlapping) network of magazines, large urban newspapers, national book clubs, and local bookstores, these readers can be hypothesized as middle-class, literate, regular book-buyers. This group would be less likely than the first to have read *Lie Down in Darkness*, *Set This House on Fire*, or *The Long March*. One might typify a member of this circle as a 1967 subscriber to the *Book-of-the-Month Club News*, reading Clifton Fadiman and Robert Penn Warren on *The Confessions of Nat Turner* and deciding to order the November selection. A third target was the growing demotic audience of sporadic, perhaps even first-time readers of "serious" fiction. Less sophisticated than the others, and less readily pigeonholed socially and economically, these paperback readers were reachable through mass media channels—advertising in local newspapers, feature stories in *Life* or *Esquire*, outlets in drugstores and supermarkets, inviting book covers promising history, romance, sex, and violence.

Some clues to the actual size of Styron's and his managers' targets of actual or intended customers lie in publishers' statistics. As we have seen, *Publisher's Weekly* announced (in late summer 1967) a Random House first printing of 75,000. Many, though by no means all, of these initial copies must have found their way into the eager hands of Styron's sophisticated supporters, from whom came the early reviews, endorsements, and interviews. Later that year, the Book-of-the-Month Club reported that 350,000 copies were to be distributed to members. Finally, in February 1969, the *New York Times Book Review* announced printing figures for the most popular paperbacks of 1968. New American Library reported that it had received 1,544,069 paperback print orders for *The Confessions of Nat Turner* during the past year.[19] By this point, of course, Styron's book had become a cause célèbre. All kinds of curious customers (including students) were by now drawn to the cash register and into the network. However, it seems plausible to assume that a great many "ordinary" American readers, neither highly educated nor widely read in modern experimental fiction, helped swell this impressive total.

What expectations, and therefore what incentives, do these diverse audiences present to an author and his publishers, and what challenges are they for the cultural historian struggling to interpret such transactions? An appropriate beginning would be to look at the author within and behind his text. How might Styron, in other words, be imagined in the act of anticipating his several circles of readers while completing the text of *The Confessions of Nat Turner*? Barbara Herrnstein Smith offers a general scenario in *Contingencies of Value* for this sort of cultural convergence when she points out that "the reader's experience of the work is prefigured—that is, both calculated and preenacted—by the author." The writer is never, however, in complete control of this preemptive process,

> for, in selecting this word, adjusting that turn of phrase, preferring this rhythm to that, she is all the while testing the local and global effectiveness of each decision by impersonating in advance her various presumptive audiences, who thereby themselves participate in shaping the work they will later read. Every literary work—and, more generally, artwork—is thus the product of a complex evaluative feedback loop that embraces not only the ever-shifting economy of the artist's own interests . . . but also all the shifting interests of her assumed and imagined audiences, including those who do not yet exist but whose emergent interests, variable conditions of encounter, and rival sources of gratification she will attempt to predict—or will intuitively surmise—and to which, among other things, her own sense of the fittingness of each decision will be responsive.[20]

From this viewpoint—one almost tailor-made for the case in point—we are invited to treat the text of *The Confessions of Nat Turner* as a narrative response to a set of questions raised not only within Styron's private consciousness but also from the three distinct but overlapping segments of prospective readers.

Styron and his elite inner circle could be expected to agree to grant him wide artistic license and sympathetic support for his bold project to meditate freely (that is, subjectively and imaginatively) about American history, and to do so psychologically, from inside the mind of a black slave. Better trained to appreciate complex fictional texts than to expertly criticize historical arguments and sources, these predominantly white academicians and intellectuals could, in turn, be expected to endorse and interpret Styron to other reading groups. Many would do so out of familiarity with the author's previous works and/or on the basis of his reputation as one admired model of the post-Faulkner southern novelist. Hence many distinctive features of this narrative must initially be thought of as deliberately and (as Herrnstein Smith would argue) jointly chosen elements in a complex, sophisticated transaction among a canonically minded elite.

Reconstructing the prefigurative collaboration between Styron and a larger audience, his Book-of-the-Month Club readers, is more speculative and sociological. However, two scholars, one a historian, the other a cultural critic of popular literature, have recently examined the club's history, internal structure, and ideology. Joan Shelley Rubin studies the formative decades of this cultural-commercial institution, whereas Janice Radway takes a closer, mid-eighties look at the subject. Though Styron's connection falls roughly midway in this history, the areas of agreement in these studies are considerable and instructive.[21] The club's cultural function, they emphasize, has from its foundation in 1926 been to make literature as social commodity widely accessible to an audience of literate Americans desiring the club's services: expert advice, convenience of purchase, maintenance of literacy skills, and social awareness. While Rubin stresses the social and economic "middleness" of the membership, Radway is more precise; she cites a 1958 survey revealing that 83 percent of BOMC membership had a college education but only 13 percent were teachers of any kind. These readers expected, and paid for advice about, books that would serve different functions from what elite literature normally does for professional intellectuals. Not identified with this "highest cultural authority" group, they sought help from the editors in keeping up with "serious" but not "trashy" writing. While novels were their favored reading, BOMC readers expected fiction to be as useful as the advice, self-help, or even reference books also offered as club selections. They regarded reading good novels as entertaining and informative experience, as encounters with real life problems and instances of appropriate responses to them. They respected the cultural elite but felt less distanced from everyday concerns and less skilled in interpretation. They would, therefore, approach Styron's story seeking entertainment, knowledge, and moral and social education. The book would, Radway suggests, be expected to operate transitively in their white middle-class lives as a set of coping strategies for dealing with social change. The protagonist would be expected to be an interesting, integrated personality. As one of a number of "serious fiction" selections, therefore, *The Confessions of Nat Turner* (though mentioned by neither scholar) would share a particular social domain and function desired by the members: "the stories they are led to select may tell us much about the particular problems of middle-class life and thus something about the utopian longings it generates in some of its subjects."[22]

A complementary study of one subset of this reading group is Elizabeth Long's analysis and description of the reading habits of Texas women's book clubs.[23] She points out that these middle-class white associations—many of whose thousands were spawned during the sixties—included, like BOMC members, those who buy, read, and respond to books quite differently from academics and professional intellectuals. But they also differ sharply from mass-market book buyers. From Long's discussion of Houston clubs I assume they respond to serious fiction much like *Harper's* readers; they are attentive, regular, but unsystematic consumers of high-culture products defined by them as "good books." Though in their selection process they often rely on advice from cultural authorities (such as college-age children and their professors), these women feel free as interpreters to respond quite subjectively. As their discussions indicate, they are not coerced socially into group thinking. Indeed, they are frequently more tolerant and more critical than their own children. The novels normally chosen for discussion share several features with BOMC selections such as *The Confessions of Nat Turner:* historical settings, strong focus on character development of protagonists, socially relevant themes and conflicts.

If scholars like Rubin, Radway, and Long are helping to clear away some of the clouds surrounding certain past middle-class reading formations, the popular or mass audiences for Styron's emerging novel remain harder to predict. In part this was true because the author lacked a large fund of experience in appealing to and receiving feedback from casual paperback consumers. Nor should feedback be much expected from such audiences. These readers would be ill-prepared for an encounter with *The Confessions of Nat Turner* by prior familiarity with John Jakes's Kent family chronicles or Frank Yerby's plantation fiction. Furthermore, paperback purchasers in the mass seldom resolve themselves into small groups for discussion; they do not join book clubs or read their magazines for advice. Nor do they write many letters to the editor of newspapers. Seldom are they swayed by reviews in the *New York Review of Books*. But publisher's lore, built upon the sales figures of books sharing certain plots, themes, characters, and stylistic patterns, would have been available to Styron. From such sources he could anticipate many New American Library readers to enjoy an exciting, fast-paced narrative. Chronological plots, unfolding in linguistically uncomplicated language, would be other desiderata of best-selling paperback fiction of the mid-sixties. Much dialogue, a diverse cast of characters, detailed and often remote or exotic settings are still other qualities a demotic audience, hungry for information as well as sensation, would crave. New American Library editors might also mention this audience's allegiance to traditional gender and racial roles and identities. Historical subjects, especially those likely to appeal later to movie or TV audiences, would provide inviting possibilities for authors anxious to appeal to popular taste and tap (in Herrnstein Smith's words) "rival sources of gratification."

Through and into some such combination of sixties consumers, critics, and superintendants, Styron's novel was completed and issued on October 9, 1967. It was immediately greeted by greater public attention than any of his previous novels, all three of which are in significant respects southern historical fictions. The newly finished narrative once more raised issues and ideas already communicated to previous readers of certain periodicals. But for even this subset of readers, as L. O. Mink has argued, following a story for the first time and having followed the same story before are quite different mental acts.[24] Now certain numbers of readers would be doing both as they tried to fit a partly (or perhaps vividly) recollected fragment or two into its larger, and largely unfamiliar, whole. Complicating such elite and demotic encounters in late 1967 and early 1968 was a series of widely experienced public events, including marches on Washington, ghetto riots, and the assassination of Martin Luther King, Jr.

Three thematic clusters, it seems to me, help connect and organize authorial vision, readers' expectations, and socio-historical contexts into something like a single cultural expression. These themes surface again and again in discussions and debates among academics and political activists (white and black). They are repeated in editorial statements and other acts of audience superintendence in magazines like *Harper's*, *Life*, and *Book-of-the-Month Club News*. Moreover, Styron himself articulates them in many formats and on many occasions. As announced beforehand, expressed within, and reiterated after publication, the book's central claims and concerns include, first, the assertion of historical truth or fidelity to actual nineteenth-century Virginia reality for this imaginative re-creation. This leads to a second claim: the necessity and adequacy of the psychological penetration of this historical figure's mind. The voyage within finally reaches and transcends the limits of historical, political, or psychological explanations of the man (and event) and asserts spiritual transcendence as the ultimate "fact" of Nat Turner. Each of these interlaced assertions—historical veracity, psychological plausibility, and "ineffable otherness"—involves literary choices and strategies. As literary historian Styron answers both the ordinary reader's question, Is this the way it was in 1831?, and the more recondite question raised at the SHA: Will an actual fact, character or story lend itself to the particular method by which a (great) novelist conveys his historical faithfulness? Then as psychological writer, Styron explores at length the question first posed in "This Quiet Dust": did Nat Turner become a man in the act of bloody revolt (which included the murder of Margaret Whitehead) or did acts of violence rob this slave of his dearly won humanity? Finally, as spiritual amanuensis of another's "confessions," Styron dramatizes the thrust towards timelessness in a nineteenth-century black man's life and thought: "Is this rebel's goal of freedom actually realizable in this world by these means?" might be a more popular inquiry about a Baptist preacher's actual and spiritual life. All of these assertions and audience expectations are putatively claimed in the author's oft-repeated phrase: *The Confessions of Nat Turner* is first and last "a meditation on history."[25]

Opening Signals and Strategies

In the narrative's opening pages Styron quickly introduces and connects these problematic themes. Before Nat Turner's autobiographical voice is heard in a long reminiscence in the form of a dream-vision at the head of part 1, the author sends several advance signals about the nature of the forthcoming tale. This elaborate overture comprises title, dedication, an emblem page and biblical quotation, author's note, table of contents, and an italicized section called "To the Public." Few historical fictions go to such lengths to lead readers along multiple avenues into the main narrative.

"The Confessions of Nat Turner" is a deceptively straightforward and bold title. Appropriated from Gray, it promises first a faithful, if far longer, retelling of the 1831 version. Gray is likewise the source of "To the Public," a carefully edited excerpt from the first *Confessions*. This introduces the reader to the style and mind-set of Nat Turner's original amanuensis, now a fictional figure. More than a historical reminder, however, the word "confession" is also a legal term prefiguring the Jerusalem courtroom in which, on his way to the hanging tree, Nat Turner hears his "confession" to Thomas R. Gray introduced as prime evidence in his trial for insurrection and murder. Is not a judgment of "guilty" also implied by the borrowed title? Furthermore, "confessions" denotes not only a criminal in the dock but also a sinner in repentant address to God, father confessor, and reader. Here Styron's title carries modern literary and clinical implications, since confession can be a secular and psychological communication as well as spiritual exercise. The autobiographical mode of first-person narrative keeps both options open. Thus Styron's audience may anticipate a story either along the lines of Saint Augustine's or Thomas Merton's—accounts of sin and redemption—or its twentieth-century secular counterpart: a retrospective account of a life seen as the unfolding of a personality or identity.

Complicating but not replacing these foremeanings is Styron's choice of an almost-empty page following the dedication (which is a conventional acknowledgment of debts to wife and children and to friends James Terry and Lillian Hellman). On the blank page appears the emblem

$$\text{\AE}$$

denoting the alpha and omega of New Testament Christianity. It points the reader toward both the apocalyptic historical event Nat plans and the timeless realm of death which is his fate and desired destination. The emblem's meanings are then reinforced with biblical texts on two later pages. The first text precedes part 1 and with the second one Styron closes the novel. Both are quotations from the twenty-first chapter of the Revelation of Saint John the Divine. The second makes a fictional finale of verses 6 and 7: "And he said unto me, It is done. I am Alpha and Omega, the beginning and the end. I will give unto him that is athirst of the fountain of water of life freely. He that overcometh shall inherit all things; and I will be his God and he shall be my son." Between biblical parentheses, then, the slave's life, mission, and death are suspended in the same tensions the Book of Revelation exhibits among prophecy, apocalypse, and a timeless utopia of forgiveness and love.

For most readers, however, these predictions are less immediately significant than the author's note. As the ensuing controversy was to underscore, this one-paragraph statement of Styron's historicism drew more attention and fire than all other preliminary devices:

> In August, 1831, in a remote region of southeastern Virginia, there took place the only effective, sustained revolt in the annals of American Negro slavery. The initial passage of this book, entitled "To the Public," is the preface to the single significant contemporary document concerning this insurrection—a brief pamphlet of some twenty pages called "The Confessions of Nat Turner," published in Richmond early in the next year, parts of which have been incorporated into this book. During the narrative that follows I have rarely departed from the *known* facts about Nat Turner and the revolt of which he was the leader. However, in those areas where there is little knowledge in regard to Nat, his early life, and the motivations for the revolt (and such knowledge is lacking most of the time), I have allowed myself the

utmost freedom of imagination in reconstructing events—yet I trust remaining within the bounds of what meager enlightenment history has left us about the institution of slavery. The relativity of time allows us elastic definitions; the year 1831 was, simultaneously, a long time ago and only yesterday. Perhaps the reader will wish to draw a moral from this narrative, but it has been my own intention to try to re-create a man and his era, and to produce a work that is less an "historical novel" in conventional terms than a meditation on history.

The note appears to be a forthright and plausible claim of artistic and historical intentions, duties, and freedoms. It is also an explicit act of superintendence deliberately paralleling Gray's "To the Public." Both are clever appeals. Gray's is to an apprehensive southern public in 1831 (Styron misdates the first publication of Gray's *Confessions;* it appeared in Baltimore only weeks after the revolt). Styron's is directed to a modern audience also excited by current happenings but strangers to this remoter part of the past. Styron's notion of history and historiography and his obligations to both are summarized boldly: his subject is virtually unique in American experience; he will be faithful to its known but scanty facts—scanty respecting not only this man and his era but slavery generally and motivations for rebelling against it. Once again his prerogative as an artist is insisted upon, though at the same time history will impose limits on imagination. That his intended audience is a general rather than a specialized one seems clear from the scope of these historical claims and the looseness of his language. Students of American history (college undergraduates included) might react differently from ordinary members of Book-of-the-Month Club to his argument's weaker points. Was the Southampton slave revolt "the only effective, sustained revolt in our history?" What do these adjectives mean in comparative perspective? What are "*known* facts" and how might one recognize an unknown fact? Have Americans in 1967 only "meager enlightenment" about the institution of slavery given libraries' well-stocked shelves of southern history, surely one of the livelier areas of interest in American universities and their presses? Why does Styron tie "the motivations for revolt" so tightly to Nat and his early life? What about less idiosyncratic reasons for opposing slavery with violence? What does the author mean precisely by the relativity of time allowing elastic definitions; is not this his, not time's, elasticity? Finally, many readers, white as well as black, expert as well as lay, all too aware of the serious splits in society, might raise eyebrows at Styron's repetition of "us" in his credo. Who is intended by this not-so-innocuous pronoun? Some literate Americans might even wryly recall Mark Twain's witticism on the subject—that only kings, newspaper editors, and people with tapeworms are licensed to use "we." Such mixed responses may have been precisely what this author wished to evoke from his audiences. In any case, his "meditation on history" already begins before the reader turns to Gray's preface, "To the Public."

The decision to open with an italicized excerpt from a nineteenth-century document serves several ends at once. Most obviously, it introduces readers to an authentic source whose historical and literary weight is underscored by the court's six judges, who affirm "that the confessions of Nat, to Thomas R. Gray, was read to him in our presence, and that . . . furthermore, when called upon . . . to state if he had any thing to say, why sentence of death should not be passed upon him, replied he had nothing further than he had communicated to Mr. Gray." Gray argues his own case as well by declaring his work "a full and free confession of the origin, progress and consummation of the insurrectory movements of the slaves of which he was the contriver and head." Nat's testimony had been published, he insists, "with little or no variation, from his own words," and bears one stamp of truth and sincerity. He makes no attempt . . . to exculpate himself, but frankly acknowledges his full participation in all the guilt of the transaction."[26]

Styron's own agenda is likewise advanced through Gray's self-serving preface. Despite his claims to be a reliable reporter, Gray's preface paints a highly emotional and slanted picture of his subject. Wrapped in mystery like the revolt itself, Nat Turner stands revealed in Gray's words like a villain from nineteenth-century stage melodrama.

> It will thus appear that whilst every thing upon the surface of society wore a calm and peaceful aspect; whilst not one note of preparation was heard to warn the devoted inhabitants of woe and death, a gloomy fanatic was revolving in the recesses of his own dark, bewildered, and overwrought mind, schemes of indiscriminate massacre to the whites. Schemes too fearfully executed as far as his fiendish band proceeded in their desolating march. No

cry for mercy penetrated their flinty bosoms. No acts of remembered kindness made the least impression upon these remorseless murderers. Men, women and children, from hoary age to helpless infancy were involved in the same cruel fate. Never did a band of savages do their work of death more unsparingly. (App. 410)

Such overripe rhetoric, direct ancestor perhaps of James Hamilton's a century later in the *DAB*, is a far cry from the existentialist voice of Styron's narrator. Nevertheless, several of Styron's own attitudes and arguments are here articulated. Crucial to both storytellers is the mysterious interior of Nat's mind, the true seed and seat of the revolt. Gray acknowledges that "motives of revenge or sudden anger" cannot explain the brutal episode but rather "long deliberation, and a settled purpose of mind,"—"offspring of gloomy fanaticism, acting upon materials but too well prepared for such impressions" (App. 411). Though not content with the reassuring simplification of Nat Turner as a gloomy fanatic, Styron, too, is struck by the paradox of the rebel's remorseless cruelty and what Gray calls "not the least remarkable feature in this horrid transaction, that a band actuated by such hellish purposes, should have resisted so feebly, when met by the whites in arms" (App. 410). But whereas Gray reports a specific instance of this weakness—"more than twenty of them attacked Dr. Blunt's house on Tuesday morning, a little before daybreak, defended by two men and three boys. They fled precipitately at the first fire"—Styron silently omits this passage.

Styron sandwiches between the author's note and Gray's "To the Public" a table of contents. Not entirely conventional, it promises no usual sequence of chapters but rather four parts. Three are very lengthy, the fourth a brief finale. Thus "Judgment Day," "Old Times Past," and "Study War" greatly outweigh "It Is Done." As already announced in *Harper's*, part 2 has a revealing subtitle, "Voices, Dreams, Recollections." This, we now discover, accurately summarizes not just a part but the entire narrative. "Voices" signifies Nat's distinguishing endowment of several voices or modes of expression (each with its vocabulary and social persona) with which to address other voices from his past. "Dreams" underlines not only the central dream motif that opens and closes the story but other dream sequences that exert pressure on the overt actions. Finally, "Recollections" reminds the reader that Nat's backward gaze had been deliberately chosen not just for part 2 but to provide the whole narrative its autobiographical (hence, historical) perspective. Although retrospective narration is the customary medium of history, Styron here redirects readers' expectations away from a chronological and dramatic account of events. The historian's nominal task of creating a convincing picture of a public, sharable reality is to be overridden by a stronger imperative—the evocation of one putatively mysterious inner and timeless reality.

Through this elaborate overture the author reminds readers repeatedly of the experimental nature of this narrative. In this vein, part 1, "Judgment Day," establishes at once a powerful tension between this Nat Turner's thoughts and psychic state and his interactions with four figures known from history. These are Thomas Gray, Jeremiah Cobb (the presiding judge), Hark (his wounded comrade in the next cell), and Margaret Whitehead. Even the initial dream and several flashbacks take place inside Jerusalem jail as well as inside Nat's mind. The presiding image of this narrative action, therefore, is historical: an infamous black slave in chains telling his story to a white lawyer. The transaction, we note, fits exactly Hernnstein Smith's model of all retellings. Hence we should be alerted to examine statements by both tellers and listeners for motives, interests, circumstances, and guiding principles. At the same time, the consciously ahistorical, formal language continually reminds readers that these are Styron's motives and principles, as much as Nat's or Gray's.

Only gradually do Nat's and Gray's distinct reasons for their exchange become clearer, though even at the end there is still some mystery. Nat learns quickly that his confession is legally futile and the trial a mere formality. He and most of his followers are "guilty as sin itself with nothin' to mitigate their guilt whatsoever."[27] Moreover, as Gray explains, many of Nat's army "was either youngly or innocently dragooned or mere tagalongs or they out-and-out *balked* at this crazy scheme of your'n" (23). Their discussion of this issue discloses the white lawyer's multiple role as conduit of historical information, fictional scribe, and dramatic antagonist. Both reader and prisoner need to learn from Gray that of the sixty-odd culprits only seventeen have been or are to be hanged, the rest either acquitted or convicted but transported. "Dad-burned mealy-mouthed abolitionists say we didn't show justice. Well we do. Justice! That's how come nigger slavery's going to last a thousand years" (25). (Here is Styron's first linkage of American slavocracy and the Third Reich.)

Since Nat Turner's "goose is cooked already" (29), he and Gray must negotiate his confessions on other grounds. Gray solicits Nat's story simply as information for the prosecution as "a history of the motives which induced me to undertake the late insurrection" (30), as Nat explains. Consequently part 1 consists chiefly of Gray reading portions of the original *Confessions*, punctuated by queries and answers. The whole fictional-historical transaction is suffused with Nat's emotions and memories and enlivened by his observations of the white man seated opposite.

"Of course, Nat, this ain't supposed to represent your exact words," Gray observes at the outset. "Naturally, in a court confession there's got to be kind of, uh, dignity of style, so this here's more or less a reconstitution and recomposition of the relative crudity of manner in which all of our various discourse since last Tuesday went" (30). Hence when Gray recounts Nat's arrival at one bloody scene during the revolt where he "viewed the mangled bodies as they lay, *in silent satisfaction*," Gray adds "my emphasis. Well, that last item, gildin' the lily, maybe?" (40). Gray's need to gild the captive's words is driven home by his blatant proslavery racism. This bias constitutes the burden of his running commentary on the futility of the revolt and the scientific fact of black inferiority. The lawyer raises moral questions, too, demanding to know how Nat could have killed Travis, "a man who you admit is kind and gentle to you and you butcher in cold blood!" (34). Nat is discomfited by the query. Present-day readers, too, might be discomfited by his response: "For a moment I was so surprised that I couldn't speak. I sat down slowly. Then the surprise became perplexity, and I was silent for a long time, saying finally even then: 'That—that I can't give no reply to, Mr. Gray.' And I couldn't—not because there was no reply to the question, but because there were matters which had to be withheld even from a confession, and certainly from Gray" (34).

If there are indeed matters withheld even from *this* confession, then fiction itself seems to lie at the service of other realities than history or the ideology of liberation. What these realities are comes only gradually into view in part 1. When Gray repeats familiar proslavery arguments—"This is *Virginia* in the year anno Domini 1831 and you have labored under civilized and virtuous masters" (35)—Nat again summons no rejoinder: "I stared long and hard at Gray. Little different from any of the others, nonetheless it was a matter of wonder where this my last white man (save one with the rope) had come from. Now, as many times, before, I had the feeling I had made him up. It was impossible to talk to an invention, therefore I remained all the more determinedly silent" (35).

Silence cannot fend off Gray's deeper probes, however. If not Travis as undeserving victim, what about Margaret Whitehead? "How come you slew only one? How come, of all them people, this here particular young girl?" (37). As Gray reads the account of her murder and other bloodthirsty acts, Nat cries out, "Stop! We done it! Yes, yes, we done it! We done what had to be done. But stop recitin' about me and Will!" (39). Then he apologizes: "It's just that I don't think you understand about this business, and I don't know but whether it's too late to make it all plain" (39).

Again, Styron's readers might feel variously confused. Why is Nat unwilling, even inside his own thoughts, to debate Gray's view of slavery? Yet he stubbornly insists that these confessions constitute no admission of guilt. Disingenuously he explains to Gray why his words must be reported exactly:

> But as I sat here in these chains, with this neck iron and these leg irons and these here manacles eating at my wrists, as I sat here in the hopeless agony of the knowledge of what was going to befall me, why, Mr. Gray, I'll swear that the Lord came to me in a vision. And the Lord said this to me. The Lord said: *Confess, that all the nations may know. Confess, that thy acts may be known to all men.* . . . For a brief instant I thought the falsity of these words would reveal itself, but Gray was lapping it up. . . . "What'd the Lord say to you again, Nat? 'Confess your sins that'—what?"
>
> "Not confess your sins, sir," I replied. "He said confess. Just that. Confess. That is important to relate. There was no *your sins* at all." (15)

As the plea of not guilty makes plain later, Nat is hindered from openly defending the revolt not simply out of a desire to gain temporary relief from his chains but, more profoundly, by his spiritual state of "hopeless agony." In the jail he can neither pray nor recite his beloved

Psalms, so deep is his sense of separation from God—"a separation which had nothing to do with faith or desire, for both of these I still possessed, but with a forsaken solitary apartness so beyond hope that I could not have felt more sundered from the divine spirit had I been cast alive like some wriggling insect beneath the largest rock on earth, there to live in hideous, perpetual dark" (10).

Bitter despair marks and masks all Nat's thoughts, including those toward his fellow slaves, "my black, shit-eating people" who are, he feels, "surely like flies" (27). The flies in his cell are emblems of "God's supreme outcasts, buzzing eternally between heaven and oblivion in a pure agony of mindless twitching" (26). How this mood of agonizing alienation is related to his gnawing remorse (if not guilt) over the murder of Margaret Whitehead is a question postponed. But it is clear that these existential emotions are tied more explicitly to sympathetic whites he has known, including Margaret, than to injustices suffered as a slave. Though the young white woman and his adored master Samuel Turner are the two figures chosen for intense emotional investment, there are several lesser characters distinguished also in his memory by their superior understanding of his personal plight and the true nature of slavery. Of these, part 1 presents Jeremiah Cobb as the first and most striking specimen.

As elsewhere in this novel, weather and landscape augur social and psychological states, and this symbolism is apparent in Nat's early recollections of the man who later pronounces his death sentence. The November day is "a vast gray globe of silence" (48), out of which Cobb appears in a sudden whirlwind of leaves. Nat sees the crippled and drunken judge while crouching to clean a rabbit. As Cobb questions him, Nat fears a white man's "nigger-needling." Should this happen, he vows silently to strike back. But Cobb's sympathy for the young slave makes premature violence unnecessary.

> As he continued to speak I slowly stood erect, but even at my full height he towered over me, sickly, pale, and sweating, his nose, leaking slightly in the cold, protruding from the stormy and anguished face, the brandy bottle clutched in one huge mottled hand against his breast. . . . Speak you of the yoke of bondage? How then, country magistrate, do you answer this? Ephesians Six, Five: *Servants, be obedient to your masters according to the*

flesh, with fear and trembling, in singleness of your heart, as unto Christ. . . . There, friend,—*there*—is that not divine sanction for the bondage of which you rave and prattle? Merciful God in heaven, will such casuistry never end? Tell me in the honesty of truth, preacher: is not the handwriting on the wall for this beloved and foolish and tragic Old Dominion? (63–64)

Cobb's rhetoric, to some readers almost a parody of the conscience-crippled southern liberal's language, becomes even more ironic as his diatribe settles upon the future rebel-criminal: "this prodigy, this *paragon*, a Negro *slave*—oh, perish the vile word!—who had acquired the lineaments not just of literacy but of knowledge, who it was rumored could almost speak in the accents of a white man of breeding and cultivation; who, in short, while still one of this doomed empire's most wretched minions, had transcended his sorry state and become not a thing but a person—all this is beyond the realm of one's wildest imagination. . . . Tell me, preacher, how do you spell *cat*?" (67).

Despite, or perhaps because of, the judge's sympathy, Nat is terrified by the Gothic figure prophesying general doom. Virginia, Cobb insists, has become "a monstrous breeding farm to supply the sinew to gratify the maw of Eli Whitney's infernal machine" (69). His words at first awaken hope and awe in the young slave, but these feelings quickly turn to fear.

I could only smell the musky scent of danger—flagrant, imminent danger—and feel a sense of suspicion and mistrust such as I had rarely ever known. Why? It is perhaps impossible to explain save by God, who knows all things. Yet I will say this, without which you cannot understand the central madness of nigger existence: beat a nigger, starve him, leave him wallowing in his own shit, and he will be yours for life. Awe him by some unforeseen hint of philanthropy, tickle him with the idea of hope, and he will want to slice your throat. (69–70)

But it is with another runaway, of an apparently different breed of black slave, that the rest of the scene with Jeremiah Cobb unfolds. For crouching at the white man's feet—but also lying wounded in the next cell to Nat as he recalls the past—is Hark. In between these narrative moments, Hark's ludicrously inept attempt to run away to Pennsylvania serves as ironic commentary on slave narratives like Frederick Douglass's, in which the flight to freedom is the central action. Hark's escape proves instead an exercise in futility. Wholly ignorant of geography, he wanders, terrified, in circles and is easily caught by a fellow slave's betrayal. Here, however, Hark gives no more hint of this future than of his far more historic transformation into rebel and martyr. In the present scene Hark typifies for Nat all "bad-assed" slaves whose bondage has made them feel "devoid of character or moral sense or soul" (53). As Cobb approaches, Hark is admitting this. "Figger when I gets to heaven like you says I is, de good Lord hisself even *He* gwine make ole Hark fell bad-assed, standin' befo' de golden throne" (54). When Cobb speaks to him, Hark becomes, in Nat's words, "the unspeakable bootlicking Sambo, all giggles and smirks and oily, sniveling servility. . . . Can't you see the *difference*? The difference betwixt plain politeness and bootlickin'?" (55–56).

At the story's outset, then, Hark epitomizes the problem Nat faces as future and failed leader. With "the face of an African chieftain—soldierly, fearless, scary, and resplendent in its bold symmetry," Hark has "the eyes of a child, trustful and dependent, soft doe eyes mossed over with a kind of furtive fearful glaze, and as I looked at them now—the womanish eyes in the massive, sovereign face . . . I was seized by rage" (56). How to rid his future lieutenant, and others like him, of this "fawning and servile abasement" becomes a fateful issue throughout Nat's brief career. In Hark's case (as Nat rather improbably finds himself explaining to Cobb) degradation involves a series of childish acts of disobedience. These are his response to the bitter memory of the sale of his wife and beloved son by a hated master. On hearing this, the drunken white man bursts out with further imprecations against slavery, "*the ultimate horror!*" (73). "Great God! Sometimes I think . . . *it is like living in a dream!*" (74).

Dreams and dreamers are indeed crucial to several dimensions of this historical tale. But Nat's dreams differ from Cobb's, despite their common detestation of slavery. Their secret unity and public opposition are dramatized in the courtroom when, at one point in the tedious proceedings, Nat lapses into daydream. This one differs from the opening dream-float down the river, which is serenely soundless, by being terrifyingly noisy. Nat imagines himself wandering alone in a swamp desperately seeking his lost Bible. Suddenly he hears voices.

They were the voices of boys . . . half a dozen black boys trapped neck-deep in a bog of quicksand, crying aloud for rescue as their arms waved frantically in the dim light and as they sank deeper and deeper into the mire . . . while I stood there a voice echoed out of the sky, itself partaking of that remote sound of thunder: *Thy sons shall be given to another people and thine eyes shall look, and fail with longing for them all the day long, so that thou shalt be mad for the sight of thine eyes.* . . . Screaming their mortal fright, black arms and faces sinking beneath the slime, the boys began to vanish one by one before my eyes while the noise of a prodigious guilt overwhelmed me like a thunderclap. (76)

Though no equivalent to this vivid daydream is to be found in Gray's *Confessions,* Styron's fictional vision finds a striking poetic parallel in Robert E. Hayden's poem on Nat Turner, a contrasting treatment of white and black imagery discussed below. In the present context, Nat's "prodigious guilt" at the plight of the bogbound boys finds an echo in Gray's derisive taunt about the failed insurrection:

Here's what it got you, Reverend, if you'll pardon the crudity. It got you a pissy-assed record of total futility, the likes of which are hard to equal. Three-score white people slain in random butchery, yet the white people still holdin' the reins. Seventeen niggers hung, including you and old Hark there, nevermore to see the light of day. A dozen or more other nigger boys shipped out of an amiable way of life to Alabama. . . . I've seen them rice layouts too, Reverend—niggers up to their necks in shit from day clean to first dark. . . . This is what you brung on them kids, Reverend, this is what Christianity brung on them boys. . . . Nineteen hundred years of Christian teaching plus a black preacher is all it takes—Is all it takes to prove that God is a God durned lie. (112–14)

Though laced with heavy irony, Gray's accusations play a more important role than simply supplying historical details and white southern rationalizations. Gray's crude questions expose and exacerbate Nat Turner's private doubts and spiritual despair. His weak, evasive rejoinders keep reinforcing the impression of a self-accused culprit. Never, for example, does Nat state simply and openly, even to himself, that slavery is the monstrous and justified cause of his massacre—as do Frederick Douglass and his ilk in their slave narratives. The psychological burden of defending himself and thereby filling in gaps in Gray's *Confessions* appears as heavy as the chains on the slave's body. As here established, Styron's portrait of Nat Turner denies readers their possible desires for a forthright hero or prophet.

Nat's burden of responsibility and remorse is, in fact, twofold. The heavier weight, despite his daydream, seems not to be his fellow slaves but rather Margaret Whitehead. She is the fourth and in several respects crucial historical figure Styron fleshes out with his imagination in part 1. She enters only in the prisoner's memory, of course, occupying space "in some fragrant summery context of dappled light and shade" (87). Escaping the ominous atmosphere of the Jerusalem courtroom, Nat returns in dreamy reverie to two particular memories of Margaret Whitehead. In the first, the schoolgirl and the slave share their love of poetry and the Psalms on a carriage ride. The second is of a mission Sunday at her brother's church. In both, Margaret is evoked with a flood of erotic and romantic feeling, followed by an equally genuine surge of hatred for the "innocent and sweet and quivering young girl" (92). These conflicting emotions reflect several pressures. Most immediate is the young slave's exquisite consciousness of a desirable, unattainable "demure and virginal beauty" with its "faintest touch of wantonness" (89). But just as powerful is their spiritual and literary friendship; *"when I tell the girls at school they just don't believe me when I say I go home on weekends and the only person I can talk to is a darky!"* (91). Yet Margaret's sympathy is maddeningly naive. She thinks it merely strange that Nat's temporary services at the Whiteheads have been swapped for a yoke of oxen. Yet at the church she sees through her brother's annual sermon to the slaves—*"Just folderol for the darkies!"* (104).

In the church scene, Margaret's character as adolescent tease and ignorant sympathizer is contrasted with Nat's exasperation, fear, and loathing of his fellow slaves. As Richard Whitehead enjoins the blacks to serve their masters with their bodies and God with their souls—a message Styron has lifted from an actual southern bishop—the slaves sharply divide into two groups in Nat's mind.[28] The majority is "a score of faces popeyed with black nigger credulity, jaws agape, delicious shudders of fright coursing through their bodies as they murmur soft

Amens" (97). Then there are the select others—Nat's future rebels, Hark, Nelson, Sam, and Will. The latter's voice whispers hoarse, obscene accompaniment to the sermon: *"get me some of that white stuff, yas"* (102). Nat suddenly overflows with hatred and distrust—hatred of the house servant, "docile as a pet coon" (98), distrust of Will's "foaming and frenzied . . . madness" (102). With relief, and forgetting his recent outburst against Margaret's naïveté, his eyes pick out her figure, "her dimpled chin tilted up as, with one arm entwined in her mother's, she carols heavenward, a radiance like daybreak on her serene young face" (104). While the white maiden in the country church seems to promise spiritual communion without community, his fellow blacks promise Nat only a community of domesticated or feral animals.

Nat's disturbing daydreams and romantic reveries conclude abruptly with Judge Cobb pronouncing sentence. "We gazed at each other from vast distances, yet close, awesomely close, as if sharing for the briefest instant some rare secret—unknown to other men—of all time, all mortality and sin and grief" (106). While Cobb can only hint his pity, Gray continues to assault Nat's conscience with accusations of failure and guilt. The rebel is, therefore, left alone in spiritual despair. *"Then what I done was wrong, Lord? I said. And if what I done was wrong, is there no redemption?"* (115). Alone in his alienation, Nat suddenly speaks in slavish accents, for at this crucial moment Styron has stripped him of his usual literate voice, the chief mark of his achieved identity.

The novel's early sections, then, present an extended sequence of scenes and dreams unified by the transaction of telling and listening, questioning and responding (or remaining silent), and, above all, of brooding on the past. As the framework for Nat's future meditations and farewell interactions, part 1 creates a variety of images, emotions, and arguments from which Styron's several audiences must construct their own responses to the historical-fictional characters and their fateful relationships. It is a communication guaranteed to provoke strong and divergent reactions.

Beyond Revolt: Love, Hate, Death

Although it would be a simplification to believe Styron consciously constructed his novel to appeal to a tripartite white (or white-oriented) audience, any more than he wrote *The Confessions of Nat Turner* to fit the formula of successful Pulitzer Prize winners, the author's main preoccupations, especially in four successive parts of his long narrative, do nicely fit many expectations shared by mainstream as well as elite and mass readerships. In part 2, "Old Times Past," and also in large sections of part 3, "Study War," the focus shifts from the discernibly historical to a necessarily more fictitious history of Nat Turner's early life. In the *Harper's* excerpt we have already witnessed several episodes and relationships in this fictional black man's growth toward his historical roles of preacher, prophet, and rebel. We have yet to trace the final trajectory of his consciousness, beyond revolt and retribution to transcendence at the brink of death.

Reviewing "Old Times Past" from the perspective of its likely audience in the sixties and early seventies, it is clear that white readers could—and did—identify successfully with Styron's version of Nat Turner, the slave who became a "man" and a rebel. One familiarizing feature is the narrator's anchor in Nat's childhood and youth. Not simply in deference to Gray's opening—"You have asked me to give a history of the motives which induced me to undertake the late insurrection, as you call it—To do so I must go back to the days of my infancy, and even before I was born" (99)—but also in recognition of present-day expectations, this multilayered history of a psyche begins in early experiences and the individual's significant identifications. This is, of course, not exclusively a white assumption about fictional biography or autobiography. What makes Styron's version particularly acceptable to white readers, though, is the nature of the black child's imagined upbringing and consequent emotional attachments. (These are wholly social and psychological happenings in real time, for Styron ignores one "superstitious" detail in Gray's *Confessions*—that the three- or four-year-old child remembered events that occurred before his birth.) Nat's early turn away from the black community and from what might be considered mature heterosexuality, together with his passionate embrace of an idealized white plantation culture, encourage white readers to feel at home inside this black consciousness. Though deviant in gender identity, he is one of "us" culturally, many could say. Homosexuality was, to be sure, a risky though by no means taboo subject. But in its single and almost childish expression here it was likely less threatening or abhorrent to sophisticated white readers than to the vast majority of black readers. Sixties audiences—and not merely the subscribers to the highbrow *New York Review of Books*—would probably assent to Eugene Genovese's reply to the outraged ten black writers on this issue: "Twenty years ago the *Kinsey Report* reported that the majority of white males had homosexual experiences during pre- and early adolescence. By assuming that black men follow similar lines of development, Styron merely gives Nat Turner something of a normal early life. Perhaps black men do not share with decadent whites these delightful early encounters. *Che Peccaio!*"[29] Genovese's irony by no means disposes of all questions about the motives for marking Nat Turner's maturation in this particular ahistorical fashion. But his remark underlines Styron's practice of measuring black men against white, in terms here of "a normal early life." One aim is clearly to render the Preacher less remote and unique a figure than in previous retellings.

Styron also invests Nat's attachment to white women with ambiguous excitement for white readers. His erotic fantasies doubtless disturbed as well as titillated many. But in the context of the slave's commitment to white southern cultural ideals, these sexual longings might seem pardonable, unthreatening, perhaps even admirable. After all, Nat never acts out his fantasies and even his secret dreams can be justified as homage to the southern white lady as the embodiment of purity and beauty. The cornerstone of cultural myth and literary tradition, the southern belle still flourishes in some forms of American twentieth-century fiction. As a mythic figure from a very different cultural story, Nat Turner has been carefully shaped to be safely refined and repressed. In Styron's depiction, he stands as the polar opposite of Will, the revolt's bestial axeman and would-be rapist. Both men's preoccupations with white women's bodies as erotic (and political) targets would not seem strange to many groups of readers. A staple of sensationalist popular fiction like the Falconhurst and Bondmaster series is the theme of black man/white woman sexual relations. This feature of what Houston book club members call "trashy" novels had become commonplace since at least the success of Kyle Onstott's *Mandingo* in 1957. For somewhat more sophisticated readers as well, the sixties saw several bestsellers dealing with interracial sex, including Calvin Hernton's pop psychology paperback, *Sex and Racism in America*, in 1966. Eldridge Cleaver's autobiography *Soul on Ice* (1967) dramatized even more harrowingly one bitter black man's career as an ideological rapist of white women. Styron's black rebels serve some of the same psychological functions as this popular literature of fear and desire. Nat and Will balance each other in this transaction just as they conflict with each other within the plot. Nat is clearly the more complex but less threatening figure. Not only does his homosexual past "soften" his sexuality in some readers' eyes, but his religious convictions and inhibitions and his freight of remorse (but not guilt) over the murder of Margaret Whitehead temper some of the horror of Nat's turn toward violence. White readers of "This Quiet Dust" would have encountered these fantasies with the advance knowledge that Nat did succeed in controlling Will's lust and brutality.

Two key scenes in the novel's second half vividly illustrate Styron's exploitation of public and private preoccupations in this troubling psychosocial realm. Each episode juxtaposes Nat's feelings and actions so as to explain his lifelong conflicts and contradictions as these come to focus upon white women.

The first indication—and prime symbolic cause—of Nat Turner's turn toward violence occurs on the street in Jerusalem. There, at the opening of part 3, Nat witnesses a shattering display of white liberal guilt, pity, and withdrawal in the face of the brutal reality of slavery. A rich northern woman who has arrived in Jerusalem as Major Ridley's bride-to-be is the medium and object of Nat's passionate witnessing. At this moment (1825 as he believes) Nat felt "'on the fence,' so to speak, toying with the notion of slaughter and already touched with the premonition of a great mission" (259). The future rebel was on the fence in other respects as well. For he had begun to separate himself from his fellow slaves, preferring, when in town, to read his Bible rather than join the other men in idle chatter or, worse, in group fornication with some willing Jerusalem black woman.

The major's fiancée appears on foot and asks directions from Arnold, an oafish free black. In Nat's eyes, Arnold is a scathing illustration of manumission's futility, for he has been freed by "the grace and piety of his late mistress" (261). Yet Nat wonders: "What could freedom mean to Arnold? Unschooled, unskilled, clumsy by nature, childlike and credulous, his spirit numbed by the forty years or more he had spent as a chattel" (261). To this groveling "incarnation of freedom" the New Haven woman addresses her question: "'I seem to have lost my bearings'—the accent now touched with vague anxiety—'Major Ridley told me the courthouse was next to the market. But all I see is a stable on one side and a dram shop on the other. Could you direct me to the courthouse?'" (262). As the confrontation unfolds, the implications of her query translate into a thinly veiled synecdoche of southern society itself. To this stranger, that world is organized around the law, which stands cheek by jowl beside the (slave)market and serving (and enslaving) a populace, black and white, of animals and drunkards. Poor Arnold exemplifies but comprehends nothing of this. Nor can the lady comprehend a word of his "nearly impenetrable . . . stunted speech" (262). She is suddenly struck dumb by the abased, stammering apparition before her:

> "I don't seem to know what—" And she halted, her expression now full of chagrin, sorrow, something even more disturbing— perhaps it was horror, but it seemed even more to be akin to pity. At any rate, it was what then took place—and it had to do not alone with Arnold and the Northern lady but with the sudden upheaval in myself that caused this encounter to be graven upon my brain as long as I was possessed of memory. For the woman said nothing more, simply stood there while her arm went limp and the parasol clattered to the road, then raised her clenched fists to her face as if she were striking herself—an angry tormented gesture—and burst into tears. Her whole frame—back-bone, shoulders, rib cage— . . . seemed to collapse inward with a rush, and she became helpless and shrunken as she stood there in the road, fists pressed to her eyes, shaken by loud racking sobs. It was as if something long pent up within her had been loosed in a torrent. (263)

Nat's response is as visceral as hers.

> I was seized by a hot convulsive emotion that I had never known so powerfully before—it was like a roaring in my ears. For what I had seen on this white woman's face was pity—pity wrenched from the very depths of her soul, and the sight of that pity, the vision of that tender self so reduced by compassion to this helpless state of sobs and bloodless clenched knuckles and scalding tears, caused me an irresistible, flooding moment of desire. And it was, you see, pity alone that did this, not the woman herself apart from

the pity.... It was as if divesting herself of all composure and breaking down in this fashion—exposing a naked feeling in a way I had never seen a white woman do before—she had invited me to glimpse herself naked in the flesh, and I felt myself burning for her. Burning! (263–64)

In Nat's fevered imagination, sexual passion, "which I knew to be abominable to the Lord" (264), turns instantly to rage and violence, as "in a swift fantasy I saw myself down on the road beginning to possess her without tenderness, without gratitude for her pity but with abrupt, brutal, and rampaging fury, watching the composure melt from her tear-stained face as I bore her to the earth, my black hands already tearing at the lustrous billowing silk as I drew the dress up around her waist, and forcing apart those soft white thighs, exposed the zone of fleecy brown hair into which I drove my black self with stiff merciless thrusts" (264).

Nat's imagined rape not only identifies him temporarily with Will but also with (and against) the drunken Irish overseer of early childhood memory. For it cannot be pure accident that he explains his desire thus: "I conceived not of any pleasure I might cause her or myself, but only the swift and violent immediacy of a pain of which I was the complete overseer" (265). Yet the subliminal quid pro quo is subsequently cleansed of actual desire by the preacher's sternly repressive ideology, which he succeeds in imposing on himself, Will, and the others. In this way, Styron dramatizes the sexual dynamics of American interracial violence without violating the recorded facts of the historical event. This is a strategy well suited to his several white audiences, whose own subliminal wishes in the scene are completed by the northern lady's final gesture: "I later learned that she left town and never came back" (265).[30]

The rich lady on the Jerusalem street joins a chain of women, white and black, whose galvanizing presences are part of Nat's past and, along with other forces, eventually impel him to violent action on the stage of history. Nat's mother Lou-Ann, Miss Emmaline, and Margaret Whitehead have already contributed their legacies to the explosive chemistry of Nat's consciousness and unconscious. Sexuality as fateful female attractiveness is one catalyst for catastrophe. Moreover, its power must be experienced or observed at close range. Nat Turner reaches this conclusion in a meditation on white pity and black rage that prefaces the northern lady's encounter with poor Arnold. "Many conditions are required for the full fruition of this hatred, for its ripe and malevolent growth," he declares, "yet none of these is as important as that at one time or another the Negro live to some degree of intimacy with the white man.... For without knowing the white man at close hand, without having submitted to his wanton and arrogant kindnesses, without having smelled the smell of his bedsheets and his dirty underdrawers and the inside of his privy . . . without having known all these cozy and familial truths, I say, a Negro can only pretend hatred" (257).

Committed to this truth, Styron necessarily makes Nat a house servant and skilled craftsman. Proximity to whites is absolutely vital to Styron's story. It affords the child and youth opportunities to experience his mother's rape, Miss Emmaline's godless coupling with her cousin, and Margaret Whitehead's naive flirtations with her favorite "darky." Yet though his experiences also include several incidents of Samuel Turner's "wanton and arrogant kindnesses," these acts arouse Nat's burgeoning hatred only after the fact. At the time, the boy is unable to blame his master for complicity in a brutal institution—perhaps because the beloved white deity of Turner's Mill is unconsciously an object of erotic desire. But, if so, the emotional-ideological current surging within and beneath this slave's consciousness is diverted into (and defused by) the episode with Willis. Thus it becomes more momentous that the chief turning points of the rebel's history involve white women. Why a woman's sympathy and pity, of which the northern lady is the general prototype and Margaret Whitehead the particular instance, should outweigh similar liberal sentiments in Samuel Turner and Jeremiah Cobb is a question raised but not fully resolved. There are, to be sure, scenes in part 2 in which the young apprentice and his saintly master are united in momentary intimacy. But by the time of Nat's crisis of identity Samuel Turner has been removed to Alabama. His embittered slave, robbed of his idyllic life and hopes (and fears) of manumission, has simply put the white man out of his mind. Well before this repression takes place, Nat's mother has died and the small boy who once fled her kitchen "bound for the ends of the earth" has become the Baptist preacher whose Bible and visions instruct him to eschew erotic attachments and become God's avenger. To some extent Nat has also outgrown his infatuation with white culture, though not his disgust for the community of the slave quarters. Thus the encounter with the northern lady's wrenching pity is the decisive moment "when I felt this hatred at the most deranging and passionate" (259). For at this point personal and general experiences have merged. Borne forward on a wave of religious inspiration, bitter experiences of the cruelties and ineffectual kindnesses of slaveowners, and a series of profoundly frustrating relations with white women and black men, Nat Turner embarks on the revolt. His account of this climax of his personal and political history is, as we have seen, suffused with overpowering feelings of remorse, guilt, fear, and failure.

What other factors explain these all but crippling emotions? How are they finally dissipated or transcended in part 4, "It is Done"? There are several answers to these vital questions. Apart from the feelings of fear and despair that Nat carries with him into the sleeping Travis household, one devastating memory of the revolt accounts for much of the storyteller's despair. That is the dismaying evidence that his insurrection, far from releasing the suppressed desire for freedom among the slaves of Southampton County, failed because, at a crucial moment at Major Ridley's, loyal slaves joined in the battle that halted the rebels' march toward Jerusalem. Styron's description of this crushing blow represents his authentication of Gray's derisive taunts and the claim on the Virginia highway marker that faithful slaves fortified the houses. This memory at least temporarily replaces Nat's "entombed frustrate rage" at the whites with bitter resentment toward the blacks. They, too, brought about defeat on "that Wednesday afternoon, when after having finally laid waste to two score buildings and our force of fifty had rallied in the woods to storm Major Ridley's place, I had caught sight for the first time of Negroes in great numbers with rifles and muskets at the barricaded verandah, firing back at us with as much passion and fury and even skill as their white owners and overseers who had gathered there to block our passage to Jerusalem" (398). In this crucial engagement Hark falls wounded. Nat recalls what happened there to his brave lieutenant: "I saw three bare-chested Negroes who were dressed in the pantaloons of coachmen charge from the house under covering fire and kick him back to earth with booted feet. Hark flopped about in desperation but they kicked him again, kicking him with exuberance not caused by any white man's urging but with rackety glee, kicked him until I saw droplets of blood spray from his huge and jagged wound. . . . *yes, Gray was right*" (400). In fact, the *historical* Gray was neither right nor wrong. For, as we have already noted, there is no mention of this episode in the 1831 *Confessions*, where, indeed, it might have been used to great propagandistic effect. Styron's protagonist credits a *fictional* Gray with these damaging claims—which, of course, readers might mistake as historically accurate.

Nat's second, even more anguishing remembrance of the revolt is of a different murderous attack, one executed with neither exuberance nor rackety glee. The ineffaceable image in the storyteller's consciousness is of his own killing of Margaret Whitehead. Its attendant emotions are utterly opposite from the black defenders' at Major Ridley's, despite Will's taunts with which the description is prefaced—"Go git her, preacher man! If'n you cain't make de red juice run you cain't run de *army*!" (412). Nat's response climaxes in this scene:

> *Ah, how I want her*, I thought, and unsheathed my sword. . . .
> I ran headlong into the field. . . . I heard for the first time her hurtful, ragged breathing, and it was with this sound in my ears that I plunged my sword into her side, just below and behind her breast. She screamed then at last. Litheness, grace, the body's nimble felicity—all fled her like ghosts. She crumpled to earth, limp, a rag, and as she fell I stabbed her again in the same place, or near it, where pulsing blood already encrimsoned the taffeta's blue. There was no scream this time although the echo of the first sang in my ears like a far angelic cry. . . .
> I stopped and looked back. "*Die*, God damn your white soul," I wept. "Die!" . . .
> "Shut your eyes," I told her quickly. Then when I raised the rail above her head she gazed at me, as if past the imponderable vista of her anguish, with a grave and drowsy tenderness such as I had never known, spoke some words too soft to hear and, saying no more, closed her eyes upon all madness, illusion, error, dream and strife. So I brought the timber down and she was swiftly gone, and I hurled the hateful shattered club far up into the weeds. (414–15)

As if her death were not already sufficiently symbolic of a long-wished-for union between murderer and victim, the scene concludes even more explicitly in the lush language and tone of popular romance.

> For how long I aimlessly circled her body—prowled around the corners of the field in haphazard quest for nothing, like some roaming dog—how long this went on I do not recollect. . . .
> And once in my strange journey I thought I heard her whispery voice, thought I saw her rise from the blazing field with arms outstretched . . . as she cried: "Oh, I would fain swoon into an eternity of love!" But then she vanished before my eyes, melted instantly like an image carved of air and light—and I turned away at last and went back to join my men. (415)

If this denouement pleases—or at least does not offend—readers of drugstore romance, what about historically minded readers who, provoked by Styron's pyrotechnics, decide to check his scene against Gray's account? The contrasts in detail, tone, and meaning between modern novel and antebellum journalism are never more striking than here. In the earlier of the two *Confessions*, Gray writes that Turner recalled:

> as we approached the house we discovered Mr. Richard Whitehead standing in the cotton patch, near the lane fence; we called him over into the lane, and Will, the executioner, was near at hand, with his fatal axe, to send him to an untimely grave. As we pushed on to the house, I discovered some one run round the garden, and thinking it was some of the white family, I pursued them, but finding it was a servant girl belonging to the house, I returned to commence the work of death. . . . As I came round to the door I saw Will pulling Mrs. Whitehead out of the house, and at the step he nearly severed her head from her body, with his broad axe. Miss Margaret, when I discovered her, had concealed herself in the corner, formed by the projection of cellar cap from the house; on my approach she fled, but was soon overtaken, and after repeated blows with a sword, I killed her by a blow on the head, with a fence rail. (App. 419)

As freely acknowledged to the questioner at the SHA session, Styron's Margaret Whitehead and her death are intentionally different from this historical description. They are products of a fictional imagination. Yet she and Nat are central figures through whom Styron dramatizes his psychohistorical thesis of pure black hatred. For from Nat's first memory of the prattling schoolgirl with whom he was once thrown into close contact comes the germs of her death at Nat's hands. Even at that early encounter the young slave was baffled by contradictory emotions. Erotic and spiritual attraction switch suddenly to "the long hot desire to reach out with one arm and snap that white, slender, throbbing young neck" (92). Seeking to understand this murderous reversal in himself, Nat explains, "Yet—strange I am aware of it—it is not hatred, it is something else. . . . It is closer to jealousy, but it is not even that. . . . Then all at once I realize that from just that sympathy, irresistible on my part, and unwanted—a disturbance to the great plans which this spring are gathering together into a fatal shape and architecture—arises my sudden rage and confusion" (92).

Here, Styron suggests, lies the paradoxical core of Nat Turner's historical and psychological situation. Pity and sympathy together, whether resistible in the case of men like Samuel Turner or Jeremiah Cobb or "irresistible" in the case of beautiful women like Emmaline Turner, Margaret Whitehead, or the rich stranger from Connecticut, form the weapon white liberal Christians, whether consciously or not, turn on this talented and sensitive slave. Such pity and sympathy are the most disarming of ideological weapons. Sympathetic understanding of the plight of the oppressed simply transfers to the victim the task of dealing with the historical horrors of slavery and white racism. White pity lays particular responsibility on sensitive minds like Nat's. The choice he confronts is agonizing: either to accept and forgive his oppressors in a one-way act of love—one-way because a racist white society forbids oppressors to return such love—or to vent righteous rage in revolutionary (and futile) violence aimed at bringing down the system of bondage that his pitying befrienders also hate but are impotent to oppose. Christianity cannot solve the dilemma of this devout preacher, but rather intensifies it. For Nat Turner's biblical beliefs are divided between "virile" Old Testament revenge and "womanish" New Testament acceptance and forgiveness, and these religious contradictions are reflected psychologically in ambivalence. Thus the fictional climax of Nat's murder of Margaret Whitehead epitomizes the historical, social, and psychological dichotomies while it fleshes out the vision of "being human," which Styron expressed at the SHA meeting in New Orleans: "I supplied him with the motivation. I gave him a rationale. I gave him all of the confusions and desperations, troubles, worries."

Thus as soon as Nat Turner kills Margaret Whitehead she becomes the source and symbol of all-but-consuming remorse and "obscure unshakeable grief" (417). At the same time the rebel never relinquishes his conviction that he and his fellows are not guilty of killing even white women and little children. The after-effects of this moral, spiritual, and political dilemma constitute the action of "It Is Done," the final few pages of *The Confessions of Nat Turner*. This prison drama is played out with four partners—Gray, Hark, the spirit of Margaret Whitehead, and the (italicized) voice of God as recorded in the Book of Revelation. Their transactions offer four variations on Styron's theme of reconciliation and transcendence.

Gray's is the first gesture. He signals changes in his attitude toward the condemned prisoner by defying the court's ruling and bringing Nat a Bible. "For a long moment we gaze at each other in the flickering light and I have a strange sensation which passes almost as quickly as it comes, that never have I seen this man in my life. I say nothing to him in answer. At last he reaches through the bars and grasps my hand; as he does so I know by some strange and tentative feeling in his grip that this is the first black hand he has ever shaken, no doubt the last. . . . I feel a wrench of pity for Gray and for his mortal years to come" (425). Given what we have already learned about pity, the prisoner's silent pity signals how incomplete is the rapprochement with Nat's last white man.

The second person Nat bids farewell to in the dawn light of his last day is Margaret Whitehead. Her presence is announced in the accents of the Book of Revelation, thus merging erotic and divine love in the phrase *Then behold I come quickly.*

> Her voice is close, familiar, real, and for an instant I mistake the wind against my ear, a gentle gust, for her breath, and I turn to seek her in the darkness. And now beyond my fear, beyond my dread and emptiness, I feel the warmth flow into my loins and my legs tingle with desire. I tremble and search for her face in my mind, seek her young body, yearning for her suddenly with a rage that racks me with a craving beyond pain; with tender, stroking motions I pour out my love within her; pulsing flood; she arches against me, cries out, and the twain—black and white—are one. I faint slowly. My head falls toward the window, my breath comes

hard. I recall a meadow, June, the voice a whisper: *Is it not true, Nat? Did He not say, I am the root and the offspring of David, and the bright and morning star?* (426)

Reconciliation here is simultaneously spiritual and sexual, in the shape of a remembrance of the past and prophecy of an eternal future of transfigured love. Whether Nat is reliving an adolescent masturbatory fantasy is as unanswerable as the question of the nature of the sudden rage accompanying yearning. What seems clear, though, is that Margaret Whitehead's body and youthful spirit are the medium of Nat Turner's repossession of God's favor and love. She and God—she as God?—are the resolution of the tormenting contradictions of life as a black slave and death as a failed rebel and now-repentant murderer: "*I would have done it all again. I would have destroyed them all. Yet I would have spared one. I would have spared her that showed me Him whose presence I had not fathomed or maybe even known. Great God, how early it is! Until now I had almost forgotten His name*" (428).

Hark is the third human partner in Nat Turner's final action of self-discovery and self-redemption. Through the wall Nat hears the executioners strapping the huge wounded slave into a chair to carry him to the gallows-tree:

"*Easy!*" Hark cries out, sobbing.
"Push him down!" says a voice.
I find myself hammering at the walls. "*Don't hurt him!*" I rage.
"Don't hurt him you white sons of bitches! You've done hurt him enough! All his life! Now God damn you don't hurt him no more." (427)

But Hark regains composure and goes to his death like "some marvelous black potentate borne in stately procession toward his throne" (427). " 'Hit gwine be all right, Nat,' he cries out to me, the voice fading." To this brotherly farewell Nat Turner makes an ambiguously soft reply: " 'Good-bye, Hark,' I whisper, 'good-bye, good-bye' . . . '*Good-bye, Hark, good-bye.*' " Styron's use of italics continues to be unclear so that one cannot be certain whether Nat's words actually reach, or are intended to reach, his lieutenant's ears. In any case, they fall well short of any public act of fellow love and solidarity.

Nat's apotheosis, then, is primarily internal and private, a series of incomplete reconciliations in a psychological drama of self-forgiveness. Yet the great exception to this impression comes at the last moment as God Himself speaks. His are the accents of Revelation and are recorded in alternating typefaces, roman denoting the autobiographical narrator of the whole novel and italics denoting some inner self. "'Come!' the voice booms, but commanding me now: *Come my son*! I turn in surrender. Surely I come quickly. Amen. Even so, come, Lord Jesus. Oh how bright and fair the morning star" (428). The Preacher has indeed regained his relationship with the Father and His Son. Moreover, this act apparently occurs both inside and beyond human consciousness, time, and the confines of Jerusalem jail. That this dual existence is the inescapable, final "truth" of Nat Turner's search for a man's identity is underlined by two codas that complete Styron's text. The first is a quotation (earlier cited in both *Harper's* and *Life*) from Drewry's *The Southampton Insurrection* which claims that, after his execution, Nat Turner's body "was delivered to the doctors who skinned it and made grease of the flesh. Mr. R. S. Barham's father owned a money purse made of his hide" (429). Whether fact or legend, this grisly detail nails Nat Turner into American history and its white racist ideology at the same time as it establishes an analogy between slavery and Nazi concentration camps like Buchenwald. But the second and ultimate quotation is again from Revelation and asserts this man's sonship with God. The narrative's conclusion blends human depravity and divine acceptance into all the contradictory realities of Nat Turner's racial, sexual, psychological, and spiritual existence and thus orchestrates themes meditated and acted upon from the opening pages of this ambitious translation.

3

The Public Controversy

Before and After *Ten Black Writers Respond*

> *By recognizing Nat Turner this award really honors all those of my contemporaries who have steadfastly refused to write propaganda or indulge in myth-making but have been impelled to search for those insights which, however raggedly and imperfectly, attempt to demonstrate the variety, the quirkiness, the fragility, the courage, the good humor, desperation, corruption, and mortality of all men. And finally it ratifies my own conviction that a writer jeopardizes his very freedom by insisting that he be bound or defined by his race, or by almost anything else. For one of the enduring marvels of art is its ability to soar through any barrier, to explore any territory of experience, and I say that only by venturing from time to time into strange territory shall artists, of whatever commitment, risk discovering and illuminating the human spirit that we all share.*
> —William Styron, Acceptance Speech for the Howells Medal, May 26, 1970

On May 7, 1968, William Styron's *The Confessions of Nat Turner* was awarded the Pulitzer Prize for fiction. The award climaxed more than a year's assiduous advertising by the author and his publisher, a six-month chorus of critical and popular acclaim, and "bestseller" success with American readers. Yet the Pulitzer Prize was neither the first nor necessarily the most prestigious award Styron received. His first novel, *Lie Down in Darkness*, won the Prix de Rome in 1952 and in 1970 he was presented the Howells Medal of the American Academy of Arts and Letters for *The Confessions of Nat Turner* as the outstanding work of American fiction of the preceding half-decade. Styron's acceptance speech suggests his awareness of a more discriminating public of artists, scholars, and highbrow critics than was true of the Pulitzer Prize.[1] Nevertheless, the Pulitzer conferred a public status not previously enjoyed by Styron. Its imprimatur also marked an important stage in the debate that, long before May, 1968, swirled around his version of Nat Turner's story. Although we have already identified some of the actors and issues in this debate in examining one representative episode in its history, I shall in this chapter thicken a description of the controversy, its cultural and ideological implications and, where possible, its reverberations through a widening circle of literate Americans. Disagreement, as we shall see, marked the Pulitzer Prize as it had already the book's creation and commercial marketing.

The group managing the Pulitzer includes an impressive array of institutions and influential individuals. Reading from the top down, this cultural apparatus embraces the president and trustees of Columbia University, the Columbia School of Journalism, eminent national and regional newspapers represented by their publishers or editors, as well as nationally known figures appointed to the advisory board and its various subcommittees and juries. Disagreement over Styron's novel first surfaced at the jury nomination. The fiction jury voted to nominate Isaac Bashevis Singer's *The Manor*. The one vote cast for Styron was that of John K. Hutchins of the *New York Times*. This jury decision, however, was reversed by the advisory board, and Styron's novel nominated to President Kirk and the trustees. One aspect of this mini-struggle (not unusual in Pulitzer Prize proceedings) was that literary critics, academics, and professional book reviewers were represented on the divided jury while the advisory board was almost entirely composed of editors and publishers, in many of whose journals *The Confessions of Nat Turner* had already received rave reviews.

According to William F. Stuckey, Styron's novel was in several respects an unconventional choice for a Pulitzer Prize, so that some disagreement was to be expected.[2] In other ways, though, *The Confessions of Nat Turner* was a surprisingly typical winner. Specifying its innovative and controversial features while still fitting the book into the expected pattern of Pulitzer Prize novels reinforces my argument that Styron's cultural significance derives in part from his novel's appeal to a tripartite spectrum of sixties readers, with its center in mainstream, middle-class, liberal, predominantly white book-buyers.

Stuckey points out that *The Confessions of Nat Turner* is both "better written" and deals with more explosive issues than most predecessors in the nearly fifty-year history of the Pulitzer Prize. By "better written" Stuckey identifies the narrative style already noted—most distinctively, the meditative, descriptive, relatively undramatic yet metaphorically ornate language of Styron's black narrator. Most other Pulitzer Prize winners are less obviously artful. That is, other novels tend to be "rattling good" tales that maintain the reader's interest through a straightforward story structure and brisk narrative momentum. Moreover, Styron's mix of social, historical, and psychological themes hardly fits the conventional Pulitzer pattern of upbeat narratives of personal achievement and social success achieved through hard work, self-reliance, and happy, monogamous marriages. A familiar and derisive description of this formula and set of reader expectations is Malcolm Cowley's. He once called the prizes "Mid-Victorian Crosses" awarded by a timid cultural establishment "afraid of sex, afraid of ideas, afraid of blood, revolution, and coarse language."[3] Though Styron flouts each of these shibboleths, his book does so disarmingly by also meeting other prescriptions and preferences. Some of these compliances are surprisingly specific. As Stuckey's survey indicates, Pulitzer Prize novels commonly present fairly stereotyped heroes and heroines caught in an action in which they enact only slightly unconventional gender roles while often personifying quite pressing social issues and moral dilemmas. While their heroines are frequently "sweetly aggressive"— toned-down versions of Scarlett O'Hara—male protagonists tend not to be strong masculine figures. Indeed, Stuckey contends that they are often "somewhat womanish, weak, timid, fearful of change . . . ineffectual."[4] As the controversy so far described suggests, some readers found Styron's Nat Turner fitting this pattern to a disturbingly ahistorical degree.

History is, in fact, another prominent feature of this group of popular novels. Common to many Pulitzer Prize winners is a historically "realistic" setting, frequently frontier America in the pre- or post–Civil War eras. Furthermore, the social issues and obstacles grappled with by the protagonists are significant historical problems that must, however, still possess contemporary relevance. Scarlett O'Hara again is a notable example of a nineteenth-century heroine whose struggles were as pertinent to Margaret Mitchell's Depression-era readers as to Pulitzer Prize committees.

These criteria shared by Styron and his predecessors provide plausible grounds for his success. Yet in drawing attention to this pattern Stuckey ignores other features and issues that deeply engaged Styron's imagination and aroused strong reactions in some readers. One question cavalierly dismissed by Stuckey is historical faithfulness or truth. Ignoring Styron's author's note and the vehement objections by the ten black writers and others, Stuckey insists: "Styron's book is an extended psychological interpretation of the man himself. There is no real question here of truth or untruth, for there is no way of proving an invention true or false."[5] This judgment can be seen as a familiar ideological ploy intended, as Jameson or Tony Bennett would point out, to legitimate criticism of *The Confessions of Nat Turner* largely or exclusively in literary terms. Writing a decade or more after the height of the controversy, Stuckey's comment echoes earlier instances of the same preemptive strategy. Another significant—and perhaps linked—omission is Stuckey's almost complete indifference to the complex racial and sexual motives energizing Styron's rebel. Indeed, Margaret Whitehead's name is never mentioned in his plot summary. Consequently the terms of the discussion are in this context reduced to literary features bringing *The Confessions of Nat Turner* closer to *Gone With the Wind* and *Andersonville* than many sixties readers, not to mention the author himself, would acknowledge or desire.

An intricate, sustained engagement with problematic questions like the nature of slavery and of history itself, interracial sexual feelings and rarified spiritual aspirations distinguishes this fictional history from many of its Pulitzer kin. In this respect, Styron must be grouped with the authors of other Pulitzer Prize–winning novels like *All the King's Men* and N. Scott Momaday's *House Made of Dawn,* which bend or break formulaic molds. As Stuckey admits but has no cause to explore, these matters provoked lively debate. And, as seen at the SHA, such exchanges often produced both praise and vilification for the very same features of Styron's story.

One concrete and controversial reactivation of Nat Turner was the response by New York's *Amsterdam News* to the Pulitzer Prize. As already noted, this newspaper's prepublication announcement was a guarded endorsement. During the intervening months, however, the paper's two columnists, Poppy Cannon White and Gertrude Wilson, devoted several columns to Nat Turner and the unfolding controversy. In the process, they moved to reflect (and encourage) the mounting black indignation over the white writer's audacious novel. This meant breaking ranks with highly respected black intellectuals, including James Baldwin, John Hope Franklin, Benjamin Quarles, and J. Saunders Redding, who expressed early approval of *The Confessions of Nat Turner*. This switch culminated on May 18, 1968, in the well-publicized column by Gertrude Wilson, "I Spit on the Pulitzer Prize."[6] Wilson set Styron within an ideological context very different indeed from the one assumed by most previous white reviewers and commentators. The virulence of her attack reflects not simply momentary emotions but seeks to elicit the feelings of educated, middle-class blacks caught between the dominant white culture and an increasingly alienated cadre of militant blacks.

What made Styron's award particularly offensive to Wilson was the ironic juxtaposition between President Kirk presenting a prize "to a white Southerner who successfully made a Negro revolutionist look like a 'nigger'" and the campus scene then in progress on Morningside Heights. There a student rebellion "without parallel in this country" was taking place. To make one gesture was to demonstrate unfeeling indifference to the other situation and "to the enormous problems which Columbia University faces in the grievances of its Negro students and the Harlem community in which it exists." Wilson had already been offended by the Columbia trustees overturning the Pulitzer advisory board's recommendation of a special music citation for Duke Ellington. The present "smellier award" was still more egregious since the Pulitzer committee

> has chosen to overlook the outraged reaction of the Negro community to this book; disregarding verified testimony to its historical dishonesty, and its cruel image of Nat Turner as a black buck lusting after white flesh. . . .
> And yet, despite the spotlight which the National Commission on Civil Disorders has placed on the evils of white racism; despite the soul-searching of a whole nation after the assassination of Martin Luther King, Jr., in our relations to our Negro brothers. . . . despite all—it chose to award this controversial and distorted meditation on Negro history a Pulitzer prize.
> Let that action be a measure of the kind of solutions which

President Grayson Kirk and the Board of Trustees of Columbia University will come to in regard to both the black man on its campus and in its community.

They have virtually spat in the face of both—and I spit on their Pulitzer Prize.[7]

These events of Spring 1968 point beyond Styron's text and the situation on the steps of Low Library as they heighten apparent divisions between the literate middle classes as reflected in the columns of an influential Negro newspaper. How this dramatic division emerged during the months after October 9, 1967, can be suggested by looking at other sectors of the American press and retracing different public responses to Styron's novel.

Immediate Responses and Their Networks

Though several institutions and media became involved in publicizing, praising, and attacking *The Confessions of Nat Turner*, national newspapers and magazines were the first and most persistent supervisors of this cultural process. This network of information and interpretation comprised, according to my unscientific tally, more than 110 newspapers (daily and weekly) and more than 60 magazines. Characterizing this sizable and diverse collection of print media is no simple task. For it includes, first, most major urban newspapers from the *Atlanta Constitution and Journal* to the *Wall Street Journal* and *Washington Post*. Of these, the *New York Times* and the *Amsterdam News* devoted the most sustained attention to the controversy. Next there were smaller urban and regional newspapers whose names and locales run the gamut from the *Abilene Reporter-News* to the *Youngstown Vindicator*. Another segment was composed of still smaller periodicals with specialized readerships in which appeared reviews and feature stories. Into this category fall such papers as the *Boston Jewish Advocate, Bridgeport Post, Chapel Hill Weekly, Erie Times-News, Fresno Bee, Hemet (California) News, Hollywood Reporter, Newport News Daily Press*, Olympia's *Sunday Olympian, Orlando Sentinel, Roanoke Times, Staten Island Advance*, and the *Advocate* of Victoria, Texas, and Victoria, British Columbia.

Magazine coverage, which we have noted began well before the novel's appearance, embraced an equally varied range of organs, addressing even more diverse readerships. Styron must have been astonished as well as delighted to find his book, within its first year, discussed in the pages of, for example, the *Atlantic Monthly* and *Playboy*, *Ebony* and *Hadassah Magazine*, *The Nation* and *National Review*, *New York Review of Books* and *Marquette Mining Journal*, *Seventeen* and *The Worker*. In addition to these predominantly unscholarly media, reviews in surprisingly short order appeared in scholarly journals such as the *Chicago Review*, *Hollins Critic*, *Journal of Negro History*, *Journal of Popular Culture*, *Kenyon Review*, and *Yale Review*. On the basis of this very partial listing, it seems clear that notice—and at first overwhelmingly favorable notice—reached a sizable segment of the American reading public. Few novelists of Styron's generation could point to reviews of the same book within weeks of each other in the *Hudson Review*, *Political Affairs*, and the *New York State Education Magazine*.

What common and divergent views characterize this unusual repository of literary opinion and cultural attitudes? From this distance the pattern appears plain: responses to *The Confessions of Nat Turner* include a significant majority of key readers agreeing on the importance and success of Styron's experiment in historical fiction. Discordant notes in this paean are, nevertheless, heard from the outset. Though many favorable notices were brief and undiscriminating, others were thoughtful and thorough discussions of the novel's literary and social features. The same variety can be noted in the largely negative reviews. Furthermore, no clear pattern of either unqualified endorsement or categorical condemnation can be drawn along regional, racial, or ideological lines. Even in the network's three likeliest centers of controversy—the New York media, black voices nationwide, and southern white opinions—no unanimity emerges.

Reviewers focused attention with surprising regularity on the same topics as clues to the ambiguous features of the narrative: the historical highlights of the Southampton revolt as seen through the lens of present politics; the character of Nat Turner himself as man, black, slave, preacher, prophet, rebel, and martyr; the story's accuracy and adequacy as history; the author's literary strategies including, again, the arresting gamble of a white "meditation on history" expressed as a black man's autobiography.

The Nat Turner controversy comes full blown into public view in early 1968. The first challenges are exasperated, even passionate reactions (chiefly from blacks) to an earlier body of often fulsome praise thought by the attackers to emanate from biased, ill-informed, and usually white (or white-oriented) readers and critics. But dividing these challengers is the question of whether Styron and his supporters were guilty of conscious or unconscious racism. Both groups, the original advocates and the later attackers, mobilized media networks to disseminate their views. However, Styron's admirers had greater access to mainstream media attention and support, and this became an important element in the ensuing conflict.

One might begin with an initial review representing a respected metropolitan newspaper, one that is neither black, southern, nor from New York City, engaged in its traditional task of providing readers information and advice about a brand-new book. The *Minneapolis Star*'s book review editor, John K. Sherman, rendered his confident opinion on the day after publication: "The late William Faulkner's niche as leading Southern writer has been filled by William Styron with this powerful, imaginative and moving novel about an abortive Negro uprising that actually occurred in the Virginia backwoods in 1831." Turner was "a God-obsessed fanatic like Joan of Arc and John Brown. He came eventually to see that the white man's pity and charity, wherever they existed, were even worse than his scorn because they encouraged docility and delayed the day of reckoning." Sherman concluded that this arresting new novel is manifestly "a literary work of art and not a piece of pamphleteering, it yet draws the white reader nearer to understanding the implacable hatred that Stokely Carmichael and Rap Brown express today."[8] Though Sherman left many historical and artistic matters unmentioned, his review emphasized to Minnesota readers the arrival of an important and pertinent fictional message.

Equally emphatic but a more guarded opinion was William Hogan's in the *San Francisco Chronicle*. Even more unequivocally than Sherman, Hogan told readers that a milestone book had just appeared. *The Confessions of Nat Turner*, he wrote, "is a novel exasperating, depressing, and important. Nothing like it has happened since Faulkner. . . . Styron without question takes his place in the forefront of American writers."[9] He questioned, though, Styron's use of a fictional autobiography and predicted that this was going to prove a touchy topic for many readers:

"It seems to me that Styron has been successful in this first-person 'identification' with Nat Turner, but we shall have to listen carefully to Negro reaction to the book to really know." Hogan's word "really" signals a more tentative and culturally inclusive perspective than most early white reviewers took.

The rhetorical move of promoting Styron to Faulknerian eminence was often repeated. To be sure, Styron's white critics had made similar flattering comparisons as early as *Lie Down in Darkness*. It took some months for this beatification to peak, however. One striking example was Calhoun Ancrum's review in the *Charleston News and Courier* at year's end. Ancrum declared *The Confessions of Nat Turner* "the year's most important literary event. . . . If William Styron never writes another book, he will be remembered as the author of the most significant novel ever to come out of the South. . . . [It is] the masterpiece of all American prose."[10] Then the South Carolinian argued that Styron's story was "a great purgative" for white southerners:

> The myths by which we were led astray, starting from our early childhood when we were fed "Diddie, Dumps, and Tot" and "The Little Confederate" are destroyed inexorably once and for all. Mr. Styron has written an anatomy in all its aspects and all its implications.
>
> Mr. Styron uses Nat Turner as his narrator. It is a device and one cannot object if Nat Turner occasionally seems more literate than he might have been. . . . Any device of art is perforce artificial.
>
> And what is the universal significance of this novel? It involves all mankind, and more specifically it is constructed and based on profound Biblical scholarship. Nat Turner owned one book, the Bible. He read constantly about the heroes of Judaism who lived to set men free from oppression. . . . The reader realizes, if he never has known it before, what a revolutionary book is the Holy Bible.

Ancrum was by no means alone in interpreting *The Confessions of Nat Turner* more from the perspective of art than history. Nor was he the only critic to cite the Bible as the common ground among historical actor, southern author, and present-day reader. Several other southern newspapermen likewise put themselves in Styron's shoes.

One of the more judicious of these was Roy Parker, Jr. Parker sees the novel as a double confession. Downplaying Turner's original motives and feelings, Parker speculates at some length on Styron's own emotional investment. "Every white liberal emigré from the South," he observes, "looks forward with great yearning to the day when he can climb up on that mountain and sing to the world that he has cleansed himself of the blood dripped from the Southern moon, made peace with history, and felt those . . . brother-loving arms entwining him with all his kin—black, white, highborn and mean, men women and even the chil'run."[11] Then, after guardedly praising Styron's "immense literary talent" but observing that he possesses a tongue that is neither delicate nor kind, Parker acknowledged the white writer's "confessing through one of the famous figures of Southern history," to be simply "majestic, magical, meticulous, monomaniacal." Nonetheless, the North Carolinian found *The Confessions of Nat Turner* flawed as historical fiction. "One wonders if he really feels at one with his kin yet? Has he really freed himself from history by possessing it? Or, like his mentor-admirer James Baldwin, is he rather consumed by it, haunted by it—or perhaps only wallowing in it? There is thus left a nagging doubt whether Styron views Nat Turner with understanding or merely with a sort of reverse horror." He counseled readers to ponder whether a Tidewater past, a liberal stance, formidable artistic ability and a lively historical sense, in fact endowed this son of the South with the necessary power to comprehend fully the "biracial sin" of slavery. In fact, Parker stated that Nat Turner's actual motives and thoughts are better revealed in Gray's original *Confessions*. Hence, respectful, critical attention should be paid to both accounts. Properly related to each other, Turner's dual confession—"the original and the new manifestation—will endure as a unique, disturbing, yet profoundly typical ingredient of the American Experience." Parker's notice was thus one of the first to suggest that Styron, like Gray, is the mouthpiece of Nat Turner as well as Nat Turner the mouthpiece of William Styron.

One of the most perceptive New York reviews of *The Confessions of Nat Turner* appeared in the *New York Times Book Review* on the Sunday before the book's publication. The reviewer was Wilfred Sheed, and his was one of several assessments in the *New York Times* during this week and season. Sheed's review was arguably the most searching and one of the most severe. (It was not, understandably, one Styron himself relished.) Distinguishing his discussion was Sheed's keen sense of Styron's missed or squandered opportunities. Factual faithfulness to 1831 history did not greatly concern Sheed. History's pastness must always give way to present uses, with the writer putting "his own experience into fancy dress [to] see how it looks."[12] Nonetheless, Sheed feels Styron fails to make readers recognize the true nature and full extent of Nat Turner's legacy, since "he gave the Negroes a legend which has not yet lost its potency," founded a line that stretches from Turner to Marcus Garvey and then to Garvey's disciple, Malcolm X's father, and thence "through many blood-lines to today's Negro leaders" (2). On the other hand, Sheed stresses that for Styron the Southampton slave revolt was grounded in the Bible and the Preacher's rhetorical skills, scripture being used to "weld his audience, give them some point of concentration and the energy to pursue it" (2). Feeling no need to remind readers of contemporary preachers with similar skills, Sheed asserts that "a novel on this subject has to be part politics, ours and his, at the moment" (1).

Nevertheless, as history and political parable *The Confessions of Nat Turner* is more successful in aim than execution. Styron's problems, Sheed believes, are increased rather than eased by his long-term emotional involvement with his subject. Overattachment is exacerbated by literary choices of language and viewpoint. "The message seems to be that the Negro has every right to kill the white man, but cannot escape pollution in the process," Sheed wryly asserts, adding that

> The ending is covertly sentimental, one of those chins-up sad endings, and part of its effectiveness will be determined, as I say, by your view of the race question and the other and smaller part by whether the novel has worked for you as a novel.
>
> And here we run into difficulties. There is no doubt that Turner is still worth writing and speculating about; but whether he can be successfully written about fictionally is another question. The historical novel is traditionally so clumsy a method of investigation that the reader usually winds up doubting whether the characters ever existed at all, in any form. And Styron has only exaggerated the difficulties by telling his story in the first person. (2)

For Sheed, it is less a matter of Styron's diction, "a plausible, timeless blend of Southern-Biblical, a little stiff . . . [but] generally serviceable" (2). The trouble is at once deeper and more superficial and centers in Turner's reimagined consciousness. Whatever advantage the author has achieved by squeezing "his own excellent prose into this [nineteenth-century] whalebone of rhetoric" (2) has been sacrificed to creaky devices for bringing Nat Turner alive as a fictional figure. Chief among these is the long, leisurely first-person narrative. "We are in effect being asked to spend a short lifetime in the head of one skillfully animated museum piece. . . . A long book told from one point of view is always a risk," Sheed observes, and "here the risk is prohibitive" (3). Complicating the choice is Styron's penchant for numerous nature descriptions in which "the weather is always just right for the scene: sultry for tension, cold for failure, etc." (3). Though more successful in scenes of straight dialogue, Styron's meditations strike Sheed as ultimately deadening. "[A] simple brief narration of Nat Turner's trials would be far more moving than this windy, florid elaboration of them." Readers' anticipation of the novel's publication was doubtless dampened by Sheed's final judgment. Although as novel *The Confessions of Nat Turner* "fails by default . . . it does succeed in many places as a kind of historical tone poem" (3).

Despite its strategic placement in the *New York Times Book Review*, Sheed's opinion carried less weight than it otherwise might, surrounded as it was, that same weekend, by far more enthusiastic voices, several in the *New York Times* itself. One cheerleader was George Plimpton. His interview of an old friend and *Paris Review* colleague preceded Sheed's by one day. Indeed, interviews with this suddenly famous writer became such an industry during this period that in January 1968 Art Buchwald published a parody in *Playboy*.[13] Repeating previous historical assertions and autobiographical remarks, Styron's responses to Plimpton are last-minute efforts to continue supervision of his book's reception. Several statements, in addition, prefigure the looming debate. One particularly prescient comment came in answer to Plimpton's leading question about the genesis of *The Confessions of Nat Turner:* "I remember describing it to Hiram Haydn, my editor then at Random House, with full bloodcurdling delight. . . . [Then] he said to me 'I don't think you have a real understanding of the thing' . . . [and] he was right."[14] By confessing that "the gothic part of my nature was too predominant," Styron appeared to anticipate criticism of several of his fictional creations—Jeremiah Cobb and Will, in particular.

Even more revealing are other remarks to Plimpton about his white imagination as a fit instrument for plumbing the mind of a black and the dim reaches of slavery. Though Haydn may have implied this, Styron himself retains no qualms. Years of immersion in the history of slavery, familiarity with rural southern black speech, and—most confident note of all—"rank intuition" (39) that he could bring off an inside narrative, have equipped him for the challenge no previous white American novelist has attempted. To these assertions is added Styron's firm doubt "that the feelings of the dispossessed, whatever their color, are all that different. If you can sympathize with the dispossessed you can certainly take on the lineaments of the Negro." However, he concludes that "It was a risk, call it arrogance" (37). Then he reiterates the psychohistorical principles guiding this characterization of Nat Turner. As earlier outlined in *Harper's*, the basic supposition is that Turner's revolutionary personality closely resembles other leaders' in different historical epochs:

> that is to say puritanical, repressive, and sublimated. Such impulses seem an authentic part of the revolutionary drive. Luther, Castro, Danton, Mao—all of them are basically puritanical. Nat Turner was no exception. In the book he never has a sexual experience directly with a woman. He has an adolescent homosexual experience, quite innocent. Beyond that, Turner lived a sexual life of fantasy, fantasies of women, mainly white women, which in turn led to imagined revelations, and then finally to what Turner supposed were revelations from the Divine Spirit. Of course, I can't prove that this is Nat's psychological history, but I think something like it was part of his psychic makeup. (38)

To some of Styron's antagonists, the grand hypothesis linking religion, revolt, sexual repression, and fantasies cannot be grounded in Gray's *Confessions*. Important as this source is, Styron explains to Plimpton, it skips over too many important matters, although those omissions offer opportunities to the novelist's imagination. One signal omission is the slave's knowledge of social conditions elsewhere. "Nat Turner was aware in a rudimentary way of the social horrors he was struggling against, but the wellsprings of his revolt were largely religious" (39), and thus for Styron, necessarily psychosexual. Another important gap is Nat's silence about the fact that relatively few Southampton slaves rose in revolt; indeed, many opposed and even fought against him. "It must have been the bitterest part of his ultimate feeling about what he had done," Styron's intuition tells him, "though it's nowhere mentioned in the actual confession. It's *hinted* at, and I think if you read between the lines you can feel that regret" (39). In other respects, though, Styron insists to his friend that he has been faithful to Gray and to certain plausible details found in Drewry's book as well. "Every character in the book has a prototype," he affirms, although he admits that the figure of Thomas Gray himself "is a product of my imagination" (39–40).

As their absence so far in this account suggests, historians were not prominently represented among the initial reviewers of *The Confessions of Nat Turner*, with two notable exceptions—John Hope Franklin and C. Vann Woodward. As the leading black American historian of the day, Franklin participated in the day-before salvo of Sunday reviews, October 8, 1967. We shall shortly examine his along with other early black responses to Styron's book. Woodward's role both in the book's public and academic receptions was the more influential one. It began with his notice in the *New Republic*, which, though less popularly positioned than Franklin's in the *Chicago Sun-Times* and *Washington Post*, was more strategically placed for white liberals. Moreover, Woodward had already played a specific part in the prepublication history of *The Confessions of Nat Turner*. As Dick Shaap reported in a feature story in the *San Francisco Examiner and Chronicle*, Styron, shortly after completing the manuscript, asked Woodward to check it for factual accuracy. "He caught me in one or two minor historical errors," he later reported. "I had mentioned bright leaf tobacco, which didn't exist then."[15] Furthermore, Woodward continued to champion Styron after the novel appeared. For example, he and fellow Yale professor R. W. B. Lewis interviewed the author for the *Yale Alumni Magazine*. Later, in a radio talk on a Hartford station Woodward again praised and recommended his friend's novel.[16]

The *New Republic* piece was both carefully timed and unequivocal in its approval. Concluding a three-page commentary the historian roundly declared: "This is the most profound fictional treatment of slavery in our literature. It is of course the work of a skilled and experienced novelist with other achievements to attest his qualifications. It is doubtful, however, if the rare combination of talents essential to this formidable undertaking—a flawless command of dialect, a native instinct for the subtleties and ambivalences of race in the South, and a profound and unerring sense of place (Styron's and Nat Turner's) could well have been found anywhere else."[17] Without raising the possibility of a black novelist doing it better and thus moving into territory most other early reviewers skirted, Woodward specifically endorsed Styron as historian. If students of American history or careful readers of the author's note have reservations about this dimension of Styron's achievement, Woodward dispels them. Furthermore, he underscores the subject's historical significance, declaring that of the two great nineteenth-century opponents of slavery who acted on their beliefs, John Brown must take second place to Nat Turner: "Turner's rebellion was far more bloody, both in the lives it took and in the reprisals it evoked. As a threat to the security of a slave based society, Turner's conspiracy was more momentous than Brown's. John Brown's Raid never had the remotest chance of success" (25). The paucity of detailed information on the leader and the event—besides Gray only "a pedestrian monograph or two" (25) exist—makes Styron's venture all the more valuable as a presentation of slavery from the slave's perspective. Not even Melville (the only major American novelist to treat a slave rebellion) has dared to do this.

In delivering these *encomia* Woodward reemphasizes the basic enigma: "why the greatest slave republic in the New World had by far the fewest slave rebellions; why smaller and allegedly more benevolent slave societies bred vast insurrections [while] America had one that recruited seventy-five and petered out in three days" (25). Since records are scanty about slaves' specific motives for rebelling or submitting, this story possesses special value. Even though Styron is white—another touchy issue Woodward does not elect to discuss—his artistic imagination and southern background and sensibility prove to be instruments adequate to the challenge: "It is informed by a respect for history, a sure feel for the period, and a deep and precise sense of place and time" (25). Then, with no noticeable shifting of disciplinary gears, Woodward summarizes Styron's version of Nat's life. Thus the novelist's transformations and/or additions (like Nat's boyhood as a house servant, being taught to read and write by a white mistress) are related as if historical verities. "Then when the moment came and the dread axe was poised over his master's head, Nat's hand palsied and the blow missed. Again and again between violent seizures of vomiting he tried to kill and failed. Initiative fell to a demented black monster maddened by a master's brutality. The only life Nat was able to take, among the scores slaughtered was that of the one white person he still loved, a simple-hearted and sympathetic girl" (28). Though never deliberately misleading, Woodward's description mentions neither contradictions nor inventions about those who are, after all, actual historical figures with other details attached to their historical activations in other texts. Especially problematic areas like Turner's psychosexual motivations are swept under the carpet of phrases like "the one white person he still loved" and "a simple-hearted and sympathetic girl." In deciding not to bring history and fiction into critical conjunction for this audience, Woodward neglects not only the Author's Note but also many questions serious students of American history would soon raise about it.

While the *New Republic* offered the expectant public a prestigious historian's largely undiscriminating endorsement, its liberal rival *The Nation* took quite another course. Recognizing as early as October 16 that Styron's novel was going to stir up a hornet's nest, the editors provided a pair of provocatively complementary reviews—both, however, written by whites. One was by Shaun O'Connell, a literary critic, the other a historical evaluation by Herbert Aptheker, whose *Nat Turner's Slave Rebellion* had reappeared the year before. In a box the editors explained the reasons for such unusual coverage, drawing attention to Aptheker's book with its important appendix containing Gray's *Confessions*.

The Nation's bold decision to enjoin the debate was an exception to journalistic responses to the novel. Not that O'Connell's review was unfavorable; it was not. "Styron has written an apologia for no political position," he concludes, "but a stunningly beautiful embodiment of a noble man, in a rotten time and place, who tried his best to save himself and transform his world."[18] O'Connell traces the process by which the pampered slave lad, granted "a sense of his own significance that a field hand could never know," gradually realizes that he can never become free in the way Samuel Turner has promised, and finally decides to strike back at the white man's act of "wanton and arrogant kindness." O'Connell summarizes this development in terms virtually indistinguishable from Styron's own. "The need to slaughter those who are most compassionate is, Nat says, 'the central madness of nigger existence.' Their philanthropy, however patronizing, creates a sense of self in Nat, but their refusal to accept that self as fully human creates in him the capacity to deny their human reality, to make their blood flow 'in a foaming sacrament'" (373).

O'Connell fails to point out, however, Styron's culture-bound (i.e., white) conception of "humanity." Styron's Turner is uncritically accepted; the rebel's remorse and final self-forgiveness for Margaret Whitehead's murder are expressions of an intelligence and nobility implicitly white. For O'Connell, these are literally *redeeming* qualities salvaged from the rage and violence of Nat's black self. From this perspective—whose generic roots lie in the civilization-savagery dichotomy—actual historical circumstance becomes of negligible importance. Thus O'Connell airily asserts that Nat might have killed six hundred whites instead of sixty if Margaret's murder had not sapped his will to continue the uprising. Religious motives, too, are overlooked. The visions, Nat's preacher-prophet reputation among the slaves, and the Bible's ambiguous messages of divine vengeance and meekness are left out of this retelling. "Nat is believable," O'Connell blithely concludes, "the gap between color and times can be bridged, because he is first and last a man, not a Negro slave" (374). Hence when the prisoner muses in jail about his fellow slaves—"my black shit-eating people . . . like flies, God's mindless outcasts"—these graphic metaphors of disgust become for O'Connell "marvelous associations in terms of which any man, any time, could understand. Who has not mulled the significance of flies?" (374). Where Nat's apocalyptic imagery comes from and how it might differentially affect white and black readers are historical, psychological, and social issues subsumed under the indulgent rubric of artistic freedom and a writer's "daring imaginative leap into a tormented black psyche to better understand himself and his country" (373). It is Styron, not Nat Turner, whose self-understanding matters most.

The striking differences—and certain convergences—between O'Connell the literary critic's interpretation of Styron's new book and Aptheker the historian's are nicely expressed not only in the reviews themselves but elsewhere on the pages of *The Nation*. Side by side with O'Connell's tribute appears a poem, "Historical Days," by the young black poet Jay Wright, a brief meditation on ghetto life. On the following page, in a box flanking Aptheker's "Note on the History" is an even more explicit sign of the times: a Random House ad for Tom Hayden's

Rebellion in Newark. "He is white," Styron's own publisher announces of Hayden, but his personal account shows "how the police and National Guard not only failed to cool the violence, but *actually intensified and prolonged it*."[19]

Aptheker picks up these topical resonances in his own Note, which expresses his assumptions about historical fiction: first, it should "bear some resemblance to reality . . . indeed, through the creative act it may perhaps deepen the grasp of that reality"; and, second, "each generation's historical novels tell at least as much about that generation as about the past they depict."[20] In these terms, Styron's historical fiction contains numerous and serious divergences from actual historical records of the Turner rebellion. These discrepancies produce a pattern of distortion widely representative of white racist thinking about history. In both respects, Aptheker declares, this novel is a significant cultural document of the sixties.

In sharp contrast to Woodward's sweeping endorsements, Aptheker's evaluation of Styron's "meditation on history" weighs "history" more than "meditation." To the author of *American Negro Slave Revolts*, history preeminently means fidelity to surviving trustworthy documents, critically read. By this criteria Styron is often guilty of both omissions and dubious assumptions of fact. These range from single significant details to fundamental historical hypotheses. Several of the latter are based, far too trustingly, on Elkins's and Tannenbaum's books. One important departure from the "actual" *Confessions* (Aptheker never mentions Gray's name or discusses the process by which his pamphlet was produced) is Styron's omission of Nat Turner's running away from his master for a month, then returning voluntarily. The recorded response of Nat's fellow slaves—"they 'murmured against me' as he said"—is ignored evidence of "the impact upon Turner of the anti-slavery feelings present among his peers" (375). Another significant omission is Nat's father's role in reinforcing his precocious son's sense of special capacities and a prophetic future as a rebel. Not only is the father's name silently removed but the mother replaces the grandmother as the most powerful family influence on the young slave. Such changes, Aptheker claims, reflect Styron's negative view of the slave family as cultural institution and ideological force. In contradiction, he points out that "while American slavery certainly dealt awful blows to the family structure of the slaves, it never fully destroyed it—

in large part because of the women's ingenuity and resistance," adding that "a rather unusual feature of Turner's life—well documented—is that he remembered both his father and his mother and a grandmother, too. The father, also a slave, fled and made good his escape (this fact is in the book), but he did not do so before having left a clear mark on the memory and the consciousness of his son. All this may be in conflict with the so-called Moynihan thesis, but that is the fault of the thesis—not of Nat Turner!" (375).

Other features questioned by Aptheker include the character of Will, transformed by Styron into a bloodthirsty sadist. Such melodramatic typecasting reflects a basic misrepresentation of American slavery, the same sort of misunderstanding also seen in Styron's insistence upon the uniqueness of Nat Turner's revolt. Indeed, Styron's myopia goes further as he dramatizes the failure of most Southampton slaves to join the revolt and the willingness of some to fight against it.

> But the records of history—unlike the novel—do not show efforts at recruitment other than the original handful of six. It is these six who commence the uprising, in one parish of the county; and in a day and a half of desperate struggle are actually joined by perhaps seventy more. All things considered—including the system of control, the stakes involved, the apparent lack of prior preparation—this argues for discontent so deep that scores could actually risk their lives in order to express it. The repeated references in the novel to masters arming loyal black slaves to resist the rebels are made up out of whole cloth: there is no evidence of this whatsoever and to believe it or offer it shows an utter misapprehension of the nature of American slavery. (376)

Threading this acerbic critique is Aptheker's repeated denunciation of Styron's white bias toward black culture. Instead of a fragmented and defenseless society in the quarters, Aptheker views the slave community and the historical Nat Turner as reciprocally sharing stable family structures, coherent identities, and a measure of autonomy and opposition to slavocracy. This, despite the obvious brutalities of the system. Though Aptheker fails to cite the role of biblical Christianity in forging an ideology of opposition as well as a pattern of acceptance, his counterimage of Nat Turner in his black world aims to correct what he asserts are Styron's stereotypes and misleading caricatures. "Nat

Turner, however, *was* real; perhaps a novelist will come along to do justice to him, as, about thirty years ago, Arna Bontemps did justice to another great slave rebel, Gabriel, slave of Prosser, also of Virginia, in his book *Black Thunder*" (376).

Initial Black Responses

This survey of representative early passages in the Nat Turner controversy has so far concentrated on national, popular media. One aspect of these often widely publicized discussions is the fact that the media, commentators, and (on slimmer evidence) the audiences involved were predominantly white. There were, however, black voices from the start—and which were heard well before Gertrude Wilson raised hers. In fact, their numbers grew, especially in the spring and summer of 1968, following the Pulitzer award and the publication of John H. Clarke's *William Styron's Nat Turner: Ten Black Writers Respond*. These two events mobilized black opinion and altered the whole tenor of public discussion of Styron, Nat Turner, and slave revolts in general. As this change occurred, several persistent questions emerged: Who has the power and who the right to define and discuss the issues dramatized in *The Confessions of Nat Turner*? Is the basic issue here the nature and meaning of black rage and violence—then and now—or is white racism the unifying link between slaveowners then and the still dominant ethos and cultural apparatus now?

One passionate answer to these questions came from a reader of *The Nation*. A few weeks after the O'Connell/Aptheker reviews, June Meyer (later June Jordan) sent a scathing letter to the editors.

> I have been amazed by the phenomenon of Nat Turner *alias* William Styron. Or is it: the alien phenomenon of Nat Turner *via* William Styron.... [t]here lives a man who is spoken for, imagined, feared, criticized, pitied, misrepresented, fought against, reviled *and loved*, primarily on the basis of secondhand information or much worse.
>
> This man, this object of attention, attack, and vast activity, cannot make himself be heard, let alone be understood. *He has never been listened to*....

That man is black and alive in white America where the media of communication do not allow the delivery of his own voice, his own desires, his own rage. In fact, the definitely preferred form of communication, black to white, is *through* a white intermediary—be he sociologist or William Styron.[21]

Meyer provides several examples of this ideological arrangement, which she sees as disturbingly common in white culture. Wilfred Sheed's *New York Times* review is titled "The Slave Who Became a Man," which Meyer translates as "The slave (the object) became a man: He spoke in the first person: *He spoke as subject*—courtesy of William Styron, of course" (597). She finds even more ironic and condescending Styron's own qualification for his role as humanizing intermediary—his "rank intuition." But Meyer is chiefly exasperated by Philip Rahv's comment in the *New York Review of Books*, "I think that only a white Southern writer could have brought it off. . . . A Negro writer, *because of a very complex anxiety* . . . would have probably stacked the cards, producing in a mood of unnerving rage and indignation, a melodrama of saints and sinners" (italics Meyer's).[22] To which she replies: "Are you kidding? If not, then let me make plain that you would have to reject *The Confessions of Nat Turner, by Turner*. Mickey Rooney can write his memoirs. Gertrude Stein can write the 'Autobiography of Alice B. Toklas,' but you're not having any 'confession' by Nat Turner, unless it's an outright fake" (597). She admits that Turner's own version of the revolt would indeed "have been pretty damned one-sided. And, no doubt, his mood was that of 'unnerving rage and indignation.'" On the basis of other recent white books about black experience, Meyer concludes that "Styron's stunt merely gives point to a season of fantastic black-to-white 'dialog' miscarried by white-controlled media through the 'medium' of the now professional, white intermediary" (597). When she broached this subject to a "liberal" white editor, pointing out the double filtering of black life when both author and reviewer are white, he replied, "Oh, but the reader won't know the difference" (599). To *The Nation*'s readers Meyer replies:

> Let me tell you: there is a difference. There is a difference black from white in this country. And the reader, the general public, is not going to know the human meaning of that difference as long as *dialogue-by-intermediary* rules the press and the rest of it.

The white problem will never be solved as long as American black life is an imagining, a TV spectacular, the product of rank intuition, the casualty of gross misrepresentation, and grist for statistical games. The white problem will never be solved as long as American black life remains an object, titillation, a scare, an unknown reality and an unfamiliar voice. Black people have been speaking as subjects, as first persons, as the only people we are—for longer than it took to 'radicalize' Jonathan Kozol. Is anyone, is anyone white, preparing to listen? (599)

Meyer's biting critique is underscored by the demonstrable fact that most early reviews of Styron's novel were, in fact, by whites. Nevertheless, black voices were heard, and prominent ones, too. Yet perhaps the most notable black to express an opinion did so indirectly through a white reporter's quotes. When *The Confessions of Nat Turner* first appeared, James Baldwin, unlike several others of Styron's friends, wrote no review. But he was interviewed by R. A. Sokolov in *Newsweek* and he was mentioned in *Time*. In both magazines, Baldwin's friendship with Styron was prominently cited, including his five-month stay at the Styrons' home during the period when Baldwin was writing *Another Country*. Sokolov reported that Baldwin was confident his friend's novel would prove to be a "storm center": "It'll be called effrontery . . . Bill's going to catch it from Black and white. . . . It's a very courageous book that attempts to fuse the two points of view, the master's and the slave's. . . . It's important for the black reader to see what Bill is trying to do and to recognize its validity."[23] When Styron was reported as remarking that "Jimmy broke down the last shred of whatever final hangup of Southern prejudice I might have had which was trying to tell me that a Negro was never really intelligent" (46), Baldwin grinned hugely and observed, "Yes, I think there's some of me in Nat Turner. . . . If I were an actor, I could play the part." Then he proceeded to define and defend Styron's story to Sokolov: "This is a troubling book. Styron is probing something very dangerous, deep and painful in the national psyche. I hope it starts a tremendous fight, so that people will learn what they really think about each other" (47).

Had Baldwin wished to participate more directly in the "tremendous fight," it seems unlikely that he would have been prevented by the reasons June Meyer mentions. Perhaps the more plausible explanation is that, like Ellison and others, he did not wish to place himself in the line of fire between two liberal and literate groups to both of which he had ties. Moreover, he may have recognized that his integrationist beliefs and his known homosexuality were liabilities in the eyes of certain members of both groups, who would discount his support and impugn his motives.

No such considerations apparently constrained Albert Murray, a less well-known black novelist. Murray reviewed *The Confessions of Nat Turner* at some length for the *New Leader* in December 1967.[24] His commentary anticipates several issues and attitudes subsequently voiced by the ten black writers. He reported that blacks regard reconstructed southerners as more sympathetic to blacks' problems than other whites. Nevertheless, any such altered racial attitude or behavior is "achieved rather than received" (18). Southern white assertions—whether by Robert Penn Warren, C. Vann Woodward, Walker Percy, "and, yes, Lyndon Johnson"—are often a reliable index of actual commitments to racial understanding. But Murray discovers little evidence in Styron's novel of a successful reconstruction of basic attitudes. Realistically speaking, it *would* have better served the cause of black liberation if William Styron had been able to become Nat Turner than "for Benny Goodman to become Jimmy Noone" (18). Instead, "what Negroes will find in Styron's 'confessions' is much the same old failure of sensibility that plagues most other fiction about black people. . . . they will find a Nat Turner many white people may accept at a safe distance, but hardly one with whom Negroes will easily identify" (18). Styron's failure to penetrate the core of Turner's self and soul results from a double error. To begin with, he has bought Stanley Elkins's narrowly prescriptive profile of the black slave—"emasculated and reduced to fit snugly into a personality structure based on highly questionable and essentially irrelevant conjectures about servility, to which Styron has added a neo-Reichean hypothesis about the correlation between sex repression and revolutionary leadership" (19). More serious than such naive use of dubious historical theses, however, is Styron's own ignorance of the *black* conception of Nat Turner and the cultural context within which that conception was and is reactivated. This social domain, Murray points out, reaches across several sectors of the black community, embracing eventually southern black schoolchildren, Negro History Week as observed by adults and young, and folk expressions like Nat Turner's Old Song:

> You cain't keep the world from movering around
> or stop old Nat Turner from gaining ground.

For Murray, the cultural distance is simply too vast between this black construct of Nat Turner, the tragic folk hero as man of direct action, and the isolated, repressed rebel of Styron's vision: "Instead of the man of meditation who fasted and prayed to become the Moses of his people, instead of the good shepherd who bequeathed a heritage of activism to American ministers (never more active than at present), both black and white men of the gospel will find here a black man who really wants to marry somebody's white sister—a man with a sex hang-up who goes out into the wilderness to meditate only to get a simple thing like freedom hopelessly confused with masturbation while having fantasies about white women" (19). Styron should have seen that the Negro conception of Nat Turner was one already geared to the dynamics of ritual, myth, and dramatic literature rather than to rigid ideological formulations of an essentially white psychology and view of history.

A few black social scientists prove kinder than the novelist in their judgments of *The Confessions of Nat Turner*. John Hope Franklin acceded to the invitation of simultaneous publication in the *Chicago Sun-Times* and the *Washington Post* to review Styron's book on the eve of publication. The distinguished University of Chicago historian, whose *From Slavery to Freedom: A History of Negro Americans* had recently reappeared in a third edition, commended Styron's "skillful and engrossing book."[25] It is based, he wrote, on a "profound understanding of the institution of slavery." However, he carefully warned readers not to dismiss the rebel as simply a religious fanatic. Styron's Nat Turner is no "half-wit because he wanted to do his meagre bit to destroy human slavery" (11). He joined Murray and others only on one point, in questioning that of the "unrealistic" explanation of Turner's sexually inspired murder of Margaret Whitehead. Finally, in guarded language Franklin points up the significance of Styron's retelling: "The solution to the problem of the Nat Turners is not the indiscriminate killing of the innocents or the further suppression of the victims of injustice. Rather it is what the survivors of Nat Turner's wrath could never bring themselves to do; namely, to see the inherent injustice of the institution that produced him and to destroy it" (11).

The example of middle-of-the-road commentators like John Hope Franklin was not widely followed by other black scholars and critics. Whether uninvited or, when asked, declining, black critics were for some months as scarce as June Meyer asserted. Early in 1968, however, at the time of the appearance of *Ten Black Writers Respond*, certain black scholars and writers did voice opinions in several national media. One in a more academic venue was Michael Cooke's evaluation in the *Yale Review*.[26] Another common magazine practice typified by the *New Yorker* and the *American Scholar* was the "recommended" summer reading list, an impressionistic survey of recent books recommended to vacationing readers. Among the half-dozen prominent intellectuals invited by the *American Scholar* to suggest good books, three mentioned *The Confessions of Nat Turner*.[27] C. Vann Woodward, as we might have expected, ranked Styron's novel equal in importance and interest to recently published histories of slavery by Winthrop Jordan and David Brion Davis. Another expert was J. Saunders Redding, the black novelist and scholar who, years before, when a professor at Hampton Institute, had responded to a request from William Styron for a bibliography on Nat Turner. Redding's recommendation was laconic but favorable: Styron's story of Nat Turner's revolt is "very perceptive and true" (542). Directly contradicting these two men was the young black novelist Alice Walker, who dismissed *The Confessions of Nat Turner*, "so raved about in the white press," as "a typical Southern white man's cliché." By contrast with the original *Confessions*, she wrote, Styron's version sounds like a "fairy tale." She concluded sarcastically that "if in a hundred years someone writes a book about why Malcolm X and Stokely Carmichael revolted, it will be interesting to learn what amorous repressions for white teen-agers prompted them" (551).

Later in November, still another well-known black social scientist, Benjamin Quarles, gave his judgment in the professional journal *Social Studies*. Coming down firmly on the side of Baldwin, Franklin, and Redding, Quarles (author of numerous books and editions of black history and sociology) wrote that "Turner emerges as the man he must have been in real life, a Puritan in his personal conduct, torn between a New Testament affirmation of love and an even more consuming Old Testament passion for massive warfare against the Satanic hosts, in this instance, slavery." Though adducing no evidence for the historical accuracy of Styron's story, Quarles was confident that Styron's "lesser characters are likewise soundly realized." As an important account of "an American tragedy," *The Confessions of Nat Turner* is "an example of the historical novel at its best," in the pages of which "Styron reveals Southern slavery in its essential human dimensions."[28]

Thus during the thirteen-month gap between Franklin's and Quarles's endorsements, American readers had several opportunities to heed William Hogan's advice to listen carefully to black responses to Styron's powerful story. Surveying these early comments and critiques, the concerned reader could conclude that black opinion was nearly as divided as white opinion. One possible way to describe such reactions is to pit the two black literary artists, Murray and Walker, against the scholars and social scientists, Franklin, Redding, and Quarles. A more plausible way, however, to explain the division is to view it in generational and/or social class terms, with older, black, thoroughly middle class intellectuals more willing to sympathize with Styron's attempt. In any case, the cumulative presence of published black opinion during these first months was comparatively insubstantial.

This situation, however, changed dramatically in 1968 when Beacon Press issued John H. Clarke's collection of fiery essays. *William Styron's Nat Turner: Ten Black Writers Respond* signaled by its title a significant and major body of black opinion aimed at the white writer rather than Turner himself. Quickly reviewed in several national media, *Ten Black Writers Respond* was so widely read and discussed as to go into seven printings by 1972. These polemical essays reactivate virtually all dimensions of previous discussions of the book and its subject, and introduce an emotional, ideological, and racial edge to new dimensions of the controversy. After *The Confessions of Nat Turner* itself, the black writers' manifesto proved the most arresting and divisive expression of American attitudes and cultural values that Nat Turner's return occasioned in sixties America. Indeed, the book possesses permanent significance as a model of black-white communication within a multiracial society that shares a common historical legacy of chattel slavery. "No event in recent years has touched and stirred the black intellectual community more than this book," Clarke observed of Styron's novel, and the same can also be said of *Ten Black Writers Respond*.

Ten Black Writers as Critics of History

When Clarke's collection appeared, its contributors were, with few exceptions, less widely known to the general reading public than either the black political activists whose headlined names—Carmichael, Brown, McKissick, Cleaver—were often linked to Nat Turner or the established scholars and artists already on record with favorable opinions of *The Confessions of Nat Turner*. Within the black community, however, Clarke and his associates were well known. One by-product of the unfolding debate was to acquaint white Americans with a black cultural network recently developed and now competing with older voices, institutions, and ideologies for power and influence. As their language shows, these were "black" rather than "Negro" intellectuals, and this meant that their views were initially regarded with suspicion if not outright hostility by many sixties Americans.

John Henrik Clarke, editor of the anthology, was most prominently connected to *Freedomways: A Quarterly Review of the Negro Freedom Movement*, of which he was associate editor. Established in 1960, *Freedomways* had by 1968 become a vigorous voice of left-wing black political and cultural criticism. Among its contributors were at least three other of the ten black writers. Clarke himself was active in educational circles as teacher, writer, and director of the Heritage Teaching Program of Haryou-Act, the antipoverty program in Harlem. Even more visible to the general black audience was Lerone Bennett, Jr., senior editor of *Ebony* magazine and author of several popular works of black history and social commentary, which included *Before the Mayflower*, *Confrontation Black and White*, and *Black Power, USA*. Through *Ebony*, Bennett reached more middle-class black readers than any of the other ten writers. Indeed, his opinions may have carried greater popular weight at this moment than John Hope Franklin's or James Baldwin's, which may explain why his essay opened the attack on Styron.

Several prominent social scientists were also numbered among the ten. The most famous (or notorious) was the senior academic member, Charles V. Hamilton, then of Roosevelt University but soon to become professor of political science at Columbia. His book *Black Power: The Politics of Liberation in America*, written with Stokely Carmichael, was a cause célèbre of 1967. Even more than Bennett's book, this manifesto helped make "black power" a household phrase, the source of pride and unity for many younger blacks, of fear or anger for many whites. A younger social scientist destined for a different kind of visibility and influence when he moved to Harvard and began appearing on television talk shows was Alvin F. Poussaint, a psychiatrist at the New England Medical Center. With James Comer of Yale, Poussaint was subsequently to publish *Black Child Care*, a pioneering childrearing manual known to many as the "black Dr. Spock." Still a third social scientist and academic radical was Vincent Harding of Spelman College. Later associated with the Martin Luther King, Jr., Center in Atlanta, Harding was a widely experienced activist, a Mennonite minister, historian, and sociologist. As contributor to *Negro Digest* (also a Johnson Publishing Company enterprise like *Ebony*), Harding was in the process of formulating a definition of black history later to appear in *Amistad-I: Writings on Black History and Culture* and eventually in *There Is a River: The Black Struggle for Freedom in America*.

Clarke's group also numbered two prominent black novelists, both espousing more radical politics than Ellison or Baldwin. In 1968, John O. Killens had already published three novels and a book of essays. Of these, *And Then We Heard the Thunder* and a recent collection, *Black Man's Burden*, had earned critical praise. John A. Williams, too, was a novelist and essayist, most widely recognized for *The Man Who Cried I Am*. Williams's travel book *This Is My Country, Too* was, like so many other works in this cultural history, a 1967 publication. Both writers reached a wide range of black magazine readers through articles and reviews in *Ebony* and *Freedomways*.

The final subgroup within the ten black writers were freelance writers publishing essays and reviews in various periodicals including *Negro Digest* and *Freedomways*. Loyle Hairston was a member of Harlem Writers Guild while Ernest Kaiser was a librarian at the New York Public Library's Schomburg Collection in Harlem. Finally, Jamaica-born Mike Thelwell was a younger writer and teacher at the University of Massachusetts who also published in *Freedomways* and the *Massachusetts Review*.

Though some white critics and reviewers referred, often derisively, to these black writers as unknown, radical, and irresponsible, it should be clear from their biographies that, as a group, Styron's black critics were scarcely wild-eyed radicals. They were associated with a wide spectrum of respectable, as well as some more radical, institutions both within and beyond the black cultural communities of New York, Chicago, Boston, and Atlanta. They were articulate, angry, and deeply disillusioned with white America. While some were in the process of assuming positions of status in the dominant culture's intellectual cadre, others were just as decisively distancing themselves from white institutions, preferring less secure separatist positions in the black world. Integration was emphatically not on their political and social agenda at the time.

Given their professional diversity yet fundamental ideological consensus, the black writers, not surprisingly, ranged in their individual critiques well beyond the boundaries of academic history and literary criticism. In addition to questioning, often vociferously and rudely, Styron's motives and accomplishments, they also asked general questions about the social uses of history and fiction, as well as about the relevant cultural contexts and concepts underlying Styron's narrative. They freely passed ideological judgment on cultural practices such as current American book reviewing. Indeed, it was not simply Styron's subject and its reception that aroused these critics, but the fact that *The Confessions of Nat Turner* was tied so intimately to white commercial literary practice. For Mike Thelwell, the novel, its commercial marketing, and its rapturous public reception by the white establishment were significant events: "Clearly, we are in the presence of no mere 'fiction' but a cultural and social document which is both 'illuminating' and potentially definitive of contemporary attitudes."[29]

These writers were most aroused to assail Styron and the white cultural ethos on historical grounds, as is signaled by the opening lines of Clarke's introduction. Clarke quotes Aptheker's review of *The Confessions of Nat Turner* in which the historian of slavery characterized in widest terms the threat Styron poses: "History's potency is mighty. The oppressed need it for identity and inspiration; oppressors for justification, rationalization, and legitimacy. Nothing illustrates this more clearly than the history writing on the American Negro people" (vii). Lerone Bennett also echoes Aptheker in his own essay's epigraph which quotes Maurice Merleau-Ponty and anticipates Ellison's comments at the SHA: "History takes still more from those who have lost everything, and gives yet more to those who have taken everything. For its sweeping judgments acquit the unjust and dismiss the pleas of their victims. History never *confesses*" (3). Both mottoes reflect the almost desperate sincerity with which these critics reclaim the history of slavery as, first and foremost, *theirs*. This cultural treasury of black history has been pilfered by Styron, just as Ulrich B. Phillips did in generations past. "We are not quibbling here over footnotes in scholarly journals," Bennett declares. "We are objecting to something more insidious, more dangerous. *We are objecting to a deliberate attempt to steal the meaning of a man's life*" (5). Or, in the spirit of Vincent Harding's review, "You've taken my Nat and Gone."

These accusations are leveled not just at one historical novel but at white history in general, which Killens characterizes as "millions of *little white lies* manufactured through the years to rationalize the Western Paradox and the Great American Tragedy." The tragic irony at white culture's core, Killens asserts, is the brutal fact that America's founding fathers were "freedom-loving slave-masters" (34–35). All black historical and political thought begins with this fact. For "most men came to America to be free. We came in chains, were brought here to be slaves. There is the irony. And there is the basic cause for Nat's rebellion. There is the fundamental cause of the current black rebellions in the northern cities, the so-called Long Hot Summers" (35). Given this inescapable circumstance, black Americans cannot help but see 1831 and 1967 as a continuum and single reality. In the struggle for liberation, the past, properly understood, is a vital resource. Misrepresented, history can forge a fresh set of chains. Styron's bestseller is the latest weapon in a continually replenished arsenal of oppression. With ironic resignation, Williams predicts the chances of blacks' successfully reclaiming their own past: "Black writers, it appears, have lost the race, if there ever was one, to air the truth. The likes of Styron are already past the finish line" (49).

In vigorous counterattack, the black writers find common ground in their firm belief in the primacy of fact. There *is* a truthful version of the Southampton slave revolt just as there is likewise an accurate portrait of its heroic leader. Truths and deviations can both be confirmed by the proper use of historical records. Although these sources are, in the case of black history, usually written by whites and often few in number, their individual importance—especially of Gray's *Confessions*—is, paradoxically, all the greater. Styron claims to honor this principle but, in fact, signally fails to do so. In Bennett's words, he has not worked "within the tensions of accepted facts" (5). He has ignored key details and interpretations found in other relevant nineteenth-century records. Bennett and others identify Thomas Wentworth Higginson, Joshua Coffin, Samuel Warner, and William Wells Brown as among these neglected authors. Cavalierly omitting, substituting, and distorting, Styron's historical imagination has spawned a fantasy. "Styron *dreams*, but he refuses to confront history and that refusal defines his book," Bennett insists. "We know—he confesses it—that he is trying to escape the judgment of history embodied in Nat Turner and his spiritual sons in the twentieth century" (4). The outlines of that judgment from the past are clear:

> According to the historical data, the real Nat Turner was a virile, commanding, courageous figure. Styron rejects history by rejecting this image of Nat Turner. In fact, he wages literary war on this image, substituting an impotent, cowardly, irresolute creature of his own imagination for the real black man who killed or ordered killed real white people for real historical reasons. The man Styron substitutes for Nat Turner is not only the antithesis of Nat Turner; he is the antithesis of blackness. In fact, he is a standard Styron type: a neurasthenic, Hamlet-like white intellectual in blackface. (4–5)

Bennett's accusations are echoed by other historically oriented critics, especially Killens, Hamilton, Kaiser, Harding, and Thelwell. "At every crucial point," Harding writes, "it is almost embarrassingly obvious that Styron is unable to comprehend Nat Turner's real stature and meaning, that he does not perceive Turner's role as a tragic-triumphant hero in the biblical genre" (25). Harding and others are not only confident about which documents support this "true" image and confirm the historical significance of the revolt, they are equally clear as to which vital facts Styron has misused, denied, or ignored. Each of these data relates to the two conflicting images of the historical figure at issue—Nat the leader, one with his people in the slave community and in military command of the insurrection, versus the isolated, self-obsessed, white-oriented protagonist of Styron's story. To these men no contrast could be clearer or more revealing of cultural relations between blacks and whites in sixties America.

Other vitally important details and outlines have been passed down through written sources like Gray and through the oral folk tradition of blacks. To begin with, the historical Turner, the manly leader, was not celibate but had a black wife and son (this from Higginson; the black writers do not mention other sources such as contemporary newspapers that verify this fact). There exists, they insist, no evidence whatsoever for Styron's Nat's erotic attraction to white women or for his homosexual episode. These are simply fantasies. They compose the core of explicit or implicit denigration and emasculation by which the historical Nat has been robbed of his social identity.

A second, more general but closely related "fact" denied is that Turner had strong ties to the slave community, particularly his own family, an unusually close-knit slave family. Nat learned early to read and write from his parents and grandmother, rather than the master's family in the Big House. The implication in Gray's *Confessions* is that other members of Nat's family were literate; he was, therefore, not unique. From them the future rebel also acquired the conviction that his precocious powers augured a special destiny. This belief was shared by the other slaves, as revealed in a third relevant historical fact Styron ignores. Running away and voluntarily returning to bondage after thirty days astonished his fellows, perhaps engendered a false confidence about this remarkable slave in white minds, but above all demonstrated Nat's entire trust in divine guidance, the true source of his personal and political power.

From a variety of viewpoints, therefore, this event is crucial. Its absence from Styron's narrative illustrates the white writer's deliberate refusal to recognize and record Turner's full role within the community of which he is the voice. This role is early demonstrated on a smaller scale by Nat's boyhood leadership in the slaves' various nocturnal acts of thievery, a detail from Gray signifying his masterminding as typical, symbolic expressions of slave discontent and opposition. These forays by no means contradict another fact of Nat's early maturity that Styron has misunderstood—his consciously political decision to stand apart from the other slaves in order to emphasize his prophetic identity as a kind of black Moses with authoritative visions.

Turner's public role as Baptist preacher is, moreover, still another facet of his historical character that Harding in particular argues is absent or misrepresented in *The Confessions of Nat Turner*. The position of the preacher is an important "accepted fact" of historic black community life during as well as after slavery. The real Nat Turner exercised this power through the spoken word, religious rituals, and the example of his own deeds. Renowned for fiery preaching, the Preacher-Prophet of history is seldom heard or seen in these roles in this latest reincarnation. "For though William Styron-Turner talks about religion a great deal and though he quotes biblical passages in excellent style, the 'divine fury' of Old Testament experience is almost totally absent. Though Nat Turner is a preacher, only one major attempt at a sermon is made in *The Confessions*, and it fails to catch any of the peculiar rhythmic and thematic strengths of this black folk art form. Equally striking is the fact that the religious music of Afro-Americans never enters as a major structural element of the novel" (29). By this failure Styron sacrifices not only historical verisimilitude but dramatic immediacy as well.

Just as dismaying to Harding are the fictional Turner's ritual performances of baptism, so central to his time, region, and sect. Baptizing the young and the penitent provided repeated demonstrations of the preacher's God-given authority and the community's cohesion. Neither divine forgiveness nor a sinner's repentant return to full communion with other believers is enacted in Styron's story. This is especially notable inasmuch as the narrative contains not one but two baptismal scenes. The first takes place in the creek on whose banks Nat and Willis have just made love. Far from a communal act, this ceremony *à deux* scarcely includes Willis at all, so patently is its function to bind the power of Nat's own sexuality through a private ritual. The second baptism is even less a communal rite of cleansing and reunion, involving as it does Ethelred T. Brantley, the one white man who in Gray's narrative seeks forgiveness for his sins from the black preacher. In Styron's version, Brantley is a pitiful pederast, a repulsive outcast from the white community. His baptism, in a manure-filled pond from whose shores derisive whites throw rocks at the two men, is a parody of a spiritual transaction. "Again we see the driving force of his search for baptism not in the power of Nat's religious message or personal charisma," Harding observes, "but in Brantley's own sense of futility, fear, and sexually confused guilt. Since there is very little description of Brantley in the historical records, Styron alone chose to create such a pariahlike personality for the one white man who is drawn to Nat Turner's religious teachings. How else can this be read except as an act of diminishing the power of William Styron's black 'hero'?" (27).

Spiritual power issuing from the core of a religious life is, then, conspicuously absent, in normal, historical terms, from Styron's retelling. Nothing illustrates this lack more clearly to the black writers than Styron's omission of the two moments in Gray's *Confessions* when, against his will and prejudices, the white lawyer records his awestruck impression of the prisoner. The first is the historical Turner's reply when asked if he was not mistaken in reading natural signs as divine instructions for revolt: "Was not Christ crucified?" The second moment comes with Gray's final description of the unrepentant prisoner, "with a spirit soaring above the attributes of man" (15). Bennett speaks for others in remarking on these striking gaps in the record as history: "In the 428 pages of William Styron's *Confessions*, there is not one single image to compare with Gray's image of the defiant rebel raising his manacled hands to heaven" (16).

To these specified and "accepted" facts of Turner's life and career (most attributed to Gray) the black writers add several larger historical statements on slave revolts and the motives for rebels like Nat Turner. The most sweeping accusation is that the Southampton slave revolt was by no stretch of the imagination—except Styron's and his credulous reviewers'—the only effective, sustained slave insurrection in American history. To ignore evidence in Aptheker and elsewhere of a 250-year record of plots, murders, and outright uprisings is, they declare, to traduce history. Styron's justification by recourse to Elkins's and Tannenbaum's "fraudulent and untenable thesis," as Kaiser calls it, is to commit still another error—to assert "that American slavery was so oppressive, despotic and emasculating psychologically that revolt was impossible and Negroes could only be Sambos" (54). Styron's semantics thus distort and limit the actual pattern of continuous slave resistance in the past. "The reality of slavery . . . by testimony of the slaves themselves," Thelwell observes, "was that the slaves were constantly resisting and rebelling, whether by sabotage, malingering, escape to the North, physical retaliation to attack, plotting insurrection (with a frequency that caused the masters to live in a state of constant apprehension and under conditions of continual vigilance and security), running off to join Indian tribes, or forming small bands of armed guerillas operating out of swamps and remote areas" (87). This truer history is proof of a deep-seated desire for freedom, the bedrock of all violent resistance and revolt. This universal motive Styron either denies or defines narrowly in terms of specific individual traumas like those attributed to Nat, Hark, and Will. "It should not now be necessary to search for the motives, personal and otherwise, for the Nat Turner revolt," Clarke concludes (x).

"Historical figures cannot move in a historical vacuum," Williams the novelist asserts. "Is the vacuum surrounding Styron's Nat Turner the result of the failure of the author to thoroughly research his material? A novelist embarked on a historical work becomes a historian in effect, and he must evaluate his character in terms of the time in which his character lived" (46). By this simple but stringent criterion Styron stands condemned. For he has closed in the world around Nat Turner's solitary consciousness, excluding from view a host of facts and factors concerning the antebellum world in which the slave lived. Sacrificed to interior reality are such other realities as Santo Domingo, Haiti, and other Caribbean uprisings. Thus Nat calls himself a "nigger Napoleon"—another sign of his insatiable eavesdropping on the white masters—but his creator never once mentions Toussaint L'Ouverture, Walker's *Appeal*, the *Liberator*, antebellum apocalypticism, or the colonization movement. The actual number (surprisingly large) of free blacks in Southampton County and whether records prove that slaves actually fought alongside their masters against Nat's followers—these, too, are relevant facts or questions regarding 1831 that Styron's "meditation on history" has no room for or treats dishonestly. Their absence or abuse, these critics assert, undercuts the author's announced aim to "recreate a man and his era."

Even if the historical Nat Turner were, in fact, unaware of such outside events and forces, they *were* influences and circumstances affecting his and others' behavior. By systematically sacrificing context and ethos to pathos and an implausible, anachronistic psychology, Styron has repeatedly shown indifference or hostility to history, just as his depictions of most Christians (except Samuel Turner) and clergymen in the novel demonstrate hostility to what Harding calls the "religious core" of the historical man and his insurrection. What these acts of commission and omission add up to is nothing less than a repudiation of the revolutionary impulse itself. "Turner's rebellion is depicted as a worse crime than slavery!" Hairston exclaims with horror (67). Killens asks:

> What's the big mystery about Nat's motivation? He was a slave, PERIOD, which meant, no matter how you sugar-coated it, he was a non-man. Every slave is a potential revolutionary. The only reason Styron failed to see this fundamental truth is that the color of Nat's skin stood in the way. The most obvious way for a non-man to become a man is to wreak violence upon the man who had raped him of his manhood. Let me speak plainly. Every black American, then and now, was and is, a potential Nat Turner. . . . And the failure to face this truth is the fundamental failure of Styron's *Confessions*. (37)

For this complex of reasons, Styron likewise fails to articulate anywhere in his story the ideological result of the Southampton slave revolt. "Nat Turner was a revolutionary who did *not* fail, but rather one who furthered the idea and cause of freedom precisely because he chose to act for freedom" (73–74). So the political scientist Charles Hamilton avers. "The important thing is that the desire for human freedom resides in the black breast as well as in any other. No amount of explicating about the harshness of slavery or the gentleness of slavery, about the docility of the masses of slaves, etc. can keep that desire from exploding. Man—black or white or yellow or red—moves to maximize his freedom: THAT is the lesson of Nat Turner that Styron did not deal with" (74).

Ten Black Writers as Literary Critics

If Clarke and colleagues seem unified in their attack as historians, this is less clearly the case when it comes to dissecting *The Confessions of Nat Turner* as a literary text. However, the occasional disagreements appearing among the ten usually derive from their common recognition of the inextricable connectedness of this narrative as simultaneously historical recreation and imaginative creation. Thelwell speaks for the others by opening his essay, the book's final piece, with recognition of the interrelated issues to be resolved in criticizing Styron's story as a social and cultural document: "When a work of fiction is cast in the form of a novel, utilizing techniques of narrative, situation, and structure that we associate with that form, and is about an important historical event, but is defined for us as 'a meditation on history' rather than a 'conventional' historical novel, certain questions are forced upon us" (79). Though the reading public has been taken in by Styron's straddling of two genres, he adds, such public reception does not remove questions about historical and symbolic truth. As "fiction" Styron claims freedom from the very historical claims and responsibilities that his author's note and ordinary readers assume. This claim is, therefore, real as well as self-serving, since others accept and act upon it. So it necessitates the kind of textual, intertextual, and extraliterary analyses several of the ten attempt in their review essays. Connecting these discussions are three or four recurring questions, to which each of these critics offer different answers.

Dealing with *The Confessions of Nat Turner* as an imaginative act, the black writers first raise a patently ad hominem issue. Is it possible for a southern white liberal imagination to enter the mind of a particular black man and probe its mysteries of motivation and consciousness? Does William Styron even have the right to try? If he does, what dangers and possible benefits accrue from his use of certain literary techniques and artistic insights? Finally, has Styron overcome or succumbed to the acknowledged dangers? With respect to each of these matters the critics subject *The Confessions of Nat Turner* to stern scrutiny. Frequently they draw comparisons with other writers, texts, and techniques as different, more or less adequate solutions to what they concede is the formidable task of recreating this rebellious slave in fictional narrative.

Consideration of these loaded questions proceeds differently, with each literary critic or practicing novelist employing a slightly different terminology. Their common commitment remains, however, to the primacy of historical criteria, which in their eyes entails fidelity to representational or "realistic" fiction as the most appropriate mode for treating the Nat Turner subject. In this emphasis the ten diverge from many earlier reviewers who, as we have noted, are inclined to grant Styron virtually unquestioned latitude as an artist dealing experimentally with history.

As might be expected, the three writers of fiction—Killens, Williams, and Thelwell—devote most attention to Styron's successes and failures with narrative structure, language, and characterization. Yet even the less sophisticated critics offer plausible insights on the problematic nature of historical fiction. For instance, the librarian-bibliographer Ernest Kaiser who, many readers have felt, makes some of the more outrageous statements in denouncing Styron, points out that "the problem of creating Negro characters in historical fiction (within the veil and in slavery) is very difficult even for Negro writers. . . . Historical fiction about Negroes that has real characters and is true to history is almost impossible even for the most understanding white writers in the racist, separatist United States" (50). Nevertheless, Kaiser is unequivocal in denouncing Styron's attempt. "The unspeakable arrogance of this young southern writer daring to set down his own personal view of Nat's life as from inside Nat Turner in slavery! . . . Styron, who doesn't really know the Negroes living in Virginia today, deigns to speak personally for the slaves" (56).

Directly contradicting Kaiser's dogma, Williams defends his fellow novelist while at the same time criticizing the white reading public's preference for white writing on this aspect of American experience. "Since I do not believe that the right to describe or portray or in other ways delineate the lives of black people in American society is the private domain of Negro writers, I cannot fault Styron's *intent*," he observes, adding wryly that "white writers by the score have been taking over that function anyway" (45). But Styron's book was not honest, and Williams has doubts that even in intent it was honest. For Williams, grounds for this judgment are found not only in the novel's thinness of historical context (a result of the author's failure to utilize all available sources) but also in stock characterizations of key figures. Characters like Jeremiah Cobb, Will, and Margaret Whitehead are so stereotyped that Faulkner (who is often cited in these essays as Styron's forefather) would never have stooped to creating them. Moreover these figures are grouped in simple contrasts and oppositions: "Styron's bad people are bad, and his good people are good and there is very little mix except in Turner" (48).

As for Styron's fictional language, the black writers disagree vehemently as to its effectiveness while agreeing that the narrative voice in this story provides the clearest evidence of the author's artistic and historical priorities. To Williams, Nat Turner's voice does not ring as false as it does to several others; it "is full-bodied, slow, it seems, and often beautiful" (48). But he laments that the earthy and anachronistically profane speech usually issues from black mouths. Hairston, too, is guardedly impressed. "The writing is graceful and often moving in the lyrical beauty of many descriptive passages," he admits, adding this important reservation, "somehow it is deficient in that interior quality which is needed to breathe the illusion of life and human warmth into the work. And because of the elaborate, and sometimes heavy, style, the work seems to be more tapestry than historical literature" (68). Styron's stance toward his black subjects is either the cause or consequence of this remote style. "When depicting black people in fiction," Hairston generalizes, "white writers are guilty of two fundamental faults, to which William Styron is no exception. First, they are incapable of portraying black characters as human types, and second, they look upon the black man's condition of social degradation as being natural to his *inferior* character, rather than resulting from the racial oppression of the American social system" (68). Hence Styron's protagonist, despite what Hairston calls his "good grammar and ivy league accoutrements" (68), illustrates the "white American writer's concept of the 'Negro'" (69) no more believably than Mark Twain does with "simpering" Jim or Faulkner with "obstinate" Lucas Beauchamp or the "matriarch" Dilsey.

Qualifications of this sort do not satisfy others in *Ten Black Writers Respond*. Many of the contributors choose to see in the "glossy surfaces" of Styron's prose a deceptive and inappropriate mask covering an "ambiguous substructure" of attitudes and values, as Harding puts it (23). To Killens, the quality of writing in *The Confessions of Nat Turner* is quite uneven, "inspired, in spots, dull and repetitious oftentimes, tiresome even" (43). As the expression of a particular black consciousness, Styron's Nat's voice is "a monumental failure," for Killens sees only contradiction and confusion in a Turner "who is sometimes thinking and speaking in biblical or Victorian English and at other times lapsing into an Amos-and-Andy dialect" (43). Whereas Styron's announced aim is to dramatize through changes of voice and vocabulary the various verbal masks the black slave must don to cover his intelligence and rage, Killens perceives only ineptitude in catching the actual subtleties and peculiar cadences of black American speech. Killens appears convinced that no white writer is able to replicate faithfully these rhythms of black language—"the manners of formulations and of thinking through and the special way of saying things, the unique-to-our-blackness methods of expression; the Afro-American psyche. Amos-and-Andy dialect is easy, too easy. On the other hand, black idiom, Afro-Americanese, is more difficult to achieve, but it is also more authentic, more rewarding and profound; it is historic and creative. Styron in attempting to write Afro-Americanese, is like a man who tries to sing the blues when he has not paid his dues" (43–44).

These strictures are endorsed and expanded by Mike Thelwell, whose essay contains the fullest critique of *The Confessions of Nat Turner* as historical fiction. Of the ten, Thelwell is the most explicit in locating language at the very center of culture—black culture and especially folk culture:

> When black people were brought to America they were deprived of their language and of the underpinnings in cultural experience out of which a language comes. It is clear that they developed two languages, one for themselves and another for the white masters. The latter has been preserved (parodied is a better word) as the "Sambo" dialect. . . . The only vestiges we can find of the real language of the slaves are in the few spirituals which have come down to us, which give a clue to its true tenor. It is a language produced by oppression, but one whose central impulse is survival and resistance. And it is undoubtedly the language in which Turner's rebellion and the countless other plots for insurrection were formulated. . . . Lacking complicated syntactical structure and vast vocabulary, it depends on what linguists call para-language; that is, gesture, physical expression, and modulation of cadences and intonation which serve to change the meaning—in incredibly subtle ways—of the same collection of words. It is intensely poetic and expressive, since vivid simile, creative and effective juxtaposition of images, and metaphor must serve in the absence of a large vocabulary to cause the audience to see and feel. It is undoubtedly a language of action rather than a language of reflection, and thus more available to the dramatist than to the novelist. (80–81)

This "real" black language does not appear in *The Confessions of Nat Turner*. For various reasons, Thelwell argues, Styron's Nat "speaks, or rather meditates in no language at all." His creator, instead of living speech, has fabricated "a sterile leaden prose . . . a strange fusion of latinate classicism, a kind of New England Episcopalian prissiness" (81). Perhaps intended to replicate Gray's official lawyerly language, it is more likely an imitation of the prose voice of James Baldwin, "the Negro Mr. Styron knows best, or Faulkner at his least inspired." Either way, the construct—though not without its charms inasmuch as it is "clear, even elegant in a baroque Victorian way, especially in the functionally inexplicable passages of nature writing that continuously interrupt the narrative"—is inappropriate. For "it is the language of the essay, heavy and declarative" (81). Compounding the problem of vitality is the retrospective narrative structure, in obedience to which "much of the book is in the form of long, unbroken monologues. Even the most violent action or intensely felt experience seems distanced and without immediacy, strangely lumpen" (81).

Clearly this disagreement between Thelwell and Styron is cultural in origin and implication. The young black critic and fiction writer protests against artistic choices that he acknowledges are culturally determined and probably inevitable for a white author. Styron's fictional language, narrative structure, tone, and characterizations all reflect the white author's conception of his protagonist as the prototype of present-day middle-class blacks rather than a nineteenth-century slave whose character and mission both reflect a community-based spiritual and military leader. "As his language is 'white,' so are his values and desires" (82), Thelwell asserts. Turner's attitudes do, in fact, reflect social reality that black Americans have experienced both before and since slavery—"close to but isolated from whites" (82). Hence the fact that this Nat Turner speaks like a nineteenth-century plantation owner naturally means that he reflects his master's values. It is plausible for him to hold in contempt the society and folk culture of his own people whom he considers "dumb, mindless, unsalvageable brutes unfitted either for freedom or salvation. . . . What this Nat Turner really wants is to become white, and, failing that, to integrate. As a type this Nat certainly exists *today*. 1831 is a different question. There is nothing in the historical record to justify such a characterization of Turner" (82).

Language, then, is one key to Styron's success and failure about which the ten are in large agreement. It mirrors an essentially "white" protagonist who in turn generates a distanced and fastidious view of the very slaves Turner energized into revolt. Instead of a fictional universe peopled by believable humans, white and black, inhabiting a realistic social setting and addressing each other in believable social idioms, Styron has created an implausible mixture of historical reality and dream. (None of the ten, in fact, shows much interest in Nat's dreams.) Most of his colleagues agree with Hairston that this "first-person narrative of a slave recounting the vicissitudes of his life in a very literary prose destroys whatever plausibility his Nat Turner might have had. The method has the effect of reducing the character to an abstraction, a kind of literary conduit through which the author transmits the white man's emotionally charged involvements with the black man. But with all the work's sorrowful tone, its pathos has a hollow, disquieting ring" (69).

Psychology and the Ten Black Writers

A "white man's emotionally charged involvements with the black man" is a phrase that suggests succinctly the black writers' contention that *The Confessions of Nat Turner* must be read as a personal and cultural psychogram. To those critics—Poussaint, Harding, Hairston, and Bennett, in particular—interested in the psychological depths beneath the story's ambiguous surfaces, the tale suggests one told by an analysand to his analyst. It is an overdetermined confession. In the first case, the historical Nat Turner seeks to record his version of the past using Gray's words, which inevitably reflect the white lawyer's thoughts and feelings. Now and simultaneously, the words represent a fictional Nat Turner's meditation on his past as reimagined by the white author, William Styron. Since white writers control both confessions and project their own beliefs, knowledge, fears, and desires onto both Nat Turners, the black writers understandably devote more space to Styron and Gray than to the two Turners. To them, the historical Turner's motives were relatively uncomplicated. They do not, therefore, discuss in any detail freedom, the Bible, visions, and violence as psychic phenomena. The psychological processes here at work are social, reflecting public thought and behavior, not the private, unconscious drives arising, as perhaps a Freudian would say, from childhood memories and family dynamics.

For these critics, it is a sufficient psychosocial explanation to say that Nat Turner was a slave. Theological, spiritual, and psychological complexities in the historical figure's Christian mind-set are of surprisingly little concern to them. With the notable exception of Harding, most of the ten treat *The Confessions of Nat Turner* in thoroughly secular terms. Lerone Bennett is representative in condemning Styron's ignorance of the "true" psychology that "makes slaves rise up and cut their oppressors' throats from ear to ear. Styron evades this dynamic; he refuses to come to grips with the institutionalized violence of an oppressive status quo and the inevitable counter violence of the oppressed" (13). Bennett does not choose to imagine the personal feelings and moral reflections that might precede or follow the act of cutting someone's throat, and hence dismisses Styron's extended exploration of the mixture of rage, righteous vengeance, remorse, and guilt in the mind of his fictional figure. Nor is Bennett greatly interested in this imaginary black man's reactions to the arrogance, obliviousness, sympathy, pity, and fear that mix and boil in the minds of the whites he encounters in the novel. That this mental turmoil may or may not resemble the historical experience of an actual Baptist preacher is a matter likewise of little concern to the black writers. Thus though Harding observes that "the Old Testament is present only as a collection of words in *The Confessions*" (29), he ignores New Testament references to the Book of Revelation, which also fill Styron's preacher's thoughts—and which may have been pondered, preached on, or even sung about by the historical Nat Turner. (To be sure, Styron seldom raises these issues within the social context of black religious ritual and music that Harding and Thelwell miss; instead he does so characteristically in his rebel's solitary musings.)

The black writers' critiques of "pure hatred"—that rare state of intense emotion, thought, memory, and intention which Styron's Nat meditates about and dramatizes in the opening scene of part 3—are similarly skeptical or perfunctory. Why this emotion—in its relative rarity and its power—should figure so largely in Styron's Nat's revolt is a question Hairston raises only to condemn:

> And why is our slave so concerned about "pure hatred"? Because in order to make good his "divine mission to kill all the white people in Southampton" he must find "Negroes in whom hatred

was already ablaze" or can be cultivated. Men who would reduce fellow humans to brute-animals, in their lust for wealth and privilege, are worthy of nothing less than pure hatred. But William Styron has a different purpose in mind: by pure hatred, he is suggesting a criminal state of mind for the purpose of reducing the insurrection, in the reader's mind, to the baseness of slavery. (69–70)

Many of these psychological perceptions and assertions are manifestly ideological and political arguments thinly disguised as quasi-scientific opinions. More significant than such amateur attacks is the commentary of Alvin Poussaint, the only psychiatrist in the group. His essay, entitled "The Imaginations of William Styron on the Life of Nat Turner," tries to link specifically psychological arguments with ideological ones: "How will we ever know how well the author has freed himself of his own white supremacist attitudes as he attempts to project himself into the mind of a black slave?" (17). In pursuing more or less systematically this common concern, Poussaint concedes that "in many parts of the novel I detect a strong empathy which the author has for his protagonist" (22). Ignoring the psychological processes of identification and introjection that the character Nat exhibits during his early years at Turner's Mill, Poussaint examines the white writer's projections. The emotions, qualities, and attitudes thus attributed to Turner can only be this white man's own fears and desires; only in this form can they be acknowledged.

Upon examination, Styron's projections prove to be age-old anxieties and impulses of the classical white racist. The tacit result, though not necessarily the conscious aim, is to degrade, infantilize, and emasculate a black man whose historical image threatens white mental and emotional constructs evident in racial myths and stereotypes. In thus confirming his colleagues' more intuitive or ideological descriptions, Poussaint never uses the term "southern" to characterize Styron's racism. Indeed, the phobias, associations, and fascinations expressed or symbolized in *The Confessions of Nat Turner* are, Poussaint believes, widely shared by Styron's white readership who will, he fears, conclude that, since this is a historical account based on facts, their fantasies and fears are similarly grounded: "Thus, the psychological impact on the American public of this widely publicized literary work will be considerable" (18).

Poussaint also identifies the devices Styron's fiction utilizes to articulate these projections. The first narrative choice is to create plausible evidence about the influential others in the small slave's life. During these decisive years Nat's mother is relegated to a secondary role. In her place, "all the people he seemed to 'worship' were white" (18). Modern psychologists, himself included, must find this situation surprising. It would be more convincing to hypothesize that the future greatness and strength of this historical figure came along more traditional lines from a mother and father. "Yet, the wanderings of Styron's mind seem to focus mainly on his relations with white people. Is this because of a commonly held racist view that a Negro who achieves must be primarily doing so because of his associations with whites?" (18). Such suspicions are strengthened by Nat's improbable gift of "white" speech and his recurring fantasies of actually becoming white. This process of identification is not pure fabrication. Over the generations, Poussaint points out, the mental behavior of house servants, Uncle Toms, and today's middle-class blacks often exhibit similar patterns. "However, Nat Turner was a unique and great individual. It could be that what really distinguished him was the fact that he was not indoctrinated with the psyche of a 'house nigger.' It is just as reasonable, from a psychological viewpoint, to speculate that he did not hate his blackness and that it was self-love that made him a revolutionist revolting against the abominable institution of slavery. There is certainly little in the original confessions of Nat Turner which suggest that he ever played the psychological role of a 'house nigger' or 'Uncle Tom'" (19).

Stereotyping and role-playing, Poussaint goes on to assert, operate on two levels in Styron's narrative. Ordinary blacks are metaphorically children or animals while the superior protagonist becomes a willing protégé and imitator of certain well-born whites. This process then extends to the adolescent's erotic-spiritual aspirations and objects. "Why does the author choose to depict Nat Turner as a celibate pining for white women?" (20). Why, too, so much emphasis on Will's desires for white female flesh? Neither fixation is extractable from Gray's *Confessions*. "In fact, Turner and his troops did not sexually molest or rape any white women whom they had slain or encountered," a particularly telling detail in light of the drunkenness often reported and acknowledged by Nat about his followers. "As anyone acquainted with the behavior of conquering soldiers will testify, this is amazing self-restraint for a band of 'drunken' and 'undisciplined' black troops. Why didn't these white-women-hungry slaves take advantage of their opportunity? Why does Styron in his tale go so far in distorting the actual historical facts?" (20).

Such queries lead inevitably to Margaret Whitehead. She is, in Poussaint's opinion, the novel's most transparent projection. Why has the author gone to such lengths to imagine such "an enormous tale of Turner's overwhelming, erotic, and quasi-religious attachment to this young girl and her 'whiteness'"? (20–21). This creation of "Miss Margaret" as the divine symbol of alienation and reconciliation—"I would have spared *her that showed me Him* whose presence I had not fathomed or maybe never even known" (Poussaint's emphasis)—is the most extreme, least supportable instance of white rationalization in this narrative. "Once again we see propagated the hackneyed racist belief that Negroes who are strong, successful, and masculine must also want to possess a white woman in order to give final sanction to their manhood. Why is not the author able to 'imagine' that Nat Turner had a young, feminine, beautiful, and courageous black woman who stood by his side throughout his heroic plan to revolt against slavery!?" (21).

Instead of a heterosexual hero with a black wife or lover, Styron has substituted a character whose sexual identity is complicated by a homosexual experience with a young slave, Turner's only erotic encounter with another person. "What is the communication here?", the psychiatrist asks. "Naturally, it implies that Nat Turner was not a man at all. It suggests that he was unconsciously really feminine. Styron underscores this image by depicting Turner as a bungling, awkward soldier who is unable to kill his oppressors and pukes at the sight of blood during combat. Thus, throughout the book he is revealed as an emasculated and 'abnormal' character" (21). Are not readers to infer that "the whole revolt against slavery and racism was somehow illegitimate and 'abnormal'"? (22). Such plausible speculations suggest that Styron's imagination works to alter, reduce, and emasculate his chosen historical figure. "Yet given the facts and contents of the novel, one wonders if Styron was an unwitting victim of his own unconscious white racism for which he alone cannot be held fully accountable" (22).

Poussaint's restraint in identifying and interpreting psychological clues in Styron's historical fiction is not shared by others in *Ten Black Writers Respond*. Ernest Kaiser's emotional fervor and polemical language are more typical: "This novel is a witches' brew of Freudian psychology, Elkins's 'Sambo' thesis on slavery and Styron's vile racist imagination that makes especially Will and Nat Turner animals or monsters. . . . Styron cannot see Turner as the hero he was and as the Negro people see him; as a slave who led a heroic rebellion against the dehumanization of chattel slavery" (57). Though in more discriminating language, Thelwell concurs. He, too, condemns the "Freud, moonlight, and magnolia view of history" (85), adding that in this version events and relationships "which did not happen" (90) become all too often central motifs in Styron's account. These substitutions inexorably suggest the operation of wish fulfillment. Authorial projections take literary and social forms long familiar to readers of American and especially southern writing on slavery. "If this book is important," Thelwell sums up, "it is so not because it tells much about Negro experience during slavery but because of the manner in which it demonstrates the persistence of white southern myths, racial stereotypes, and literary clichés even in the best intentioned and most enlightened minds. Their largely uncritical acceptance in literary circles shows us how far we still have to go. The real 'history' of Nat Turner, and indeed of black people, remains to be written" (91).

Counterresponses to Clarke et al.

Almost at once, Clarke's anthology drew public attention in ways the other social and literary commentary by black intellectuals had not done. Amiri Baraka, Harold Cruse, even perhaps James Baldwin scarcely ruffled as many white feathers as did the ten black writers.[30] During the summer and fall of 1968, national newspapers and magazines reviewed and discussed the passionate responses. Areas of sharp dissent never really engaged by earlier white commentaries flared as Styron's admirers and defenders took on the black essayists. Half a dozen lively exchanges took place within a few months in bellwether metropolitan media like the *New York Review of Books, New York Times Book Review, Saturday Review, The Nation,* and *Freedomways*. With astonishment, ordinary readers, college students and teachers, and others inside and beyond the academy felt the unexpected force of a concentrated assault on basic white values and assumptions. In the process, the grounds for black rage and resentment were widened to include subjects on which many whites, by insulation, ignorance, or failure of imagination had blithely assumed agreement. After all, had not the great majority of reviewers and commentators, respected scholars and noted intellectuals proclaimed Styron's book a landmark? Had it not truly captured "the agonizing essence of Negro slavery"? For their part, black readers discovered fresh reasons for deciding a white man's book to be a serious threat to cherished (or newly perceived) values and ideals. If some of these blacks did not actually read Styron, many, like Ellison, did read *Ten Black Writers Respond*. Clarke's collection sold briskly, going quickly into several reprintings. Beacon Press no doubt was delighted that its liberal Unitarian policy of encouraging minority literature was paying off in this case; its editors doubtless relished both the controversy and the sales.

Two early assessments of the issues and emotions here reawakened or initiated appeared in key periodicals. One was Ossie Davis's review in *Freedomways* 1968 summer issue. More prominently placed and more widely noted, however, was Martin Duberman's lead review in the Sunday *New York Times Book Review* of August 11, 1968. The white Princeton historian had already reviewed Styron's novel for the *Village Voice* the previous December. Not noted as a specialist in southern history, Duberman was nevertheless well known as the author of the docudrama *In White America*. Though never directly addressing each other, the black actor and the Ivy League historian voiced opinions about the black writers as different as the media in which they appeared.

"In ten essays, brilliantly written, closely reasoned, thoroughly researched . . . these men accuse Styron of nothing less than cultural aggression against black people," Davis begins, adding "these retaliatory essays [express] more than anger here, more than blackness, there is scholarship, justice, high confrontation, and there is warning!"[31] By contrast, Duberman's lower-keyed critique begins as if treating an entirely different book. "This is a depressing volume," he asserts solemnly, "for those who believe the past can and should be protected from the propagandists, for those who have regarded the blacks as a saving remnant that might help our country become something better than what it has been."[32] The term "commentary" being inadequate, Duberman suggests that "attack" is the more accurate description. "One hoped it was going to be different this time around," he mourns. "But that, I suppose, was one of the more recent myths: that blacks in this country could somehow transcend the destructive racism that permeates our culture" (27). Far from doing so, Duberman asserts, the ten black writers have extended racism's reach and enhanced its power to blind American eyes. With few exceptions, these essays are little more than self-deceiving and deceptive polemics dressed as historical and literary criticism. The book bodes ill for future American cultural politics.

The opposite judgment is reached by Davis, in whose eyes *Ten Black Writers Respond* exemplifies an engaged black intelligentsia expressing convictions at the highest pitch of intellectual precision and emotional passion: "At every turn, you feel their command of craft, their sureness of aim"; theirs is a "cool professional fairness of judgment" producing "literary criticism of the highest order and responsibility" (230). Realizing the gravity of Styron's threat to black cultural pride, these writers demand that such aggression cease forthwith. Styron and his ilk must take their "hands off our history and our heroes" (232). Davis claims that Styron's novel, like other works by such white writers as Harriet Beecher Stowe and Thomas Dixon, is a dangerous directive on race relations, offering models of black character and behavior that blacks ignore at their peril: "Hand-me-down heroes and devils from the white man, his hopes and fears done up in black face and passed along for our instruction" (231). He believes blacks in the past have too often capitulated.

> We imitated in order to survive, but deep down in our secret selves—in our stories, our humor, and our music—it was a different story. Deep down inside, even when we didn't know his name, Nat Turner was always alive. Nat, by whatever name we called him, or dreamed of him, or told stories about him, Nat was our secret weapon, our ace in the hole, our private consciousness of manhood kept strictly between us. Our sacred promise to ourselves that someday . . . somehow . . . we would all rise up, black and beautiful, and throw off our Tomish ways, and stand up against the white man like men, even if it cost us our lives! Hence

the battle between these writers and William Styron's America for the meaning of Nat Turner's life is a matter of life and death to us. Nat was the black man's conjure. We can't afford to lose him! (231)

Styron's "white liberalism does not stop being racist by putting black on its face, before it speaks." Today it is doubly insulting "to have the white man foist his literary bastards upon us and say: 'This is your identity!' The Hell it is!" (231). Davis's rhetoric eloquently emphasizes that his is more than a review. It is a passionate denunciation of the shaping power of an enduring cultural myth and an endorsement of black mythic self-determination as a stimulus to action. "Like Nat, black men have grown tired of waiting. And like Nat we are prepared to gain our freedom by any means necessary" (232). Thus did Davis alert *Freedomways*'s readers about the implications of a controversy perhaps dismissed as merely academic.

As befits a professional historian, Duberman is less categorical and more specific in his critique. Ultimately, however, he is no more willing than Davis or the ten writers to place himself, except fleetingly, in the shoes of the racial Other. Though he emphasizes at the outset that "there are legitimate complaints, historical and literary, to be made against Styron's book, and as presented by two of the ten essayists, Vincent Harding and Mike Thelwell, these complaints are cogently, even poignantly set forth" (1), he never details those legitimate criticisms. He concedes that Styron invites legitimate criticism by claiming that his book is "a work of history as well as one of fiction" (1), but attacks almost wholesale the black writers' counter-model of Nat Turner, the historical figure. "My own feelings about Styron's book are that, although seriously flawed as a novel, it is, at the same time, superlative history. By that I do not mean that Styron cannot be faulted for the occasional omission or distortion of detail (an inescapable by-product of *any* work of history, no matter how rigorous and scrupulous the historian), but that the 'Confessions' provide the most subtle, multifaceted view of antebellum Virginia, its institution of slavery and the effects of that institution on both slaves and masters, available in any single volume" (1).

What dismays Duberman most about *Ten Black Writers Respond* is the authors' insistent presentism and political ideology, which, he believes, blind them to Styron's actual achievement in drawing the portrait of a complex and convincingly human figure: "It is unthinkable to them that Turner could have been irresolute in battle or ambivalent about committing murder, as it is that he could have hankered after a white woman or not 'dearly loved' his wife. . . . In any case, they see Turner not as a human being, but as an epic force, a figure immune to the usual range of error, compassion, and desire" (26). Therefore, "if this is what blacks mean by 'rediscovering' black history and finding historical figures with whom black youths can identify, then the prospects are grim, for in the case of Turner at least, the figure they present for emulation is frighteningly one-dimensional, even pathological. It is a question, moreover, whether the new emphasis on black heroes really will demythologize our past (as is claimed and needed) or whether it will replace one set of myths with another" (26).

The black writers, says Duberman, err in their independent opinions but tend also to duplicate Styron's sins. One error is elevating Gray's *Confessions*—the "chief source, with the exception of a few scattered references in contemporary accounts" (26)—into absolute Truth. He lauds the reprinting of Gray in an appendix, for the original confessions confirm certain "facts" such as Turner's family lineage, which contradict Styron. But even the black writers "should have been the first to remind us (as they do in so many other contexts) that Turner's confessions were filtered through the eyes and words of a white man and are therefore automatically suspect" (26). A second dubious source uncritically embraced is Aptheker's *American Negro Slave Revolts*. This is a book most historians consider suspect, "based as it is often on inference and rumor" (26). But pitting one source or item against others does not remove the central problem Nat Turner's story dramatizes: "Since there were millions of slaves and very few revolutionaries, the phenomenon of Nat Turner does need further exploration—as does the failure of the vast majority of Negroes to rebel. Evidence of Negro apathy or acquiescence will not disappear by the mere reiteration that it never existed" (26).

Styron, he insists, has squarely confronted an issue about which the black writers are also inconsistent. "By insisting all slaves 'craved freedom,'" the latter "are forced into a bizarre view of slavery. For slavery could not have been as barbaric as they otherwise insist if it inculcated self-love and masculine assertion in the slaves, rather than the self-hate and loss of identity more usually taken to be its products" (27). However, Duberman does not discuss the alternative clearly implied throughout *Ten Black Writers Respond*, especially in the several attacks on Elkins. Slavery *was* barbaric, but it did not totally determine slave character and culture; it was not, in other words, a parallel institution to the Nazi concentration camp. Had Duberman engaged more directly the arguments of Harding and Thelwell, not to mention the others, he might have suggested to *Times* readers in what respects these were serious counterstatements to Styron's historicism.

Instead, Duberman declares that Styron dramatizes the central paradox of slavery that, despite its relative mildness in some cases, it was always harsh enough to produce "serious character disorders" in slaves. (Like many others in this controversy, Duberman is less interested in examining the "character disorders" of the slaveowners and their women, which is one rich theme in Styron's story.) *The Confessions of Nat Turner* is "superlative history" because it demonstrates vividly the uncomfortable truth that "some slaves had kind masters *and* that slavery was abominable. . . . Styron recognizes that slavery produced Uncle Toms and rebels" (27). Far from being "an unreconstructed Southern rebel," a charge Duberman calls "obscene," Styron does not "bury or minimize the complexities of past experience in order to serve some presumed contemporary need" (27).

Tag-Matches: Aptheker vs. Styron; Genovese vs. Harding

While clearly divided on many issues arising from the black writers' attack on Styron's Nat Turner, Davis and Duberman never address each other. Neither *Freedomways* nor the *New York Times Book Review* arranged direct exchanges of views. Nevertheless, other print media soon filled this gap. One of the first direct confrontations took place in *The Nation* where Styron and Aptheker traded arguments about slavery, slave revolts, and Nat Turner's historical character. This was in April 1968. Later, in the fall, a more heated and more widely publicized exchange occurred in the pages of the *New York Review of Books*. Precipitated by Eugene Genovese's lordly review of *Ten Black Writers Respond* in the September 22 issue, a debate took place in November, with Vincent Harding as spokesman for the ten and Genovese having the last word. Then Styron continued the controversy the following spring when he and the director of Beacon Press exchanged tart accusations and rejoinders in the *Boston Globe*, during which the rights and privileges of authors, publishers, reviewers, and the press were aired. Perhaps these three episodes can be said to represent a somewhat drawn-out climax of the Nat Turner controversy, although historians, literary critics, political activists, and others more removed from the disciplines of history and fiction continued to derogate and defend *The Confessions of Nat Turner* all through the final months of the decade and on into the seventies.

The Nation's April exchange carries on and in certain respects extends the earlier pair of reviews by O'Connell and Aptheker. As previously in his "Note," Aptheker speaks as historian rather than literary judge, again assailing Styron's cavalier treatment of Gray's "facts." The "authenticity" of the original *Confessions* is reaffirmed and other sources are mentioned, which Styron knew and should have respected.[33] The three most serious errors are familiar ones: Styron's omission of Nat's wife; having his fictional rebel taught to read and write by "a benevolent white master"; and the episode at Major Ridley's (really Dr. Blunt's) in which armed slaves help quash the revolt. In each instance Styron had, or should have had, "indications" from history denying the choices he made as literary artist. Like the black writers, Aptheker is still concerned that what was conceivable to Styron and convenient to his fictional aims will be accepted by readers as uncontested historical fact. As always with this historian, truthfulness in all details as revealed in available, trustworthy documents is the overriding criterion of responsible historical fiction. He is, as usual, less explicit about the ideological arguments these "truths" support. The implicit assumption is that if, in Nat Turner's case and in line with Lerone Bennett's formula in *Ten Black Writers Respond*, the novelist works "within the tension of accepted facts," the results will prove ideologically correct as well.

If Aptheker sticks to his guns, so, too, does Styron. The novelist answering in *The Nation* strenuously refuses to don the straightjacket the historian prescribes for his imagination. "I at no time pretended that my narrative was an exact transcription of historical events; had perfect accuracy been my aim I would have written a work of history rather than a novel" (545), he replies. Whereas Aptheker finds certain situations in his novel "inconceivable" because they contain inaccurate historical data, Styron (sometimes on the very same historical evidence) *can* conceive of such different behavior and belief. Indeed, the historical novel, he believes, is precisely the literary form through which to *re*imagine the past and thereby construct alternate or supplementary explanations of human motivations and actions. In justification, Styron again quotes Georg Lukács, whose *The Historical Novel* contains authoritative answers to Aptheker's narrow literalism:

> Every really original writer who portrays a new outlook on a certain field has to contend with the prejudices of his readers. The image which the public has of any familiar historical figure need not necessarily be a false one. Indeed, with the growth of a real historical sense and of real historical knowledge it becomes more and more accurate. But even this correct image may in certain circumstances be a hindrance to a writer who wishes to reproduce the spirit of an age faithfully and authentically. It would require a particularly happy accident for all the well-known and attested actions of a familiar historical figure to correspond to the purposes of literature. (545)

This "flexible theory," and no desire to resort to "subtle trickery," has afforded Styron the justification for his choice of historical options and fictional means. On the matter of Nat Turner's wife, the novelist defends her absence on less theoretical grounds, however. Against the dubious authority of Thomas Wentworth Higginson (writing "thirty years later" than the revolt) and the *Negro History Bulletin* (an article written 125 years after the event by a "descendant"),[34] Styron sets not only artistic prerogative but his knowledge as serious historian. He declares that "there is not a shred of contemporary evidence—no hint, not a single statement either in the original 'Confessions' or in the few newspaper accounts—to show that Nat Turner had a wife. . . . She remains to me as illusory and as insubstantial as those dozens of 'great-grandchildren' of Nat who, since the publication of *The Confessions of Nat Turner*, have written me from all parts of the country, each of them claiming proof of kin" (546).

As for deciding to have his Nat educated by Samuel Turner instead of his own parents, Styron ignores Aptheker's citation from Gray, insisting instead that "it remains clear that almost nothing is known of

Nat Turner's childhood and upbringing" (546). Far from intending to reawaken memories of benevolent paternalism or white superiority, his artistic motives were quite different. For one thing, "'enlightened benevolence' did in truth, alas, exist." For another, Styron doubts not the "authenticity" but the "accuracy" of Gray, and so does not share Aptheker's belief in "the gospel truth" of the account by the southern racist and court functionary. Most important of all, "chance dictated my setting Nat in [the] environment" of the Big House. This was done in order to illustrate one historical irony of truly Lukácsian dimensions—"that it was precisely this enlightened benevolence which in the end ameliorated nothing, instilled a false hope, brought Nat to disaster, and constituted a betrayal at least as cruel as the nightmare of captivity in the Deep South" (546). So much, Styron adds, for Thelwell's accusation that *The Confessions of Nat Turner* perpetuates Old Dominion stereotypes about slavery.

One stereotype Styron does admit perpetuating, however, derives from his fictional elaboration of the obscure historical figure of Margaret Whitehead. The stereotype of "the black man's hang-up on white females" is used quite deliberately "because I feel it was—quite probably—true. . . . Nat's fateful impulse valid then as now [was] that Nat Turner *was* hung up on Margaret Whitehead, bashing her brains out because of the same hatred and love and despair that make Americans today as then all hopelessly hung up—black and white—one with the other, wedded inseparably by the error and madness of history" (547). On such (to him) plausible grounds, and refusing blind fidelity to any suspect historical document to the contrary, Styron refuses "to apologize for any liberty I took with the 'facts' concerning a man who still, to me, whatever the fictional transmutations, was a figure of tragic magnitude and nobility" (547).

This rejoinder indicates that, even if convinced of the historical reality of Nat's wife, Styron would still have insisted on the presence and function of his Margaret Whitehead in order to dramatize a historical and psychological "fact" of even greater relevance. Against both this white historian and a young Black Muslim in a New Haven audience who also accused Styron of this mendacious cliché (while "accompanied by a pretty white girl" [546]), the novelist sticks to his original assertion. "To me such an eventuality was logically and eminently *conceivable*" (547). With similar self-confidence, the novelist also maintains his prerogative to suppose "that armed Negro slaves might, at their master's behest or even voluntarily, rise to defend the only homes they had ever known" (547). This, in answer to Aptheker's equally dogmatic assertion that "never in the history of slavery in the United States were black slaves armed by their masters for slave-suppressing duties" (544).

Inasmuch as Styron refers in this same exchange to Thelwell's forthcoming essay in the *Massachusetts Review* (later reprinted as his contribution to *Ten Black Writers Respond*), it is appropriate to introduce at this point in the debate another perspective on this stand-off between the historian's "never" and the novelist's "eminently *conceivable*." One of Thelwell's arguments in "Back with the Wind: Mr. Styron and the Reverend Turner" is that, faced by the contradiction, as Styron inevitably is, between social cliché and hard historical evidence, the reader should look at the wider literary context that justifies either inclusion or omission. In the case of the loyal slaves at Major Ridley's, Thelwell agrees with Aptheker that, "contrary to any historical evidence" Turner's ultimate defeat did not turn on this action of loyal slaves. Rather, "this thing which did not happen" is an unwarranted invention.[35] What makes it unwarranted is the emphasis Styron gives the episode as a crucial piece of evidence not only about the benign nature of "aristocratic slavery" but also about the sadistic satisfaction the slaves take in their violence. Consequently, "dispirited and broken, Nat sits in his cell feeling himself betrayed by his people and his God."[36] Thelwell does not dwell on the excess of authorial emotion clearly invested in this imagined scene or its psychic origins as a white man's projection. But he does point out how far from Gray's *Confessions* the novel's conclusion is; instead of Turner feeling broken and separated from God, Gray records at this place the arresting image Styron omitted from his book—that of Nat in chains raising his manacled hands to heaven.

Styron stoutly defends his literary and historical principles and priorities. This slave revolt—in conception, execution, and catastrophic failure—is (to echo Lukács) one of the great collisions or turning points in American history. Hence, in order to "express this historical conception in an adequate artistic form the writer may treat individual facts with as much license as he likes, for mere fidelity to the facts of history without this connection is utterly valueless" (547).

If this comparatively mannerly exchange between Aptheker and Styron (with Thelwell's imported contribution as quoted by Styron) typifies the balanced liberalism of the venerable magazine in which it appeared, the later debate in the fall is similarly representative. Far more contentious in tone and more wide-ranging in content, the debate between Eugene Genovese and Vincent Harding seems equally in character for the *New York Review of Books*. As compared to Woodward's earlier choice by *The New Republic*, Genovese speaks less for fellow historians than for himself. Nevertheless, this socialist sounds more representative and mainstream than the marginalized and more radical Aptheker. Yet like his fellow Marxist, Genovese begins his critique not with historical issues relating to antebellum slavery raised in *Ten Black Writers Respond* but "what it reveals about the thinking of intellectuals in the Black Power movement."[37] Ignoring substantive questions on history and literature, he declares that "what is at issue here is the ferocity and hysteria of the attack, which claims Styron to be a racist, a liar, an apologist for slavery, and a man who displays 'moral cowardice' and 'moral senility'" (34). Then, like Duberman, Genovese makes exceptions of Thelwell and Harding, "two young and gifted writers" whose arguments do merit discussion. "Except for occasional entertainment . . . of the rest, the less said the better" (34).

Genovese's truculent and derisive tone is further exemplified by an abrupt dismissal of Clarke's introduction with its quotation from Aptheker about history's ideological roles for the oppressed and their oppressors. "This nonsense sets the tone for the book," he announces. "I should respectfully suggest that although the oppressed may need history for identity and inspiration, they need it above all for the truth of what the world has made of them and of what they have helped to make of the world. This knowledge alone can produce that sense of identity which ought to be sufficient for inspiration" (34). Against the shrill contentions of black ideologues Genovese asserts that "revolutionaries do not need Nat Turner as a saint; they do need the historical truth of the Nat Turner revolt, its strength and its weakness" (34).

One basic historical truth Genovese recognizes is that, quite contrary to assertions here that "Black America has always known of and admired the historical Nat Turner," no evidence exists to show "that slaves and postslavery blacks kept alive a politically relevant legend of Nat Turner or any other Southern slave leader" (34). Instead, the uncomfortable truth the black writers refuse to acknowledge is that "if Nat Turner is now a name widely known to black and white America, and if the existence of armed resistance to slavery is now generally appreciated, William Styron deserves as much credit as any other writer" (34).

Of Styron's command of the history of American slavery Genovese is equally confident. Again contrary to most of the black writers' strictures (in which, he declares, history and ideology are disastrously mixed), "the novel is historically sound. Styron takes liberties with fact, as every novelist does, but he does not do violence to the historical record" (34). Thus, for instance, Styron understands very well that Virginia slavemasters did not deliberately breed slaves for export to the Deep South. If Thelwell has consulted the historical literature on this issue "he would have found there a distinction between a system of deliberate breeding and the process of transferring surplus populations. Styron understands the distinction, which is of great importance to the moral question of slavery, but Thelwell misses it completely" (34). Though Genovese adds that "there is no disagreement on this matter among historians, black and white, radical, liberal, or conservative," he does not explain the distinction to readers of *New York Review of Books*.

Another contested "fact" revealing Styron as "a better student of history than his critics" (35) is the much-discussed scene showing loyal slaves "helping to shoot down the insurgent blacks" (34). On Aptheker's authority, the black writers deny this ever happened. "This is nonsense," Genovese again retorts. Records show that during "the War for Southern Independence some loyal slaves defended their masters' families with guns in hand" (34). Passing silently over striking differences between the two circumstances, he tries to strengthen his case by turning from Virginia in 1831 "to Brazil and the Caribbean, where large black slave revolts were frequent [and where] we find all the evidence we need. Armed loyal slaves often fought against insurgents, as every historian of those regions knows" (34). The larger truth behind Genovese's dubious refutations is then adduced: "It is pardonable for Styron to take liberties with the particular history of the Nat Turner revolt, so long as he does no violence to the history of the slave revolts generally" (34). This generous grant of authorial freedom to a historical novelist does not go unchallenged by other historians like Harding or, for that matter, by a historical novelist like Fred Chappell, to whom the essence of the historian's art is to "do justice to the historical record" by respecting particular data and distinguishing among and between circumstances.[38]

Like Styron, Genovese is further annoyed at the black writers' failure to appreciate—indeed, even to see—the multiple ironies in Styron's complex fiction. One such is the character Gray's comment to Nat that "nigger slavery will last a thousand years." For making such statements, clearly intended to invoke parallels between Hitler's twelve-year Third Reich and the less than thirty years remaining before the Civil War, the novelist is branded "a Southern racist." Even more sadly misperceived is the contempt and hatred Styron's Nat expresses for his fellow blacks. "The critics of Styron's book insist that love not hatred must have driven Turner forward. Such love for his people is also in the novel," Genovese declares. "Had he not loved them, he would not have protested so much against their weakness in the face of oppression; he could not even have perceived them as victims of oppression. No revolutionary could be free of such feelings of hatred, which is essentially a hatred for the oppression rather than for the oppressed" (35).

On this and related points Genovese is well aware of the cultural grounds the black writers have for denouncing the (to them) whitewashed rebel depicted in Styron's retelling. But he refuses to accept their conclusions. In his eyes, Styron has simply but subtly reimagined, out of skimpy and sometimes dubious data from Gray, a historically and psychologically convincing profile of a revolutionary. Should not black readers feel proud of such flattering comparisons? "Turner's aspiration to white culture is not the same as hatred for things black. Slaves of any race normally reach out for the culture of the class above them. So do colonials, as Fanon shows. So do industrial workers, for all their freedom and leisure, unless they are organized in a struggle to develop a larger view. Again, consider the example of Toussaint and other black leaders who were, at one bad moment, prepared to betray their army back into slavery" (35). Furthermore, the particular ways culture is communicated to the child Nat are less important than the prophetic facts themselves of precocious intelligence and literacy. "How much can we make of Turner's having been taught to read by his parents? Who, after all, probably taught them? Turner himself says that he used white children's books. Styron did not invent paternalism" (35). Nat's "white" language and dreams, too, are the typical attributes of a colonial revolutionary, for which Frantz Fanon again "provides adequate theoretical justification" (35). It is, therefore, unrealistic of Thelwell to rely on Turner's testimony in Gray regarding his early and steadfast alienation from the slavery system; every revolutionary says something similar and Gray should not be read so literally. Since "it is impossible to expect the *Testimony* [his term for Gray's *Confessions*] to yield more than unconscious hints" (35), Styron is entitled to incorporate them into his fictional recreation who is "a believable Nat Turner, although by no means the only possible one. But then, nothing prevents (or has ever prevented) black intellectuals, who claim to have the living traditions of black America at their disposal, from creating their own version" (35). Genovese's debater's dig appears to shift blame from Styron's white shoulders to the black writers themselves. Speaking for his fellow whites, the historian continues in the same vein:

> Since we know so little and can say so little, the anger and hostility toward Styron, who has created something out of what we do know, seems absurd. One is tempted to say, especially to such a talented and eloquent young historian as Harding: If you say that black folk life can be unearthed and made relevant, then do it; if white historians—for whatever reasons—have been blind to whole areas of black sensibility, culture, and tradition, then show us. We can learn much from your work, but nothing from your fury. (35)

Hindsight and distance may soften the edges of Genovese's truculent language for later readers, but it still should not be difficult to reimagine sixties resentments—and not only on the part of blacks—of this patronizing white rhetoric. The historian's "we-you" oppositions here between knowledge and ignorance, reason and rage, define and illustrate the nature and extent of cultural blindness, which is of particular interest given Genovese's own radicalism, his professional dedication to black history, and personal familiarity with blacks. One wonders how many historians, even in the heat of the sixties, would share Genovese's indifference to the social fact of black rage—surely a significant historical phenomenon desperately in need of careful understanding by both whites and blacks.

The magisterial tone of Genovese's critique, and its theoretical underpinnings, emerge most pointedly in his discussion of the role of sex in Styron's novel. On every aspect—the presence or absence of rape in the revolt, Turner's homosexual episode, Margaret Whitehead in life and death, Nat's fantasies and dreams, and black-white sexual stereotypes—Genovese rejects the black writers' accusations and ridicules their emotional heat. Conceding that no rapes did occur in this uprising, he points out that Styron has actually introduced no such scenes into his fictional account. Will's characterization and language should not, therefore, constitute an affront to black readers. If the novelist's language suggests hatred taking the shape of sexual violence, that is historically justified, for "as his black critics ought to know, the evidence of rape appears frequently in the histories of slave revolts.... To deny these common occurrences during social struggle is to betray an ignorance not only of history but of life" (36). Genovese's argument, resting upon the basis of Saint-Domingue and Toussaint L'Ouverture, remains pointedly silent on the obvious question about Southampton: Why, then, was this revolt unusual?

Just as peremptorily the historian dismisses the matter of this Nat Turner's homosexuality. Surely a mountain is being made of a molehill. As we have earlier noted, Genovese dismisses or condones what the black critics condemn: in imagining the episode with Willis, "Styron merely gives Nat Turner something of a normal early life. Perhaps black men do not share with decadent whites these delightful early encounters" (36).

On two other central matters, involving Styron's Nat's celibacy and his emotional fixation upon white rather than black women, especially Margaret Whitehead, Genovese continues the strategy of arguing that the novelist's protagonist is less the historical Nat Turner than a representative revolutionary. Celibacy, therefore, is a plausible state, reflecting "Turner's single-mindedness, his devotion, even to the point of monomania, to his revolutionary calling. This characteristic, in its general if not necessarily specific form, may be found in many great revolutionaries. As a literary device, it may or may not be successful; it is clearly meant not to denigrate, but to link Turner with a great historical tradition of revolutionary heroes. And those who think sexual abstinence deprives a man of his manhood have a few questions to answer themselves" (36).

Finally Genovese deals with the heaviest issue raised by the ten, the case—in their eyes as gratuitous as it is revealing—of Margaret Whitehead. He fails to see much point in their denunciation, for to him the character of the young woman and her location at the center of Nat's drama of revenge and remorse, alienation and reunion, are private psychological issues, not historical or racial ones. Even less is she a spiritual symbol or theological statement. Given the fictional situation Styron has created, "it would have been perfectly natural for Turner to focus his feelings on a lovely girl who seemed to embody everything in life that was desirable and unobtainable. . . . The Margaret Whiteheads of the WASP bourgeoisie have long fluttered before working-class boys of other ethnic groups quite as much as they must have fluttered before black slaves" (36). What distinguishes Nat Turner from the white chick-infatuated black males of today—whose numbers and motivations are authenticated in creditably researched books like Calvin C. Hernton's "indispensable" *Sex and Racism in America*—is that

> to some extent Turner does come to see Margaret as a particular human being, rather than as a social type. That, I should suggest to Harding, is the reason he must repent of her murder before he can re-establish a relationship with his God. In repenting, he does not repudiate his revolt; he repudiates that hatred which led him to deny the love he felt for a human being who was as trapped as he. This may or may not be convincing artistically, but the charge that this part of the novel stamps Styron as a racist is outrageous. If anything, it may stamp him as an integrationist—which for some may well be his ultimate crime. Certainly it stamps him as a man who has the courage to confront the depths of America's racial tragedy. (36)

Genovese ends his review with a highly qualified recognition of the importance of *Ten Black Writers Respond* and also a warning. The book "needs to be taken with alarmed seriousness, no matter how absurd most of the contributions are" (36–37). He thinks Thelwell and Harding partly redeem the rest by their combination of passion and intellectual power.

> But it is clear that the black intelligentsia faces a serious crisis. Its political affinities lie with the black-power movement, which increasingly demands conformity, myth-making, and historical fabrication. No one need believe that any of these writers would resort to deliberate falsification—which they so readily accuse Styron of—but the intellectual history of popular and revolution-

ary movements has overflowed with just such crises, in which dedicated, politically committed intellectuals have talked themselves into believing many things they later have had to gag on. The black intellectuals seem to be going through what Marxist intellectuals went through in the 1930s and 1940s. Let us hope they come out a good deal better. (37)

Nearly two months later, the *New York Review of Books* at last published a reply to Genovese by Vincent Harding, one of his chief targets.[39] Speaking both for himself and his colleagues, Harding articulates their deep resentment of the white historian's tone and substance. One of his own original complaints against Styron, Harding reminds readers, is the novelist's assumption of the role of white advisor and interpreter of black experience. If Styron elected himself one of "the official keepers of our memories and the shapers of our dreams" (32), Genovese has unfortunately compounded the problem by following the same well-worn path, "trailing behind him all the ironic humor and strange blindness" (32) of many previous white arbiters.

Among the multiple examples of white arrogance and rationalization in Genovese's remarks, Harding declares, three are of prime historical and political significance to Styron's story. The first and most insulting is Genovese's condescending white language and viewpoint, with its "we" who have yet to be shown the political relevance of Nat Turner. This is but the most recent instance of whites grandly deciding for blacks (and everyone else) what is "obscurity" and "what is alive and well in the continuing traditions of black America" (32). In this same America, Harding declares, there is another "we" with experience of and viewpoints on slave revolts and their relevance to contemporary issues. Whites may confidently declare the tradition of Nat Turner dead or useless. But this other "we" wonders if the white historian knows the writings and words of former slaves and other black abolitionists like Frederick Douglass, Samuel Ringgold Ward, Henry Highland Garnet, Harriet Tubman, or H. Ford Douglass, "to name only a few of those ancestors in whom Turner's memory lived and was offered to black people as an inspiration to resistance" (32). Moreover, this other "we" possesses also a post–Civil War tradition of rebel slaves.

We urge him to peruse the pages of Marcus Garvey's widely read *Negro World* or to read the poetry and fiction of Sterling Brown,

Robert Hayden, Arna Bontemps, and Margaret Walker, if he wishes to find a vital tradition concerning Turner, Vesey, and others. Let him settle down among the pages of the recorded slave recollections in the Federal Writers' Project papers. Let him listen to the black people from Virginia, North Carolina, and Georgia who speak of the Sunday School and Lodge pageants and plays of their childhood which dealt with the life and work of Nat Turner. Finally, let him listen again to the voice of Malcolm X. (32)

To Harding and the black "we" across the decades, Nat Turner has not languished in the obscurity and irrelevance Genovese assumes, any more than sixteenth-century Africans really languished in European "darkness." Both viewpoints reflect the cultural blindness of white observers, just as the fictional picture of Nat Turner reflects Styron's. Moreover, the black "we" of the American past possessed a folklife and culture within which versions of Nat Turner's story were preserved in slave narratives, spirituals, work songs, and folktales. "Significant portions of the folklife," Harding admits, "are available only to the folk, but much is out in the open" (32) for those with eyes and imaginations to see and appreciate their significance.

The most vital and powerful component of black folklife was, and remains, black religion, the realm of public and private experience central to the life and character of Nat Turner. Herein lies Styron's signal failure. For a variety of apparently personal motives, the white novelist "snatched Nat Turner out of the nineteenth century, out of the community of black religious rebels, and placed him totally into our own age of nothingness and fear" (33). Yet Genovese asserts that Styron understands well the dynamics of black religion. "How, I wondered, did Gene Genovese know? Where has he demonstrated his scholarly competence in the understanding of the religion of black America?" More important, "when was the last time he tasted the peculiar experience of one of those rural-urban black churches where Africa, the American South, and the concrete hardness of the urban North leap and play in dazzling juxtaposition? How can he know what was missing from Styron's nineteenth-century exhorter if he has not known his twentieth-century counterparts?" (33).

In place of black religion, Harding reiterates, Styron has put Margaret Whitehead, "the now celebrated white teen-ager" (33). Styron's Nat, according to Genovese, can only be reunited with God after repenting for the "hatred" which led him to kill her. Though one should expect such emotions in a slave revolt, they simply are not found in Styron's fictional version.

> There is no emotion so powerful as hatred given to Turner in the entire episode (or, one must say, in the entire book). Instead there is the indecisive, sexually symbolized impotence, the killing without conviction which marks Styron's black-white man indelibly as a twentieth-century antihero. This indeed was at the heart of my quarrel: Styron's Turner has no hatred to repent for. Margaret Whitehead is a false, sometimes ludicrous and forced figure in the novel. She is about as real as the two other white women Styron creates for no other observable purpose than to start Nat's sperm on its wasted pathway into the dirt. (33)

To be sure, there is here the matter of interracial sex, which Genovese accuses Harding and others of ignoring. But "Genovese has missed the point of my essay again, so eager was he to lecture us on the role of interracial sex in America. The issue for me was not simply how many white women Turner desired, nor whether or not he was married. The crucial flaw resided in the fact that the black leader was offered no meaningful love relationship with a black woman in the novel, not even in the fantasy world he so often shared with awkwardly imported white women. Indeed it was clear that he despised black women" (33).

Harding's rejoinder ends by addressing Genovese on the subject of the "splitting" of the American intellectual community. Though decidedly leftist, Genovese sounds to Harding like many another white American liberal lamenting the recent advent of black power with the consequent separation of that "wonderful community of loving black and white people which existed in peace and harmony since at least 1865" (33). The unsentimental reply to all this is plain: "the intellectual community has always been racially split" (33). Furthermore, one prime cause of that chasm is the double presumptuousness typified by *The Confessions of Nat Turner* and Genovese's review. Their patronizing insistence on speaking for blacks, delivering "countless lectures and sermons on how black history and culture ought to be seen and used" (33) is more at fault than black impatience, anger, and separatism. In fact, separatism has until recently been forced upon black authors by "a publishing community which thought it knew very well how to judge matters of blackness with no help from black people" (33). Such ostracism is exemplified, for instance, by the failure of a leftist journal like the *New York Review of Books* to mount a "symposium of articles by black intellectuals in response to Harold Cruse's valuable *Crisis of the Negro Intellectual*" (33). Recent changes in this isolationism and exclusion have, to be sure, begun to occur, affording Harding and others the opportunities to be heard in national media tragically withheld from their cultural predecessors. Yet even for younger black writers and scholars the same obstacle remains: "the many mediators who continue to stand in the way, insistently—almost evangelically—waving their own definitions of the black past in our faces, calling us at least mistaken and at most absurd" (33).

Genovese's coda to the *New York Review of Books* chapter of the controversy is by turns conciliatory, evasive, and staunchly defensive of *The Confessions of Nat Turner*.[40] The white historian now invoking his "working-class Italian-American origins and socialist politics" (34) is deeply dismayed at being associated with older, proslavery historians. Since he has been at work "for many years on a book on the life of the black slave, including his religious life" (34), Genovese would have hoped not to be identified with those who view the institution only from the masters' perspective and records. Furthermore, he resents the assertion that blacks alone can understand and write about the black experience, especially their ancestors' experiences during slavery. "A black man today," he observes, "no matter how oppressed or close to his people, is not a slave, and there is a class as well as a racial distinction here" (35). To be sure, a common body of "experience, traditions, and historically conditioned sensibilities tie together black people, past and present, and that alone makes it essential for white historians to listen to what black historians have to say" (35). Nonetheless, Genovese denies addressing his review as a specific admonishment to blacks; "my historical writing is for those, black and white, who care to read it" (34–35). On this occasion, in fact, his chief audience was the white, leftist readership of the *New York Review of Books*. This suggests that Genovese's actual aim was to argue class bias as the more significant historical category than racism. Consequently he agrees with the ten black writers: "much history has been written with a class and racial bias; that black people have left their own kinds of historical evidence, which every honest historian must take into account; that to write history without its cultural dimension is to write superficial and misleading history; and that a rising generation of black intellectuals, for a variety of reasons, is able to see these things more clearly than most whites seem to be able to do" (35).

Genovese's last word also contains a defense of his defense of Styron as historical novelist. The reason for supporting many of Styron's historical data and emphases is, quite simply, that he is a novelist and so the artistic relevance of many contested historical facts or interpretations "remains to be established." Thelwell and Harding have not granted the novelist that right, so have "seriously undermined their important message by framing it in what I frankly think is an irresponsible attack on a novelist who does not deserve it" (35). Rather than pontificating about "the black mind," as the ten insist he does, Styron is actually "trying to make a statement by using a particular incident as a focus. To do so he had to reconstruct the people involved, most of whom were black, and had to speak through them. For doing so, he has been denounced as presumptuous and worse. . . . the central question is whether Styron makes his characters believable as black men, as slaves, as rebels, and as human beings?" (35). Genovese's recourse here to particular human characters instead of a generalized "black mind" is ironically at odds with his previous historical defense, which, as we have noted, moves quickly from particular details of Southampton to general features of slave revolts and their leaders. Furthermore, Genovese's description of Styron's representation of various particular black points of view is inaccurate, for Styron had a number of other narrative options besides the exclusive first-person perspective he uses. Genovese's implication that Styron actually speaks through black minds other than Turner's is, furthermore, dubious, since no other black mind is entered and recreated in *The Confessions of Nat Turner*. That is one of the contentions of several of the black writers, in addition to their central charge that Styron fails to make his protagonist a believable black, slave, rebel, or human.

To the crucial literary question about credible black characters, Genovese's answer remains firmly affirmative. In Nat's growth and movement toward violent resistance to slavery he finds "the hatred, slowly and ominously building up, that Harding demands and cannot find" (35). This reply, however, misses Harding's central point, which targets Styron's failure to show Nat's hatred for Margaret Whitehead alone, especially before and during her murder. As for Nat's character as a whole, Genovese insists again that his depiction represents "the triumph of black humanity that some seem to think is denied" (35). On the other hand, he agrees with Harding that Styron does not show a "deep grasp of black religion and its social role," adding "this may or may not be a major criticism of the novel. For myself, I think the novel did many things superbly, and there is a limit to what ought to be asked of a single work" (35).

Genovese ends with another, more subdued, lecture to Harding and the others: "If Styron's novel suffers from insensitivity to some important aspects of black life, I see no reason to assume that he would close himself to criticism from those who present their ideas in a constructive spirit, and without personal attacks and impossible demands on the novel as an art form" (35). In retrospect, this too may ring hollow in some ears since on the day before Genovese's words were published, Styron in New Orleans was giving indications, as I have traced in Chapter 1, of his limited openness to "constructive" criticism. In any case, the print and electronic records of these years report more than a few occasions when, faced with pointed and hostile questioning by black audience members, Styron vehemently defended his book and his artistic integrity, but seemed notably less concerned to elicit and listen to opponents' arguments. In these exchanges, Styron's "we" sounds much like Genovese's rather than Harding's. If so, this underlines the continuing reality of racial battlelines and antagonistic cultures as well as individuals arguing with one another.

One characteristic instance of Styron the controversialist occurred in the wake of *Ten Black Writers Respond*. On April 20, 1969, the *Boston Globe* carried another of Styron's numerous interviews, his favorite arena for replying to detractors. Conducted by Robert Taylor, this interview was aptly titled "The Contentions of William Styron: The Novelist Responds to Critics of 'Nat Turner.'" Their talk took place in Styron's Connecticut study, where, incidentally, Taylor noted a copy of *The Autobiography of Malcolm X* on a shelf. The author's tone on this occasion was sorrowful rather than truculent, though in repeating earlier arguments he again used emphatic terms. Deprecating the "regrettable and malignant totalitarianism I have encountered," he confessed disappointment that so many blacks have rejected his novel without reading it. "If a black man had written my book he'd be a black cultural hero," he observed wryly. Countering their accusations, he insists once again that he has faithfully met a novelist's fundamental obligation to a historical subject by devoting years to immersion in the relevant records. "In fact seldom has a novel based on history hewed so close to basic evidence."[41] Later, he went further by repeating "I know as much as anybody about slavery in the South in 1831" (12). Then in striking reversal of several 1967 statements he adds that many black arguments of fact are invalid since Gray's *Confessions* is "totally suspect as history anyway" (6). Hence fictional details like Nat learning to read from his white master's family are quite defensible inasmuch as "common sense told me that given the time and circumstances, it would not be unnatural for Nat to learn under the conditions I describe" (8). Even more striking is Styron's continuing defense of Nat's sexual history. This time, as often before, his evidence comes from twentieth-century sources. "The white woman is a source of obsessive erotic concern throughout black society," he declares to Taylor. "Look at Chapter One of Eldridge Cleaver's 'Soul on Ice,' for example," adding that "Cleaver isn't singular in recording the hang-up" (8).

This weight of supporting evidence makes Styron resentful but not resigned to black attacks. Recalling the title of the *Amsterdam News* column on his Pulitzer Prize, he believes the contributors to *Ten Black Writers Respond* have been similarly carried away; "the idea of the book is hysterical."[42] As he told Taylor, "responsible critics, black and white, have refuted them" (10). As additional evidence of his recognized honesty and artistic achievement, he recalls that when recently awarded an honorary degree from predominantly black Wilberforce University in Ohio, the president's citation read: "You have initiated all Negroes into their fearsome and wonderful heritage" (11).

One matter sticking still in this successful author's craw, however, is the Beacon Press. The publishers of *Ten Black Writers Respond* behaved disgracefully, he told Taylor. Not only did they issue a "hysterical" book of irresponsible criticism but advertised it dishonestly as well. "It smacks of Fascism" (11), he declares, pointing out that Beacon did not accord him the standard decency and fair play of a rebuttal. Ten days later, the *Globe* published Beacon Press's reply in a tartly worded letter from the director, Gabin Stair, who asked: Why does this author make such groundless accusations? The book is far from hysterical: "What we did and are proud to have done is to publish the views of ten men who wanted to challenge the moral certainties of Mr. Styron. Our advertising was an attempt to reflect their views and most, if not all of them, see Mr. Styron as either a conscious or unconscious racist." Clarke's collection "is one of our contributions to the thoughtful reconsideration which so many people are giving to the problem of racism in America today. . . . Our function as we see it, is to provide a platform for those hard questions of our national life. Mr. Styron's remarks suggest that we have succeeded." Stair was equally firm in rejecting Styron's complaint that he was not afforded the right to see and rebut *Ten Black Writers Respond* before publication. The Beacon book was a collection of reviews, which are never submitted to an author before being published. Furthermore, Styron was incorrect to accuse Beacon Press of asserting that no black reviewer was allowed to criticize *The Confessions of Nat Turner* on its publication in 1967. Stair declares:

> We said no such thing. What we did point out was that "no black novelist or black historian has been persuaded to review the book in the national press." . . . We were simply commenting on the fact that the most important national book reviews, such as the *New York Times*, *New York Review of Books*, and *Saturday Review*, and other journals of opinion, either did not choose or could not persuade black historians or black novelists to review the book. . . . At the national level, was it a failure of imagination on the part of the editors who commission reviews or a basic decision on the part of black intellectuals who may have been approached?

Though here ignoring John Hope Franklin and Albert Murray, among several others, Stair's rejoinder reinforces, from a liberal white publisher's viewpoint, June Meyer's contention that *The Confessions of Nat Turner* was from the outset a white literary and commercial product, created, marketed, and possibly chiefly consumed by white Americans. Stair's letter does not deny Beacon Press's role which, while commercial in seeking to capitalize on the Nat Turner controversy, and both commercial and academic in wooing new markets like the new black studies movement, was also an ideological act. Beacon's lists of new books in the late sixties like Clarke's and reprints like Bontemps's *Black Thunder* were clearly part of a white liberal policy of encouraging communication, if not integration, between the two races and cultures here in conflict.

Cultural Controversy: Style as Substance

Several tentative and a few certain conclusions can be drawn from this truncated history of the Nat Turner controversy as a public press event of the late sixties. One thing seems clear: the Beacon Press publication of *William Styron's Nat Turner: Ten Black Writers Respond* widened, focused, and polarized discussions already circulating in American newspapers and magazines and at various meetings and airings. In particular, Clarke's collection brought home to a national audience—modest compared to Styron's, to be sure, or the *New York Times*'s—that disagreements about Styron's return of Nat Turner were not merely racial or academic but cultural. The social functions of historical and fictional narratives in building and maintaining consensus and in precipitating conflict were dramatically displayed in ways that had not been seen since perhaps the theatrical season of 1953–54 when Arthur Miller's *The Crucible* reminded many Americans of the continuing relevance of the Salem witchcraft trials of 1692. Though pooh-poohed by Eugene Genovese, Aptheker's assertion that "history's potency is mighty" stands up well as an explanation for many—though not all—dimensions of this controversy. So, too, do Genovese's complementary statements in his reply to Harding that "a novel, sociologically considered" can enrich understanding, as this instance proves, of the history of slavery and slave revolts. A corollary must also be recognized, however. With fictional history even more than in conventional history writing, objectivity is impossible. Readers of both traditional history and fiction will continue to "insist on reading things to suit their own prejudices."[43]

The perspectives these two modes of historical narrative provide on past and present reality are often complementary but sometimes in direct conflict and contradiction. To begin with, the creators, critics, and consumers of the two forms of storytelling are never identical. The suitability of history and fiction for specific emotional, intellectual, and ideological purposes also varies from one social group to another. The debate precipitated by Styron's prizewinner was carried on in the national press for and by certain segments of the American book-buying public. Almost simultaneously, other discussions and analyses were published and read in elite circles—principally academic periodicals and books. *Ten Black Writers Respond* began as perhaps the most striking example of this latter form and forum. Partly because the black writers found a national mainstream publisher and then reaped the benefits of dramatic, controversial, and well-placed reviews by Genovese and Duberman, their audience was significantly enlarged from the one Beacon Press may have realistically expected. In this process, the social domain of Styron's novel was widened by the very vehicles through which its cultural influence (though probably not its sales) was challenged—and, in certain minds at least, diminished. A possible parallel suggests itself between *The Confessions of Nat Turner* and *The Crucible*. Though Miller's medium was the stage and his subject and historicism very different from Styron's, the popular success of *The Crucible* as historical and political theater brought strong reactions from both historians and drama critics who faulted Miller's penchant for simplification and slanting of the issues. Herbert Blau once trenchantly described the result: "This absence of doubt reduced the import of *The Crucible* for those who thought about it, while increasing the impact for those who didn't."[44]

One cannot apply Blau's judgment to Styron's novel and its readers without more extensive analysis of the positions and influence of others in this controversy, especially literary critics and historians writing in elite, scholarly, or low-circulation publications serving specific audiences, white and black. *Freedomways*, *New York Review of Books*, and *The Nation* simply represent three models of such media. The principal actors in this portion of the controversy are also models and types. Different and even flatly contradictory as their arguments have proved to be, the black writers, Genovese, Aptheker, and Styron are readily comparable in one respect: the way their specific arguments about history, fiction, and culture fit their modes and metaphors of expression and argumentation. To return to the concepts of Chapter 1, the ideas of these several cultural spokesmen are actions, and their actions in debate incarnate their ideologies.

That specific lines of argument find fitting rhetorical acts may be seen most clearly in the case of the ten black writers. Since their two common contentions are that Nat Turner represents in black culture, present and past, an emotional symbol of mythic manhood, heroism, and martyrdom, and this figure's potency as political weapon has been diminished by a distorted white retelling of his historically verifiable story, it is appropriate to find their attacks on Styron's version, as on the author himself as symbolic white southerner, expressed with emotional passion and ideological intensity. Rage and "intemperate" discourse are essential features of their message to white America and to each other as black brothers. The tone and temper *are* central elements of the argument. Ossie Davis's review, in this perspective, could as plausibly be printed alongside the ten essays as in *Freedomways*. This is not to underestimate the investment Styron's black critics have in history as factually based narrative. But the public rhetoric of Lerone Bennett and of Herbert Aptheker are subtly different, although their common ideological and intellectual ground is devotion to "accepted facts." Rage through radical, even to some outrageous, criticism is more characteristically a black stance than even a white fellow traveler's. From a black perspective, rage stands for the simplifying, unifying motives and actions of Nat Turner himself. It is the emotional equivalent, then and now, for black power, confirmed by history and ritually rehearsed in a myriad of forms and storytelling occasions. For Styron to resort, as he does in *his* version, to oversubtle, often unsupported, psychological motive-hunting to explain Turner's and his followers' violence is to dilute the purity and power of black rage, diverting attention away from the enormity and inhumanity of slavery toward individualized responses to it—anger and vengeance, surely, but also sympathy, pity, impotence, sexual longing, remorse, guilt, forgiveness. These emotions are precisely the "human" qualities with which the white novelist has endowed or confronted his protagonist. Rage, divinely inspired and socially supported, is, on the contrary, *the* hallmark of Nat Turner's humanity for Styron's black critics and their champion Ossie Davis.

White responses to the black writers' discourse of fury are more varied. For Genovese, the key statement is "We can learn much from your work, but nothing from your fury." Though less sarcastic than other put-downs, this assertion neatly represents the white historian's rhetorical strategy of defusing black fury by dismissing eight of the ten as too "hysterical" to merit serious reply, then dividing the issues Harding and Thelwell raise into "rage" statements—to be likewise derided and dismissed—and "reason" statements. His tactic for dealing with the latter is to acknowledge the brutality but also the complexity of chattel slavery and black responses to it in continental North America. Then, leaving the particular and enigmatic case of Nat Turner's revolt largely to Styron (where it can be freely treated as *fictional* history), he generalizes a historical defense on the basis of other societies, revolts, and theoretical models of the revolutionary leader. In this role as cross-cultural historian of slavery, he can play the wise expert telling young but promising black provincials like Harding and Thelwell what black culture and black violence mean in the Caribbean, South America, and other colonial contexts. Caught uncomfortably by Harding's spirited and specific retorts in a linguistic stance of "we-you" superiority, one that sounds as racial and cultural as professional, Genovese invokes his class identity and adds working-class analogies to strengthen his general argument and to avoid sounding too white. Throughout, he avoids detailed defense of Styron's novel by shifting responsibility to a future (or perhaps an undiscovered past) black novelist who might do fuller justice to Nat Turner. His review reads at times like a high school debater's brief which twists and turns in order to avoid serious discussion of black fury and black history.

Aptheker's argument and rhetoric are similarly interconnected, though to ends very different from those of Genovese or Duberman. Eschewing the sorrowful or sarcastic tones of his fellow white historians, Aptheker's low-keyed prose sticks closely and relatively unemotionally to two arguments. First, any historical writing must respect the historical records on which it is based—in this case, Gray's *Confessions* most of all. Gray is not only the closest thing we have to a firsthand contemporary document but its contents, despite being the work of a white Virginia racist, can lend themselves as readily to today's black liberation as to the abolitionists' cause in antebellum America. Containing sufficient evidence of a vigorous slave culture and community support for Turner and his followers, Gray's account also contains two politically potent images of the rebel as Christ and as manacled martyr. Aptheker does not deny the power of historical fiction to plumb depths of this symbolic past event left unexplained by Gray or other historical sources. But he is profoundly convinced that Styron has not respected the available historical and cultural data on which an adequate imaginative reconstruction of Nat Turner's slave revolt must be constructed.

William Styron's role in the aftermath of his novel's publication and reception also reflects his characteristic style of argument and the historicism and aestheticism that style serves. His polemical strategy is to dismiss even more comprehensively than Duberman or Genovese the black writers' contentions as too hysterical, biased, inaccurate, or malicious to merit serious reply. It seems that, as he was later to write in *This Quiet Dust and Other Writings,* Styron believes "it is beneath a writer's dignity to discuss his critics in print."[45] In interviews and other informal situations, however, his practice is to continue to insist on his novel both as responsible history and as a conceivable reimagining of the man and his era. In the face of mounting evidence that *The Confessions of Nat Turner* was, almost willfully, not written for black readers or out of familiarity with black social and literary tradition, Styron remains convinced that his white imagination has penetrated to the universal bedrock of human motivation and experience. Hence he rejects Harding's accusation that he has been unable "to eat and digest the blackness, the fierce religious conviction, the power of the man."[46] He shows little willingness to acknowledge his story as a white man's legitimate psychological projection and go from there to an open discussion about black perspectives on the same putatively "bedrock" beliefs. What seems to stand most clearly in the way of such dialogue is Styron's fierce, protective investment not in his racial, regional, or political identity but in his artistic prerogatives and powers. These combine most appropriately with the obscurities and dramatic highlights of Nat Turner's history. Hence the author rejects all attempts to challenge this sometimes obscure conjunction. His defense is nicely summarized in a concluding remark to Robert Taylor in the *Globe* interview: "Then, too, I sensed a resonance about Nat Turner when I grew up in the James River region of Virginia. I could feel the presence of a way of life, 35 or 40 years back not much removed from slavery. There was a buried quality, a furtive, whispered eloquence attached to Nat, which charged my interest. He was a shadowy mythic hero. He wasn't like John Brown with tons of stultifying testimony and documentary credentials: Nat Turner was ideal for a writer because so little was known about him."[47]

Styron's behavior and argumentation in the controversy are thus congruent. His truncated and often truculent public confrontations and seemingly arrogant withdrawals from direct encounters represent actions designed to protect *and* publicize his vision. His Turner expresses the resonating presence of a buried, furtive, eloquent myth of his own remaking, freed largely of conventional historical impediments but wide open to philosophical and psychological meditations. Given this deep-seated desire for privacy and distance from black cultural criticism, Styron does not, like others in the Nat Turner controversy, suggest or recognize fruitful comparisons and contrasts between his own novel and other imaginative recreations of Nat Turner or slave revolts. Following several earlier remarks by reviewers, both the black writers severally and Genovese propose this wider scope as one appropriate way to clarify issues raised in the debate. Vincent Harding, as we have seen, is one who invites Styron's readers, defenders, and critics to familiarize themselves with other works, especially by black writers. Killens, Williams, and Kaiser echo Harding's call. Setting Styron within and against this tradition—particularly of reactivations written during the sixties, or republished then, or whose presence and special relevance became known to sixties readers and librarygoers—provides a wider literary *and* sociological horizon of images and stories against which to interpret the ideological arguments and cultural assumptions of the controversialists introduced here, as well as of others waiting in the wings.

4 Other Images, Other Imaginations

As the preceding chapter suggests, the literary record of North American slave revolts long remained largely terra incognita. As a body of cultural data it was widely disregarded as inconsequential. Such ignorance (which, like all cultural knowledge, is selectively distributed) must be interpreted within the larger context of the relative neglect, until well into the present century, of slavery as a subject for American authors. Many late sixties readers of *Ten Black Writers Respond* were, therefore, surprised by Ernest Kaiser's impressive list of titles, names, dates, and genres in his essay "The Failure of William Styron."[1] This subliterature first emerged during the antebellum era with three novels: Harriet Beecher Stowe's *Dred: A Tale of the Dismal Swamp* in 1856, and two years later G. P. R. James's *The Old Dominion* and Martin Delany's *Blake: The Cabins of America*.[2] Kaiser identifies two later periods that saw imaginative retellings of stories about Nat Turner and/or American slave revolts. In the 1890s, two now-forgotten novels were published: Mary Johnston's *Prisoners of Hope* and Pauline Bouvé's *The Shadows Before*. Both were issued in 1899, one year before William S. Drewry's monograph, *The Southampton Insurrection*.[3] Then during the Depression came a small flurry of literary activity, this time embracing not only novels but plays and poems as well. Frances Gaither's popular novel *The Red Cock Crows* (1934) was followed by Arna Bontemps's *Black Thunder* (1936). Two even more obscure works were dramas: Randolph Edmonds's *Nat Turner* (also in 1934) and Paul Peters's *Nat Turner* during World War II. Kaiser missed Edmonds's one-act play and also failed to cite a number of poems on the theme of the rebellious slave, the most widely known of which, Sterling Brown's "Remembering Nat Turner," appeared in the NAACP's *Crisis* magazine in 1939.[4]

Though helpful, Kaiser's bibliography by no means tells the whole story. A striking pair of omissions are Herman Melville's "Benito Cereno," first published in 1857 in the proabolitionist magazine *Putnam's*, and Robert Lowell's 1965 poetic retelling in *The Old Glory*. Melville's account of an actual shipboard slave uprising is considered a masterpiece (and widely anthologized for the past three generations of American students) of psychological prose in the nouvelle form. Lowell's own "Benito Cereno" is the final part of a historical triptych created for the modern stage out of historical fictions by Hawthorne and Melville. For many playgoers at New York's American Place Theatre during the 1964–65 season, "Benito Cereno" was the most compelling of the three. Kaiser also overlooks another off-Broadway success of the earlier sixties by a prominent contributor to the later controversy. Martin Duberman's *In White America*, a docudrama, opened at the Sheridan Square Playhouse on October 31, 1963. Kaiser's omissions are perhaps understandable as these works by white authors were more likely to be familiar to white readers, students, and theatergoers than the earlier versions of Nat Turner's story, which Kaiser was at pains to return to public notice.

Exploring and expanding this slender corpus and reconstructing, where possible, its continuing presence and influence for sixties Americans provides more than some fresh viewpoints on Styron's "meditation on history." A closer look at imaginative treatments of slave rebellions leads beyond Styron's reactivation to broader consideration of the linkage among literary modes, actual circumstances of creation and reception, and the kinds of cultural work performed. Statistics on a book's sales or a play's run are always relevant social data but can prove deceptive indices of cultural values. How, or whether, a given piece of historical imagination actually sees publication or performance, remains in print and becomes readily available in public libraries, is reprinted in paperback editions, becomes anthologized or revived on later stages—these socioeconomic questions generate revealing speculations. Indeed, obscure or neglected works—whether Melville's books in the decades before his rediscovery in the 1920s, or black plays like Edmonds's or Thomas Pawley's *Messiah* (a work so obscure that no observer of the Nat Turner controversy has, to my knowledge, mentioned it),[5] or historical novels or romances of strictly ephemeral popularity—are all valid reflectors of some groups' shared values as they are of their creators' historical awareness. As both private imaginative acts and collective ideological formulations, these works were once—perhaps still are—received and transmitted, ignored or suppressed, by a culture's multi-filiated network of communication, and always for discernible reasons.

Furthermore, since the returns of Nat Turner are necessarily historical as well as imaginative transactions, light is thrown through this seemingly narrow aperture onto certain larger cultural questions. How can any act of imaginative retelling deepen understanding of a given portion of historical reality? In particular, what unique insight or special perspectives are brought to events like the Southampton slave revolt through the literary modes and genres of fiction, lyric verse, and realistic or poetic drama? Conversely, how do the surviving records of such historical happenings exert pressure on literary and imaginative expressions? That is, how do common literary genres and historical documents comport to provide readers historical information, instruction, and indoctrination? As the preceding pages indicate, such queries were by no means confined to the mandarin class in sixties America. Rather, these issues and activities became integral to the cultural rethinking and repositioning of different groups in American society.

The Other 1967 Novel: Daniel Panger's *Ol' Prophet Nat*

Styron's success, both commercial and cultural, underscores the assumption that novels were—and may for many remain—privileged carriers of cultural messages. Besides *The Confessions of Nat Turner*, another example of a fictional work defining and testing the social agency of sixties fiction is Daniel Panger's *Ol' Prophet Nat* (1967). Published in the same year, this narrative of the Southampton slave revolt by a white author exploited much of the same historical material and utilized several of the same fictional techniques as did Styron. *Ol' Prophet Nat*, a modest 159-page narrative, is an early publication by a young, previously unknown writer. Its publication history and reception differ significantly from that of *The Confessions of Nat Turner*. Far less popular (and much less publicized) than Styron's story, it was issued by John F. Blair of Winston-Salem, North Carolina, and was later reissued as a Fawcett paperback, which sold reasonably well. It even earned its author a modest advance on a movie contract, though nothing ever came of that. The book's greatest impact was on black readers and in black college classrooms.

Nevertheless, more than one perceptive reviewer brought Panger into the discussion as a foil to Styron. Perhaps the first was Loyle Hairston, one of the ten black writers. For one sector of the black intelligentsia, Hairston's review was timely and strategically placed. *Freedomways*'s Summer 1968 issue was a central venue for raising historical and cultural issues, containing Ossie Davis's salute to *Ten Black Writers Respond*, a provocative essay by the black psychiatrist Lloyd Delaney on "The White American Psyche—Exploration of Racism," and Hairston's notice. The three pieces reinforce each other as characteristic ideological statements by the new black cultural cadre.

The psychiatrist Delaney vilifies Styron's imputation of his own fantasies to Nat Turner, yet implicitly provides grounds for black readers to trust another white imagination. "Styron's projection of his sexuality into the character of Nat Turner required not only a distortion of history but an emasculation of this revolutionary figure."[6] Hairston's review echoes Delaney's (and Poussaint's) charges and holds up Panger as a counterexample to Styron, without mentioning that Panger is white. Styron's book "was nurtured in the envenomed atmosphere of American racism" (267); Panger, on the contrary, has to a remarkable degree escaped or transcended this American poison. In fact, he has written "a refreshing book worthy of a place on every bookshelf," one told "simply and without literary pretensions." Panger captures "the passion and the spirit" of Nat Turner, creating a "human being" where Styron conceived "an ogre." Hairston especially commends the treatment of Nat Turner's "religious mysticism as the catalyst which steels his resolve to free himself."[7] Nonetheless, Hairston concludes that Panger's treatment "falls short of what must have been Nat Turner's full measure as a man. . . . There is a magnificence about such men which is almost impossible to describe."[8] The implication hovers in Hairston's evaluation—as in Davis's review of Styron—that no historical or fictional language can recapture the mythic dimensions of the figure these modern minds imagine. Nonetheless, as several fellow essayists in *Ten Black Writers Respond* do not, Hairston tacitly acknowledges that a white writer can indeed do justice to Nat Turner's historical identity and cultural meanings, thereby satisfying black as well as white readers. Hairston's failure to raise the question of Panger's race suggests not so much deception as the desire to create common ground on which to stand with white liberals.

As in 1968, readers of *Ol' Prophet Nat* today possess little biographical data and critical commentary about Panger, unlike that which clustered about William Styron. This disproportion may tempt readers to ignore Panger's novel as a mere footnote in 1960s literary history.[9] Who Daniel Panger was and is, what social contexts and historical activities surrounded and preceded his book, why this northerner's book was published by a small southern press, remain legitimate questions. Only this is readily known: Panger once worked in a governmental agency in northern California, and his early novel was followed by several others.

But emotional if not biographical facts may be inferred from the persona Panger created to take the reader inside Nat Turner's story. In the italicized introduction, a white narrator relates how he first came upon Nat Turner's account of his insurrection. In a North Carolina secondhand store, he found an old Bible inscribed by Benjamin Turner "*to my man Nat to further his Christian education.*"[10] Two previous encounters with Nat Turner's name and history make this discovery an epiphany. Hitchhiking in rural Virginia some years earlier, the narrator was picked up by a dark-brown truck driver and warned against getting lost in the nearby swamp where, in generations past, black folks hid for years in safety. "*Had Nat Turner reached the swamp, they never would have catched him*" (4), the driver remarks cryptically, then identifies Turner to his fascinated passenger. A second encounter occurred in the New York Public Library where the narrator, now "*doing some research on the pre-Civil War South*" (5) came upon T. W. Higginson's 1861 *Atlantic Monthly* essay. "*It was a fascinating account of a man whose story I had never read in any history textbook*" (5). Turner's tattered Bible is thus the kind of invaluable find of which historians dream, for it includes a historical figure's heretofore unknown autobiography, in this case composed while hiding in the woods following the collapse of the revolt. "*As I began to read, taking care to identify each word, I felt a whisper in my brain—a whisper of words from a mouth stopped with earth these 130 years*" (8).

As an imaginary dialogue between a present-day white amateur historian and a nineteenth-century slave, *Ol' Prophet Nat*, unlike Styron's story, endows both its white editor and the black preacher-rebel with unsophisticated but effective voices. The narrator's unprepossessing diction is displayed at once in his description of Nat in hiding:

> *As if a curtain were suddenly pulled away from my eyes, I could see the man crouched in his burrow with a tiny piece of candle that had run its wax on the page. I could see the momentary vexation on the face of the man as he was forced to skip the waxed portion that could no longer hold the ink. I closed my eyes for a few moments to make his image sharper, a poor lost man totally abandoned by all—hiding not with hope of escape, but only trying to coax a little more time, a few more days so that he could tell his story, if not to all men at least to his God. I felt an ache in my chest as I prepared to read on.* (11)

The slave in this case uses much the same language to express his own sentiments. Temporal, racial, and intellectual gaps are thus narrowed by the slave's direct discourse. An unobtrusive vernacular integration results. Panger's Nat characteristically thinks and writes in this vein: "All these thoughts have been recorded as a base for understanding what has taken place since the time when I received the last and greatest sign of all. To be true, I have a certain vanity that desires me to set down the facts of my life so that long after I am dead men will know of my youth and growing up. But more than anything else I am concerned in telling all men who may chance to read these recordings why and how I led my people into battle" (98). Turner's often plodding prose becomes at key moments heightened and readily distinguishable from the narrator's commentary by its aphoristic economy. His account is sprinkled with colloquial country phrases, often carrying powerful emotional weight. Thus he writes that upon the death of his little sister, "Mother was taken so bad I thought she would bust her chest and die too" (17). Reflecting on the rightness of his cause, "as I thought of the unnumbered poor black people pouring the years of their lives into their white masters' hands, I was filled, for perhaps the thousandth time, with rage at the unfairness of it all" (156). Contemplating escape and guerilla existence in the Dismal Swamp, he fantasizes: "We would not fight the whites in their way. We would make them fight in ours. Our black skins would be a shield of safety during the dark night. The day would be for sleeping, the night for killing" (147). Neither archaic nor anachronistically modern, this autobiographical voice is reminiscent of slave narratives and Gray's *Confessions* more than of most twentieth-century historical novels. Moreover, a complex retrospective viewpoint is no more necessary to Panger's project than highly metaphoric language. Along with Styron's rich interior consciousness, Panger has stripped his story of melodrama and, in fact, much of its actual bloody violence. He prefers instead to highlight as concisely as possible the historical circumstances within which a particular individual, institution, milieu, and moment intersected.

At the center of Panger's reconstruction is Nat Turner's personality, a portrait drawn in stark outline. He is, simply and deeply, the Preacher-Prophet whose experiences of slavery and God's guiding presence eventually come together in the act of violent rebellion. His is, however, no childlike, unchanging Christian faith. From the small boy who first gazes at his mother's bloody face swollen by some white man's fist, to his night of agony in the cornfield following the defeat and scattering of his band, Nat is repeatedly subject to doubt and despair. But he never succumbs. Consequently, the shape and sequence of Panger's paragraphs are repetitious: typically a scene or emotional state is depicted as a plunge or sinking, followed by realization of the higher truth by which hope and determination are restored. The pattern is set early when the half-grown lad sees his mother's battered face:

> As I stood by a certain tree getting my wind, a special tree that I always went to on my way to the mill, the thought came to me that He didn't care . . . everything is bad and no one cares. . . .
>
> It hit me like a whip handle thrust in my belly—THERE IS NO GOD!
>
> The awfulness of this thought expelled the breath from my body and I sank down cold with my hands and teeth shaking. The idea of a world without God had never come to me before. For ten minutes altogether Satan himself must have had hold of my very soul. No God—no God—no hope—no reason to live—nothing. . . .
>
> For ten minutes Old Satan had me but he was chased away. First he was there and then gone—gone and I knew, I really knew for the very first time, and ever since I have known, that God is real, God does care, but many of His most wondrous works

are done by His poor creatures. I knew that God can lead a man, God can lead men, that one man or many men led by God, loving God, can change things, can crush the Serpent. (12–13)

Much the same pattern of thought and imagery reappears in moments of defeat and despair:

As I lay in a field of tall corn hearing their shouts and curses I felt such hatred towards the whites that my eyes were filled with burning tears. I picked up the rusted sword I had been carrying and slashed at the stalks around me—slashing and cutting with all the strength of my arms, calling on the Lord, all the while, to rain His most terrible plagues down on their vile and hateful heads. For twenty minutes my madness boiled out of my body. . . .

Later I lay on the ground exhausted, weak, more weary than I ever remembered being. I kept saying to myself, "We will quickly build back our strength and then fight on." But all the while I felt the cold water of uncertainty running inside my body. I searched my knowledge of the Bible for portions that might give me comfort. My mind rested on the story of King David. (145–46)

Throughout the revolt, in fact, Nat's resolve is repeatedly threatened. Occasionally, he is as appalled at his own violence and as sickened by his white victims' blood as Styron's Nat. "I stood before the third house; angry flames shot into the sky from holes in its roof," he recalls. "Grouped about me were black men and women carrying all manner of fearsome weapons. Half the people were astride horses which were nervously pawing the ground and shying as the flames grew brighter. They all waited on my next command. I felt a dizziness tear through my body, bringing a foul taste to my mouth." Then the crisis of leadership passes. "The faces of the slaves were shiny with sweat. They all looked at me, waiting, none daring to speak. The momentary chill of loneliness dropped away; its place was taken by the presence of my Lord. I could feel Him everywhere. The bitter taste was in my mouth no longer" (131). Though the flames lighting this uncharacteristically melodramatic scene are fictional, not historical, details (signaling Panger's artistic freedom with his sources), this moment is a true synecdoche of this slave's characteristic state of mind. Throughout his ordeal, Nat's earlier spiritual experiences keep returning to sustain him, as in his first encounter with the Divine Spirit:

> All at once I heard a loud noise in the heavens. It was greater than the fiercest thunder, yet there were no clouds in the sky. The day grew dark around me, the sun's heat turned into icy cold. I was filled with fear and dread, but was rooted to the spot unable to run or shout.
>
> The next moment there appeared before me a flashing light so bright that I was almost blinded. The light shimmered slowly, taking the shape of a Spirit in long white robes. I fell to my knees before this Spirit, covering my eyes with my hands to save me from blindness. The Spirit spoke to me in a wondrous voice that had the sounds of the wind. It said the Serpent was loosened, and Christ had laid down the yoke He had borne for the sins of men. Then the Spirit told me to take on the yoke and fight against the Serpent, for the time was fast approaching when the first should be last and the last should be first. (73)[11]

As a modern translation of Gray's nineteenth-century lawyerly idiom, Panger's language is arguably more faithful, though less adventuresome, than Styron's—or Robert Hayden's. Other free, yet believable, uses of historical data occur in *Ol' Prophet Nat*, which seldom strays far from its moorings. An instance is Gray's reference to Nat Turner's familiarity with gunpowder. This folkloric item is naturalized in Panger's retelling: "On the day of February 12, I was breaking boulders loose from a pasture that Mister Travis intended to use for planting. I had learned how to use charges of gunpowder to shatter boulders that could not be freed by digging out" (100). Whether or not geologically accurate to southeastern Virginia, this homely farming activity is introduced in order to underscore the symbolic meaning of gunpowder implicit in the original source. Nat's skill with gunpowder prefigures his explosive attack on the boulder of slavery. A similar simplicity of metaphor heightens the symbolic overtones of a more prominent moment in the revolt—the sun's eclipse.

> As the sun was blotted out completely, the screams and cries of the slaves rent the air while the wind whirled clouds of icy dust all about. My face was streaked with tears—but not from fear. The moment for which I had waited so very long had finally come. I looked up into the blackened sky murmuring blessings on His sacred name. The sky was the sky of night; stars were scat-

tered everywhere—never had such a thing been seen before. I knew that this wondrous sign had been given me. That when I told those I had chosen to assist in my plans they would know, because of this sign, that I spoke in the name of the Lord God Himself. (101)

Here symbolic resources of a mysterious reversal in nature of the normal powers of light over darkness are subtly suggested in words that enrich Gray's version—and perhaps Styron's as well. Emblematic of the coming "victory" of black over white, the eclipse exults the fearless, faithful leader even as it terrifies the others. These contrasting responses, of course, prove decisive factors in the subsequent uprising. Yet at this ecstatic moment, Nat is unaware that the fears of his fellow slaves, and the eventual collapse of the insurrection, are foretold by the sun's return a few minutes later. Nevertheless when he later remarks of his lost cause that "if we wait for the whites to give us our God-given rights, we will wait until the sun grows cold" (156), it is clear that he is aware of the ironic implications of his own natural imagery.

These connections are reinforced by still another dimension of Nat Turner's reimagined humanity. The corollary to Turner's indomitable though troubled faith in God is a deep but sometimes frustrating love of his fellow slaves. Unlike Styron's Nat, Panger's protagonist is never out of fundamental unity with his community. A special feeling for his people is an innate character trait. "From the time I was a tiny boy I felt the hurts of others keenly," he recalls. "The black slaves were all like members of my family. When one got hurt, was sick or was dying, I cried, feeling the slave's pain within me. I knew a profound sense of loss when one was taken by death" (81). Having been taught to read and write by his Christian master, he knows and feels "certain things that my poor people could not" (8). Yet Nat refuses opportunities to escape, becomes a dedicated minister to his people, and finds a wife, friends, and followers within the slave quarters. The day the revolt begins finds him in a characteristic (though fragile) harmony with God and the slave folk:

That day I stood before my people; their silent faces were eager for my words. I looked at their dark features and felt my chest bursting with love for them. They had spent their lives without hope, an existence no better than that of the beasts that stood in the fields. They waited for me and I knew it was within my power to lead them into a far, far better life. That or lead them to death as they fought for their freedom. . . . They would no longer face the years running out of their muscles like blood, years that might end as they did with Old Luke as he lay dying alone in the woods, his back torn open from the lash. They would no longer have their children sold away to places a thousand miles distant. They would not be separated at the master's whim from their wives or husbands. The love I felt at that moment made tears bubble from my eyes. (118)

Panger's hero (the term here is clearly appropriate) is superior to his brothers and sisters not by superhuman energy, imagination, or rhetoric but rather by virtue of specific skills like writing and reading, by stronger and steadier feelings of affection and hatred, and by a capacity to generalize from particular victims to the slave system itself. Added to steadfast piety, these ordinary qualities make him an extraordinary figure, a revolutionary. The transformation is quantitative, rather than qualitative. Social or sexual frustration at not being considered the equal of whites is so foreign to his outlook that Margaret Whitehead's name is never once mentioned. His wife, however, is evoked in lovingly sentimental detail.

The transition from small boy witnessing his mother's punishments to righteous avenger rallying his followers by the light of burning farmhouses is traced with prime emphasis on God's guidance but also the support of fellow slaves. "I must study how to die in a manner fitting to one who has served his Lord" (49) epitomizes Nat's prime inspiration. But the fuel of his righteous rage is human oppression. "If I had a second chance, even if I knew it meant certain death, even if I knew I could be free and safe if I ran away right now—if I had a second chance I would strike another blow for my poor people. I would smite the rock with such a force that its sound would reach a thousand miles" (156). Nat's "rock" recalls not only Moses in the wilderness but also the "boulder" earlier blown to pieces by Nat's gunpowder.

Given their common subject and reliance on Gray, Panger and Styron, not surprisingly, sometimes create the same scenes and use similar images. Likenesses, however, almost invariably underscore basic divergences. One example is the young slave's feelings of loss when told he has been sold to Putnam Moore. Whereas separation from Turner's Mill, promising a Richmond carpentry apprenticeship and eventual manumission, sends Styron's Nat into a frenzy, Panger's Nat feels anguish at the thought of being wrenched from family and friends. Thus the two writers' expressions of slave emotions are strikingly divergent. Here is Styron's youth reacting to Samuel Turner's unwelcome news:

> *A free man*! Never in a nigger boy's head was there such a wild sudden confusion. For surely as the fact of bondage itself, the prospect of freedom may generate ideas that are immediately obsessed and half crazy, so I think I am being quite exact in saying that my first reaction to this awesome magnanimity was one of ingratitude, panic and self-concern. And the reasons were as simple and natural as a heartbeat. Because such was my attachment to Turner's Mill . . . that the idea of leaving it filled me with a homesickness so keen that it was like a bereavement. To part from a man like Marse Samuel whom I regarded with as much devotion as it was possible to contain, was loss enough, it seemed almost insupportable to say goodbye to a sunny and generous household which, black though I was, had cherished me as a child despite all the unrelenting fact of my niggerness, the eternal subservience of my manner and the leftovers I ate even now and my cramped servant's room and the occasional low chores I was still compelled to do, and the near-drowned yet lingering and miserable recollection of my mother in a drunken overseer's arms—had been my benign and peaceable universe for eighteen years. To be shut away from this was more than I thought I could bear. (193–94)

The analogous moment in Panger's version is equally emotional but so vastly different in ideological implication that one remembers with surprise that both writers are white:

> In spite of my manhood my eyes filled with tears. This was the only place I had ever known. My mother had birthed me on the cabin floor. I had never spent one whole night of my life in any other cabin than this one. Twenty-two years I had lived, each day right here. I was the only one alive of five and I comforted my poor mother; she would be poorly after I was gone.

My cheeks were wet as I gathered my belongings, Mister Moore tapping his high boots with the leather whip all the while. He mounted up and ordered me to walk out in front of him. I left Master Turner's place with all my goods slung in a blanket over my shoulder. My breath steamed the air, my wet cheeks burned from the cold wind. As I passed the other cabins I could see the doors opened just a tiny crack, too small to be noticed by one who didn't know. (40)

Though aware of slavery's cruel realities, Styron's Nat envisages the moment as banishment from a peaceable kingdom presided over by a beneficent white god. Panger's Nat, on the other hand, is more plausibly disheartened at leaving his birthplace and long-suffering mother and friends. Instead of a god, Mister Moore is a satanic figure in boots and whip. Yet Nat's thoughts characteristically settle on the black slave community imaged by the hidden ones peeping at him from behind their doors. The threatening white man, now his owner, neither notices nor cares what is actually taking place under his horse's nose.

This sense of racial solidarity and cultural unity chiefly distinguishes Panger's from Styron's protagonist. The emotional freight, often of quite common and conventional words, ideas, and experiences, in *Ol' Prophet Nat* is different because the story's perspective (created jointly by narrator and central figure) is black, communal, and altruistic, whereas Styron's standpoint is self-consciously inward and culturally white. This contrast holds true despite several common themes and episodes. Thus, both protagonists (*contra* Gray) are taught to read and write by their masters; both are enraged at the passivity of other slaves. Panger's Nat goes on bended knee to ask Master Turner to teach him to read the Bible, the skill eventually deployed on behalf of his mind-darkened fellows. Instead of opening the door on white culture, however, this "supreme day of my life" (26) depicts Nat's white teacher as the instrument of spiritual revelation. "The Lord was speaking from his lips; it was a sign just as if He had touched me with the point of His fiery sword" (26). It is thus immaterial *how* the word comes into Nat's possession. Though in hindsight victory has not crowned Nat's literacy, he remains without bitterness: "Had old Mister Turner denied me, I expect I wouldn't be crouched hiding here today. No parcels of white men with their dogs would be seeking me out. Without the Good

Book, Old Nat would be back there working a plow or sunning himself or lying safe and warm with his sweet woman" (26).

Once caught in the whirlwind of insurrection, the two Nats frequently feel and act in similar ways, though again, from different memories and motives. Like Styron's, Panger's Nat has his puritanical side. "And above all there would be no traffic permitted with any woman in the houses along the way," he warns Hark and the others. "This was to be no lustful orgy or occasion for satisfying the needs of the flesh. We were to strike our blow for liberty, we were to march beneath the sacred banner of the Lord and I expected all to behave as His soldiers" (123–24). Since sexuality figures only puritanically in *Ol' Prophet Nat*, there is no hint of interracial love or lust. Furthermore, Panger's hero behaves at times as unheroically as Styron's character when it comes to personal leadership in acts of violence. Although Styron's Nat sweats, gags, and vomits, he does attempt to wield a sword and is at last capable of murdering Margaret Whitehead. In Panger's version, the rebel leader is carefully shielded from all direct bloodshed. Shrieks of the dying are occasionally heard offstage, but Hark (rather than Will) is the chief axe-wielder and executioner in this surprisingly sanitized insurrection.

At the revolt's decisive moment, which occurs at Dr. Blunt's, the rebels are confronted not only by better-armed whites but by black slaves armed with guns as well. The kernel of this episode comes from Gray but, as we have noted, is changed in Styron's story so as to take place at Major Ridley's. Though the two white writers reimagine almost the same past (one, as we have seen, Herbert Aptheker strenuously denies ever happened), for Panger's Nat the rebuff is as much a military setback as an act of racial disloyalty. In fact, he understands all too well why the slaves "who had known so much pain, were shooting at other black men instead of turning their guns on their masters. They had been beaten so often that they were no longer human. The whip had made them into willing beasts. . . . I shouted for them to join us, that together we could conquer the entire county. My words were answered with more gunfire. The poor slaves knew not what they were doing. . . . I was filled with sick tears but my face showed nothing" (151–52).

By comparison with Styron's scene, Panger's description is briefer, more didactic, far less dramatic. Its brevity and tone contrast with Styron's three-page depiction. Rather than imitating Gray's laconic account, which simply asserts that "more than twenty of them [the rebels] attacked Dr. Blunt's house on Tuesday morning, a little before daybreak, defended by two men and three boys. They fled precipitately at the first fire; and their future plans of mischief were entirely disconcerted and broken up" (411), Styron embroiders the scene to heighten several uncomfortable "truths" about slavery and revolt. Nat recalls, *"It was the niggers that beat you! You might have took Ridley's. You might have made Jerusalem if it wasn't for those bootlickin' black scum of white men's ass-suckin' niggers!"* (401). Panger, too, repeats newspaper reports confirming such white assertions about loyal slaves and cowardly, ineffectual rogues. His Nat is well aware of slavery's hold over the minds as well as bodies of its victims. "How can I be harsh, how can I condemn my poor people?" he remarks of their fears and obsequiousness. "The lot of a slave is so cruelly hard that who can fault those who try to ease their lot by finding favor with their master? . . . It is the master and not the slave that bears the blame. . . . I concluded that slavery can rob a man of his pride and manhood both when he is fattened, petted and kept in shiny livery; or when he is beaten, cursed and starved until nothing matters except the peace of sleep or the greater peace of death" (56–57).

What, then, brings Panger's Nat's mind and will to a boil? What sustains him beyond the betrayal at Doctor Blunt's and the dispersal of his followers? Despite his night of anguish in the cornfield "empty of faith" (153) in God, Nat's despair does not persist. Hiding beneath the woodpile, he reflects on failure: "My people were still in bondage and would remain so until some other one again struck out for liberty" (155). But something enduring has been accomplished: "They did rise up at the proper time. They did follow Old Nat. The white folks swarming over all the land looking for this black man know the truth of these very words. The slaves, even those a thousand miles away, must know it too, just as I knew of Denmark Vesey. Perhaps, like in Vesey's time, my doings have brought a heavy hand down on the slaves. But as with Vesey, Ol' Prophet Nat brings hope to his people. They whisper and are glad. They sleep at night while the whites go riding through the darkness" (54).

These reflections distinguish one 1967 hero from the other, for Panger's Nat is more aware of events beyond Southampton and shares fully in the underground network passing around news like Vesey's 1822 insurrection: "The slaves were extra silent during the day save for singing, which always pleased the whites and made them think that all was well. At night in the cabins or at small gatherings in the woods Vesey's name was on every man's lips. The most fantastic stories were told as gospel, each new tale making the one before look small and puny" (38). Since he can read, Nat recalls seeing a Richmond paper and passing around the news, "Vesey Hanged." References to white patrollers, arbitrary whippings, and even hangings, like other threats and restrictions, made the whole slave community aware of slave plots. That this situation obtained long before his own plotting began underscores still another contrast between Panger and Styron. Such social and historical awareness, moreover, is not added by the white editor but informs Nat's own words as fictional memoirist.

Nevertheless, Panger's narrative, by its brevity and occasional clumsiness in introducing material beyond Ol' Prophet Nat's ken, reveals the young author's awareness of the dangers of a first-person narrative. One internal clue to his need for other narrative strategies is the character of Old Luke, an aged slave beaten by Major Ridley "once too often" who dies alone in the woods. The parallels between this figure and Bundy in Bontemps's *Black Thunder* are strong. In both stories, the rebel leader later uses the memory of a weak, pitiable old slave brutally killed by his master to arouse the feeling of his followers. But although Panger may have been inspired to write *Ol' Prophet Nat* by Bontemps's example, his historical sensibility is quite different from the thirties novelist's. How differently the older black writer dramatizes another slave rebel may be seen as we turn to the work more familiar to many black and white readers of 1968. *Black Thunder*'s reissue in that year allowed a whole new generation of American readers to think about Nat Turner, and to see Styron's and Panger's heroes in a new light by contrast with a fictional history of Gabriel Prosser.

The Thirties and the Sixties: Arna Bontemps's *Black Thunder*

Bontemps's reappearance illustrates one way in which segments of thirties expression became embedded in a later generation's imagination. Like Henry Roth's *Call It Sleep* and John G. Neihardt's *Black Elk Speaks*, both thirties publications of life on the fringes of mainstream

American experience, *Black Thunder* achieved wide recognition only when reborn under radically different social circumstances. We cannot be sure how directly this return was occasioned by Styron; nevertheless the new *Black Thunder* had by 1970 gone into four printings. Though cover blurbs for Bontemps's book do not mention Styron, the connection is made in Beacon Press's other contribution to the now-flourishing debate. On the back of *Ten Black Writers Respond*, Bontemps's *Black Thunder* is advertised as "a black writer's novel of Gabriel Prosser's slave revolt, rich in the pride and integrity which black writers feel Styron's novel ignored."

For his book's reappearance, Bontemps wrote a new introduction, which makes historical and personal connections backward and forward. Its dateline, "Chicago, April 1968," carries an ominous ring, especially in light of Martin Luther King, Jr.'s recent assassination and other tragic reminders of the continuities of violence in our history from September 1800 to 1968. "Time is not a river," Bontemps asserts. "Time is a pendulum."[12] Recurrence, not progress, is the bedrock of this writer's historicism, in his own life as in the nation's. Repeatedly shattered dreams mark the young novelist's struggle in the thirties to find his voice and have it heard. These repressions are linked backward to Prosser, Vesey, and Turner, then to the eclipse of the Harlem Renaissance and the thirties cause célèbre, the trial of the Scottsboro Boys in Alabama, and finally to ghetto riots in the sixties and the gunning down of the latest black preacher-prophet in Memphis.

Looking back, Bontemps recalls that "in the gloom of the darkening Depression settling all around us, I began to ponder the stricken slave's will to freedom" (xii). First in Alabama, then in Nashville, Bontemps immersed himself "almost frantically" in slave narratives and other records. He was seeking inspiration and information for a historical novel and had to choose which slave revolt would best focus his imagination:

> Denmark Vesey's effort I dismissed first. It was too elaborately planned for its own good. His plot was betrayed, his conspiracy crushed too soon, but it would be a mistake to say nothing came of it in Vesey's own time. The shudder it put into the hearts and minds of slaveholders was never quieted. *Nat Turner's Confessions*, which I read in the Fisk Library across from Schom-

berg's desk, bothered me on two counts. I felt uneasy about the amanuensis to whom his account was related and the conditions under which he confessed. Then there was the business of Nat's "visions" and "dreams." (xii)

For reasons partly personal but also historical, Bontemps turned to Gabriel Prosser. The Henrico County uprising of September 1800 "seemed to reflect more accurately for me what I felt then and feel now might have motivated slaves capable of such boldness and inspired daring" (xii). For one thing, "Gabriel had not opened his mind too fully and hence had not been betrayed as had Vesey" (xii). For another, Gabriel himself stood out as a commanding figure who "by his own dignity and by the esteem in which he was held inspired and maintained loyalty" (xii–xiii). Instead of Nat's religious visions, disturbingly foreign to Bontemps's skeptical temperament, Gabriel "had not depended on trance-like mumbo jumbo. Freedom was a less complicated affair in his case. It was, it seemed to me, a more unmistakable equivalent of the yearning I felt and which I imagined to be general. . . . He had not been possessed, not even overly optimistic" (xiii). Finally there was the plan itself with its bitterly ironic outcome—"a strategy which some contemporaries, prospective victims, felt could scarcely have failed had not the weather miraculously intervened in their behalf. Gabriel attributed his reversal, ultimately, to the stars in their courses, the only factor that had been omitted in his calculations" (xiii).

The history Bontemps reenacts in fictional form from sources in the Fisk Library was pounded out in his father's tiny house in Watts in 1934–35. Published the next year, *Black Thunder* earned no more than its publisher's advance. But with quiet pride the author recalls the recognition it received. In the Midwest came reviews and radio broadcasts by John T. Frederick, director of the Illinois Writers Project, as well as favorable mention in classes at the University of Chicago taught by Robert Morse Lovett. Bontemps's introduction does not mention, however, Richard Wright's enthusiastic review in *Partisan Review*.[13] In general, though, "the theme of self-assertion by black men whose endurance was strained to the breaking point was not one that readers of fiction were prepared to contemplate" in 1936 (xv). Thirty-two years later, the author still wonders "if its story will be better understood by Americans, black and white" (xv). Two decades later still, the same question hovers, although *Black Thunder* survives on Beacon Press's in-print list and the novel's place as an exemplary black work of historical fiction seems secure.

Though we can speculate about the factors, commercial and political, affecting Bontemps's still modest success with white readers, there is no question of *Black Thunder*'s relevance to the literary issues and ideological forces mobilized in the Nat Turner controversy. An understanding of this cultural history begins with an examination of Bontemps's fictional strategies. Briefer than Styron, longer than Panger, *Black Thunder* is a 224-page mosaic of brief chapters, vignettes of action grouped into five books to make a chronological narrative of the few weeks during which the Prosser uprising ran its course. The author's aim in dividing his tale into small units (many scarcely more than two or three pages) becomes clear as we note that each succeeding book contains fewer subdivisions. The nineteen in book 1, *Jacobins*, are needed to introduce a sizable cast of characters and establish multiple perspectives on the slave unrest in and around Richmond during the presidential contest between Thomas Jefferson and John Adams (incorrectly called by his grandson's name, John Quincy Adams, in the text). Gabriel and his fellow conspirators compose one group (mostly rural) of blacks. Richmond townspeople include slaves, free blacks, and the town's mulatto prostitute, but also white militiamen, French emigrés, northern liberals, and a notorious political publicist in jail for his radical views. The two aged figures of old Ben and his aristocratic master Moseby Sheppard precede and follow the others, thus raising and dropping the curtain of history. At the story's climax, too, old Ben kneels tearfully before his master to disclose the plot Gabriel and his fellows are beginning to execute. If Ben's opening act of winding the ancestral clock symbolizes Bontemps's theme of cyclical time, it also represents how faithful slaves historically preserved the aristocratic Virginia order. Bontemps thus encloses the revolt itself within fictional bookends that exhibit the continuing power of fear and loyalty. This contrasts with Styron's device—made virtually inevitable by a rigorously first-person narrative—of locating similarly conflicted motives inside Nat Turner's own mind. Fears of revolt and visions of violent black intruders breaking into the Sheppard mansion and spilling mud and blood across its polished floors are specters haunting the minds of both slaveholders and slaves as Bontemps's action unfolds.

Within the parameters of such carefully established social circumstances stands Gabriel Prosser—a black giant with Roman (but not mulatto) features. A man "too old for joy, as a slave's life went in Henrico County, Virginia, too young for despair as black men despaired in 1800" (16), he is energized by an infectious desire to be free. After the plot's failure, the white prosecutor seeks to uncover foreign agitators (from France, the Caribbean, or the North) at the helm of this horrifying conspiracy. Gabriel calmly rejects such rationalizations:

> "I tell you. I been studying about freedom a heap, me. I heard a plenty folks talk and I listened a heap. And everything I heard made me feel like I wanted to be free. It was on my mind hard, and it's right there the same way yet. On'erstand? That's all. Something keep telling me that anything what's equal to a gray squirrel wants to be free. That's how it all come about."
>
> "Well, was it necessary to plot such a savage butchery? Couldn't you have conceived an easier way?"
>
> Gabriel shook his head slowly. After a long pause he spoke.
>
> "I ain't got no head for flying away. A man is got a right to have his freedom in the place where he's born. He is got cause to want all his kinfolks free like hisself." (210)

In Bontemps's hands Gabriel is depicted as a man of great muscular and moral tenacity, but he is not particularly pious. He stands apart from the other conspirators' Christian, African, and American Indian modes of transcendent thinking. He employs biblical rhetoric, however, picking it up from Mingo, the literate and devout free black. Gabriel is, quite simply, a *natural* rebel. The term "natural," repeated in many mouths and in various images and events, means much more than the stereotyped associations of sexual potency and naive pastoral existence. Nature becomes a charged ideological sphere enclosing black slaves, white and black free men, animals and the landscape and geography of Virginia. Nature gives rise to a dialectic of innate desire and artificial or social constraints, as exemplified early in several episodes in which men and animals are metaphorically linked. When Old Bundy, the rum-soaked Prosser slave, is trampled to death beneath his master's horse, Gabriel ponders this latest brutality. Standing in his coachman's livery by the meadow in which Araby, the same master's beautiful colt runs free, he soliloquizes: "That's all right for you, Araby. . . . You ain't a horse yet, and you ain't a nigger neither. That's mighty fine for you, feeling yo' oats and trying to outrun the wind. You don't know nothing yet. Was you a white colt, I reckon I'd have to call you *mister* Araby" (15–16). "As glossy and black as anthracite" (15), Araby joins the lowly gray squirrel as an emblem of natural freedom that is denied to Gabriel and the others by their bondage. The horse and squirrel head a procession of animals whose states of captivity or liberty bring their names spontaneously to black lips and white. At the height of the storm—the worst in a third of a century—a frightened bird is trapped inside the Sheppard mansion's kitchen. To the house servants this is a sign of bad luck and death. But Gabriel changes that meaning as he remarks to Mingo: "A wild bird what's in a cage will die, anyhow, sooner or later. He'll pine hisself to death. He just is well to break his neck trying to get out" (69). Later, after the revolt has been delayed and betrayed, Gabriel reluctantly joins the others in flight. He stows away on a James River schooner bound to Norfolk and the Atlantic. In the fetid hold he confronts a gigantic rat at close quarters. The confrontation is strikingly prophetic of Bigger Thomas's encounter with the rat in the Chicago tenement, which is the opening scene of *Native Son*, published four years later. Man and rat face each other in mortal combat. "Bad, hunh? Wants something to set yo' teeth into, do you? Try this here blade one time . . . Showing me them teeth so big—you got to use them now. . . . There now, see what you done? Kilt yo' self. Jumped right straddle across my blade. Well, suh, that's you all right. Look just as nachal as can be. You got on yo' last clean shirt, too" (190).

Gabriel's dual perspective, by which he sees himself as black rat/rebel and white avenger, repeats a pattern from the preceding action, in which multiple viewpoints on slavery and freedom are as frequently combined as opposed. Animals—a black colt in a fenced meadow, gray squirrels annoyed by bluejays, a frightening jackass and cornered rat—are favorite tropes of human desire and frustration. Over and above the systematic frustration of black desire by oppressive institutions is the power of nature itself, manifested in the stars and the deluge that chokes every creek in the countryside and prevents Gabriel's thousand recruits from reaching the Richmond arsenal. If it is "natural" for summer drought to be ended by a titanic rainstorm, it will be equally "natural" for another pendulum to usher in the Civil War after the long dry centuries of chattel slavery. Thus Bontemps deems it appropriate to both the historical event and its participants to use natural and meteorological tropes. In one of the last, he depicts Pharoah, the "pumpkin-colored mulatto" conspirator who also betrays Gabriel and the others, first as a hog and then as a mad dog perched in a tree.

If *Black Thunder*'s tapestry of natural imagery is one major fictional device by which a particular historical action is generalized, the other conventional yet equally apt pattern of metaphors also enlarges meaning of the human figures and their actions. For slaves as well as the free, clothing symbolizes both social conditions and dreams (or nightmares) of change, and these implications are communicated both in the act of wearing and shedding garments. In his servant's role as Thomas Prosser's coachman, Gabriel wears a resplendent uniform and top hat that are gradually soiled, soaked, and discarded in the storm and strain of the revolt. By its deterioration Gabriel's garb is transformed into the uniform of General Gabriel. As his magnificent black body emerges from beneath the trappings of servitude, this American Toussaint L'Ouverture displays his natural power. Simultaneously, however, his vulnerability is made pathetically visible in the tattered garments of his lieutenant, old General John. The same process of nobility displayed and failure made public occurs with Juba, Gabriel's woman. Her lithe legs and seductive torso are scarcely covered by her slave rags. But as the messenger of revolt Juba bestrides Araby, wearing a discarded pair of her master's boots. Her skirt almost around her waist, she rides through the rain to signal the start of the attack on Richmond. Still another signal of social identity is Melody's black and white striped stockings, which the "apricot-colored mulatress" stuffs in her trunk as she flees Richmond just before the storm. Perhaps the beautiful whore, whose "enameled black hair" contrasts suggestively with Juba's wild mop, may actually be trying to shed her marginality in the act of hiding the garments that signify her compromised role.

Like Mingo, the literate Bible-quoting rebel whose presence in this secular story may be a shadow of the rejected figure of Nat Turner, Juba and Melody are fictional figures Bontemps has imagined to fill particular places in the historical mosaic. Melody is a conventional type of the half-black, half-white beauty whose body is at once her prison and passport to freedom in Philadelphia. Juba is not quite so conventional, inasmuch as her role as Gabriel's lover and ally do not include being his muse. In her relationship she answers Alvin Poussaint's later query aimed at

Styron: "Why is not the author able to 'imagine' that Nat Turner had a young, feminine, beautiful, and courageous black woman at his side?" More significantly, Bontemps creates a natural beauty whose ties to the rebel hero are not primarily sexual but political. Juba's participation in the revolt is very much her own choice. Indeed, as Juba rides Araby along the road giving the signal to assemble, she is well aware that her sexual energy and appeal are natural qualities more likely to distract and disarm than incite insurrection. To the "shadows" hiding along the highway she addressed a silent sermon: "And you knows what this here means. Gabriel said it plain. Dust around now, you old big-foot boys. Get a move on. Remember how Gabriel say it: you got to go on cat feet. You got to get around like the wind. Quick. On'erstand? Always big-talking about what booming bed-men you is. Always trying to turn the gals' heads like that. Well, let's see what you is good for sure 'nough. Let's see if you knows how to go free; let's see if you knows how to die, you big-footses you" (81). Here as elsewhere in *Black Thunder*, sex, manhood, and freedom are linked in dramatically different ways from in Styron's story. Similarly, Bontemps's pervasive animal imagery—his use even of lowly animals like squirrels, rats, groundhogs, and frightened birds—never robs his black characters of their essential dignity, as is for many readers the effect of Styron's metaphoric flies and mules.

Bontemps's basic fictional choices, then, consist of a multiple perspective or "cross-section view" of a historical action and cast of characters recreated in their particular and universal contexts by a unifying pattern of nature and clothing imagery. Other fictional devices for dealing with history include combining in his cast of characters actual historical figures and imaginary representative ones. He sometimes collapses the two by giving historical personages slightly altered names. Bontemps also occasionally moves slaves from one actual plantation to another, although this exercise of authorial freedom is often masked by the fact that slaves with the same name were commonplace.

These modest exercises of fictional authority call attention to Bontemps's credible combination of respect for history and his own imagination in reembedding Gabriel Prosser in a 1936 narrative. The impression readers acquire is of a fruitful, relatively unconflicted relationship between history and literature. This sense is supported by a look at Bontemps's chief historical sources and the ways he has exploited them to make larger historicist statements about time, place, and zeitgeist.

Most of the official documents he decided to use are assembled in the *Calendar of Virginia State Papers* whose volume 9 covers the period from 1799 to 1807.[14] (He seems, like Styron, reluctant to rely on newspaper accounts.) Writing in 1934 and 1935, Bontemps did not have access to Herbert Aptheker's *Negro Slave Revolts in the United States, 1526–1860*, since that pioneering monograph, first published by Columbia University Press, did not appear until 1939. However, from other historical accounts Bontemps may have learned of the widely publicized but probably legendary reply Gabriel Prosser made to the court that condemned him to death: "I have nothing more to offer than what General Washington would have had to offer, had he been taken by the British officers and put to trial by them. I have adventured my life in endeavouring to obtain the liberty of my countrymen, and am a willing sacrifice to their cause; and I beg, as a favour, that I may be immediately led to execution. I know that you have pre-determined to shed my blood, why then all this mockery of a trial?"[15] Not only is the speech of Bontemps's Gabriel very different from such stiffly heroic rhetoric, but historical parallels with Washington and the American Revolution are never pursued in the novel. Rather, as befits the slave's viewpoint chiefly represented, Toussaint L'Ouverture is the patriot-rebel's name repeatedly on the lips of Gabriel and his followers.

While not slavishly followed, the *Calendar* served Bontemps's historical and artistic needs by providing extensive correspondence and court testimony dealing with Gabriel Prosser's leadership, the plot's careful planning, and Gabriel's escape and capture in Norfolk. To be sure, this testimony presents the official white account of the event. While extensive black testimony is included, these words are from informers or others trying to save their own skins. One such self-serving collaborator was Solomon Prosser, Gabriel's brother, whose postrevolt behavior is omitted, plausibly enough, from a chronological account that ends with Gabriel's death. Other potentially embarrassing details in a heroic story are also left out, as well as several pertinent and powerful statements about the rebel's motives and ideals.[16]

Nevertheless, Bontemps's historical researches provided a variety of viewpoints, authentic details, and apt quotations by which he particularizes setting, a cast of representative figures, and a crucial historical moment. From his immersion in history Bontemps makes Gabriel himself less a legendary individual than the public embodiment and nexus of forces working broadly in and on the new nation's slaveholding society of 1800. Though working without a narrator (like Panger's) to voice generalizations, Bontemps uses various resources of fiction to articulate a comprehensive vision of an event in the American past seen principally but not exclusively from the slave quarters. Through *Black Thunder*'s mosaic narrative, 1800 is represented as a true turning point. By means of this abortive insurrection of a thousand ill-armed slaves, Americans were made to confront the tensions between their revolutionary ideals and the economic and racist realities of chattel slavery. Just seven years before the official termination of the slave trade, Gabriel's revolt represented a genuine threat narrowly averted. Though the institution itself could not have been overthrown by the sacking of Richmond, this southern capital might well have experienced a bloodbath that could have extended across a sizable territory of the Old Dominion. Accidental forces overwhelmed a simple but plausible plot. Though psychological conflicts (expressed in Gabriel's will to freedom and Old Ben's fearful devotion to the status quo) were vital, sexual violence toward white women is confined to a single slave's ruminations in the darkness outside a poor white's cabin. Though less puritanical about violence and sexuality than Styron or Panger's protagonist, Bontemps's Gabriel exemplifies the consensus of historians about American slavery, as later articulated by Winthrop Jordan: "In fact, during this entire period of slave unrest [1790s and the following decade] there is no evidence of negroes sexually assaulting white women."[17]

The year 1800 was a turning point in slave culture as well. If under pressure from events in France and the Caribbean, white America was searching its revolutionary soul and yet hardening its hold on black slaves, the people in the quarters found themselves caught between an African past still alive in folk beliefs, religious rituals and their Christian religion. Yet these fictional figures are aware, as Styron's never are, of *Les Amis des noirs;* they talk about Toussaint L'Ouverture, have some sense about differences between the Democrats and Federalists, and make roughly accurate distinctions among the various Christian denominations.

For both blacks and whites, then, the summer of 1800, in Bontemps's imagination, is dramatically full of cultural challenges. As the commonwealth's official responses and Governor Monroe's private opinions both attest, many whites were divided over slavery, emancipation, colonization, and the righteousness (within limits) of Gabriel's cause. Natural rights philosophy was still strong enough to encourage sympathy for the slave's cause, and this response was enhanced by the dignity of Gabriel Prosser's death. Bontemps's vernacular language distinguishes itself most clearly from Styron's ornateness or Panger's pallid prose in evoking the rebel's reflections as he lies in jail awaiting his death.

> Suddenly there was silence outside. A brief hush blanketed the men with the flambeaus and sabers.
> Them is the mens with the milk-white horses, I reckon. I ain't seen nara one of them, but I know right well how they looks. H'm. I got a good mind how they come. . . . Galloping down a heap of clouds piled up like mountains. I know them milk-white horses, me . . .
> Put yo' key in the lock, Mistah Man. Give the sign and come in, please you, suh. I hear a nigger say Death is his mammy. His old black mammy is name Death, he say. Well and good, onliest thing about it is Death is a man.
> Come on in, suh, if you's a-mind to. I'm ready and waiting, me. I ain't been afeared of a nachul man, and I don't know's I mind the old Massa hisself. I ain't been afeared of thunder and lightning, and I don't reckon I'll mind the hurricane. I don't know's I'll mind when the trees bend down and the tombstones commence to bust. Don't reckon I'll mind, suh. Come on in. (220)

As Gabriel rides to his death in a cart, seated on his oversized coffin, feet thrust out, his three confederates in jail send farewell soliloquies after him. "Good-by, Gabriel," Ditcher says silently. "Don't nobody need to tell *you* how to die, I reckon. You's the gen'l, you" (221). Mingo, the man of the Book, recalls that the Bible "was all for abused folks like Negroes. Other books, too, in fact. Mostly them men what write books was a little better kind than them what made speeches at the town meetings" (221–22). Mingo also offers a prophecy: "Toussaint was first across yonder; Gabriel's first here. The first robin going north. It was too soon for Gabriel, though. It wasn't summer. The cold caught us here, the rain and all" (222). Finally, old General John, scrawny as a hawk, adds his voice: "Was I a singing man, I'd sing me a song now . . . I'd sing me a song about lonesome, about a song-singing man long gone.

No need crying about a nigger what's about to die free. I'd sing me a song, me" (222).

These earthly prayers celebrate the community of black men praising each other and prophesying in the face of apparent defeat. Thus, their silence is a sign neither of separation nor surrender. Unlike Styron's version of the analogous moment on Nat Turner's last morning—at which Nat's "'Good-bye Hark' I whisper, good-bye, good-bye" (427) reiterates to the very end an inner distance between himself and his followers—Gabriel's silence signifies nobility. "Let the rope talk, suh" (223) is his laconic farewell address. The ax's arc and the humming rope speak eloquently enough. Old Ben the betrayer saw "that arc, inscribed by the ax, lingering there against the sky like a wreath of smoke. . . . Even when Ben closed his eyes, he could see that arc, hear that violin string" (223).

Through a variety of conventional narrative techniques, *Black Thunder* anticipates arguments by several of the ten black writers and other critics of Styron. Indeed some of these later criticisms may have been occasioned by this book's reappearance. Bontemps thereby demonstrates the historical and ideological persistence of certain retellings within a culture. Originating in a Depression-era ethos, Bontemps's novel once reflected thirties cultural concerns clustering about the significance of folk culture and counterviolence in American history. Gabriel Prosser's story was disembedded from the *Calendar of Virginia State Papers* and various slave narratives like Gray's *Confessions*. Then it was reembedded in a new context defined by contemporary questions regarding the Depression, oppression, and, more directly perhaps, certain thirties political causes like the Scottsboro trial in which blacks and whites worked together. In these terms Bontemps's "cultural work" was to dramatize to blacks and sympathetic liberal whites the continuing symbolic meaning of a remote historical event and personage. Gabriel Prosser's revolt raised possibilities in certain imaginations of successful (yet potentially bloody) action toward self-determination by black Americans. The milieu of 1800 was reconstructed in some respects to resemble the 1930s—troubled yet dynamic, multifaceted yet open to changes, a society in delicate balance between its humane ideals and its capitalist and racist imperatives.

When reprinted in 1968, *Black Thunder* became not a bestselling rival to Styron's *The Confessions of Nat Turner* but, in Jane Tompkins's term, a less "privileged" narrative with respect to the mainstream audiences Styron attracted and spoke for.[18] Considerations of race and a disadvantaged access to the dominant communications network do not, however, explain why, despite respectable reviews and sales, Bontemps still failed to achieve privileged status. Unlike Styron, Bontemps never deeply plumbs the "undocumented inside" of his rebellious slave. Nor has he reimagined a fictional denouement transforming a secular parable of political violence into one of psychosexual and religious transcendence. His is in this respect a less comforting story, even though Nat Turner's revolt was the more violently troubling event. Showing little interest in exploiting the sexual or bloodthirsty behavior of his subjects, Bontemps largely subordinated his artistic imagination to the requirements of the historical records. Hence many readers, whether in 1936 or 1968, might assume that he has worked more closely than Styron, yet more imaginatively than Panger, "within the tension of accepted facts."

Between them, Panger, Bontemps, and Styron illustrate the resources fiction possesses as a relatively popular and accessible form of historical thinking. *Ol' Prophet Nat* typifies in some respects a modest but not really pedestrian work of art that demonstrates one way fiction and history can do cultural work in tandem. The sympathetic white editor/narrator and the grandly simple Preacher-Prophet openly collaborate in retelling Nat Turner's story. As white cultural work, Panger's novel speaks to and for an integrationist historicism and aesthetic, which in some respects are similar to Styron's but more deferential to the radical Christianity of the nineteenth-century protagonist and to Gray's *Confessions*, as its prime source. *Black Thunder*, by its author's choice of subject and use of multiple perspectives, sidesteps certain risks as well as certain ambiguities in Nat Turner's historical character and situation. As reprinted with a fresh introduction, Bontemps's novel embraces a wider historical horizon than either of the white writers' accounts. It illuminates two remoter pasts, 1800 and 1831, connecting them to the sixties through the lens of 1936. Fiction's power to appeal through the same narrative to different readerships and historical contexts is thus freshly exemplified. *Black Thunder* has never matched the sales or notoriety of Styron's bestseller, but it has already shown surprising adaptability. As one model of black historical fiction, it further demonstrates how unprivileged narratives reflect and affect culture by "providing society with a means of thinking about itself . . . expressing and shaping the social context that produced them."[19]

Pioneer Playwrights:
Randolph Edmonds, Paul Peters, Thomas Pawley

Stage plays are retextualizations of history that usually point more explicitly than novels or poems to the social transactions in which they principally function as cultural work. Their occasions and circumstances of performance provide visual evidence of collective feelings and values, although this does not mean that the published script of any play is necessarily an accurate index of performance or audience response. Nor can we generalize from one kind of audience to a general theater-going public. But in tracing the means of production and modes of dramatic expression of the half-dozen plays dealing with Nat Turner's or other slave uprisings, we enter a variety of theatrical settings which are also social contexts for the transmission of information and interpretation of the past. As was the case with Daniel Panger's readership, several of these theatrical occasions bring together relatively small groups, whether black or white. Even the publicized New York City presentations in this theatrical history took place off-Broadway, in small theaters, before elite or specialized audiences. These plays reenacting slave violence never enjoyed extended runs or many revivals as has, for example, Miller's *The Crucible* (1953) or Saul Levitt's *The Andersonville Trial* (1960). They remain muted or minority voices. One of them, Paul Peters's *Nat Turner*, exists perhaps exclusively within the covers of an out-of-print book. Even more obscurely, the script of Thomas D. Pawley's *Messiah* rests as a University of Iowa doctoral thesis in but a handful of university libraries. Thus the discussion that follows will not argue (*contra* Eugene Genovese) that the black playwrights (or, for that matter, most of the whites) represented here were nationally known or politically influential. What is claimed is that the stage allowed particular but varied groups of Americans to witness reenactments of slave rebels. Furthermore, these emotional and cognitive transactions took place at least a generation before *The Confessions of Nat Turner* appeared or *Black Thunder* was reprinted.

This little-known chapter in theater history opens, as I can best determine, in 1934. At the moment when Bontemps was immersing himself in black history at Fisk, another black man in the South, even more intrigued by Nat Turner, was deciding upon a different mode of communication to address fellow blacks about their heroic past. In part because he was born in Virginia, the child of ex-slaves, Randolph Edmonds was drawn to Nat Turner's revolt as a dramatic subject. Formally educated in the North, he was later schooled by years of menial labor before becoming a playwright and teacher at Morgan State College in Baltimore. Edmonds's deep roots in black folklife led to his participation and leadership in the Negro Little Theatre movement of the 1930s and 1940s. "There has been for many years a need for plays of Negro life written by Negroes," he recalls in the preface to *Six Plays for a Negro Theatre*.[20] Answering this need, he composed a number of short folk dramas, of which *Nat Turner* is one of two dealing with slavery. In the process of turning history into popular theater for ordinary black audiences and amateur actors, Edmonds chose to write "dialect" or "peasant" drama. However, as he explained in the preface, this decision did not entail exploiting "the psychology of the inferior." Rather it was one response to the need to bring together "worthwhile themes, sharply drawn conflict, positive characters and a melodramatic plot" (7). At the same time, like other socially conscious artists of the thirties, Edmonds aspired to reach "above the narrow confines of the nation or race of the cast of characters" (7).

As an experiment in folk melodrama, *Nat Turner* is apparently the first black play about "the famous Nat Turner Insurrection" (63). The adjective suggests that the southern students, teachers, and townspeople who composed Edmonds's first audiences were already familiar with Nat Turner's name and were prepared to respond knowledgeably to his re-creation as folk hero. In any case, the Negro Intercollegiate Dramatic Association became another cultural institution preserving this portion of the past and providing not only enthusiastic audiences for Edmonds' collegiate actors but potential readers of *Black Thunder* as well. In pointing out such possibilities, it is worth noting that educated, essentially middle-class Negro playgoers in the thirties celebrated their past through the life of Nat Turner, *not* Frederick Douglass or Booker T. Washington.

Six Plays for a Negro Theatre was not widely reviewed or ever, so far as I can determine, reissued by its Boston publisher. Today, it is rarely found in public libraries. Another indication of obscurity is this plaintive announcement beneath the copyright: "There is no royalty fee for the amateur stage use of these plays provided that a sufficient number of copies of this printed book are purchased by the producing group to supply each member of the cast with a copy." This meant that Baker marketed only eleven copies each time *Nat Turner* was legally performed. These eleven roles bear, with but two exceptions, the names of actual historical figures mentioned in Gray's *Confessions*, which, from internal evidence, is Edmonds's chief source. Nat, Hark, Will, and Nelson are the leaders while two other insurgents represent the outer circle of the ignorant, reluctant, or disenchanted slaves of Southampton.

Nat's first stage action is to win over these lukewarm noninitiates. His speech in an awkward black dialect recalls that already popularized by Dubose Heyward and Paul Green:

> NAT: One day while Ah was walkin' in de field behind de plow, all ob a sudden de sperit said, "Seek ye furst de kingdom ob heaven and all of dese things will be added unto yuh." Ah said, "Lawd, dat cain't be Yuh talkin' 'cause Ah want de things ob dis worl'!" So Ah ran away frum ma Moster. Ah wanted to make my way tuh freedom lak ma father befo' me. Ah tried to dodge de Moster's will; but one day de sperit came tuh me agen . . . So I came back heah tuh ma Moster. Ah come back tuh you.
> HENRY: You came back tuh lead us tuh freedom. (73)

Only the wordplay on "Moster" individualizes this crude translation of Gray's version of the historical Turner's words. To signal changes in the actor's emotional pitch Edmonds uses script cues such as "(*Eloquently*)" or "(*Fiercely*)." His call-and-response interplay between speaker and followers is likewise—though often effectively—trite.

> NAT: Ah hates tuh kill folks, too; but war ain't no barbeque feast. Yuh thinks 'cause yuh is gut a belly full and a place tuh lay yo head dat day is nuff; but hit ain't nuff fah men made in the image ob Gawd. No real man ain't willing tuh be wurked lak a mule in the fields, whupped lak a dog, and tied tuh one farm and one Moster. (*Eloquently*) Is yuh willing tuh continue dis servitude,

> dis slavery? . . . Is yuh willing tuh be beaten, enslaved, debased? Is yuh willing everybody?
>
> VOICES: No!! No!! (71)

Edmonds's play rides on such rhetoric, which replaces actual violence. Nat recruits and rouses his band with Old Testament vehemence, but on stage his sword is sheathed and no blood is shed. Stage directions, for this brief drama, signify the course of the revolt. In the two scenes three days pass, during which "the many assassinations take place" (77). Between scenes, the audience sits in "absolute darkness" before a dropped curtain hearing but never witnessing the "guns, the glee of the army and the moans of the dying" (77).

What is more arrestingly dramatized later is the revolt's failure and Nat's anguish at recalling that "when de white soldiers fired on ma army up dere near Jerusalem, dey all deserted and run lak cowards. . . . Deh ought tuh knowed dey couldn't lose. Nobody can lose when deh fight de battle ob de one true Gawd ob Hosts" (78). Then follows the melodramatic climax enacted through two fictitious characters. Jessee Harris, mortally wounded, brings Nat word of the revolt's collapse. When Lucinda (the young slave girl who may be thought of as Edmonds's anticipation of Bontemps's Juba) enters, Jessee dies in her arms. She then turns on Nat:

> Yuh killed him, Ah said. Yuh wid yo' fine notions 'bout slaves should be free. . . . But yuh'll get yours. See ef yuh don't. De white folks is all 'round in dese woods. Deh is gwine ketch yuh and stretch yo' nake on de gallows. . . . Well, see whut Gawd tells yuh when dey start stretchin' yo' nake. Ah'm gwine tell de white folks whar yuh is . . . Yuh ain't nothin' but a beast, dat's whut, a beast. (*She rushes off*) (81)

But Nat is only momentarily shaken by Lucinda's threats. As the curtain falls on the moonlit scene, the rebel preacher finds consolation in its bright beams.

> Hit is big and round an yellow. Hit done dripped out all hits blood. Ma hands is full o' blood, too. Will dey ever be clean? Was Ah wrong, Lawd, tuh fight dat black men mout be free? Whut is Ah gwine to do now? Show me a vision, Lawd, lak yuh did when de sperits was fightin' in de air. . . . (*He stops suddenly*) Whut's dat

noise? Hit mus be de soldiers lookin' 'bout in the woods fuh me. Ah can't let dem catch me. Ah is gut tuh git me a army and fight some mo' fuh freedom. Ah wants freedom! . . . Show me how to git hit, Lawd! (*Shouting wildly as he goes out*) Sperit ob Gawd! Show me de way! Guide me! Lead me! Lead me! (82)

By itself, Edmonds's one-hour melodrama witnessed on a Hampton Institute or Morgan State stage contributed but slenderly to the historical consciousness of many black Americans in the thirties. It is of continuing significance chiefly in being the first play to demonstrate the possibility of translating Gray's *Confessions*, however tritely, into folk drama. Though I have no proof, this *Nat Turner* may also have been adapted for amateur performances and actors under those other social circumstances—school plays, lodge or church pageants, and similar ritual occasions mentioned by Ralph Ellison and Ossie Davis. However dimly, Randolph Edmonds lit a candle in a dark space soon illuminated more brightly and steadily—and in different, more popular media— by Arna Bontemps and Sterling Brown. Perhaps few in Edmonds's audiences were familiar enough with Gray to note how gingerly the playwright handled the violence and Old Testament vehemence of the 1831 account, or how much more pallid is the theatrical moonlight on his stage as contrasted with Gray's transcriptions of the solar eclipse and spots on the moon. Nor do Edmonds's ideological caution and academic stagecraft ever produce images of freedom, fate, and hope to match the hangman's ax and vibrating rope in Bontemps's novel.

A vision of history and politics much closer to Bontemps's is articulated in the other early drama, Paul Peters's *Nat Turner*. But instead of live performances before collegiate audiences of black students, teachers, and the general public, Peters's play (copyrighted in 1940) came into existence within the pages of an anthology of experimental literature. Edwin Seaver was editor of *Cross-Section: A Collection of New American Writing*. Though its publication date was 1944, the collection reflects both the vigorous literary life of the late thirties and the left-wing politics of World War II. In the pages of this left/liberal anthology appeared new writing by a variety of established authors and those destined to be so, among them Ralph Ellison, Arthur Miller, Langston Hughes, Norman Mailer, Richard Wright, and Shirley Jackson. Of the thousand or more submissions, Seaver wrote, "an astonishing number of the manuscripts received, for instance, had to do with racial injustice in this country, specifically with what we call the 'negro problem.'"[21] Though not as well known as most of the other contributors, Paul Peters already enjoyed a modest reputation for dramatizing working-class life and American racism. In some ways a conventional mainstream author and drama critic—working for the *Literary Digest, Life,* and Twentieth-Century Fox's New York office—Peters showed his radical sympathies for the oppressed by coauthoring a play about working-class blacks, *Stevedore,* put on by the Theatre Union (557).

Perhaps Seaver's own leftist sympathies influenced his selection of Peters's play, a work possibly never performed. His was a playwright's name that never again graced a table of contents alongside Ellison and Mailer. Yet this *Nat Turner* is a far more ambitious and dramatically effective work than Edmonds's, as well as politically more in tune with Nat Turner's own radicalism. Like Styron, Panger, and Edmonds, Peters relies upon Gray for his representation. Yet he treats the 1831 *Confessions* at times quite freely, raising broader historical and cultural issues through the introduction of characters either unknown to historians or, in one case, in direct violation of historical probability.

This freedom and modernity are visible in the opening scene which discovers Nat's wife and Redic, his son, on the edge of the Great Dismal Swamp in whose depths Nat is hiding. They encounter an itinerant Yankee peddler who becomes the *éminence gris* of the ensuing action. The hunchbacked peddler is an abolitionist covertly encouraging Nat's uprising with heartening speeches and copies of the *Liberator*. He and the slaves are pursued by a group of slaveowners whose names and ideological allegiances make them a representative spectrum of whites, from a poor overseer to a foppish FFV. Joseph Travis, Nat's owner, is poorer than the others and more lenient in his treatment of his slaves. Salathiel Francis, a brutal money-grubber, comes into early conflict with the white man most sympathetic to the blacks—his own overseer Jim Press, who once owned thirty acres but is now reduced to one acre and one pig. The white class system of Southampton County and its opponents are thus presented in the first ten minutes of the action.

When accused by the Virginians of knowing Nat's whereabouts, the Yankee replies: "Prime field hand. Worth a thousand dollars. Six foot three and powerful. . . . Smart, too. Too smart to be a slave, your niggers say. You see, I know everything. An old dog gets in every garbage pail" (232). Peters's mythification here indicates a willingness to work freely with Gray's account which, of course, endows the historical Nat Turner with much less heroic physical dimensions. Furthermore, it is speedily apparent when Nat himself appears that, despite being addressed as a "black Moses" by his followers, he behaves more like a secular leader. Throughout the play, his religious nature, visions, and rhetoric are subordinated to social and political demands of the reimagined plot. Thus when the Peddler repeats the French motto "Liberty, Equality, Fraternity," Nat declares: "Don't need no white man to give me liberty." The Yankee eggs him on: "No. Nat Turner's big and powerful. Smart, like they say. Prophet Nat, the slaves call him. He *takes* his liberty. Big shiny horse flings the bit from his mouth, and whoo! there he goes!" (234). One suspects, but cannot be certain, that Peters's horse imagery owes something to Bontemps's *Black Thunder*. In any case, this reinscription reflects more class consciousness than does Edmonds's play. Thus the sequence of Peters's dramatic action is first to establish Nat Turner's political significance and self-awareness, then to dramatize his carrying out of "the business of the Lord" (246). This begins when the Yankee introduces Turner to an appropriate military model.

> PEDDLER: Once there was a slave who could run but didn't.
> NAT TURNER: Fool, that slave.
> PEDDLER: Instead, he called all the blacks together and he said to them: "Brothers and friends! I will avenge your wrongs. Liberty and justice shall reign. Come and unite with us, brothers!"
> NAT TURNER: And they kill him.
> PEDDLER: They sent soldiers and generals, muskets and cannons. But he was a fox by day and a lion by night. He fell on them in the mountains. He consumed them with fire and sword.
> NAT TURNER: And he free them blacks?
> PEDDLER: Free as the skies.
> NAT TURNER: Musta been some far-off country.
> PEDDLER: His name was Toussaint L'Ouverture.
> NAT TURNER: Hmn. Guinea nigger. In Virginia they string him up. (235)

As elsewhere in this literary domain, Peters's actors (black and white) use familiar animal tropes to characterize themselves and others.

Recruiting followers, Nat whispers that "the Lord sent me a serpent with a message for you . . . a sweet-talking little hump-back serpent" (247). Other slaves, too, become convinced the Yankee is Satanic; as Hark puts it, "Lord send Nat a serpent, Peachy say. Lord never say kill white folks" (257). The same natural metaphors connect members of a community but also divide them into the daring or desperate and the undecided or timid. When Wagoner Sam, for instance, hesitates at the prospect of killing white children, Nat laconically (and accurately, according to Gray) retorts, "Nits make lice" (253). Then follows a passionate exchange between two groups:

> BLACKSMITH NELSON: All my life I preach freedom. Time I practice some now.
> HIGHGRASS: I'll be there, General Nat. Count on me.
> DRED: (*Turning frantically on them*) What's the matter? You staying? You lost your mind?
> NAT: Your life worth more than theirs, Wagoner Sam?
> WAGONER SAM: I know things ain't good. But I ain't got it so bad, either. For thirty years I inch along. Mind flies, first. Next, I water boy. Start plowing when I had to reach up to hold the handles. Then I learn wagoning from old Mingo. I'm Wagoner Sam now. Best wagoner in the county. That's something.
> NAT: Would be if you owned the hands you work with. (254)

The range of black attitudes toward freedom and violence, as well as the terse directness of Peters's protagonist's speech that is reminiscent of Gabriel's, again suggests the influence of *Black Thunder*. This possibility is strengthened as the action unfolds. The uprising is reported—soon enough to constitute betrayal—by old Willie Witcher. The terrified old slave bends over and begins to kiss Salathiel Francis's hand (266). But although Willie's speech and actions evoke Bontemps's Ben Woolfolk, he retains at a crucial moment a measure of dignity among his fellow blacks that the two Judases, Ben and Pharoah, never demonstrate. Peters arranges Willie's capture by the rebels. When brought before their leader Willie pleads for understanding and mercy.

> NAT: How I know you won't play Judas again?
> WILLIE WITCHER: I'm an old dog. I want to go off and die somewhere.

> NAT: Don't you want to be free?
> WILLIE WITCHER: No.
> NAT: Even a rabbit want to be free.
> WILLIE WITCHER: What do I want with freedom? Where I go? How I act? I cain't live without Marse Francis. I want to die too.
> NAT: You love him so much?
> WILLIE WITCHER: Love him? No. But all my life I live in his house. I break his bread and eat his salt. He my cloud by day and pillar of fire by night. When he live, everything in the world have its place. Even an old dog like Willie Witcher. I was Marse Francis' personal valet. (276)

The wordplay on the Moses Bible story here is explicit and ironic. Shortly after, it reappears just as naturally, in Nat's own mouth. The revolt begins to unravel when the band decides to follow Hark down the road to the Parker plantation in defiance of Nat's orders. Left alone, Nat breaks into a biblical lament: "Moses, Moses, high on Pisgah, look down on the land of Gilead, but thou shalt not go thither" (277). More characteristic of his language, though, is his return to the secular rhetoric of Toussaint L'Ouverture, as in the portentous accents of his final words to the Yankee peddler at the window of his jail cell.

> PEDDLER: I bring you an apple, Nat Turner.
> NAT: Sweet-talking little hump-backed snake.
> PEDDLER: See my apple? My perdy little apple? Won't you eat from my apple? . . . I was up North when I read about you . . .
> NAT: Read about me?
> PEDDLER: Ten million people know your name, Nat Turner.
> NAT: The Liberator!
> PEDDLER: Everywhere up north. From Maine to farthest Kansas, that's all people say: "Did you hear? Did you hear about Nat Turner? He tried to free the slaves" . . . And everywhere down south. In New Orleans, whole city sitting up all night with guns in their laps. In Norfolk, in Richmond, in Raleigh, on every plantation: "Run, run! Nat Turner's coming. Nat Turner's coming!"
> NAT: He tried to free the slaves. And look what he done. His own people, beat and burned and hanged.
> PEDDLER: What they'll remember is that he tried. Not just your

people, but white folks too. . . . They used to say the slaves were happy. Nat Turner wasn't. They used to say the slaves were satisfied. Nat Turner wasn't. They used to say the slaves didn't want no freedom. Nat Turner was ready to die for freedom. . . . (*The sound of tramping feet on cobblestones*)

NAT: That's the guard coming.
PEDDLER: It's soldiers they're sending.
NAT: Goodbye, little snake.
PEDDLER: (*Starting to slip down*): Goodbye, 'prisoned lion . . .
NAT: Was you wrong, little snake, about armies marching?
PEDDLER: (*Head reappearing a moment*): Sleep easy in the ground, Nat Turner. They'll be marching. (279–80)

Peters's melodramatic (and more than faintly Miltonic) message of proletarian solidarity, revolt, and bittersweet postponed triumph echoes against other thirties' literary/political texts like Archibald MacLeish's *Land of the Free*, John Steinbeck's *Grapes of Wrath*, and Bontemps's *Black Thunder*. Playgoers, if there were any, could only *hear* the Peddler's final promise of what history holds as the legacy of Nat Turner, but readers of Peters's text (perhaps his only audience) are treated to one final burst of heroic prose in the last stage direction: "(He vanishes. *Nat* remains at the window. Now the footsteps are loud in the hall; they halt at the door; the door is thrown open. *Nat* resolute and straight steps into line, marches off)" (280).

As these early plays variously demonstrate, drama as a mode of cultural history is of necessity very selective history. Indeed, Edmonds and Peters largely turn their backs on the chronological historical narrative of the Southampton slave revolt with its (for fictional purposes) compact yet varied sequence of actions: planning, killing, panicking, hiding, retelling, dying. Both playwrights employ a small cast of characters and choose carefully among possible themes. Edmonds emphasizes Nat Turner the folk figure—the Preacher-Prophet dismayed but not disheartened by the collapse of his revolt, caused more by the failure of his followers than by the superior fire power of the whites. His is a brief, severely selective action set almost wholly in the out-of-doors and told in a (to later listeners, at least) outdated theatrical dialect. Peters, on the other hand, selects a wider segment of the same historical event and emphasizes the prophetic-political implications in his free adaptation. He produces a political text rather than a working script. If both playwrights once activated limited audiences, they did demonstrate the popular uses of the theater as a locale for the reenactment of selective history—chosen for symbolic significance and direct visual and auditory appeal.

Sixties Americans, if curious to recover these little-known dramas, could at least do so by visiting a well-stocked library. Such would hardly be possible in the case of the third pre-sixties playwright attracted to Nat Turner as a stage hero. Thomas D. Pawley, like Edmonds, worked in academic settings and wrote for academic audiences. But his *Messiah*, written and first produced in July 1948, never was commercially published. It therefore contributes to the cultural dialogue in mid-twentieth-century America only as a doctoral thesis deposited in the general library of the University of Iowa. A few copies may be found in the libraries or drama departments of predominantly black institutions where its author went on to teach. *Messiah* enjoys one advantage, however, over all its dramatic counterparts save Lowell's "Benito Cereno": the bound copy of Pawley's play contains photographs of the original production in E. C. Mabie Theatre. Together with reviews of its initial performances in the *Daily Iowan*, these photographs document the visual appeal of this very free adaptation of Nat Turner's story. The most noteworthy feature of Pawley's version of the Southampton slave revolt is the leader's dual role as medicine man in an African tradition and a New Testament figure who repudiates his own violent opposition to oppression.

Edmonds, Peters, and Pawley are indeed obscure names in the history of the commercial theater in the United States. To sixties readers, as to Styron and his critics (including probably most of the ten black writers) their plays were neither known nor readily found in libraries or bookstores. Oddly, Pawley's *Messiah*, the least public of all, was at least once revived at a 1954 black college theater competition in Virginia—the sort of cultural transaction at which Edmonds's *Nat Turner* originally appeared and might conceivably have been revived. (Again, no record of such an event has come to my attention.) Like Panger's *Ol' Prophet Nat*, these plays are buried artifacts whose social significance can be assessed only by the cultural archeologist.

Theater at the Cultural Hub:
Martin Duberman and Robert Lowell

Records of the commercial theater, especially at its capital, New York City, provide a different and vastly richer historical resource. This fact condones the greater use, if not superior value, of these sources. Two sixties plays thus centrally located at the nexus of American cultural life are Martin Duberman's *In White America* and Robert Lowell's *The Old Glory*. Both authors were white, left-wing, and had broad cultural ties—Duberman's to Princeton University and the history profession; Lowell's to many academic, literary, and prize-giving institutions here and abroad. When Duberman the historian turned to writing for the theater, his imaginative treatment of the American past found audiences in Greenwich Village's Sheridan Square Playhouse. There *In White America* received wide attention from newspapers and cultural journals in the fall of 1963, shortly before the height of the civil rights conflicts and four years before Styron's novel made slave resistance a fashionable and compelling literary topic. *In White America* was published in January of 1964, intended to do for the public and the history profession what Styron was later to attempt for American literature: "My starting point was the wish to describe what it has been like to be a Negro in this country (to the extent that a white man can describe it). . . . Neither popular journalism nor professional history had made much effort to tell this story. . . . The revelations are painful, but they must be faced if the present is to be understood and the future made more tolerable."[22]

On behalf of black subjects and victims, then, Duberman addresses a largely but not exclusively white urban audience. Hence he assumes June Meyer's white intermediary role, as the preface's earnest tone and claims of authority both intimate.

> Negroes are themselves often unfamiliar with their history. The truth has not been easy to come by in a society dominated by whites, nor easy to digest; old wounds, old degradations, must in the name of self-respect, be avoided. Yet if there is much in this history to enrage or sadden the Negro, there is also much to make him proud: here is a people who maintained their humanity while

being treated inhumanly, who managed to endure as men while being defined as property.

I chose to tell this story on the stage and through historical documents, because I wanted to combine the evocative power of the spoken word with the confirming power of the historical fact. The spoken word is able to call forth the binding emotions of pity and sympathy. (i–ii)

Duberman, though less sensitive than some others about the touchy topics of white pity and sympathy, was sensitive to the conflicting claims of his double role. As historian he meant to treat black American history comprehensively, with careful respect for pertinent records. As dramatist, however, he claimed the right to select and use sources for particular artistic and emotional effects. The text of a play constructed largely if not exclusively from historical documents reflects these sometimes conflicting obligations. Of the book's 126 pages, over sixty are dedicated to the acting script, while over forty are given to historical paraphernalia—preface, notes, an appendix of sample documents, and an afterword entitled "History and Theatre." These supporting sections deliver readers of *In White America* an academic and didactic message sometimes at variance with the emotional intensity of the stage version.

Another conflict Duberman obliquely records is that between the historian who traditionally researches and writes alone and the playwright who shares his script with a team of collaborators—producer and director, cast members and technicians, songwriters and musicians. Both as performed in 1963 and as a 1964 transcription, *In White America* is a deceptively interracial transaction. Although the cast included blacks and whites and although the role of narrator was, by authorial instruction, shared alternately by all actors, key members of the rest of the theatrical team were predominantly white. For example, Oscar Brand, a white composer, was in charge of the music sung or played by black actors. From the playhouse seats, therefore, Duberman's reactivation looked more thoroughly integrated than it actually was.

A different contrast between appearance and actuality is articulated dramatically as the play opens. By way of a prologue, Duberman samples current social attitudes (specifically dated January 12, 1964), which the actors read or recite from current newspapers. These quotes juxtapose official Johnson Administration policy with its mildly integrationist ideology against unofficial white racism and black cynicism. Thus a particularly virulent outburst from a southern newspaper's letter to the editor—"The white people have shown remarkable restraint in not killing niggers wholesale"—is succeeded by a black actress singing "Oh, freedom" (20). These words are direct quotations from letters, editorials, and articles in *Time, Newsweek,* the *New York Times,* and the *Atlanta Constitution*. Thus, before being transported from a present place and moment back to an eighteenth-century slave ship, Duberman's audiences are sobered by the realization that virtually every word spoken has its verifiable source and contemporary resonance.

The Southampton slave revolt occupies a central spot in the first act's history of black America. But the spot is a small one inasmuch as two-and-a-half centuries of black American experience are touched upon in the play. So Nat Turner is bracketed by 1964 opinions of ordinary Americans and, at the close of act 1, an emotional moment from T. W. Higginson's diary of Civil War service in a black regiment. A slave insurrection is thus historically antecedent to contemporary racial attitudes but dramatically follows them and the singer's declaration: "And before I'll be a slave, / I'll be buried in my grave, / And go home to my lord / And be free" (20). Immediately preceding these two pages (perhaps five minutes of stage time) of Nat Turner's testimony is an exchange of letters between a runaway slave and his former mistress.

What follows is a very different slave response to degradation in form of a concise précis from Gray's *Confessions*. The recitation is introduced by the narrator's words: "*Some Negroes reacted to slavery not by fleeing but by rising in rebellion. In 1831, the slave Nat Turner, and his followers, turned on their masters in Southampton County, Virginia*" (35). Then, in four short paragraphs, a plausible and sympathetic synecdoche is recited, carrying the audience from Nat's childhood ("Being at play with other children, when three or four years old, I was telling them something, which my mother, overhearing, said had happened before I was born. . . . Others being called on, were greatly astonished and caused them to say, in my hearing, I surely would be a prophet"), to his adult role ("I obtained influence over the minds of my fellow-servants . . . but by the communion of the Spirit . . . they believed and said my wisdom came from God"), and as visionary ("About this time I had a vision—I saw white spirits and black spirits engaged in battle"). Then he speaks as avenger: "It was my object to carry terror and devastation wherever we went. We killed Mrs. Waller and ten children." Finally Nat is fugitive and captive: "Finding myself defeated . . . I gave up all hope for the present. . . . I am here loaded with chains, and willing to suffer the fate that awaits me" (35–36). Nat's speech is concluded by a black actor singing "Follow the Drinking Gourd." Later vignettes in the play also extend the intertwined themes of religion and revolt. Colonel Higginson's recollections of his devout black soldiers acquire a retrospective and prophetic edge when he remarks: "Their religion also gives them zeal, energy, daring. They could easily be made fanatics, if I chose; but I do not choose. Their whole mood is essentially Mohammedan, perhaps, in its strength and its weakness" (43). John Brown's speech to the court and Mrs. Chestnut's diary also carry Nat's message forward into other times and locales. Thus Turner's is a central presence and example in this pre-Reconstruction capsule history of black Americans.

Duberman's afterword to *In White America* defines docudrama as a bridge between history and drama. History's goal, he says, is to embrace *all* human behavior—to make us "aware of the range of human adaptability and purpose" (124). The contemporary American theater, on the other hand, in its preoccupations with irrationality, vice, and absurdity, often denies humans the powers of will and purposeful action: "Currently, historical study is fixated on past patterns and the theatre on present ones; neither is sufficiently concerned with the future. If the variety of past experience could be communicated with an immediacy drawn from the theatrical idiom, both history and drama might become vehicles for change rather than only the recorders, respectively, of past and present attitudes" (126). Negro history—and Nat Turner in particular—demand to be represented imaginatively to a public unfamiliar with its events and actors, who can thus be taught to "see that men (even if only *sometimes*) can give purpose and structure to their lives; can use the tensions of existence creatively, or at the worst, accept them with dignity" (126).

This upbeat didacticism underscores striking differences between Duberman and his more well-known contemporary, the poet Robert Lowell. Though *In White America* received critical kudos and enjoyed a respectable run, it did not match the reception, almost exactly a year later, on November 1, 1964, of *The Old Glory*. Lowell's play was hailed as a major cultural milestone. A highlight of the 1964–65 theatrical season, it won five Tonys, including one for best play. "The American drama has finally developed an important subject and an eloquent voice," declared drama critic and director Robert Brustein. "*The Old Glory* may well mark the beginning of a dramatic renaissance in America."[23]

The immediate impact of *The Old Glory* (at least on the New York intelligentsia) was the more remarkable because the play is historical in subject but quite unrealistic in its theatrical form. It resembles an opera or oratorio about obscure events whose current relevance is chiefly symbolic. Though the play echoes Duberman's in consisting heavily of deliberate recitative, Lowell's actors do not deliver selections from actual historical documents. There are no musical interpolations of spirituals. Instead, *The Old Glory* is a triptych of imaginative retellings of short fictions (each dealing with the American past) by Nathaniel Hawthorne and Herman Melville. Of the three adaptations, only "My Kinsman, Major Molineux" and "Benito Cereno" were actually performed, for the third treatment, of Hawthorne's "Endecott and the Red Cross," proved too static and talky for that season's playgoers.

Thus this dramatic history is twice filtered through literary imaginations. Lowell, in fact, is at times more committed to playing off his revered artistic ancestors than to reviving historical characters and actions for their own sake as uniquely significant occurrences. In the case of "Benito Cereno" Lowell does not even cite in his note on sources Captain Amasa Delano's *Narrative of Voyages and Travels* (1817), Melville's source for his novella of 1855.[24] Lowell was not ignorant of Delano's book, but was more concerned with mixing his own historical consciousness with Melville's as cointerpreter of the Yankee seaman's recollections. Few playgoers or readers would be familiar with both of Lowell's sources, yet few could miss the ironic interplay between the different aspects and eras of American history evoked on the decks of the *San Domingo*.

The play revisits Melville's pre–Civil War world of 1855 (the moment, we recall, of several other literary treatments of slave insurrections) largely by way of contrast with Lowell's world of 1964. The action of the play occurs during the historical moment already seen by Arna Bontemps as a turning point in American culture—the turn of the nineteenth century, the presidential contest between Jefferson and Adams, and Gabriel Prosser's plot. All three literary artists—Melville, Bontemps, and now Lowell—see this moment as a crucial intersection of politics, culture, and racial violence, with prophetic results for the American national character. The shifts in dates and locales among Delano, Melville, and Lowell are small but significant. Delano encountered the slave-trading vessel *Tryal* in February 1805. Melville moves the date back to 1799 and renames the Spanish ship the *San Dominick*, while Delano's ship, the *Perseverance*, becomes Melville's *Bachelor's Delight*. Lowell rechristens the two vessels *San Domingo* and the *President Adams* and changes the locale from Chile to the Caribbean. The action in his version takes place on July 4, 1800. In keeping with this heavy-handed symbolism, Lowell's Captain Delano is dressed in blue and white uniform, suggesting both George Washington and the United States Navy. His crew is also dressed in military garb, and, in the violent rescue of Don Benito Cereno from the clutches of his rebellious slaves, the American seamen mow down black men and women with muskets, bayonets attached. The playwright furthers the political allegory by introducing into the dialogue echoes of many other times, persons, and events. These include the American and French revolutions, Toussaint and Gabriel Prosser, the election of Jefferson, Civil War, and Emancipation. Caribbean history, gunboat diplomacy, and the contemporary civil rights struggle are still other political parallels proposed or hinted at. Lowell's cultural perspective also reaches into the future. Readers (if not 1964 playgoers) may note how neatly Lowell's mordant view of American violence anticipates the American military intervention of 1965 in the Dominican Republic and, somewhat later, the rhetoric (in the mouth of Babu, the red-clad leader of the rebellious slaves) of the Black Panthers.

The force of Lowell's sweeping reimagining of a maritime revolt (reminiscent for Melville's Americans of the *Amistad* mutiny of the 1830s) is to widen the gap between this and previous plays dealing with Nat Turner or other black rebels. Lowell's dramatic devices drawn from musical theater and political cartoons (such as his substitution of unrhymed poetic speech for the original Delano's homely prose and Melville's intricately meditative language) separate his "Benito Cereno" from the more pedestrian, realistic plays of Edmonds, Peters, Pawley, and Duberman. Despite differences, however, all five plays are bound by a common fascination with slave uprisings and the earnest desire of their authors to bring history and theater together as dynamic public transactions.

One way to see divergence and common commitment is to consider how and why this particular story of a slave insurrection led Lowell to choose drama, and especially poetic drama, as his mode of re-creation. Shortly before commencing *The Old Glory*, Lowell held a fellowship as poet-librettist with the Metropolitan and New York City operas. Lowell often remarked that much of his verse is "imitation" wherein the reader is invited, in the author's words, to hear "one voice running through many personalities, contrasts, and repetitions."[25] "Benito Cereno" is such an imitation; the modern poet's voice runs as undertone to Melville's, recapturing essential qualities of the original and yet saying something new.

Looking back on "Benito Cereno" from the viewpoint (only three or four years later) of the Nat Turner controversy, as many sixties Americans could, other comparisons come to mind; such as one between Lowell and Styron. Both the New England poet and the southern novelist have a nose for the obscure but revealing episode from history. Each retells a violent event with a mixture of respect and disregard for previous versions. Both transform straightforward prose narratives by the amateur authors Delano and Gray into highly literary, often deliberately "unrealistic," accounts. Although the central agent of each action is a black slave, these writers shift focus (sometimes subtly, often nakedly) toward the whites involved in each episode. In the process, each retelling introduces sexual language and motivations into the psychodrama of a slave revolt. Lowell, like Styron (and indeed Melville), seems to be deeply ambiguous about the violence he evokes with such liberal indignation. Finally, both writers are wedded to mystery and mystification as essential truths that complicate (and undercut) the political messages their respective stories generate in the minds and circumstance of the sixties.

Lowell's decision to turn a leisurely paced eighty-page novella into a shorter one-act play was also a response to Melville's own cues. When Melville's Amasa Delano boards the *San Dominick*, he reflects that the scene "seems unreal; these strange costumes, gestures, and faces, but a shadowy tableau just emerged from the deep, which directly must receive back what it gave" (50). The sense of life as "shadowy tableau"—

triggered by the slaves' plot to appear to be obeying their captain, Don Benito Cereno, who, all the while, is a captive held at hidden knifepoint—provides the key to Lowell's reinscription. In keeping with the formal poetic speech he gives the Latin American, North American, and African characters, Lowell creates actual tableaux which are enacted on the ship's deck by the cunning slaves. Their aim is to bewilder (and inform) the naïf Yankee about the perplexing behavior of his host and crew of the crippled ship. Other actions during the day likewise function as theatrical performances. Thus during his daily shaving ceremony at the hands of Babu, the slaves' leader, Don Benito wears a "theatrical aspect . . . in his harlequin ensign" (87). These effects of theatrical enchantment or charade are crucial to Melville's story, describing as they do not only atmosphere but the shape of action, the revelation (or masking) of character, and ultimately the meaning of experience itself. Everything in Melville's prose sea-world is "dreamy inquietude" as the American visitor is entertained and fooled by the slaves who have, in fact, killed most of the white crew and taken possession of the ship. Lowell was inspired to adapt "Benito Cereno" not only by its potent theme but also because he saw that a disquieting tone and ambiguous atmosphere could be effectively translated into a modern parable of racial rage and fear.

There is no doubt that "Benito Cereno," as the climactic part of Lowell's play, closes with a brutal directness more reminiscent of Juvenal or Amiri Baraka than Melville or Amasa Delano. The twentieth-century captain, having finally seen through the charade and rescued Don Benito, advances upon Babu who has surrendered. The white American empties six quite anachronistic pistol shots into the defenseless slave's body. This from the bluff seaman in whose "enduring innocence" many American readers of Melville have been taught to believe.[26] The "rockslide force" of such scenes go far toward stripping innocence wholesale from the American past by suggesting parallels with present-day racial violence. Significantly, stage violence here is most visibly white upon black, with the bloody reality of black rebellion lurking in the mysteries of the ship's and the play's past. When the slaves' plot to capture Captain Delano and force him to sail the *San Domingo* to Africa is unmasked, one grisly revelation is the ship's figurehead mysteriously shrouded in canvas. When the cover is removed, the ship's patron saint proves to be the bone-white skeleton of Don Aranda, the slaves' owner. When out of temper, he "used to snap pieces of flesh off us," Babu explains, adding "Now I hold the whip" (186).

Babu's insurrection, like Nat Turner's, proves short-lived, lasting on stage but one slowly passing day. Moreover, the brutal realities of oppression and violence are both dramatically expressed and channeled formally through poetic diction and imagery. Lowell's language constitutes through its distinctive rhythms and economy a medium at once Melvillean and modern. In its own way, the play's idiom is as distinctly literary and "white" as the meditative voice of Styron's Nat. Individual differences in white and black speech are subsumed under cultural formalities of opera and oratorio. A distinctly modern combination of soliloquy and dialogue results. This is seen and heard, for example, in Don Benito's recollection of a recent nightmare:

> I was taking my siesta,
> I dreamed I was a boy back in Lima,
> I was with my brothers and sisters,
> and we were dressed for the festival of Corpus Christi
> like people at our Bourbon Court.
> We were simple children, but something went wrong;
> little black men came on us with beetle backs.
> They had caterpillar heads and munched away on our fine clothes.
> They made us lick their horned and varnished insect legs.
> Our faces turned brown from their spit,
> We looked like bugs, but nothing could save our lives! (162)

Cereno's Kafkaesque insect imagery appears earlier in *The Old Glory* and now returns to epitomize the mysterious situation aboard the *San Domingo*. As the speaker contrasts the innocence of his Spanish Catholic childhood with Delano's memories of a Yankee youth on Duxbury beach, each dreamy detail furthers the play's mood and dramatic irony. Yet Captain Delano completely misses the message the sickly Spaniard is sending; indeed, its full meaning is hidden from Don Benito himself. The comprehending consciousness clearly is Lowell's, whose poetic voice, avoiding extremes of both elegance and flat naturalism, communicates to his audience the thematic shape of the entire action in this single part. Both play and dream begin in innocence and stasis and modulate through mystery and black animal-imaged defilement to arrive suddenly at violent death. The poetic technique of synecdoche tightens rather than distracts from the dramatic form.

These literary and cultural devices and usages are manifestly European, a fact that suggests another parallel with Styron. Three cultures—New Spain, New England, and Africa—are locked together through their common legacy of slavery. But the powers of speech, costume, cultural forms, and habits of thought are formidable forces for Babu and the other Africans to overcome. They must, like most colonials, manipulate the oppressive European words and ways in order to sustain the energy and rage of their insurrection. Thus, Babu, the slave, mimics the role of a Spanish valet as he counsels Don Benito to sit quietly for the shaving ceremony:

> BABU: You mustn't shake so, Master.
> Look, Don Amasa, Master always shakes when I shave him,
> though he is braver than a lion and stronger than a
> castle.
> Master knows that Babu has never yet drawn blood.
> I may, though, sometime, if he shakes so much.
> Now, master!
> Come, Don Amasa, talk to Master about the gales and
> calms,
> he'll answer and forget to shake. (165)

Babu's razor and wordplay mock the waning powers of Spain, "this absentee empire" (134). Its demise is prophesied through threatening references to fear, inertia, blood, and the besmirched castle-and-lion flag of Spain, which is here used as Babu's barber towel. With similar irony, the tableaux presented for Captain Delano's entertainment during his tedious hours on board exhibit the racial exploitation on which Spain's three-hundred-year rule has been based. Each of these brief plays-within-the-play has its source in Melville yet each bears a modern meaning as well. The not-so-secret significance of each tableau is slavery itself, seen most vividly under the heading of miscegenation. Slavery's saffron hue is literally and symbolically everywhere present on the *San Domingo:* in the Spanish flag and on the cheeks of Francesco, the mulatto waiter at Don Benito's table who is "as yellow as a goldenrod" (174). In the living color of sexual exploitation he manifests the linked economic and sexual dynamics of slavery. These meanings are extended historically through the images of Don Benito's yellow aristocratic hands, Delano's gift of yellow pumpkins, the stately African chieftain Atufal's golden ear-wedges, and the rising and setting sun, all of which hint at the cursed legacy of greed for gold that America was inheriting in 1800 from Spain's crumbling empire. History's bequest is also dramatized in the tableaux by the white doll. This doll is first dipped in tar, then cuddled by a black Virgin Mary while a white Saint Joseph looks uncomfortably on. Thus slavery is simultaneously a black, yellow, and white plague linked to royalty, economic exploitation, and Christianity. Yet Delano's northern racist blinders prevent him from even imagining Babu's viewpoint on these aspects of the dominant culture:

> I don't know how I'll explain this pomp
> and squalor to my own comfortable family of a crew.
> Even shaving here is like a High Mass.
> There's something in a Negro, something
> that makes him fit to have around your person.
> His comb and brush are castanets.
> What tact Babu had!
> What noiseless, gliding briskness! (167)

Amasa Delano in his sixties reincarnation, though echoing words and whole phrases from his Melvillean ancestor, is the most altered and deceptive of Lowell's cast of characters. All the actors are wearing masks, but Delano's amused, condescending tolerance masks only superficially his basic racism. His untested prejudices about the primitive blacks insure the success of Babu's impersonation of the humble, cheerful servant. But the depths of Delano's cynical and dangerous character are revealed well before the climax in remarks to Don Benito: "Sometimes I think we overdo our talk of freedom"; "If you looked into our hearts, we all want slaves" (177). When he adds, "This old world needs new blood and Yankee gunnery to hold it up" (178), Delano confirms his underlying white Eurocentric belief in "civilized" law and order. This very modern figure differs markedly from the bluff, good-hearted optimist of Melville's story; indeed, he is in some respects more reminiscent of the autobiographical self of the *Narrative of Voyages and Travels*. The original captain, writing in 1817, presents himself as a tough disciplinarian and a ready flogger of his motley crew. In the original event, he offered Benito help but expected to be well compensated for his succor, for he fancied himself a canny businessman, one well capable of violence. Melville plays down this sinister side of the historical Delano's character, as he also ignores some brutal facts about Don Benito as recorded in the *Narrative*. Don Benito, too, is sacrificed to the modern poet's preoccupation with the confrontation between the white Yankees and the African slaves.

In the process of refocusing Melville's story, therefore, Lowell reverses the emphasis Melville gave to this historical event as a mythic and psychological study of American innocence, European morbidity, and African perfidy. Lowell, instead, moves in the opposite direction, away from mythic suggestion toward ideological assertion. The play's finale vividly articulates this simplified but dramatically chilling vision of history. After the American seamen have rescued the whites with musket fire and bayonets, an unwounded defiant Babu shouts:

> I freed my people from their Egyptian bondage.
> The heartless Spaniards slaved for me like slaves.
> (BABU *steps back, and quickly picks up a crown from the litter*)
> This is my crown.
> (*Puts crown on his head. He snatches* BENITO's *rattan cane*)
> This is my rod.
> (*Picks up silver ball . . .*)
> This is the arm of the angry God.
> (*Smashes the ball*)
> PERKINS: Let him surrender. Let him surrender.
> We want to save someone.
> BENITO: My God how little these people understand!
> BABU: (*Holding a white handkerchief and raising both hands*)
> Yankee master understand me. The future is with us.
> DELANO: (*Raising his pistol*)
> This is your future.
> (BABU *falls and lies still.* DELANO *pauses, then slowly empties the five remaining barrels of his pistol into the body. Lights dim.*)
> CURTAIN (193–94)

The voice of John Perkins urging surrender (and by implication mercy or at least understanding) is that of the *President Adams*'s bosun. He is a young, puritanically moral relative of Captain Delano. No such figure exists in Melville's novella. His creation here personifies Lowell's sense of an abiding split in the American national character. Although the promise of American democracy was once brotherhood, its actual fulfillment in history has too often been genocide. More cynically, the audience can view Perkins as also wearing a mask. His boyish, well-meaning sixties altruism will inevitably be lost; as he grows older this green Yankee liberal may move closer in outlook to his urbane, racist relative. If John Perkins represents Lowell's bow to Melville's original man of obtuse good will, Amasa Delano as his own captain expresses the grimmer realities of American experience that Melville could not have anticipated in 1855. Lowell's recognition of American history as simultaneously innocent promise and corrupt fulfillment is embodied in the two Yankee characters he has put in the place of Melville's one.

As these similarities and divergences among three historical/fictional/theatrical narratives imply, Robert Lowell was as committed in 1964 to the white cultural perspectives on this slave revolt as were his nineteenth-century predecessors. In all three versions, the black slaves are represented as the primitive and dangerous Other. Though Babu, Atufal, Francesco and the others mount and maintain, until the last violent moment, an imaginative charade, they are, in fact, trapped from the beginning in a Euro-American work of art. Their voices—even Babu's—are subordinated to those of the whites. Despite Lowell's fiercely liberal politics (a stance older and more radical than Styron's), his drama succeeds in containing black violence as tightly as do the language and cultural allegiances of *The Confessions of Nat Turner*. Following Melville's example, Lowell has chosen from historical sources a violent event that can be dramatized ultimately as black failure. As historical literature it is titillating but not truly threatening. As with Styron's readers, the audiences of *The Old Glory* are given a sharper realization of the justice of the black cause but left with secret or unacknowledged relief at the continued frustration of that threat. Blacks are here safely contained within the age-old civilization-primitivism conception.

One explanation and illustration of this conclusion is that the American Place Theatre production of "Benito Cereno" was dominated by white artists and technicians. Besides Lowell himself, the chief architect of the play's success was Jonathan Miller, the brilliant young British director. In his director's note to the Noonday edition of *The Old Glory*, Miller emphasizes the weight of white European conventions and effects: "As regards staging and diction, it seemed to me that Lowell had written an opera without music and the four principal actors were directed to move and speak as if they are soloists in an oratorio and they should be placed on the stage as if they were delivering Mozartian quartets and duets—very formal with no restless modern naturalism" (xviii). Miller conceived of this story of a slave revolt as "a new Tempest with the Spanish captain playing a sort of drugged Prospero held captive by his Negro Babu. . . . Everything in this production must be bent towards creating this sense of lethargy. The Negroes need only to be seen on stage in ones and twos, mending nets and so on, unless otherwise indicated. Then from time to time they should all hum on one note in unison so as to create a vague off stage murmur like hives on a summer day. The entertainment should be baroque and courtly with no concession made to modern nightclub negritude" (xviii).

The ideological implications of these directions and assumptions are clarified when reread from the perspective of the subsequent controversy. The defusing of black violence by encasement in European cultural forms extends even to the sound effects of "Benito Cereno." The black actors all humming like bees in a hive represent cultural domination. The implication of Miller's metaphor is that blacks, far from being wasps or killer bees, are honey-children. Perhaps, however, their offstage murmurs signal the lull before the storm, as is suggested by Miller's final comment on the play's staging. "When final violence comes," he concludes, "it should puncture the poisoned atmosphere which ought to have been slowly and lingeringly inflated throughout the evening." Whether this poisoned air is the miasma of black or white violence remains unclear, even after the last stage effect is produced. "Finally, when everything is still on the deck, Babu dead, and Delano upright amongst the bloody debris, a Negro girl should come on stage slowly, pause and give a long, awkward ghastly scream—like a wounded albatross" (xviii–xix).

Poetry as Cultural Politics: Ophelia Robinson, Sterling Brown, Robert E. Hayden, Alvin Aubert

Robert Lowell's "Benito Cereno" stands out in the cultural history of the 1960s as a sui generis artifact at once historical in subject, poetic in language, and operatic in form. Of the three features of Lowell's achievement, verse places him almost in a class by himself within the larger literary community, for he was the sole white artist to engage poetry with history and contemporary social issues through the subject of slave insurrections. There was no past tradition of white poets exploring this subject. As already noted, when *The Nation* reviewed Styron's novel, it published as counterpoint to the reviews of O'Connell and Aptheker a ghetto lyric by the black poet Jay Wright. Few available alternatives addressed Nat Turner and his brethren. Among those poets who did, the most prominent were Sterling A. Brown and Robert E. Hayden, each of whom published meditations on slave history before the sixties controversy erupted. Like Bontemps's *Black Thunder*, Brown's "Remembering Nat Turner" is a product of thirties' political and cultural consciousness. Hayden's "The Ballad of Nat Turner" was written "several years before Styron's book appeared," and largely reflects the poet's pre-sixties concerns and techniques.[27] Both lyrics, along with a handful of others (one of which appears as an epigraph to this book), reappeared in anthologies and collections as part of the literary ferment of the late sixties.

Though theirs were never prominent voices like those of the novelists or playwrights, the presence of black poets in the cultural dialogue and debates of 1967–68 and after is significant for several reasons. Brown, Hayden, and their less familiar fellow poets illustrate how lyric narrative verse exploits historical themes and sources in ways distinct from novels and plays. Black poets, too, engaged vigorously in cultural transactions with, and on behalf of, their audiences. Hence we need now to ask what cultural work American (and, in this instance, chiefly black) poetry did for various publics—fellow artists and the intelligentsia, readers of magazines and books, students in schools and colleges, and general audiences on various ritual occasions—during these years.

As poetry, the renewed literary life of Nat Turner generated passions equivalent or even stronger than those triggered in prose, unsurprising inasmuch as poetry traditionally is understood as a specialized medium for communicating emotional valuations of central human concepts and cultural values. Patterns of feelings more than extended formal thought distinguish lyric poetry in its social and ideological transactions. This was especially true of black poets in the sixties. One representative expression of this precept is Walter Lowenfels's acerbic 1970 article "The White Literary Syndicate," which did for poetry what Addison Gayle's *Amistad* essay of the same year, "Cultural Hegemony: The Southern White Writer and American Letters," did for literary politics in general.[28] Both critics bitterly attack the combination of white domination and indifference manifested in contemporary cultural and literary life. "The white poetry scene in the United States is in control of a literary syndicate," Lowenfels declares. "It is divided up into different families, each of which has its favorite critics and anthologists, all of whom exclude nonwhite poets" (8). He goes on to link this "poetry junta" with major opinion-molding publications such as the *New York Times, New York Herald Tribune, Saturday Review,* and publishers of American literature anthologies including the sarcastically retitled "Oxford Book of (White) American Verse" (9).

Typical proponents of establishment attitudes toward black poets were Louis Simpson and Seldon Rodman, both practicing poets as well as influential reviewers and editors. Simpson's basic attitude is quoted by Lowenfels from the *New York Herald Tribune:* "I am not sure it is possible for a Negro to write well without us (white people) aware he is a negro; on the other hand, if being a negro is the only subject, the writing is not important" (8). Lowenfels also cites Rodman who, writing in the *New York Times* on November 9, 1969, was more specific though no less patronizing: "Until recently there hasn't been any Afro-American verse that was more than that—verse. When I was editing anthologies in 1938, and again in 1946, I remember going through the complete works of Countee Cullen, Claude McKay, Langston Hughes, and the others, hoping desperately to find a *poem*, and falling back reluctantly on the spirituals and the blues" (8). Such cultural myopia was denounced by June Meyer Jordan, whose opinions on the subject of white intermediaries we have already encountered in *The Nation*. Her unpublished letter to the *Times* pointed out that Rodman's search for a poem by "real poets" overlooked the works of Jean Toomer, Margaret Walker, Sterling A. Brown, Melvin Tolson, Gwendolyn Brooks, Paul Vesey, and Robert Hayden. Later she wrote of "the *difficult* miracle of Black poetry in America. . . . we are frequently dismissed as 'political' or 'topical' or 'sloganeering' and 'crude' and 'insignificant' because, like Phillis Wheatley, we have persisted for freedom."[29]

Another manifestation of ignorance and prejudice on the part of influential white junta members is cited by Lowenfels from the *Saturday Review*, whose poetry editor asserted that "most of the black poets I have read are full of enormous intensity and huge assertion but fail to awaken the full resources of language. . . . It is conceivable that the force of their conviction and energy could create a new school of poetry. I cannot believe however that school will be worth anything until the black poets care as much for the language as they do for their angry energy" (8–9). Caring for "the language" meant explicitly working within "the great tradition of poetry in English" (8)—clearly that of Euro-Americans. Devotion to this tradition evidently outweighed other modes of expressing anger and energy along with specifically political and racial subjects.

Black American poets were not alone in being chastized with such ethnocentric assumptions about poetry, passion, and politics. Hispanic and Native American poets are similarly ignored or chided, as are various groups of radical white poets. Lowenfels cites several prominent black poets who denounce such domination, including Gwendolyn Brooks, Don L. Lee (soon to become Haki Madhubuti), and Nikki Giovanni. To the familiar refrain of "Isn't all poetry just poetry?" Brooks rejoined that black poetry is of necessity different: "The fact that a poet is black means that his life, his history and the histories of his ancestors have been different from the histories of Chinese and Japanese poets, Eskimo poets, Indian poets, Irish poets. The juice from tomatoes is not called merely *juice*. It is called *tomato juice*" (9). In keeping with his radical politics, Lee drew the cultural lines even more sharply by insisting that poetic language is indeed crucial.

> Black poetry in its purest form is diametrically opposed to white poetry. Whereas, Black poets deal in the concrete rather than the abstract (concrete: art for people's sake; Black language or Afro American language in contrast to standard English, etc.) Black poetry moves to define & legitimize Black people's reality (*that* which is real to us). Those in power (the unpeople) control and legitimize the negroes' (the real people's) reality out of that which they, the unpeople, consider real. . . . Black poetry will move to expose & wipe out that which is not necessary for our existence as a people. (9)

Nikki Giovanni echoes Lee's militant definition of the black poet's social role in her oft-quoted slogan: "There is no difference between the warrior, the poet, and the people" (9).

For all black texts treating Nat Turner as real history, the pertinent questions again involve culture and social function: who writes to legitimize which aspects of black historical experience for which audiences? The first impression emerging from such interrogation is that none of the poets Lowenfels quotes had addressed Nat Turner in his or her poetry. This is, of course, no reflection on any poet; Nat Turner as subject is no litmus test for any writer examining the black American past. As it turned out, those who wrote about slave rebels were few and consisted chiefly of amateur poets writing for specific community occasions or else older recognized poets not specifically identified with the black nationalist movement. (Alvin Aubert is an exception to this generalization.)

To begin with verses used didactically to mold the minds of American schoolchildren, the little-known name of Ophelia Robinson surfaces in an anthology as early as 1950. Robinson, a midwestern schoolteacher, was hailed by the editor as a true pioneer. "She is the first Negro in America to write an epic poem," the editor asserted. "Her 'Nat Turner' is a poem of forty pages with a sustained dignified style."[30] As evidence, the prologue to this epic was reprinted. From this excerpt it is clear that Robinson's artistic debts are to the language and traditional forms of white poetry of the nineteenth century, most particularly to Longfellow.

> I shall tell you how Nathaniel
> How the sage, devout, young prophet
> Gave his life to save his people
> Gave to them his time, his talents,
> Gave to them his youth, his courage
> Gave his all for love of freedom
> That his people should not suffer,
> Should not wear the yoke of bondage.
>
> Even as the Hebrew Children
> Found a saviour in their Moses;
> Even as the ancient Grecians
> Found a hero in Achilles;

> As the brave ill-fated Trojans
> Placed their hope, their faith in Hector;
> As the Indians famine ridden
> Looked for aid to Hiawatha;
> So did God's most swarthy Children
> Find their saviour, this Nathaniel,
> Trust in him for strength and courage,
> Foresight, faith, and fearless action.
> And Nathaniel gave them gladly,
> Never for one moment failed them.

Whether black fourth-graders in Saint Louis were expected to memorize the remaining pages of Robinson's "Nat Turner" is unlikely, but the social circumstances of reading aloud in group or individual recitation are evident. The cultural values these lines were intended to inculcate are more significant than issues of appropriate diction, imagery, or meter. Before the advent of black studies, such lyrics—together, perhaps, with appropriate readings from histories by George Washington Williams and Carter G. Woodson—were probably used in many segregated classrooms. Ophelia Robinson thus stands for two or three generations of twentieth-century black schoolteachers who strove to equip their charges with a usable literature of cultural heroes equivalent to the whites' Miles Standish and Paul Revere.

Performance rather than private reading of texts frequently characterizes the popular domain of poetry in America, and this must have been just as true of black poets and their sixties audiences as of white writers like Allen Ginsberg. Nikki Giovanni's rhetorical alliance of the warrior, poet, and people points directly toward public occasions such as rallies and demonstrations, sit-ins and teach-ins as well as academic lectures and evening readings. In such settings black poets (sometimes including politicians like Julian Bond) read and chanted their verse to educate and arouse listeners. How often older, less militant poets like Brown and Hayden participated in such sixties "happenings" is a matter even biographers and newspaper reporters may find difficult to answer. What is easier to document are the occasional appearances of Nat Turner in magazines, anthologies, and volumes of verse.

In the case of Sterling Brown's "Remembering Nat Turner," these venues had long been open. The poem was first published in 1939 in

Crisis magazine, a key location for reaching chiefly activist though not particularly literary audiences of middle-class blacks and liberal whites who supported the NAACP.[31] However, Brown's tribute contains some internal clues to an earlier public existence. In the opening lines the narrator reminds readers of Turner's "angry stab for freedom a hundred years ago" (199). This may indicate that the poem was originally written and perhaps read as a centennial song of 1931 or shortly after. Whether literally true or not, "Remembering Nat Turner" uses the centennial as an occasion for recasting the man and event in contemporary terms.

In each reactivation since then, "Remembering Nat Turner" evokes a situation already familiar to us—the speaker's recent visit to Southampton County. Like Styron three decades later, Brown's poetic persona seeks Nat Turner's contemporary existence in the minds and memories of county residents. Inevitably, in retrospect, parallels and contrasts between the black poet and the younger white novelist suggest themselves. One of the most obvious is a shared feel for the particular and symbolic resonances of the southern landscape of woods, swamp, river, sunset, and moonlight. Brown, like Styron later, carefully connects scenery to history.

> A watery moon was high in the cloud-filled heavens,
> The same moon he dreaded a hundred years ago.
> The tree they hanged Nat on is long gone to ashes,
> The trees he dodged behind have rotted in the swamps. (200)

The speaker recalls circling the countryside on an excursion similar in intent and itinerary to Styron's, though one distinctly not taken in a white sheriff's squad car. The "we" of Brown's meditation identifies neither black nor white but establishes a collective experience very different from Styron's self-absorbed viewpoint. The "we" may incorporate "RCL" to whom the poem is dedicated. If so, a pair of old(?) friends are there to test black and white familiarity with their own past. At Cross Keys, "where the march began" (199), the blacks interrogated can summon only the faintest of recollections. One remarks,

> The old folks who coulda told is all dead an' gone.
> I heard something, sometime; I doan jist remember what.
> 'Pears lak I heard that name somewheres or other.
> So he fought to be free. Well. You doan say. (199)

White residents retain no clearer memories, although their historical information is richly embroidered with fantasy and unrelated facts.

> An old white woman recalls exactly
> How Nat crept down the steps, axe in hand,
> After murdering a woman and child in bed,
> "Right in this here house at the head of these stairs."
> (In a house built long after Nat was dead.)
> She pointed to a brick store where Nat was captured,
> (Nat was taken in a swamp, three miles away.)
> With his men around him, shooting from the windows
> (She was thinking of Harper's Ferry and old John Brown). (199)

Brown's irony sharpens as the old woman derides her interlocutors' interest in "an old nigger fool":

> Ain't no slavery no more, things is going all right,
> Pervided thar's a good goober market this year.
> We had a sign post here with printing on it,
> But it rotted in the hole, and thar it lays,
> And the nigger tenants split the marker for kindling.
> Things is right, now, ain't no trouble with the niggers.
> Why they make this big to-do over Nat? (199)

As the day comes to a close, the poetic narrator contrasts Southampton's rural quiet and ignorance with "The bus from Miami . . . heavy tires snarling on the pavement"; modern noise drowns out the frogs piping in the marsh. The lyric closes, conventionally enough, with a meditation on past and present.

> As we came back the way that Nat led his army,
> Down from Cross Keys, down to Jerusalem,
> We wondered if his troubled spirit still roamed the Nottaway,
> Or if it fled with the cock-crow at daylight,
> Or lay at peace with the bones in Jerusalem,
> Its restlessness stifled by Southampton clay.
> We remembered the poster rotted through and falling
> The marker split for kindling a kitchen fire. (200)

Whether reembedded in fifties, sixties, or early eighties contexts, Brown's modest meditation of the thirties concentrates within fifty-four lines little emotional or ideological bite. The retrospective imagination here at work accumulates relatively few resonances for future retellings. The implied reader of whatever era or outlook is invited to see a distinct rural setting and share a limited range of ideas and feelings about this hazy past. The "we" who take the county's historical temperature find no fever of memory there. The "bloody sunset" in the opening portends a passion and bloodshed that leads only to "watery moonlight" and yellow lights at cabin windows. The violence lurking in such collective memories is perhaps hinted at in images of heat and color, but the poem skirts the dangerous realities of bloodshed, rage, and religious fervor. What remains at the end are the kitchen fires kindled from the historical marker, predecessor of the metal sign Styron apparently saw some three decades later. Such reverberations are, of course, unintended, yet Brown's poetic language continues to generate new meanings in subsequent rereadings. In this intertextual context, we note that Brown avoids self-conscious ruminations that Styron's essay and novel employ to introduce complexities in Nat Turner's historical character. Indeed, "Remembering Nat Turner" is notable for largely avoiding the man himself. The rebel leader is present chiefly as an absence and the violence of his history is substantially defused by an old white woman's confused fantasies. What remains is a "troubled spirit" (of revolt? of remorse?) whose restlessness but not righteous fire lies stifled in Southampton clay. Little ideological ammunition for latter-day activists is stored in such a lyric, which may explain why Ernest Kaiser forgot to mention it in his list of literature about slavery.

Sterling Brown is a major black poet of this century and, though inadequately exploiting all possibilities of this subject, has written other, more powerful lyrics about history and slavery. In his *Collected Poems*, for example, the reader can set beside "Remembering Nat Turner" a dozen or more poems on historical subjects. In "Legend" and "Bitter Fruit of the Tree" he recaptures scathing parallels between black heroes and black Judases. One pairing is an old black in slavery faithfully serving his master while his rebellious descendant cries "I wish you both in hell / Your fine day is over."[32] In "Memo for the Race Orators," the poet's anger at black history's records of "the traitor, the spy, the coward, the renegade" pours out freely:

> When Gabriel led his thousand on Richmond
> Armed with clubs and scythe-swords fashioned in spare time,

> Down on the well-stocked powder-house and arsenal,
> Remember Tom and Pharoah, who blurted the news
> To Mister Mosby, and sought as reward
> What Gabriel wanted to fight and die for.
>
> . . . .
>
> Put this man where he belongs
> In your corridor of history
> Put this rat in the hold
> Of your ship of progress . . . [33]

Brown's successor, Robert E. Hayden, was on occasion no less restrained yet at other times just as vehement. He, too, often incurred the ire of radical younger blacks for refusing to speak with unequivocal voice in support of black nationalism. Nevertheless, accusations of ideological and cultural timidity do not square with Vincent Harding's praise in *Ten Black Writers Respond* of "Robert Hayden's marvelous poem about Nat Turner." In retrospect, "The Ballad of Nat Turner" is indeed a powerful lyric, the richest of historical meditations in verse on this theme. Written about 1963, the ballad derives much of its passion and precision from Hayden's familiarity with Gray's *Confessions of Nat Turner* and also from his determination as poet to delve deeper into the prophet's mind than the white lawyer's pseudo-biography. "As I studied accounts of the rebellion," he said later, "what interested me was not the bloodshed but Nat Turner himself, his characteristics, his personality."[34] Hayden's poetic imagination, like Styron's as a novelist, dictated the point of view and focus of his poem. "I let my imagination have full play over the facts I gathered," he explained. "In the ballad I imagine him talking to his followers, preparatory to the revolt."[35] Though accounting for the first-person narrative voice, this comment fails to explain the formality of the traditional four-line stanza or the oracular, allusive diction whose literariness may remind readers of Styron's very literate narrator. Hayden's poetic imitation (to borrow Lowell's usage) mixes African, biblical, and Miltonic images and rhythms as they might have been in the historical figure's mind. The result is a poetic confession in sixty-eight lines.[36]

> Then fled, O brethren, the wicked juba
> and wandered wandered far

> from curfew joys in the Dismal's night.
>   Fool of Saint Elmo's fire.
>
> In scary night I wandered, praying,
>   Lord God my harshener,
> speak to me now or let me die;
>   speak, Lord, to this mourner. (8)

The first strand of imagery evokes an African presence in Ibo warriors hanging "shadowless" in "livid trees,"

> Their belltongue bodies dead, their eyes
>   alive with the anger deep
> in my own heart. Is this the sign,
>   the sign forepromised me? (16)

This is succeeded by a Miltonic description (one closely based on Gray) of the airy battle between black and white angels.

> The fearful splendor of the warring.
>   Hide me, I cried to rock and bramble
> Hide me, the rock, the bramble cried . . .
>   How tell you of that holy battle?
>
> The shock of wing on wing and sword
>   on sword was the tumult of
> a taken city burning, I cannot
>   say how long they strove. (40)

This recalls a dreamlike projection of the preacher's unconsciousness:

> And wild things gasped and scuffled in
>   the night; seething shapes
> of evil frolicked upon the air.
>   I reeled with fear, I prayed. (24)

Each strand contributes lines and colors to Hayden's picture of a visionary man and moment. His Nat Turner, far from experiencing alienation from God, praises Jehovah who hones and harshens the prophet's consciousness during a decisive anticipatory event in his life. At the close, the preacher awakens "free and purified."

>   ... I rose and prayed
>   and returned after a time
>   to the blazing fields, the humbleness.
>   And bided my time. (68)

   Though the point is not specifically underscored, Hayden's poetic retelling may be his version of the account in Gray's *Confessions* of the time Turner once ran away for thirty days, then voluntarily returned to plan the revolt. Whatever the reference point, this dramatic and spiritual climax occurs, after the opening emotions of anger and fear have worked upon him, at the dazzling sight of angelic warfare, a scene bathed in "sudden brightness . . . so bright that it was darkness." Both the preacher and the animals of the swamp

>   ... were held like creatures fixed
>   in flaming, in fiery amber.
>   But I saw I saw oh many of
>   those mighty beings waver
>
>   Waver and fall, go streaking down
>   into swamp water . . .
>   . . . .
>   Then that massive light
>   began a-folding slowly in
>   upon itself, and I (54)
>
>   Beheld the conqueror faces and, lo,
>   they were like mine, I saw
>   they were like mine and in joy and terror
>   wept, praising, praising Jehovah. (60)

   No suggestion of sympathy or love binds this awestruck prophet to his Old Testament God. Still less does purification in the wilderness involve expiating sexual sins or shameful attachments to white people (who are, in fact, never mentioned—even the white angels on the Miltonic battlefield have hidden faces). The only common ground with Styron, then, lies in the two writers' penetration inside this prophet's mysterious mind. Except for oblique references to "blazing fields" and "humbleness," slavery is neither mentioned nor its evils dramatized. The only trace of white brutality are the imagined bodies of Ibo warriors hanging in the trees of his post-Edenic New World. Thus all social and historical details of the actual event (as recorded in the 1831 *Confessions*, that is) are treated with extreme indirection. Unlike Brown's retrospective meditation, this dramatic reactivation of a key moment in the revolt consists of poetic imaginings and symbolic suggestions.

Hayden's economy of reference to a real world in "The Ballad of Nat Turner" does not mean this poet was either ignorant of or oblivious to historical circumstance. In *The Poet and His Art, How I Write*, Hayden justifies a psychological focus in terms strikingly similar to Styron's. Of Nat Turner he remarks: "He was a quiet, deeply religious man—a preacher, in fact—a strange, lonely 'other-worldly' man. He brooded, he kept away from others. . . . I read somewhere that he was never known to smile, never laughed."[37] Moreover, like Styron, Hayden detects a puritanical strain, though this entails none of the sexual repressions or fantasies of Styron's Nat. Since such evidence was lacking in his sources, the poet apparently felt unconstrained to invent a sexual history for his ascetic protagonist. "You have to do your homework," he told an interviewer, "study your character so closely that what you imagine him saying or doing is undergirded by the facts you've gathered. . . . I want to emphasize the point, however, that although the facts, the background information, are important—important as armature, scaffolding—it's not the facts per se that make the poem. Or even get you started writing it. It's what the imagination does with the facts. It is moreover, the poet's attitude, his vision, his emotional response to the material that lead to the poem."[38]

These afterthoughts have a familiar ring because Robert Hayden, between composing "The Ballad" and reflecting later on the experience, followed the Nat Turner controversy with great interest and sympathy. During the late sixties, too, "The Ballad of Nat Turner" was an often-requested staple of Hayden's public readings. As he points out with quiet irony, "nobody has attacked it yet as being untrue to history."[39] He made an explicit connection between his poem and the cultural debate:

> William Styron's *Confessions of Nat Turner* became a storm center when it was published a few years ago, because there were those who thought the author deliberately misrepresented Nat Turner—emasculated him. Styron's motives were questioned,

were indeed condemned as racist. And a group of writers brought out a volume denouncing him. My ballad, by the way, was written several years before Styron's book appeared—was written, interestingly enough, long before the revival of interest in this figure. . . . And at this point I would like to say for the record that the attack on Styron, the extremely harsh criticism leveled against him, should give all writers pause. We have reason to be alarmed. Are we to be restricted in our choice of subjects? It's true that Afro-American history has been traduced. And it's true that as a people we have been stereotyped and caricatured in literature almost beyond recognition. And we're therefore hypersensitive. But even if Styron's book were as gross a misrepresentation as some people consider it, would chauvinistic censorship be the proper remedy?[40]

If Robert Hayden carefully researched and meditated long on the history of Nat Turner, a younger Louisiana poet, Alvin Aubert, conceived his contribution to this literature in the heat of a moment. "Nat in the Clearing" was, as its author has recalled, the first successful poem of his career.[41] As a teacher in Baton Rouge, Aubert encountered in *Negro Digest* a reprint of Gray's *Confessions*, probably in the summer or fall of 1965. "I was in my office at Southern University," he recalled, "the door shut. I put the magazine down and began writing the poem, which was to be accepted for publication in its first draft form. I never changed a word of it. I refer to the occasion as mystical because it was as though Nat Turner was there in the office with me, dictating the poem."[42]

Though "Nat in the Clearing" at several points suggests in locale and mood the influence of Hayden's "Ballad," Aubert acknowledges no such relationship. Indeed, when the teenager who read little turned into an English graduate student he was influenced by Donne, Milton, Hopkins, Lawrence, and Yeats: "these are the writers I enjoyed studying most . . . we didn't read *any* Black writers then" (418–19). His encounter, through Gray, with Nat Turner flowered into a vivid conceit, compressed into few lines. The coal and ashes of the conspirator's fire represent "the word" of the Lord, become the "breath-moist word" of the prophet to his fellow rebels and are now transformed into the poet's word as "one last glow," to be read by "some dark child" of the future. At once freer in form and sparer in imagery than Hayden's poem,

Aubert's lyric quietly dramatizes Nat Turner's presence, through history, in southern white and black consciousness. It has taken its place in southern white and black literature through appearances in magazines and anthologies where it speaks to many of Aubert's generation who "came to Black history late, too" (418).

This exploration of the lyrical literature surrounding Styron's *The Confessions of Nat Turner* may encourage the conclusion that, by comparison with their fictional and dramatic counterparts, American poets and poems contributed but little to the understanding of the several heated literary/cultural issues of this epoch. Not only are the numbers and forms in this genre small but their occasional thinness of texture—at least by the standards of Seldon Rodman and the *Saturday Review*—draws attention again to commonly held (white) assumptions and distinctions between "verse" and "a poem," between "pure" English and the language of "angry energy." However, since the poetry within the Nat Turner domain is, with the exception of Robert Lowell's, almost entirely by black writers, the ideological implications of any such discrimination need to be kept steadily in view. The cultural uses of black poetry during this period were as varied as the subdivisions within the black community. For, as Gwendolyn Brooks points out, "different nuances and outrightnesses" of expression characterize black writing as they do all literature.[43] Whether by Sterling Brown, Ophelia Robinson, or Robert Hayden, poems served as instruments for defining and legitimizing social reality. What poetic discourse made real in the sixties for many blacks was the "history and the histories of . . . ancestors."[44] The same was true, of course, for novels like *Black Thunder* and plays like Edmonds's *Nat Turner*. As Jane Tompkins writes, all these expressions constitute American literature which "gives the American people a conception of themselves and of their history."[45] But as many of these artists acknowledged, reading publics consist of distinct and self-conscious groups: blacks, whites, browns, Asians, Native Americans, and others. Moreover, the popular and elite texts discussed here existed (and still exist) within, and as, specific social occasions. Only within such intersections of author, reader, setting, and historical moment do works like *Ol' Prophet Nat* and *Black Thunder*, *In White America* and "Benito Cereno," "The Ballad of Nat Turner" and "Remembering Nat Turner" emerge in their fullest noncanonical significance as activated artifacts and social transactions.

A central feature of this literature considered as cultural dialogue is the widely expressed obligation of these writers of different social and racial groups to wrestle in various genres with the tensions between historical subject and possible modes of its reexpression. Each of the artists discussed here confronted and answered the same question: how may or how must I represent this specific historical event in words and modes different from, but responsive to, those in which the event has been previously inscribed? Thus Martin Duberman's announced aim for his documentary play was to write "both good history and good theatre" so that past realities may enter the present consciousness of all witnesses. At another artistic extreme but in the same spirit, the poet Robert Hayden advised any young poet who would choose a figure from history: "You have to do your homework, study your character so closely that what you imagine him saying or doing is undergirded by the facts you've gathered—has, therefore, plausibility."[46]

As we turn to the interactions of history (as subject and discipline) and historiography (as inscription and rhetoric) we discover as many varieties of nonfictional prose retellings as have been found in fictional, dramatic, and poetic discourse. Historians, to be sure, come at the tensions between the imperatives of the actual and the possibilities of the imagined from different directions than do so-called creative artists. Yet, as Woodward's opening remarks at the SHA remind us, the overlapping between re-creation and creation is frequent, subtle, and socially significant. Narrativizing history, as Hayden White argues, always aims to make the real into the desirable by means of a satisfying, coherent story; historical explanations, therefore, "refamiliarize us with events that have been forgotten through either accident, neglect, or repression" and each does so by a symbolic narrative structure that "tells us in what direction to think about the events and charges our thought about the event with different emotional valences."[47] As writers of a specific kind of prose fiction, therefore, historians use a range of literary techniques in order to declare and prove that their textualizations and interpretations follow—and must be measured against—the surviving evidence of prior events. Furthermore, historians no less than novelists or poets work within and speak from specific social contexts. All narratives of Nat Turner and his fellow rebels are, therefore, more than individual reorderings. The accounts of slave insurrections to which we turn in the following two chapters need to be read as responses to a complex of cultural stimuli: records that show Nat Turner existed and acted; orderings of those records into explanatory narratives; intellectual and emotional conflicts within individual writers of history; notions of suitable forms of storytelling; and the needs of the cultures, peoples, or social groups to rewrite their own histories as they experience new versions of Nat Turner's history.

5

New Historical Explanations
Paradigms and Popularizers

Extra-legal practices command conformity. In communities where there is strong opposition to social and political equality for Negroes, no ordinance can be found which requires that they be shot, discharged from their jobs, or that their homes be burned down when they rebel against their position. Yet true believer whites in Northern and Southern communities have believed in this violence against infractors of the caste system.

Negroes were also true believers—but not in the caste system. They were punished for that. But to violence they cleaved. Negroes who engaged in counter-aggression in pre-Civil War days, and are exploding in ghettoes one hundred years later, show that they have believed in the American way. It has been only one part of American culture—the caste system—which they have rejected; in their use of violence they are and have been thoroughly American.
—Richard S. Stone and Jeane Loftin Rothseiden,
"Master-Slave Clashes as Forerunners of Patterns in Modern Urban Eruptions," Phylon, *1969*

Attempts by Styron and his artistic colleagues to enact the return of Nat Turner in such forms as fiction, criticism, docudrama, oratorio, and lyric meditation constitute a corpus that reached a rich variety of sometimes overlapping publics. Inevitably, this literature points both inward to its separate texts and also backward to the past reimagined and redramatized. On virtually every page, therefore, these historical reflections mirror the presence of other custodians and recreators of the same records and tribal memories. Historians (both academic and popular) and historiographers, publishers, librarians, and teachers are key actors staffing different cultural networks, composing overlapping yet distinct domains. To explore the chief contributions and the connections of these cultural cadres with their publics—and especially to examine historians on their sector of the "Homeric battlefield" of sixties cultural conflict—is the aim of this chapter.

Several hypotheses and assumptions already articulated at the SHA session, in Styron's and Bontemps's encounters with historical sources, and on public occasions like theatrical performances of *Nat Turner*, *In White America*, and *The Old Glory*, need now to be set beside historians' narratives. We may, first of all, wonder whether Nat Turner and his rebellious brethren were as unknown or forgotten as they were sometimes alleged to be. Or was there a prior, ongoing tradition within American historiography—both white and black—of explanations of Nat Turner and slave insurrections? If so, how was this lore communicated to sixties publics, including the young in schools and libraries? How were new historical explanations of slave resistance fitted into received or changing conceptions of chattel slavery generally? In revisiting such familiar issues in the sociology of historical knowledge we need to be especially alert to emotional modulations in the narratives, as well as their cognitive content. And we must be everywhere aware of racial, gender, class, and regional identities and allegiances. Moreover, as with previous occasions and reading formations involving different historical moments and social groups, gaps in vital data about this historiographical subject are to be expected. Hence, responsible speculation (a historian's right and duty equivalent to Styron's creative imagination) must sometimes be encountered or introduced to fill gaps in knowledge about past reading behavior.

Four Pioneers and Paradigm-Makers: John Hope Franklin, Kenneth Stampp, Stanley M. Elkins, Herbert Aptheker

As Fred Chappell asserts in "Six Propositions about Literature and History," an accepted distinction between the two narrative modes involves the irreducible individuality of the literary text as contrasted with the incompleteness or replaceability of all historical explanations. Styron's sturdy defense of his novelist's prerogative is rooted in this distinction. Since another novel can never replace his, he asserts claim to even egregious historical error as *his* creation. (To be sure, he is equally insistent that he has made no serious historical errors.) Historians, on the other hand, seldom make such claims. They know they write to correct or extend previous knowledge of the past and that their discoveries and revisions are in turn subject to refinement, repudiation, and replacement. Since all historical texts are retextualizations, as Fredric Jameson and Hayden White assert, any penetration into historical tradition, however arbitrary, must eventually lead backward, sideways, and forward to other published explanations and their sources. In the case of Nat Turner and his slave revolt, retextualizers share much the same core of nineteenth-century sources (notably Gray's *Confessions*) while offering new interpretations, each embedded within different social and ideological frameworks.

A plausible point of entry into the mid-twentieth-century historiography of Nat Turner as symbol and fact is via John Hope Franklin's *From Slavery to Freedom: A History of Negro Americans* (1967). This choice is less arbitrary when one recalls the historiographical implications of Styron's novel and the cultural dialogue it provoked. Styron's novel is clearly part of a generation-long movement in liberal America to recognize and redress some of the crimes and inequities suffered by blacks since slavery. However misguided or misunderstood, *The Confessions of Nat Turner* represents its southern author's attempt, through a fictional/autobiographical narrative, to reimagine slavery and white racism from inside one slave's mind. This shift in perspective from the tradition of Faulkner, Twain, Melville, and Stowe is paralleled—and in part caused—by the major shift in historical explanations that occurred during these same years. What Gene Wise might have called a "paradigm shift" in the historiography of southern and/or black history involved adopting the point of view of slaves (and later of freedmen) and enlarging the sources from which new explanations of slavery and resistance to it were written. By "paradigm" Wise refers, as do I in the following discussion, not only to a "consistent pattern of beliefs held by a person, a group, or a culture" but also to the "characteristic acts which function to dramatize those beliefs." Thus a "paradigm shift" is the historical process by which a change in patterns of belief is articulated and dramatized.[1]

This necessitated, first, the repudiation of the white histories and plantation perspectives of Ulrich B. Phillips and his followers. A sign of John Hope Franklin's discreet move in this direction is his footnote in *From Slavery to Freedom* to "Ulrich B. Phillips, *Life and Labor in the Old South* (Boston, 1929), which, like his *American Negro Slavery* tends to apologize for the institution."[2] Next came the search for new materials revealing slaves' experiences and responses. Slave narratives—both of the nineteenth century and in later collections like the WPA oral history project—proved a lode of information and insight, and it is no accident that Styron's novel (like other literary retellings) is loosely modeled on a slave autobiography. In mining this material, both historians and novelists, white and black, found themselves rethinking the nature of slavery itself and accounting for slave resistance in terms of the energy generated within the slave community and articulated by its leaders. Thus the main shift in historiographical tradition in sixties America was from white-centered explanations of slavery and slave revolts to black slave culture studies, which, overturning the image of the slave as passive deracinated victim, posited a social context and psychological "elbow room" within which a Nat Turner could emerge not as an isolated instance of a "religious fanatic" but as one expression of group resistance.

Franklin's text played a strategic role in initiating this paradigm shift. Because his personal and professional outlook was conciliatory and integrationist, he influenced the thinking of white historians and readers as much as blacks—indeed, when the sixties turned radical, even more so. As Peter Novick observes, "during the twenty years following the publication of his *From Slavery to Freedom* in 1947, Negro history, so far as the profession was concerned, was represented above all by John Hope Franklin. . . . In both his life and his work, Franklin was the model Negro historian for white liberals in the 1950s."[3] Though written originally for students and teachers in predominantly black southern colleges, his text, when revised first in 1956 and then in the twentieth anniversary edition of 1967, became more widely read, consulted, and taught than any previous history of black Americans. This success with white readers as well as black must have gratified Roger W. Shugg, the white liberal editor who, shortly after World War II, convinced Alfred A. Knopf to commission a survey of black history and personally recruited Franklin for the job.[4] As we have already seen, Franklin was part of the Nat Turner debate as one of the relatively few black scholars involved in the early superintendence of *The Confessions of Nat Turner* through his strategically placed and favorable review. Together with other readily available sources cited in its bibliography and notes, Franklin's history offered abundant evidence of the inadequacy of Styron's allusion to the "meager enlightenment history has left us about the institution of slavery."

Franklin's new preface of 1967 underlined the nature of his work as consensus by pointing out that it was "a history and not a contemporary tract" (vii). Nevertheless a new edition was called for to keep pace with dramatic developments of the past decade which were historical data in themselves as well as generative of new perspectives. By reprinting the prefaces of the first and second editions the author also acquainted new readers with his original aims and assumptions. Because he remains convinced that "historical forces are all pervasive and cut through the most rigid barriers of race and caste" (xi), Franklin reemphasizes that his history is conceived in relation to the main stream of American history. Unlike other works, he also asserted, *From Slavery to Freedom* is not primarily a record of black achievements and achievers. Rather "the history of the Negro in America is essentially the story of the strivings of the nameless millions who have sought adjustment in a new and sometimes hostile world" (xii). This demotic perspective links Franklin to the new social history that would emerge later in the sixties.

Readers disturbed by the conciliatory phrase "sometimes hostile world" are promptly reassured that Franklin does not follow in the steps of Phillips. For Franklin's is a radically bleaker record of slavery and a fuller treatment of slave resistance. "Even if there was no work and even if an opportunity for diversion presented itself, the slave could never escape the fact that he was a slave . . . almost always under the most careful surveillance," he wrote. "If a slave found it possible to enjoy the periods when he was not on the job he either possessed a remarkable capacity for accommodation or he was totally ignorant of the depth of his degraded position" (198). Few slaves developed either capacity. So pervasive and brutal were the common conditions of slave existence that evasion or acquiescence were virtually impossible. Franklin's index thus never lists "Sambo," nor does the character type appear in his history. Instead of docility and tractability, slave behavior was never more than grudging accommodation and at its extreme active, violent resistance. "Far from being a civilizing force, moreover, the plantation bred indecency in human relations; and the slave was the immediate victim of the barbarity of the system which exploited the sex of the women and the work of everyone. . . . Many masters as well as slaves got the reputation of being 'bad,' and their prevalence did nothing to relieve the tension which everywhere seemed to be mounting as the institution developed" (206). This emphasis on "bad" masters and bondsmen also departs pointedly from Phillips's partiality for benign masters and contented slaves.

Slave revolts, "which began with the institution and did not end until slavery was abolished" (210), were therefore situated at one pole of a wide continuum of resisting behavior, which for Franklin included religious escapism, loafing, feigned sickness, sabotage, arson, self-mutilation and suicide, running away, poisoning, and murder. "The times that overseers and masters were killed by slaves in the woods," he observes, "were exceedingly numerous, as the careful reading of almost any Southern newspaper will reveal" (209). Slaves' most sensational act was conspiracy to revolt by armed force, the bloody result of summoning the nerve to carry the fight to the enemy in hope of ending degradation. In the white camp, revolt was seen as "a mad, sinister act of desperate savages . . . who could not appreciate the benign influences of the institution." Blacks accepted bloodshed "as the price of liberty," while whites were so terrified of "even rumor of insurrections" that they made the "most vigorous efforts to guard against the dreaded eventuality" (210).

Though revolts were, in Franklin's view, always integral to American slavery, the growing tensions within a burgeoning economic system made such outbreaks more frequent after 1800. Gabriel Prosser's Henrico County revolt was also the new century's first enactment by blacks of the Revolutionary political belief that "a new day had arrived for the common man" (210). Franklin quotes the rebellious slave's courtroom comparison of himself to George Washington already cited above in discussing Bontemps's *Black Thunder*. The historian then proceeds to list numerous plots, conspiracies, and hangings between 1800 and 1831, which continued unabated after Nat Turner's rebellion and its bloody suppression.

To this succession of attempts and actions Franklin often applies the careful term "conspiracy to revolt." Like others involved in debates over slavery and slave resistance, he takes the whole range of behavior by both blacks and whites as the necessary context for understanding the Southampton slave revolt and its leader. He thereby equates the slaves' will to resist with completed deeds of organized violence inasmuch as both responses invited white retribution by hanging, conviction, and transportation. For Franklin, then, all aspects of this history must be viewed as interactions between members of the two groups.

But in scale and significance Nat Turner's resistance transcended all other manifestations of antebellum opposition. Franklin characterizes the leader of the insurrection tentatively as "a mystical rebellious person who on one occasion had run away and then decided to return to his master. Perhaps already he had begun to feel that he had been selected by some divine power to deliver his people from slavery" (212). The historian's reluctance, in 1967, fully to endorse—indeed, even to identify—messianic and millennialist motives as central to Ol' Prophet Nat's character is of a piece with his characterization of the slaves' Christianity as "escape through ritual and song" (207). In this attitude Franklin reflects the influence of E. Franklin Frazier and Benjamin Mays who characterized Negro religion as largely accommodation.[5] His overriding need was to tie Turner to Prosser, George Boxley, Vesey, and David Walker—all secular rather than spiritually motivated antislavery incendiaries. In any case, his succinct and dispassionate description of the actual revolt mentions astrological but neither Judeo-Christian nor African signs and portents by which Turner timed and defended his outbreak. Its violent course is rather undramatically recounted in five terse sentences:

> On August 13, when the sun turned a "peculiar greenish blue" he called the revolt for August 21. He and his followers began by killing Turner's master, Joseph Travis, and his family. In rapid succession other families fell before the blows of the Negroes. Within twenty-four hours sixty whites had been killed, and the revolt was spreading rapidly when the main group of Negroes were met and overpowered by state and federal troops. More than one hundred slaves were killed in the encounter and thirteen slaves and three free Negroes were immediately hanged. Turner was captured on October 30, and within less than two weeks, on November 11, he was executed. (212–13)

By contrast with this bare bones rehearsal, which omits nearly all complexities of motivation and behavior so fascinating to novelists and other historians, Franklin devotes more space to the revolt's repercussions:

> The South was completely dazed by the Southampton uprising. The situation was grossly exaggerated in many communities. Some reports were that whites had been murdered by the hundreds in Virginia. . . . Small wonder that several states felt it necessary to call special sessions of the legislature to consider the emergency. Most states strengthened their Black Codes, and citizens literally remained awake nights waiting for the Negroes to make another break. But the uprisings continued. In 1835 several slaves of Monroe County, Georgia, were hanged and whipped to death because of implication in a conspiracy. . . . Down to and throughout the Civil War, slaves demonstrated their violent antipathy for slavery by continuing to rise against it. (213)

Besides downplaying the dramatic particulars of Nat Turner's revolt and its leader's messianic character, Franklin's text of 1967 pays scant attention to details about the slave culture out of which the revolt arose. In the "Social Considerations" section of his chapter on "That Peculiar Institution," Franklin emphasizes the bleakness and cultural deprivation of plantation life as slaves commonly experienced it. "[T]he plantation with its inherent isolation and consequent social and cultural self-sufficiency frequently bordering on stagnancy tended to perpetuate the barrenness. For the slave there was little in the way of enjoyment and satisfaction during the months or hours he was off his job. It must be remembered that, for the most part, the slave had no time he could call his own" (198). Little space remains in these paragraphs for the varieties of slave cultural life "from sundown to sun-up" which George Rawick, for one, was later to celebrate in his 1972 study of the slave community.[6] Though occasional recreations in the form of fishing, races, fairs, and seasonal holidays with rituals like the John Canoe celebration are mentioned, virtually no attention is paid to black music, storytelling, or family life and its rituals. But Franklin's neglect of slave culture as a source of resistance to white cultural domination is most clearly exhibited in his cursory treatment of black religion. He points out that "the number of Negro preachers was always considerable, and few plantations were without at least one black exhorter" (199) but fails to connect Nat Turner's name and rebellious role to this situation. Stress instead falls upon slaves' religious life as increasingly controlled by whites, with joint services and camp meetings much more common, as the nineteenth century waxed, than separate and secret rites. Neither the revolutionary resonances of biblical rhetoric nor the possible power of African cultic practices to resist bondage is considered, even in passing: "In the last three decades before the Civil War the church became one of the strongest allies of the pro-slavery element. Slaves who found refuge and solace in the religious instructions of the white clergy had reason to believe that they were now trapped by an enemy that had once befriended them" (201).

If for growing thousands of students, teachers, and general readers of *From Slavery to Freedom* its author played no ground-breaking role in relating slave resistance like Nat Turner's to black—or, for that matter, white—community life and culture, Franklin did serve as a modulated, respected voice asserting that slave revolts were never isolated acts of inexplicable desperation but were rather part and parcel of slave experience of "that peculiar institution." For other sources and viewpoints (contemporary as well as antecedent), Franklin did point the way in his footnotes and bibliography. But, even in the 1967 edition, the other experts cited were overwhelmingly white historians. Though in his original 1947 preface Franklin acknowledged general inspiration from Negro predecessors Carter G. Woodson, Charles H. Wesley, W. E. B. Du Bois, and Luther P. Jackson, most specific citations two decades later were still to white scholars of the black past. Among these, three names stand out. Authors of particular studies rather than general surveys like Franklin's, these influential historians became prominent during the sixties.

If by the outbreak of the Nat Turner controversy in 1967 one history rivaled *From Slavery to Freedom*, it was Kenneth Stampp's *The Peculiar Institution: Slavery in the Antebellum South* (1956). Yet at that moment a second study may temporarily have eclipsed both books. Stanley Elkins's *Slavery: A Problem in American Institutional and Intellectual Life* (1959) was the first work of a young white historian who combined insights of social psychology with a willingness to speculate boldly about comparisons between American slave character and behavior and recent experiences of Holocaust victims and prisoners. As already noted, Elkins's name came repeatedly to Styron's lips before and after his novel's publication. A third white expert also mentioned in Franklin's notes is Herbert Aptheker, likewise a familiar name in sixties cultural politics. Franklin cites Aptheker's *American Negro Slave Revolts* (1943) but fails to mention a slighter but still pertinent work by Aptheker more recently issued, *Nat Turner's Slave Rebellion* (1966). These three white interpreters represent complementary historical perspectives to Franklin's. They also provide contrasting interpretations available to American audiences of the later sixties, both directly and through popularizers.

During the decade after its timely appearance in the aftermath of *Brown vs. Board of Education*, Stampp's *The Peculiar Institution* became an instant classic for most professional historians, black and white, and for their immediate audiences in schools, colleges, libraries, and book clubs. To his generation of white liberals and hopeful blacks, Stampp's study represented the culminating—and, to nearly everyone by 1967, convincing—demolition of Phillips's thoroughly white-centered, pro-slaveowners' paradigm. Its relevance for late-fifties and early-sixties audiences was underlined by the fact that its first readers could recall hearing news broadcasts of the bus boycott in progress in Montgomery, Alabama. Stampp himself stressed his book's topical significance as dealing with a problem of "peculiar urgency because Negro Americans await the full fruition of their emancipation."[7] Though his preface thanked John Hope Franklin for valuable advice, Stampp otherwise acknowledged debts only to fellow white historians. Nevertheless, the aim of *The Peculiar Institution* is to examine slavery from the slave's own experiences and viewpoints: "I firmly believe that one must know what slavery meant to the Negro and how he reacted to it before one can comprehend his more recent tribulations" (vii). As a white scholar, Stampp admitted he might seem presumptuous writing about black experience. But in mitigation he compared himself to predecessors who "did not hesitate to assert that most [slaves] were quite content with servitude" (86). Like the slaveowners, these earlier scholars hardly knew slaves intimately; indeed, they missed the most compelling evidence that slaves knew their masters better than vice versa. Stampp resolved that black voices be heard in his study. He intended also to correct the inaccuracy of received interpretations, based as these were on historical archives containing "few reliable records of what went on in slaves' minds" (88).

These archives—superintended by whites—contained multiple records of active and often violent protests by slaves. Even if rebels were few and exceptional they remain valuable historical subjects. With a liberal fervor that alienated some conservative reviewers, Stampp declared:

> The record of the minority who waged ceaseless and open warfare against their bondage makes an inspiring chapter, also, in the history of Americans of African descent. True, these rebels were exceptional men, but the historian of any group properly devotes much attention to those members who did extraordinary things, men in whose lives the problems of their age found focus, men who voiced the feelings and aspirations of the more timid and less articulate masses. As the American Revolution produced folk heroes, so also did southern slavery—heroes who, in both cases, gave much for the cause of human freedom. (92)

Though rebels like Gabriel Prosser more directly reflected the revolutionary ethos, Turner's insurrection receives first billing in "A Troublesome Property," Stampp's long chapter on slave resistance: "No antebellum Southerner could ever forget Nat Turner. The career of this man made an impact upon the people of his section as great as that of John C. Calhoun or Jefferson Davis. Yet Turner was only a slave in Southampton County, Virginia—and during most of his life a rather unimpressive one at that" (132). Explaining this slave's remarkable transformation from pious Baptist exhorter, "apparently as humble and docile as a slave was expected to be" (132), into frightening avenger, Stampp, like Franklin, sidesteps the religious motivation supplied by Gray and cited in other sources.[8] "There is no evidence that he was underfed, overworked, or treated with special cruelty. . . . If Nat Turner could not be trusted, what slave could? That was what made his sudden deed so frightening" (132–33). The prophet's dreams and heavenly visions, like Gray's jailhouse comparison of his manacled self to "Christ crucified," are all collapsed into the imprecise explanation that "somehow Turner came to believe that he had been divinely chosen to deliver his people from bondage, and he persuaded several other slaves to assist him" (133). Such vagueness recalls the similar attribution of secular motivations for slave revolts by literary artists of Stampp's generation such as Peters and Bontemps. A liberal egalitarianism is likewise intimated by Stampp's assessment that "within two days they killed nearly sixty whites. They could have killed more. They left undisturbed at least one white family, 'because they thought no better of themselves than they did of the negroes'" (133).

Stampp follows Franklin in emphasizing that the bloodiest of antebellum revolts was no singular occurrence. Indeed, he outdoes the black historian in linking Turner, Vesey, and Prosser to other occasions of actual or planned resistance. He quotes with guarded approval Aptheker's evidence in *American Negro Slave Revolts* of "many conspiracies and a few rebellions, each involving ten or more slaves, from the colonial period to the end of the Civil War" (134). In this case, "the shock of Nat Turner caused Southerners to take preventive measures, but these never eliminated their apprehension or the actual danger. Hardly a year passed without some kind of alarming disturbance somewhere in the South. When no real conspiracy existed, wild rumors often agitated the whites and at times came close to creating an insurrection panic. . . . Whether caused by rumor or fact, the specter of rebellion often troubled the sleep of the master class" (136).

In concluding his assessment of Turner's impact upon slaves themselves, Stampp reached a sobering conclusion:

> The speed with which it was crushed and the massacre that followed were facts soon known, doubtless, to every slave in Virginia and, before long, to almost every slave in the South. Among the Negroes everywhere, news generally spread so far and so fast as to amaze the whites. The Turner story was not likely to encourage slaves to make new attempts to win their freedom by fighting for it. They now realized they would face a united white community, well armed and quite willing to annihilate as much of the black population as might seem necessary.
>
> In truth, no slave uprising ever had a chance of ultimate success, even though it might have cost the master class heavy casualties. The great majority of the disarmed and outnumbered slaves, knowing the futility of rebellion, refused to join in any of the numerous plots. Most slaves had to express their desire for freedom in less dramatic ways. They rarely went beyond disorga-

nized individual action—which, to be sure, caused their masters no little annoyance. The bondsmen themselves lacked the power to destroy the web of bondage. They would have to have the aid of free men inside or outside the South. (139–40)

While these blunt assessments proved unpalatable to some (as they certainly did to black nationalists in the late sixties), Stampp concluded "A Troublesome Property" with a liberal revision of earlier conservative historiography, that the masters' "elaborate technique of slave control"—laws, patrols, and other awesome displays of force—constituted "a striking refutation of the myth that slavery survived because of the cheerful acquiescence of the slaves" (140).

Stampp's "A Troublesome Property" demonstrates how in 1956 attitudes had already begun to shift so as to invite black and white historians to consider far more systematically than heretofore the slaves' outlook and repertoire of resistance tactics. By its choice of sources, both past and contemporary, *The Peculiar Institution* confirms a familiar (rather than creating a new) rationale for phenomena like Nat Turner and his small band. More original, though also more ambiguous, was Stampp's later chapter 8, "Between Two Cultures." In this speculative essay he explored the complex cultural exchanges actually occurring under chattel slavery and their meaning for both masters and bondsmen. Perhaps for the first time many white readers were led to think of slaves as equal partners with whites in certain social relationships. If white paternalism on larger plantations afforded some domestic slaves the gift of indulgence and even genuine love (Styron's Samuel Turner comes at once to mind), this relationship was inherently unequal and demeaning to the slave: "The most generous master, so long as he was determined to *be* a master, could be paternal only toward a fawning dependent; for slavery, by its nature, could never be a relationship between equals" (327). Hence, though paternalism provided the institution some of its most seductive apologetics, the price slaves paid was high.

> Clearly, to enjoy the bounty of a paternalistic master a slave had to give up all claims to respect as a responsible adult, all pretensions of independence. He had to understand the subtle etiquette that governed his relations with his master: the fine

line between friskiness and insubordination, between cuteness and insolence. A nurse might scold the white child under her care; a cook might be a petty tyrant in her kitchen; an old servant might gravely advise on family affairs; a child pet might crawl on his master's lap and sleep in his bedroom; a field-hand and a small farmer might work together and eat from the same frying pan. But between master and slave there was still a formidable barrier. (329–30)

Unlike life on small farms, however, where slaves were "like tiny islands in a sea of suspicious and unfriendly whites" (330–31), the larger plantation afforded richer soil in which genuine slave community and culture could grow. "For here they lived together in their own substantial communities in regions where the majority of people were of their own race and status. There they had even fewer humiliating contacts with the whites; and in their free time they could be at ease, express their thoughts and feelings with less restraint, and find their diversions amid a wide circle of friends" (331). To be sure, there always existed threats and severe limits on the slave community. The sale of slaves, often following a master's death, could quickly destroy the slave family on which community and much cultural life were based. Even when this did not occur, the social hierarchies enacted by the masters' separation of domestic from field slaves created divisions among the slaves. For the more privileged house servants, however, frustrations often outweighed the advantages of status. Chief among these frustrations was close contact with the dominant culture's definition of an individual person—of a human being, in fact.

The bondsmen, of course, were cut off from the avenues which led to success and respectability in white society. The paragon of virtue in materialistic nineteenth-century America—at least in its white middle class segment, both urban and rural—was the enterprising, individualistic, freedom-loving, self-made man. Ideally he was the head of a family which he provided with the comforts and luxuries that symbolized his material success. He sought through education to give his children culture and social poise; he emancipated his wife from household drudgery; and he subscribed to the moral code of the Victorian age. (334)

This epitome contains within its key terms—"enterprising," "freedom-loving," "education," "emancipation from drudgery," "moral code"—the bitterest of ironies for the slaves' situation. Though a few slaves might aspire to these ideals (Styron's young Nat Turner, for one), their realization was doomed.

As their cultural counterpart, slaves erected their secret ideal male model:

> ... the bold rebel who challenged slave discipline.
>
> The strong-willed field-hand whom the overseer hesitated to punish, the habitual runaway who mastered the technique of escape and shrugged at the consequences, each won personal triumphs for himself and vicarious triumphs for the others. The generality of slaves believed that he who knew how to trick or deceive the master had an enviable talent, and they regarded the committing of petit larceny as both thrilling and praiseworthy. . . .
>
> Each community of slaves contained one or two members whom the others looked to for leadership because of their physical strength, practical wisdom, or mystical powers. It was a "notorious" fact, according to one master, "that on almost every large plantation of Negroes, there is one among them who holds a kind of magical sway over the minds and opinions of the rest; to him they look as their oracle. . . . The influence of such a Negro, often a preacher, on a quarter is incalculable." (334–36)

From the perspective of the Nat Turner controversy in the years after the appearance of these words, it is indeed curious that Stampp makes no connection between such dynamic aspects of slave culture with its community heroes and the career of Ol' Prophet Nat. He instead points to "Old Abram," "Old Jubas," "Sinda," and "Big Lucy" as actual exemplars of black cultural ideals. One of these, Old Juba from Mississippi, "wore about his neck a half dozen charms and . . . claimed to have seen the devil a hundred times" (336). Gray's evidence of the power Nat Turner also exemplified is not cited, despite mention two hundred pages earlier of *The Confessions of Nat Turner*. The puzzle is best explained, again, by Stampp's repeated preference for secular over Christian/religious motives in this social domain.

Equally ambiguous are Stampp's concluding remarks in "Between

Two Cultures" on the failures of slave culture. In spite of some convincing demonstrations of community identity and ideals, he ends by stressing disintegration or irrelevance in crucial areas of slaves' life: "In Africa the negroes had been accustomed to a strictly regulated family life and a rigidly enforced moral code. But in America the disintegration of their social organization removed the traditional sanctions which had encouraged them to respect their old customs" (340). The result was disastrous for the average slave and his family. "Here, as at so many other points, the slaves had lost their native culture without being able to find a workable substitute and therefore lived in a kind of cultural chaos" (340). Stampp's description of the dysfunctional black slave family—a setting equally frustrating for fathers, mothers, and children—anticipates Daniel P. Moynihan's famous (or notorious) report of 1965, *The Negro Family: A Case for National Action*, as it repeats essential assumptions from E. Franklin Frazier's earlier *The Negro Family in the United States* (1939). What surviving records of slave families often reveal, Stampp declares, is a barren life devoid of many features of truly civilized existence.

> The average bondsman, it would happen, lived more or less aimlessly in a bleak and narrow world. He lived in a world without schools, without books, without learned men; he knew less of the fine arts and of aesthetic values than he had known in Africa; and he found few ways to break the monotonous sameness of all his days. . . . His world was full of mysteries which he could not solve, full of forces which he could not control. And so he tended to be a fatalist and futilitarian, for nothing else could reconcile him to his life. . . .
>
> In slavery the Negro existed in a kind of cultural void. He lived in a twilight zone between two ways of life and was unable to obtain from either many of the attributes which distinguish man from beast. (361–64)

Compounding ambiguities in Stampp's by turns bleak, sympathetic, and often imaginative re-creation of slave experience and attitudes is the fact that he follows these harsh conclusions with a ten-page description of a sometimes vigorous black culture. Though insisting that blacks developed no antebellum tradition of cultural nationalism, Stampp points to evidence of a synthesis of African holdovers with borrowings from white culture. Despite the opposition of many slaves to Africanisms in general, others were able to blend Old and New World practices, thereby creating "a few things in the lives of slaves [which] belonged to them in a more intimate and personal way. . . . For instance, folklore was important to them as it has always been to illiterate people. Some of it preserved legends of their own past; some explained natural phenomena or described a world of the spirits" (367). Moreover in holiday ceremonies and church services slaves regularly strengthened their strongest social and spiritual ties by means of vocal and certain instrumental music, "their most splendid vehicle of self-expression" (368). As for preserving "the rituals and dogmas of his pagan faith" (371) the slave was only in the short run successful. However, by adapting white modes of evangelical Protestantism to his spiritual needs—which for Stampp meant ecstatic transport out of dull routine and promises of heavenly rewards for Christian conduct—the slave was able to give meaning and continuity to existence. "On many plantations religious exercises were almost 'the only habitual recreation not purely sensual,'" he quoted F. L. Olmsted as noting, "hence slaves poured all their emotions into them 'with an intensity and vehemence almost terrible to witness'" (372). Quoting this northern traveler is a characteristic authorizing tactic of Stampp's, for despite statements to the contrary, white sources are of equal (sometimes even greater) weight with slaves' own testimony.

What white and black writers attest to, then, is a complex of emotional ties knitting members of the two races together—and also keeping them apart. At times, relationships were warm and personal. More frequently, though, they were characterized by deep suspicion. Occasionally they consisted of an abiding animosity. Almost always, though, the tenor of the slaves' emotional life was fear. Stampp concludes his pioneering essay on slave culture with a sober look at one small and vividly symbolic detail in the historical record: the language of southern newspaper advertisements for runaways. Often these notices emphasized that the black fugitive stammered, would not look others in the face, was easily confused when spoken to: "'I feel lighter—the dread is gone,' affirmed a Negro woman who had escaped to Canada. 'It is a great heaviness on a person's mind to be a slave'" (382).

Stampp's *The Peculiar Institution*, unlike Elkins's *Slavery*, the other major fifties study, is distinguished by a genuine preoccupation with specific forms of slave character. Stampp's willingness to speculate freely about personality was equaled by his willingness to take resistance to slavery rather than passive accommodation as the norm. Though deeply divided in his own mind over the vitality and autonomy of slave culture, he seldom doubted its presence. As August Meier and Elliott M. Rudwick have concluded: "That Stampp had dealt with the cultural question the way he did was a reflection of the intellectual milieu, both among blacks and whites of his generation. In retrospect, that Stampp even made the attempt to analyze slave culture is of itself the significant thing about the chapter."[9] In light of the looming battles of the sixties, however, Stampp's failure to link explicitly his two chapters on violent slave resistance and slave culture, and to do so through the figure of Nat Turner, authorizes a sterner judgment than Meier and Rudwick's. Furthermore, Stampp's famous opening declaration that "slaves were merely ordinary human beings, that innately Negroes *are*, after all, only white men with black skins, nothing more, nothing less" (vii) contains within its well-meaning white liberalism the implications of a white-centered concept of culture and personality familiar to the future readers of Styron's novel.

In 1974, David Brion Davis summarized the postwar historiography of slavery for readers of *Daedalus*. There he named Stampp's book as the first of five turning points in white historical explanations of this subject. Despite reflecting "the unwitting arrogance of white integrationists,"[10] *The Peculiar Institution* decisively closed the decades-long domination of U. B. Phillips. "Stampp opened the way for new and more dispassionate modes of inquiry. Never again, presumably, would it be necessary to debate the moral wrongs of slavery or to rehearse the evidence concerning food, shelter, working hours, police regulations, medical care and punishments" (190). For our purposes, Stampp opened as well as ended debate on one aspect of slavery of momentous significance to readers and writers of history in the two decades after 1956: "His unmistakable theme is the conflict between the oppressed and the oppressors, between the weak and the powerful, between the innocent and the guilty. And the prevailing mood of Stampp's book is ultimately optimistic. Even a brutal slave regime, reinforced by racist ideology, could not crush the human spirit. The slaves remained 'a troublesome property,' capable of resistance as well as endurance" (191).

Stampp's history remains a permanent contribution to the study of slavery as blacks experienced its brutalities and paternalistic indulgences. During the late sixties, however, Stampp encountered the scathing attacks by black nationalists and young historians that were also leveled at virtually all white historians save Aptheker. For instance, at a historic meeting in Detroit in 1969 of the Association for the Study of Negro Life and History, Stampp was publicly denounced by "black militants insisting that because he was a white man he had no right to do *The Peculiar Institution*."[11] Stampp's younger, far more radical, but also white colleague Robert Starobin was even more harshly condemned on the same occasion by Vincent Harding, Sterling Stuckey, and Julius Lester. As Lester observed, "In these days any white man who devotes himself to teaching and writing about black history must have the fortitude and strength of a bull elephant."[12] The energy with which these younger black intellectuals repudiated white explanations of their history has already been noted in *Ten Black Writers Respond*, where the chief antagonist lurking behind Styron was not Stampp but Stanley Elkins.

Indeed a striking example of the split between black historians and the mainstream (i.e., white) profession during this decade is the radically different reception given Elkins's *Slavery*. In his survey of this historiographical battleground David Brion Davis names Elkins the second paradigm-maker of the new history of slavery and slave resistance. Recalling his own superficial exposure in graduate school, limited to U. B. Phillips and F. L. Olmsted but virtually no other historians of slavery, Davis agreed with Elkins that white scholarly "inhibitions" too long operated

> to consign slavery to a marginal place in the curriculum. . . . At best, slavery could be perceived as a variant on the history of immigration and ethnic conflict. I remained totally ignorant of the work of such black historians as W. E. B. Du Bois, Carter Woodson, Charles H. Wesley, Benjamin Quarles, Eric Williams, C. L. R. James, and John Hope Franklin. I am confident that few graduate students had at that time [the early 1950s] encountered Herbert Aptheker's *American Negro Slave Revolts* (1943) or even Frank Tannenbaum's pioneering essay, *Slave and Citizen* (1946), which Stanley Elkins rescued from undeserved obscurity. (189)

Though Elkins himself was already reexperiencing "obscurity" by the mid-seventies—a drop all the more precipitous given his rapid rise to professional prominence in the decade before—his contributions to controversies over both Nat Turner and the history of slavery were substantial. *Slavery*'s "brief but extraordinary vogue followed finally by the furor of intensive and searching criticism"[13] resulted not so much from its author's fresh data as from his combination of psychological theorizing and cross-cultural comparisons. His often novel suggestions about American slavery fell on the ears of Americans sensitized by violent political events and racial upheavals in their surrounding society as well as by scorching memories of World War II racism, which culminated in the Holocaust: "There is a painful touchiness in all aspects of the subject," Elkins noted in 1976 in the preface to the third edition of *Slavery;* "the discourse contains almost too much immediacy; it makes too many connections with present problems. How a person thinks about negro slavery historically makes a great deal of difference here and now; it tends to locate him morally in relation to a whole range of very immediate political, social, and philosophical issues which in some way refer back to slavery."[14]

Some of the "painful touchiness" can be explained by the collision between the beliefs of new historians (black and leftist) and Elkins's agenda of essentially conservative hypotheses. These include, first, that North American slavery differed strikingly from Latin American varieties in being a "closed" system whose victims resembled in significant psychological respects prisoners in the German concentration camps of World War II; second, that an unopposed capitalist power gave southern slaveowners the license to impose upon the great majority of their working property a basic personality pattern—"Sambo" as childlike, carefree, self-deprecating victim; further, that North American slaves were all but incapable of resisting and revolting because they were culturally deracinated; so that, finally, North American slave revolts were few, desperate, and futile. Sambo, then, and not Nat Turner is the prime historical personality for whom Elkins seeks to account. This can only be done by acknowledging that the North American slave system was "unique among all such systems known to civilization" (42) by virtue of the power of the "most implacable race-consciousness yet observed in virtually any society" (61).

In hindsight, it would be difficult to decide which black figure—Sambo or Nat Turner—more intrigued and infuriated Elkins's several readerships. Yet discussion of both was further complicated by Elkins's preference for generalization and speculation over reexamining primary sources and listening to pertinent voices, including those of the slaves themselves. The Sambo personality is assumed to have been historical reality, rather than a construct systematically reassembled from available evidence: "The picture has far too many circumstantial details, its hues have been stroked in by too many different brushes, for it to be denounced as counterfeit. Too much folk-knowledge, too much plantation literature, too much of the Negro's own lore, have gone into its making to entitle one in good conscience to condemn it as a 'conspiracy'" (84). Moreover, this imposed identity was more than mere accommodation or role-playing, though such responses were undoubtedly present. Sambo is the result of fundamental changes, wrought by institutionalized attitudes, in the adult personalities of its victims: "we do know—from a modern experience—that such an adjustment is possible, not only within the same generation but within two or three years" (89). Hence one should expect no great difference between responses to the traumas of the first generation of Africans and those of their descendants:

> Several million people were detached with a peculiar effectiveness from a great variety of cultural backgrounds in Africa. . . . It was achieved partly by the shock experience inherent in the very mode of procurement but more specifically by the type of authority-system to which they were introduced and to which they had to adjust for physical and psychic survival. The new adjustment, to absolute power in a closed system, involved infantilization, and the detachment was so complete that little trace of prior (and thus alternative) cultural sanctions for behavior and personality remained for the descendants of the first generation. (88–89)

Given the preponderance of Sambo, together with demonstrable differences between Brazilian and North American slavery systems, and psychological hypotheses derived from Auschwitz and Dachau, Elkins found it virtually unthinkable for a typical Virginia slave to conceive himself a rebel.

Compared with the countless uprisings of the Brazilian negroes, the slave revolts in our own country appear rather desperate and futile. Only three emerge as worthy of any note, and their seriousness—even when described by a sympathetic historian like Herbert Aptheker—depends largely on the supposed plans of the rebels rather than on the things they actually did. The best organized of such 'revolts,' those of Vesey and Gabriel, were easily suppressed, while the most dramatic of them—the Nat Turner Rebellion—was characterized by little more than aimless butchery. The Brazilian revolts, on the other hand, were marked by imagination and a sense of direction, and they often involved large-scale military operations. (136–37)

Elkins's detachment reflected a viewpoint based on hemispheric comparisons rather than attention to specific circumstance. As the sixties waned, this outlook was widely derided by blacks who resented what they took to be the condescension and hostility of a conservative white historian breathing new life into hoary stereotypes. Further exasperating readers and fellow historians was Elkins's way of skirting direct refutation. As David Brion Davis (one of Elkins's severest critics) pointed out, "his portraits of Latin American and North American slavery are essentially ideal models, illustrating the polar extremes of open and closed slave systems" (192). However, the exceptions and alternatives admitted in Elkins's paradigm are not major qualifications of his case. To be sure, in 1976, discussing the possibility of a viable black community and leadership, he conceded "that is hardly to say that something of an 'underground'—something rather more, indeed, than an underground—could not exist in Southern slave society. And there were those in it who hardly fitted the picture of 'Sambo' " (137). Furthermore, insurrections that did take place and those who engineered them are readily accounted for by his general explanation: "It is of great interest to note that although the danger of slave revolts (like communist conspiracies in our own day) was much overrated by touchy Southerners, the revolts that did occur were in no instance planned by plantation laborers but rather by Negroes whose qualities of leadership were developed well outside the full coercions of the plantation authority-system" (138). Not only was Denmark Vesey a freed artisan and Gabriel Prosser a blacksmith but "Nat Turner, the Virginian who fomented the massacre of 1831, was a literate preacher of recognized intelligence" (138). Though himself later pointing out "the emotionally loaded quality of the semantics" of this debate, Elkins's own language often provoked strong reactions. In the above passage, the dangers of revolt described as "much overrated by touchy Southerners," together with other loaded terms like "underground" and "fomented the massacre," and the implication that "a literate preacher of recognized intelligence" was a surprising anomaly—these semantic signals were frequently perceived as self-serving features of a belittling historiographical and ideological argument, derogative and racist. To several kinds of readers and historians, therefore, Elkins's basic strategy seemed clear: to delegitimize or dismiss as exceptions the whole category of community-based black leaders and rebels: "The William Johnsons [the Natchez barber] and Denmark Veseys have been accorded, though belatedly, their due honor. They are, indeed, all too easily identified, thanks to the system that enabled them as individuals to be so conspicuous and so exceptional and, as members of a group, so few" (139).

The historian most clearly attacked through Elkins's arguments was Herbert Aptheker, whose pioneering work is either dismissed or manipulated to support Elkins's diametrically different view of slave revolts. In observing that *American Negro Slave Revolts*, a "book, much of whose evidence consists of unsubstantial rumors in ante-bellum rural newspapers, is thus rather unreliable for judging how seriously any of these 'revolts' should be taken" (221–22), Elkins reflected the opinions of many white historians at the time. Nevertheless, Aptheker is cited for bringing out "one striking fact about the period: whereas the 'real' rebellions of the pre-1835 period (those of Gabriel, Vesey, and Turner) were instigated by Negroes, the 'unreal' ones in the following period almost invariably involved white men—white abolitionists, that is, created by the Southern imagination" (222). Then to underline the delusions of both Aptheker's and nineteenth-century feverish imaginations he adds: "One of the heavy coercions upon the Southern mind in this period was that men were expected to believe in these dangers, their patriotism actually coming under suspicion if they failed to" (222).

As these comments indicate, ideology became and remained a key ingredient of all subsequent discussions of Elkins's *Slavery*. These arguments and counterarguments are recorded in Ann Lane's 1971 anthology, *The Debate Over Slavery: Stanley Elkins and His Critics*.[15]

When confronted, Elkins admitted that his speculative study had not sufficiently examined antebellum American ideology, especially in comparative terms. For cultures are most profitably compared on the level of ideology, which represents "a kind of totality, the whole being more significant than its parts, and serves to exhibit in relief those very distinctions between cultures that are most worth grasping" (241–42). Characteristic of Elkins's historical explanation is this drive toward a totalizing concept organizing a whole society. Moreover, it is revealing of the horizon of this white historian's cultural imagination that his notion of an adequate culture/ideology comparison embraces Latin American and southern American configurations but leaves no room for an alternative black or slave ideology. He therefore asserts that "one may examine with fresh appreciation the slave ideology of the antebellum American South, supported as it was not only by the South's leading 'theorists'—Calhoun, Fitzhugh, Simms, Hammond and all the rest—as well as by every social, political, legal, and religious institution which that society contained" (242). But the possibility of likewise studying the writings of David Walker, Henry Highland Garnet, or Frederick Douglass—or most pertinently of all, perhaps, discussing *The Confessions of Nat Turner* as a complex expression of both a slaveowner's and a slave's ideology—is too particular to be pursued. As noted above in the Genovese-Harding exchanges over Styron's novel, and in David Brion Davis's confession, white historians' ignorance of and indifference to black historical thought was widespread in these years. Stanley Elkins was assuredly no exception.

Such insouciance respecting the significance of black culture is all the more surprising given Elkins's undefensive responses elsewhere in *Slavery*'s 1976 edition to his black critics. He acknowledged freely the weakness of his own awareness in 1959 of the extent and significance of slave folklore, music, religion, and Negro night life in the cities. "[Sterling] Stuckey's studies of double meanings in work songs, spirituals, and the Brer Rabbit cycle—all these represent a vast treasury of materials, much of it still waiting to be mined. Nor, incidentally, do I see why such a concept as 'underlife' cannot itself be extended to comparative examinations—say, with Latin America" (249). These afterthoughts on how his own work might have been made more adequate rest, therefore, on belated recognition of black ideology and slave culture as significant gaps in his earlier theorizing.

Elkins's limited awareness of black historiography and the actual richness of slave community life proved major factors in his declining importance as historian of American slavery. Elkins admitted as much in his 1976 preface. After insisting on his contributions to the ideology of slave systems he remarks wryly of his failures elsewhere: "Work by such scholars as David Brion Davis, George Frederickson, Winthrop Jordan and Eric Foner has given substance to my guess that at least one major realm of interest would be that ideology. But as things turned out, it was hardly the only one. By the end of 1974 it was apparent that another area—black culture—had come to predominate over all other concerns in the study of American slavery" (vii).

Nevertheless, even in second thoughts Elkins remained convinced of the overwhelmingly determinative power of the dominant southern culture to set conditions of everyday life, slave personality, dependency, and the range of resistances available to slaves. Responding, in Lane's *The Debate Over Slavery*, to Eugene Genovese's criticism in "Rebelliousness and Docility in the Negro Slave: A Critique of the Elkins Thesis" that Elkins's paradigm is simply too broad to encompass observed contradictions in American slavery, Elkins replied that "contradiction" must not be elevated to the level of historiographical principle.[16] Surely Genovese goes too far in suggesting that the tensions and complexities of American chattel slavery might turn, under some circumstances, a Sambo into a Nat Turner.

> With this, I fear, Genovese has shouldered a very cumbersome dialectical apparatus and at the same time pushed the argument down a road that leads nowhere. Rebellions have never been a major issue in the history of American slavery, and he himself has said as much elsewhere. There were none of any consequence after 1831, and the historical Nat Turner, from all indications, was himself anything but a Sambo. He was psychologically able to do what he did precisely because he was so situated in the system that he could resist the full impact of its Samboizing coercions. Moreover, Turner was an exception. There were few like him, and *this* is the thing that has to be explained. Genovese has not yet, to my satisfaction, located the true mechanism of rebellion, such as it was, on the North American continent; nor does he seem willing to consider the full extent to which the South was

able to organize itself—militarily, psychologically, ideologically—to discourage *all* forms of resistance, well short of open rebellion. (352–53)

Few summaries of their common subject could more clearly distinguish Elkins from the fourth pioneer in this representative pre-sixties historiography, Herbert Aptheker, who, ten years Elkins's senior, occupies a distinguished but, as we have noted above, decidedly uneven eminence in the field. Mentioned with respect by Franklin and Stampp and drawing even stronger support from younger black historians such as John Bracey and Sterling Stuckey, Aptheker was for many years dismissed or derided by the majority of his white colleagues. From J. G. De R. Hamilton (the author of the *DAB* entry on Nat Turner) to William Styron (in a negative review of Aptheker's *American Negro Slave Revolts* in the *New York Review of Books*), white southerners of diverse political generations and persuasions joined in attacking Aptheker's ideas and evidence regarding slavery and resistance.[17] As a young scholar who converted to Marxism and joined the Communist party in 1930, Aptheker had—during the Depression—participated in the noteworthy flowering of liberal and radical writings about the black past, which produced *Black Thunder* and several of the poems and plays discussed above in chapter 4. Other thirties historians joined him in bringing attention to slave revolts: the Marxist critic V. F. Calverton in his *The Awakening of America* (1939); the white college professor Harvey Wish and his 1937 essay "American Slave Insurrections before 1861"; and Joseph C. Carroll, a black high school teacher in Indiana who wrote *Slave Insurrections in the United States, 1800–1865* (1938).

While Wish and Carroll were bringing these works to limited public attention, Aptheker was still a Columbia graduate student. His 1937 master's thesis "for three decades . . . reposed on the shelves of the Columbia library"[18] before seeing publication in 1966 by Humanities Press. Two years later, and doubtless in response to the publicity over Styron's novel, it was reissued as a paperback by Grove Press, publisher of the highly successful *The Autobiography of Malcolm X*. During the early war years, Aptheker pursued his Ph.D. at Columbia, whose press in 1943 published the first edition of *American Negro Slave Revolts*. This larger, more mature work was immediately hailed by a young Kenneth Stampp "as refreshing to a minority of dissenters as it will be disconcerting to the upholders of the Southern legend."[19] Other white liberals and most black historians in the generations from Franklin to Bracey welcomed it as a milestone, as they did Aptheker's subsequent volumes on American slavery. But during the fifties and sixties Elkins was in the majority in dismissing or attacking its arguments. Not surprisingly, then, David Brion Davis did not consider Aptheker a paradigm-maker worthy of discussion in *Daedalus* in 1974.

Given such sharply divided assessments, Aptheker presents the cultural historiographer with several challenges. The first is to reexamine his texts—principally the larger 1943 work but also its slender, seldom-discussed companion—as textual cues and clues to their mixed reception and their author's dubious standing in certain professional circles. The second, more problematic challenge is to reconsider Aptheker's impact on a wider circle of readers, in light of the fact that the International Publishers reissue of *American Negro Slave Revolts* has gone through five reprintings since 1963, and *Nat Turner's Slave Rebellion* was twice inserted into the debates, literary and historical, swirling around Stanley Elkins and William Styron. The likelihood of Aptheker's sphere of cultural influence being broader than some antagonists suppose is shown by the range of magazines and journals in which his work appeared during these decades—*Science and Society*, the *Journal of Negro History*, the *New Masses*, and *The Nation* among others.

A preliminary hypothesis accounting for Aptheker's opposition and support is all too obvious in ideological terms: his work entered cultural discourse during a period of cold war paranoia over Marxist principles and Communist party affiliations. This era of generalized hostility toward radicalism was closely followed in the civil rights era by divisions over racism, blacks, and the South. In addition, a narrower, more professional explanation might focus, as Elkins's footnotes illustrate, on dubious historical practices—sources cited or ignored, unprofessionally polemical rhetoric, exaggerated claims about the causes, nature, and frequency of slave revolts. In any case, discussion of Aptheker's controversial place in sixties culture must concede at the outset that his two books together represent a more extensive treatment of American slave resistance than any his contemporary detractors produced.

To reembed Aptheker's 1963 version of *American Negro Slave Revolts* in possibly new reading formations means pointing out difficulties both professional and amateur readers may have had absorbing this

374-page monograph. By its language, narrative structure, numerous footnotes, and extensive bibliographies, Aptheker's narrative displays itself as archetypally a dissertation—detailed, documented, and (despite its sensational and touchy subject) often stylistically dull. His narrative strategy is consonant with a strenuously unsensational approach: it postpones, until midpoint in the sixteen chapters, any substantial discussion of the announced theme. Only on page 162 does he first define slave insurrections and estimate their frequency—two of his more controversial acts for many readers. He begins by rejecting an 1858 Texas legislature definition of "insurrection" as any "assemblage of three or more [slaves], with arms, with intent to obtain their liberty by force."[20] His standards are stricter, his findings more shocking. "In this study, however, the tests for insurrection or conspiracy are more severe. . . . A minimum of ten slaves involved; freedom as the apparent aim of the disaffected slaves; contemporary references labelling the event as an uprising, plot, insurrection, or the equivalent of these terms. The study, moreover, excludes, with a few exceptions, the scores of outbreaks and plots that occurred upon domestic or foreign slave-traders" (162). Observing such restrictions, Aptheker found records of approximately two hundred and fifty revolts and conspiracies in the history of American Negro history.

In working by these criteria to his arresting conclusion, Aptheker believes that rigorous scientific screening of historical evidence has dovetailed responsibly with general Marxist convictions about the ubiquity of underclass oppression in capitalist societies. Given the silent voices of these masses in past historical dialogues, he seeks new sources of facts and beliefs and takes note of previously overlooked events and uncovers the emotional responses to them. Tracing the history of slave insurrections from 1526 to 1864 raises continually the dual implications of white control of this subject: the records are full of rumors, exaggerations, and highly emotional statements by whites, and at the same time are frequently silent about other historical events whose reality is verified by slaves' experiences and responses to them. "Faced with these difficulties and uncertainties the present writer has attempted to exercise caution in handling reports of conspiracies and rebellions. . . . Yet, it is highly probable that all plots, and quite possibly even all actual outbreaks, that did occur, and that are, somewhere, on record, have *not* been uncovered. And the subject is of such a nature that it appears almost certain that some, perhaps many, occurred and were never reported" (161).

Chapter 7 of *American Negro Slave Revolts*, which most directly lays the groundwork for discussions of actual insurrections like Nat Turner's, is titled "Exaggeration, Distortion, Censorship." Here Aptheker assesses the complexities scholars and students face when sorting out the conflicting (and astonishingly rich) evidence in newspapers, sermons, speeches, diaries, court records, history books, and numerous other sources. (Indeed, Elkins's charge that Aptheker has proliferated exaggerations by exploiting dubious sources such as rural newspapers is hard to swallow, given the bulk and range of his references.) In so doing he is sometimes as critical of black, abolitionist, liberal, or radical historians' assertions and explanations as he is of those of conservatives. At one juncture, for instance, he corrects *The Communist* for a factual error and proceeds to chide the pioneer black historian George Washington Williams for being "more novelist than historian" in dressing up Nat Turner's oratory (297). Assessing this material, he is concerned to balance the emotional statements of powerful white historical figures against the dire consequences on slaves' lives resulting from even ephemeral rumors and lies. Typical of his approach is the following carefully worded paragraph:

> It has been shown that distortion and exaggeration, for political motives, played a part in the panic over the extensive slave conspiracies of 1856 and 1860, both coming in years of terrific excitement; the latter in the months just preceding and following a presidential election whose result would touch off a counter-revolutionary effort on the part of the slaveocracy. The sensational accounts of amazing quantities of poison being found among Texas slaves, and of the total destruction by incendiaries of town after town in the same State are particularly questionable—though the result in swinging black bodies is certain. (153)

Though affective terms like "terrific," "amazing," "total," and "counter-revolutionary" are heavily loaded, Aptheker's historical aim seems to be to re-create past feelings and events without sensationalizing them irresponsibly. Hence the contrast between wild white exaggerations and all-too-real black victimization is a somber-hued thread running through both books. So, too, is the contrast between the lulls and outbursts of slave uprisings during the eighteenth and nineteenth centuries—rises and falls often reflecting moods and movements in white society and political life by contrast with ongoing black determination to struggle against enslavement, which he finds even during lulls.

In this uneven struggle, both blacks and whites responded to the same larger historical forces. Thus one reason Aptheker postpones discussion of what he terms "The Turner Cataclysm" until chapter 12 of his larger study—and until page 33 in the 110-page text of *Nat Turner's Slave Rebellion*—is the conviction that even key events and extraordinary individuals are, to a decisive degree, determined by long-term economic factors and political and social institutions. These factors must, therefore, be presented before narration and explanation of the revolt and its leader can commence. He prefaces the account of the Southampton revolt in *American Negro Slave Revolts:*

> The situation, then, in the decade prior to the Southampton revolt, is one of extraordinary *malaise* in the slaveholding area. It is marked by a considerable expansion and development of anti-slavery feeling, nationally and internationally (as part of an all-embracing upsurge of progressive and radical thought and action throughout the western world), by great and serious unrest among the slave populations, in the West Indies as well as on the Continent, by severe economic depression, and by the more rapid growth of the Negro population than the white throughout the old South. Testifying to the uneasiness of the master class there appear numerous precautionary measures for the purpose of overawing or further restricting the activities of the slave population (which, in turn, very likely stimulated discontent), and, as a last resort, in order to assure the speedy suppression of all evidences of slave insubordination.
>
> It was into such a situation (one is tempted to assert, though proof is, of course, not at hand, that it was *because* of such a situation) that the upraised dark arms of vengeance of Turner and his followers crashed in the summer of 1831. (294)

As a fair synecdoche of Aptheker's style of historical discourse, this piece of rhetoric exhibits the writer's implicit assumption that careful enumeration of objective factors will accord neatly with Marxist assumptions about worldwide events, underclass unrest and master class repression, and everywhere the priority of material and economic causations. Externally, this passage and its location resemble similar passages from *Nat Turner's Slave Rebellion* in which the M.A. candidate wrote:

> What were the causation and the motivation of the Turner Revolt? The former, which, it is felt, is more deep-seated, more prolonged, more objective than the latter, has been displayed in some detail in the preceding pages. This cannot be *proven*, as can a result in chemistry, but it seems correct to say that the Turner Revolt was not merely a remarkable coincidence agreeing with the temper of the half-decade preceding it. Rather, just as the laws, petitions, plots, revolts, intrigues of that period were manifestations of the times . . . so the Turner Revolt appears to be a manifestation of this spirit, and a direct and indirect influence itself in developing the spirit and accounting for the events in the time immediately following its occurrence. (38)

Another convergence of "scientific" historical method and political ideology is Aptheker's recognition of the impossibility that even the most careful search of available sources will produce incontestable factual assertions: "No attempt will be made here to give a detailed picture of the proceedings of the Revolt. Accuracy is impossible, and the importance of it is very questionable" (47). Then he explains why a detailed narrative in this case makes questionable history: "The attempt has been made by Drewry who devotes forty pages to it. This is really too detailed, for the reader is told that one infant was temporarily spared because it 'smiled sweetly' at the assailant. Violence is too horrible to need any such artistic touches, and that such embellishments are not of a historic nature needs no demonstration" (47). Such caveats, it should be recalled, were written three decades before its author read Styron's fictional version of the same event. It is likewise worth noting that though in his review of *The Confessions of Nat Turner* for *The Nation* Aptheker only corrects a number of the novelist's factual errors, here the parsimony of historical discourse derives from fear of rhetorical excess in face of truly mysterious, truly awesome events. This conviction helps explain the matter-of-fact tone of both Aptheker narratives. Indeed, emotional images like "upraised dark arms of vengeance" crashing upon white heads in Southampton are relatively rare in either monograph. Instead, Aptheker's ideological and professional pulls lead more typically toward summarizing conclusions: "one may then, and should, consider the followers of Nat Turner not as deluded wretches and monsters (unless all revolutionaries may be thus described) but rather as further examples of the woefully long, and indeed veritably endless, roll of human beings willing to resort to open struggle in order to get something precious to them—peace, prosperity, liberty, or, in a word, a greater amount of happiness" (6). Here, as in Aptheker's maturer writings, the human factor of personal desire merges with the dialectic of history. This is quintessentially the case with Nat Turner. In Aptheker's two narratives of the Southampton slave revolt, although Turner himself is carefully described and motivated, he is not drawn with heroic strokes nor is his insurrection depicted as an act of personal vengeance. In fact, his deep religious motivation scarcely sets him apart from fellow slaves or, indeed, fellow Americans: "Turner became convinced that he 'was ordained for some great purpose in the hands of the Almighty,'" Aptheker reports in *American Negro Slave Revolts*. "The slave waited for a sign from his God. This came to him in the form of the solar eclipse of February 12, 1831" (296). Then, in a tart footnote, Aptheker takes issue with historians who have ridiculed Turner's "negro intelligence": "One must remember that Turner lived in early nineteenth-century rural America where superstition and mysticism were common for white and Negro. . . . Indeed, the eclipse that influenced Turner moved a New York City white preacher to say that 'the whole city South of Canal Street would sink. Some persons actually went to the upper part of the city'" (296–97).

A description of the revolt's course follows, which covers less than four pages. Of nearly equal importance with the narrative of killings and reprisals is Aptheker's careful documentation and questioning of sources. The initial attack is described in a dozen laconic lines.

> These six slaves, then, started out in the evening of August 21, 1831, on their crusade against bondage. Their first blow—delivered by Turner himself—struck against the person and family of Turner's master, Joseph Travis, who were killed. Some arms and horses were taken, the rebels pushed on, and everywhere slaves flocked to their standard; a result which Turner, starting out

with but a handful of followers, must have had excellent reasons to anticipate. Within twenty-four hours approximately seventy slaves were actively aiding in the rebellion. By the morning of August 23rd, at least fifty-seven whites—men, women, and children—had been killed, and the rebels had covered about twenty miles. (298)

The drama's denouement takes scarcely longer to relate. Both are critically defended in footnotes that repeat warnings first sounded in *Nat Turner's Slave Rebellion*. "*The Confessions*, and the press, especially the Richmond *Enquirer* and the Richmond *Whig* are the basic sources for the proceedings of the rebellion itself, bearing in mind, of course, that all are hostile to the cause Turner espoused. No attempt will be made to detail these since accuracy is impossible" (298). Then he takes up the apparently inevitable question of violence other than death done to the whites: "Death alone met the victims of the slaves' vengeance and wrath. Historians find great difficulty in accounting for the fact that, so far as the evidence shows, there was no instance of rape or attempted rape by Turner's followers." One historian (R. R. Howison) is quoted as saying "Remembering the brutal passions of the negro [sic] we can only account for this fact by supposing the actors to have been appalled by the very success of their hideous enterprise." Another (Drewry) "states that women were insulted and offers further, without reference, some romantic nonsense about Turner promising to save a fair white damsel if she would but marry him" (298–99). Unlike his southern white predecessors, Aptheker makes it his historian's duty to document his retelling as fully as possible. There are, for example, 109 footnotes in his chapter devoted to the revolt. At the same time he takes pains to distinguish between supported data and attributions of fact or opinion.

The impossibility of maintaining clear lines between fact and fantasy are exemplified—if not openly admitted—in Aptheker's treatment of the "Turner Cataclysm's" aftermath. He declares flatly:

> Massacre followed. Phillips simply notes, "a certain number of innocent blacks shot down," and Ballagh asserts, "A most impartial trial was given to all, except a few decapitated" in Southampton, while Drewry thought "there was far less of this indiscriminate murder than might have been expected." Just how much

"indiscriminate murder" one ought to "expect" is not clear, but General Eppes, the officer in command of the affected county, leads one to believe that these historians were rather uncritical in dealing with this phase of the event. (300)

Though properly ironic about others' interpretations, Aptheker cannot, of course, escape the same accusation. His succinct declaration "massacre followed" carries as clear a moral judgment as "a few decapitated." Similarly loaded is the rhetoric of his conclusion about the black death toll after the revolt: "It seems accurate to say that at least twice as many Negroes were indiscriminately slaughtered in that county, as the number of white people who had fallen victim to the vengeance and bondage-hating spirit of the slave" (301).

When describing the aftermath, Aptheker's almost pedantic sifting of evidence leads finally to privileging Turner's own version of the revolt's extent, even when the governor of Virginia voices a contrary opinion:

> With the news of this outbreak, panic flashed through Virginia. The uprising was infectious and slaves everywhere became restless (or, at least, it was believed that they had become restless) so that the terror, momentarily localized in Virginia, spread up to Delaware and through Georgia, across to Louisiana and into Kentucky. This naturally led some to believe that Turner had concerted measures for rebellion over a wider area than his own county. Thus, Governor Floyd wrote: "From all that had come to my knowledge during and since this affair—I am fully convinced that every black in the whole country east of the Blue Ridge, was in the secret," and again, "In relation to the extent of the insurrection I think it greater than will ever appear." A few other contemporary statements of similar purport appeared, and some later writers have adopted the same viewpoint.
>
> The final authority on this question, however, is Nat Turner himself and he affirmed that the revolt he led was local, and that his activities had been confined to his own neighborhood. He added: "I see, sir, you doubt my word but can you not think the same ideas and strange appearances about this time in the heavens might prompt others as well as myself to this undertaking?" In the absence of any evidence of equal weight to the

contrary, one must conclude that Turner possessed the characteristic of great leaders in that he sensed the mood and feelings of the masses of his fellow beings, not only in his immediate environment, but generally. (305–6)

Aptheker's reliance on Gray's *Confessions* here and elsewhere is augmented by other supporting evidence, including his own speculations. Thus regarding the above comment he observes: "It is possible that Turner insisted on this in order to protect others. It is also possible that his early associates in the plot, in the weeks prior to the outbreak, may have spread word of what was to come. Such news via the almost uncanny underground telegraph of the slaves could travel great distances in a short time" (305–6). Though slaves' underground networks left few archival traces, the historian reminds readers of their existence and importance as one piece in the historical puzzle.

Hidden (or at least not well-known) messages circulating in the white world are likewise important to Aptheker, even as misstatements or outbursts of raw emotion. In fact, by quoting liberally from such sources he emphasizes the fact that, however academic his own retelling may for good reasons be, the original event and its social ambience were charged everywhere with the strongest, and often most irrational, feelings. Among his many quotations, therefore, are a number of sensational statements. These sometimes reflect responses by leading actors like Governor Floyd or General Eppes. But frequently Aptheker also recaptures the thoughts and emotions of ordinary citizens—even, at times, those whose spelling placed them close to the illiterate white underclass. One literate response to news of the revolt was the following: "A niece of George Washington declared 'it is like a smothered volcano—we know not when or where, the flame will burst forth but we know that death in most horrid forms threaten [*sic*] us. Some have died, others have become deranged from apprehension since the South Hampton affair'" (306–7). This lady's letter to the mayor of Boston is followed by a Virginia gentleman's even more eloquent missive to a northern acquaintance:

> These insurrections have alarmed my wife so as really to endanger her health, and I have not slept without anxiety in these months. Our nights are sometimes spent in listening to noises. A corn song, or a hog call, has often been the subject of nervous ter-

> ror, and a cat, in the dining room, will banish sleep for the night. There has been and there still is a *panic* in all this country. I am beginning to lose my courage about the melioration of the South. Our revivals produce no preachers; churches are like the buildings in which they worship, gone in a few years. There is no principle of life. Death is autocrat of slave regions. (307)

Aptheker's footnotes instruct the attentive reader how to assess the ideological import of these outpourings. The first is preserved only in the mayor's collected correspondence, while the latter was speedily reprinted in the *Liberator* during the month of January 1832 as the Virginia legislature debated its response to Nat Turner's insurrection. Its poignant eloquence was thus put to work in the abolitionist cause, even as its date of publication records stiffening southern resistance. However, the modern historian clarifies as he links these responses to rebellion and abolition: "there is no evidence to show a connection between Turner's efforts and those of the Abolitionists, and it is not true that the Virginia legislature, following his rebellion, came close to abolition" (317). Nevertheless, all these actions and expressions are seen as historical elements in a critical period that, in Aptheker's account, stretched almost without break from 1831 to near the close of the Civil War:

> The era of crisis takes form . . . , remaining groups of anti-slavery people, as Quakers, leave or alter their sentiments; emancipationist societies disappear in the South, and spring up by the hundreds in the North. Anti-slavery agitators "in any shape, or under any pretext, are furious fanatics or knaves or hypocrites; and we hereby promise them, upon all occasions which may put them in our power, the fate of the pirate, the incendiary, and the midnight assassin," while in the North there begins to develop the feeling that "all who are not with the abolitionists are against them; for silence and inaction are public acquiescence in things as they are." (321–22)

In concluding remarks Aptheker continues to justify his consistent (and, to many, excessive) attention to this category of reports, which mixes rumors with plots, conspiracies, and actual rebellions. "There are few phases of ante-bellum Southern life and history that were not in some way influenced by the fear of, or the actual outbreak of, militant concerted slave action. In some cases the influences were of a minor, if not of a merely formal, nature" (368). By implication, at least, this assertion anticipates the accusation by later readers that *American Negro Slave Revolts* fails to consider adequately the cultural basis of both revolts and their suppressions. Without repudiating economic and political causes and consequences of insurrections, actual or threatened, Aptheker reminds readers that the dominant southern way of life was organized around threats to a slaveholding social order. There were two dimensions of this cultural construction: first, "the formulation of the legal, social, and theological aspects of pre-Civil War Southern life . . . to prevent . . . or . . . suppress mass Negro rebelliousness" (369); second, the institutional and intellectual structure rested upon a singular substructure, the "myth of the sub-humanity of the Negro":

> a myth basic to the entire social order, and which demanded the corruption of political science, theology, and anthropology. Acceptance of this idea had to be demonstrated by all, Negro and white, in their daily behavior, their mode of eating and speaking, their demeanor, their occupations and activities, their worshipping and love-making, their every feature and phase of living had to acknowledge the immutability, indeed, the divine origin of the status quo. Failure to abide by this meant—for the white—ostracism, both social and economic, explicit warning or overt punishment, tar and feathers, lashing, imprisonment, hanging; for the Negro, sale, torture, death. (370)

After 1959 and especially by the mid-sixties, readers of these lines already familiar with *Slavery* could hardly fail to be struck by how near Aptheker approaches an endorsement of Elkins's "total institution" construct. To be sure, the preceding 360-odd pages of *American Negro Slave Revolts* have as their insistent burden the modes of resistance slaves imagined, developed, and often carried out even in the face of "sale, torture, death." But what is all but absent from both of Aptheker's historical explanations is a sketch of the way of life in the slave community that paralleled and opposed the oppressive white culture. Despite his sympathetic advocacy of the black's cause and role in American history, Aptheker's treatment of this crucial area reflects a narrowly political rather than anthropological outlook. Though he argued (and documented) an intertwined social order of whites and blacks, Aptheker failed to flesh out in any detail the slaves' web of communal experiences, beliefs, and institutions. In this respect, *American Negro Slave Revolts* is closer to Franklin's *From Slavery to Freedom* and, curiously and to a limited degree only, Elkins's *Slavery* than it is to Stampp's *The Peculiar Institution*.

Nevertheless, Aptheker's contributions to the sixties debates over slave resistance and slave culture were and are substantial. Summarizing them again raises questions still not resolved here about Aptheker's marginal standing not only as a potential paradigm-maker but even as respected pioneer in this field. In tracing the flow of historical information and interpretation from academic fountainheads typified here by Franklin, Stampp, Elkins, and Aptheker, we should look for evidence of Aptheker's impact on sixties thought and feeling. We might suspect this influence to be at work if and where the following generalizations by Aptheker are clustered:

1. the study of a range of available sources demonstrates the frequency and importance of violent slave resistance throughout the three centuries of the institution's history;

2. much of this evidence is what some historians claim is soft data: opinions, rumors, secondhand facts, expressions of emotion and belief embracing intent, desire, fear, hatred, vindictiveness, dream, nightmare;

3. estimates of 250 or more conspiracies, plots, or actual revolts are based on all sorts of evidence, including this soft data but also newspapers, court records, government documents, census reports, correspondence, travelers' accounts;

4. lumping together real, reported, projected, or imagined acts of armed resistance to slavery is justified by the verifiable results of even false information on the behavior of whites and the lives of blacks;

5. the complex causes of slave revolts include social, economic, political, legal, and theological events and institutions and these factors are more basic and influential than private motivations like vengeance, benevolence, or divine inspiration;

6. nevertheless, a leader such as Nat Turner and the singular

event of his Southampton slave revolt are significant influences on the course of future history.

The Journalist as Popular Historian: Roger Butterfield, Lerone Bennett, Jr., Charles Silberman

In reimagining the historiographical reach and impact of these four influential historians of slavery and resistance, I have tried to fill gaps in sociological knowledge by adopting several conventional interpretive strategies. One has been to establish each writer's personal and cultural identity and professional niche as suggested by such recent historiographers as David Brion Davis, Peter Novick and Meier and Rudwick, whose *Black History and the Historical Profession* has proved especially useful because it not only complements and corrects the white-oriented analyses of Davis and Novick but is also based on interviews with more than 175 historians, including Franklin, Stampp, Elkins, and Aptheker. Now in continuing to trace the spread of information and interpretation through other channels to different audiences of sixties and seventies Americans, I shall bring other historiographical perspectives to the discussion. Though continuing to treat historians as socially active creators, conduits, and critics of explanations about the past, I shall pay closer attention to shifts in social valuations of information exchanges. To what groups of readers are what sorts of facts and interpretations transmitted and become significant? This process grows especially relevant but also more problematic during the later years of this tempestuous decade as new groups of players, along with traditional cultural elites, recharge this aspect of American history with different and often strong passions.

We need first to acknowledge that professional historians' significantly revalued understandings of the past depend for their full social influence not simply upon the sales of their own books but also on their influence upon other writers. These are sometimes fellow historians but also journalists or classroom teachers who translate historical research and new explanations for wider audiences and different consumers. Although all of the central texts mentioned above appeared eventually in readily available paperback editions, there were limits to each work's social domain and cultural impact. Addressed primarily to fellow professionals, graduate students, or college undergraduates, these texts sent signals not readily received by more general readers. Indeed scholarly monographs and university textbooks, with their paraphernalia of introduction and acknowledgments, footnotes, tables, graphs, appendices, and bibliographies surrounding a text written in relatively cool, third-person nonfictional prose, are unlikely to seize and hold the ordinary adult's attention, no matter how pertinent or sensational the subject. Even more remote from general readers' interests are references and counterarguments linking one scholarly text to another.

Nearly as clear-cut are biographical differences among the authors of academic as contrasted to popular histories. As already pointed out, Franklin, Stampp, Elkins and Aptheker are all professionally trained, university-based historians with working connections to university presses or certain liberal commercial publishers such as Alfred A. Knopf or the radical International Publishers. Despite Aptheker's often marginal location in this professional publishing scene, he, like the others, was an active participant in institutions like historical associations and the *Journal of Negro History*.

The three popularizers whose texts illustrate types and variations in the demotic distribution of historical explanations operated socially and commercially at some distance from these pioneers. Each of the three—Roger Butterfield, Lerone Bennett, Jr., and Charles Silberman—was affiliated primarily with journalism and freelance writing rather than academic activities. Butterfield, author of *The American Past: A History of the United States from Concord to Hiroshima, 1775–1945* (Simon and Schuster, 1947), was a newspaperman, writer, and longtime editor at Time, Inc. In popular books on a World War II marine and on Henry Ford, and in scores of articles and features in such magazines as the *Saturday Evening Post, Ladies Home Journal, American Heritage,* and *Reader's Digest,* he addressed a broad spectrum of middle-class readers. Lerone Bennett, Jr., was affiliated with the Chicago-based, black-owned Johnson Publishing Company, whose magazine *Ebony* appeals chiefly to the black middle class and aspirants thereto. In 1962 Johnson published *Before the Mayflower: A History of the Negro in America 1619–1962,* the first of Bennett's several histories and political essays written during the decade. Charles E. Silberman, author of *Crisis in Black and White* (Random House, 1964), was a *Fortune* editor assigned in the early sixties to work on a series of articles on urban problems. One result was "The City and the Negro," a major article in the March 1962 *Fortune* that drew wide attention. Like Bennett, Silberman received a leave of absence from his magazine to expand his study into a book addressing the underlying causes of urban dysfunction. Unlike the black writer, however, Silberman received a Ford Foundation grant through Columbia University to support his project.

The earliest of these popular histories, Butterfield's *The American Past*, was also the most inclusive, as suggested by its original subtitle, *A History of the United States from Concord to Hiroshima, 1775–1945*. This weighty, coffee-table production "contains more pictures from more different sources than any single volume ever published," Butterfield boasted. "Yet I do not think of it strictly as a 'picture history.' Pictures *can* lie, and often do; . . . A carefully chosen picture can distort almost any fact. By the same token, some pictures can tell the truth in a way that words are powerless to match. I have tried to include as many such pictures as I could find."[21] Appearing originally the same year as *From Slavery to Freedom*, Butterfield's breezy text was designed to provide "the steady factual theme of the book, while the pictures supplied the overtones in significance, drama, and humor" (v). This was, in short, American history for browsers rather than burrowers, and its setting was the middle-class living room or den rather than the library or schoolroom. Despite a once-over-lightly treatment of nearly all historical subjects, slave insurrections are at least mentioned in Butterfield's panorama. The book's central focus is politics, "by which I mean considerably more than party conventions and ward heeling and Boss Tweed. Politics, as I understand it . . . includes everything that importantly influences the fate or mood of the nation at any particular time" (v). What he might have added is that his politics deals primarily with issues and events affecting white Americans. Thus Nat Turner's name is cited only in relation (and subordination) to northern abolitionism. For the year 1831, therefore, the spotlight falls on William Lloyd Garrison, Boston, and the *Liberator*. As a less "political" event, "later that year the Nat Turner slave insurrection broke out in Virginia, causing the senseless slaughter of 55 whites and more than 100 blacks. Although such revolts were nothing new, the whole South blamed this one on Garrison. A virtual state of siege went up in the Southern states" (97). The liberation movement's first martyr, therefore, was not Turner but the abolitionist editor Elijah P. Lovejoy of Illinois. Another clue to Butterfield's beliefs—and his reading of his audience's preferences—is revealed in the illustration of a New Orleans "slave store" which specialized in domestic servants. A group of black men and women are shown sitting or posing in their best clothes, seeking to attract wealthy buyers. The caption mentions that "the black men in the silk hats at the left sold for between $600 and $800 each" (96). On the facing page, in a smaller picture of Louisiana sugarcane workers, the caption's sanitized message is again couched in financial terms: "these sugar-cane cutters were the most valuable slaves, selling for as high as $1300 each" (97). In the background of this picture, however, the grimmer realities of slavery are suggested by a kneeling slave receiving lashes from a slave master. Thus Butterfield's visual and written messages bring into the white middle-class home of the forties, fifties, and even sixties impressions of slavery and its violence weighted in favor of house servants clothed and priced as extensions of genteel white culture, with the more unpleasant realities of field hands, overseers, whips, and the "senseless slaughter" of Nat Turner kept in the background.

As with Butterfield, one social setting in which to situate Bennett's *Before the Mayflower* is the black middle-class home of the sixties. This 400-page, fairly expensive, and generously illustrated book might well serve as a social possession bespeaking its owners' cultural and racial pride. Thus one could reasonably imagine the same coffee tables holding copies of *Ebony* as well as *Reader's Digest* and *Negro Digest*. Bennett's prefatory remarks to readers of the first edition lend plausibility to these inferences. He points out that *Before the Mayflower* originated in a series of *Ebony* articles. Its title is frankly chosen to arouse pride of ancestry. "The book, like the series, deals with the trials and triumphs of a group of Americans whose roots in the American soil are deeper than those of the Puritans who arrived on the celebrated *Mayflower* a year after a 'Dutch man of war' deposited twenty Negroes at Jamestown."[22] As compared with Butterfield's white north American perspective, Bennett's story begins in the Sudan and Nile Valley and ends with a quite different contemporary climax, "the Second Reconstruction which Martin Luther King, Jr. and the 'sit-in' generation are fashioning in the North and South" (xi). Clearly, Bennett's "politics" primarily answers the needs and mood of black American readers.

Moreover, Bennett expects his audience to be more seriously concerned than Butterfield's about the conjunction of history and politics: "This history is founded on the work of scholars and specialists and is designed for the average reader. It is not strictly speaking a book for scholars, but it is as scholarly as fourteen months of research can make it" (xi). For readers unfamiliar with key facts and the basic chronology of black American history Bennett appends a section of "Landmarks and Milestones." Like his own narrative, this outline emphasizes two insistent themes—black suffering and resistance counterpointing black achievements as contributing members of American culture. Hence the entries for 1830 and 1831 emphasize four key events: the birth in 1830 of the first black Roman Catholic archbishop; the first National Negro Convention in Philadelphia; the appearance of Garrison's *Liberator;* and Nat Turner's revolt.

In marked contrast to such bare bones but carefully selected recitals of facts, names, and dates, Bennett's main text is vigorously paced, full of dramatic scenes and plentifully dotted with quotations from slaves themselves. Frequent rhetorical questions, one-sentence paragraphs, and arresting, often violent illustrations further characterize a colloquial style full of adjectives and active verbs. Yet the journalist-historian expects readers to listen respectfully to scholarly voices and arguments that are also part of his message. The combination creates a deceptively simple narrative texture. Readers are carried along on currents of vicarious emotional participation. But at the same time they are exposed to current ideas and arguments over the changed meanings of these events. This mixture, indicating that Bennett speaks simultaneously to several sorts of readers, is aptly illustrated in the passage on slave resistance that precedes chapter 5, "Slave Revolts and Insurrections." This description of "bad negroes" and cruel slave masters illustrates his characteristic authorial presence.

> That some slaves succumbed to this assault on the mind is not unusual. Faced with absolute power in a closed system, American white men and Europeans succumbed in concentration camps in Korea and Germany. The interesting thing about slavery is that so many saw through the shell game and fought back.
> There were many proud and defiant rebels who could not be broken. At one time or another, most planters ran afoul of the

"bad Negro," fabled in the traditions of slavery, who vowed that no white man would whip him. . . .

Court records speak for these "bad negroes" whom some historians would like to forget.

One slave said:

"He would be damned if he did not kill his master, if he ever struck him again."

Another was ecstatic as he dug his master's grave.

"I have killed him at last. . . ."

The court records of this period yield ample evidence that a large number of slaves refused to play the game of slavery: they would neither smile nor bow. Some bowed but would not smile. . . .

What they thought can be inferred from what they did. Stampp and other historians have uncovered a mass of material relating to their passive, "day to day resistance to slavery." (94–95)

Bennett concludes this descriptive and historiographical passage (which contains oblique references to Elkins, Phillips, Stampp, and Aptheker) by quoting key sentences from *The Peculiar Institution*'s peroration on the folk heroes of American slavery.

A black historian from an older generation than Franklin and Stampp, however, supplies Bennett's epigraph to his crucial chapter 5: "Denmark Vesey is a symbol of a spirit too violent to be acceptable to the white community," Charles S. Johnson observed ironically in *The Negro in American Civilization* (1930). "There are no Negro schools named for him, and it would be extremely poor taste and bad judgment for the Negroes to take any pride in his courage and philosophy" (96). Bennett's encomium to Vesey is matched by others to Toussaint L'Ouverture, Gabriel Prosser and, more briefly, the anonymous African slaves who in 1526, first revolted against their Spanish leaders on the Pedee River in South Carolina. Aptheker provides much of this information and is also the inspiration for the chapter's illustrations and captions. These illustrations graphically document a slave burnt at the stake in New York City after "The Negro Plot of 1741" and then depict a group of blacks, "increasingly militant" after the passage of the Fugitive Slave Act, repelling with gunfire a group of slave hunters in Christiana, Pennsylvania. But for Bennett the preeminent demonstration of a slave's triumph over degradation and betrayal is Nat Turner: "Gabriel Prosser plotted and was betrayed. Nat Turner plotted and executed" (118). In fact, "the dark, buddha-bellied man called The Prophet [who] dangled from the end of a rope in a town called Jerusalem" (125) had greater impact on the antebellum South than either Calhoun or Jefferson Davis. Bennett's borrowing of Stampp's bold comparison is part of a characterization of Turner that nicely balances mythic and heroic with thoroughly human qualities.

> A mystic with blood on his mind, a preacher with vengeance on his lips, a dreamer, a fanatic, a terrorist, Nat Turner was a fantastic mixture of gentleness, ruthlessness and piety. Of middling stature, black in color, in demeanor commanding and bold, Nat Turner was five feet six inches tall, a little dumpy perhaps, running to fat around the middle, with a mustache and a little tuft of hair on his chin.
>
> Early in life, Nat came to the view that God had set him aside for some great purpose. And he worked hard to help God. (118)

At the center of the seven pages devoted to Turner's bloody act of assistance to God, Bennett includes three revealing illustrations. Two of these depict the prophet, documenting Bennett's physical description. Their relative size and content accurately reflect the text's priorities. In the larger, upper illustration (here see p. x) Nat and his five followers are gathered in the swamp, plotting a fearful vengeance, symbolized by the eerie light falling on Nat's contorted masklike face and outstretched arm pointing toward Jerusalem—the rebels' goal on the "trail of terror" depicted by a map on the opposite page. Below this gothic scene is another, smaller copy of the often-reprinted representation of Nat Turner's capture. In this spot, the reader is led to note two details perhaps overlooked in other printings: how bravely erect Turner stands confronting his captor, and how large and daggerlike is his sword. In fact, Benjamin Phipps, the white captor, might almost be thought to cower behind his shotgun. Elsewhere the text also balances auspicious beginnings against tragic outcomes.

> He then led his men to the bedroom of his master and mistress.
> Nat struck the first blow, but his aim was faulty. Will finished the

Nineteenth-century engraving of Turner's capture by Benjamin Phipps (Courtesy of the Library of Congress).

job. Two boys in an upstairs bedroom were also killed. Nat's band appropriated guns and powder. Leaving the house, Nat recalled that a baby had been spared. Remarking that "nits make lice," he detailed two men to kill the infant.

Moving quietly and swiftly through the night, the little band cut a swath of red, chopping down old, young, male, female. At almost every stop, additional slaves joined them. . . .

All through that terrible night, men, women, and children died. No one with a white skin was spared except a family of poor whites who owned no slaves.

Monday morning dawned and Nat rode on.

When the first bodies were discovered, a nameless dread seized the white citizenry. Women, children, and men fled to the swamps and hid under the leaves. Other citizens flocked to the public buildings and barricaded the doors. Some whites left the county; others left the state. (123)

Though more briefly narrated, the revolt's failure and aftermath are similarly violent but always personalized accounts: "A massacre followed. The enraged whites shot down innocent Negroes who smiled and innocent Negroes who did not smile. The editor of the Richmond *Whig* said: 'Men were tortured to death, burned, maimed, and subjected to nameless atrocities'" (124). Indeed, Bennett's penchant for drama leads at times to bathetic extremes: "A boy rode into town and reported falsely that a hostile force [of slaves] was within eight miles. The town went up in hysteria. An old man keeled over and died. At least two other white men died of heart failure in the state" (125).

So intent is Bennett on arousing terror (if not pity) in his readers that he cuts short discussion of the long-range consequences of the Southampton slave revolt. Furthermore, though many personal and gory details derive from Gray's *Confessions*, no reference is ever made to that prime record or its problematic status as a "white" document. Thus, instead of offering Aptheker or Gray as conclusive sources of his version, Bennett concludes with an almost flattering appropriation from W. S. Drewry's *The Southampton Insurrection*, surely one of the most blatantly racist accounts of the revolt ever written. Drewry reports Nat Turner's last-minute prophecy that it would rain and grow dark after his execution. Though this proved false, Drewry was symbolically correct, Bennett insists. He then quotes Drewry's summary judgment: "Nat Turner's insurrection was a landmark in the history of slavery. . . . It was the forerunner of the great slavery debates, which resulted in the abolition of slavery in the United States and was, indirectly, most instrumental in bringing about this result. Its importance is truly conceived by the old negroes of Southampton and vicinity, who reckon all time from 'Nat's Fray' or 'Old Nat's War'" (125–26).

If Butterfield and Bennett clearly target different American audiences, Charles Silberman's *Crisis in Black and White* seems to promise—by its title at least—a more inclusive readership and a more evenhanded treatment of American racism. Such expectations are only partially fulfilled. Written in the immediate aftermath of President

John F. Kennedy's assassination, the March on Washington, and the Birmingham street riots, *Crisis in Black and White* is preeminently a social and political diagnosis of white racism and "the Negro problem," two blights on American national life. The disease, moreover, is more deeply embedded in the body politic than Gunnar Myrdal's 1944 study, *An American Dilemma*, ever discerned: "Myrdal was wrong. The tragedy of race relations in the United States is that there is no American Dilemma. White Americans are not torn and tortured by the conflict between their devotion to the American creed and their actual behavior. They are upset by the current state of race relations, to be sure. But what troubles them is not that great justice is being denied but that their peace is being shattered and their business interrupted."[23] What is essential—though not to be expected—is a radical reconstruction of American society in which New Yorkers as well as Mississippians, older whites as well as young blacks, recognize and alter age-old attitudes. If they fail to act, all Americans will suffer, not just the black or the southerner.

Basic to understanding the present situation and beginning its reformation, Silberman argues, is historical consciousness. Although *Crisis in Black and White* is more insistently contemporary (if no more political) than either *The American Past* or *Before the Mayflower*, it examines in some detail the legacy of the past, and in particular the sources of "the Negro Problem." History is employed at several points to discover the nature of black personality and identity formation. But examination of the past is less necessary for understanding the psychosociology of white prejudice and discrimination. This imbalance is typical of Silberman's approach. Negroes are ostensibly equal and respected actors in the reconstruction of modern social reality, but in practice their role as victims and the fact of their deviance from white cultural norms are heavily weighted: "White men began three and a half centuries ago to treat black men as inferiors, and they haven't stopped yet. A major part of 'the negro problem' in America lies in what these three hundred fifty years have done to the Negro's personality: the self-hatred, the sense of impotence and inferiority that destroys aspiration and keeps the Negro locked in a prison we have all made" (11). When it comes to itemizing the costs of dehumanization, Silberman asserts the sad fact that white stereotypes of blacks are by and large accurate: "Negroes *do* display less ambition than whites; . . . Negroes *do* have 'looser morals.' . . . Negroes *do* 'care less for family' . . . [and] score lower on IQ tests than whites of comparable socio-economic status and Negro children do poorer work in school" (74). Consequently, "the Negro cannot move into the mainstream of American life unless he is able to destroy the image in his own mind and in the mind of the white" (77). Recognizing these unpleasant truths, he insists, is not to accept immutable Negro inferiority: "On the contrary, every one of them can be explained by the facts of Negro history in the United States" (74).

The crucial factor, Silberman believes, has been identified by Stanley Elkins of the University of Chicago, "author of the most brilliant and probing study of slavery in the United States" (74–75). *Slavery* provides the key to the past and present norm of black personality—the childlike and dependent Sambo who remains the lasting legacy of history. Silberman supports this assertion by echoing with approval other arguments of Elkins's, including the concentration camp analogy with its contrasts between "open" and "closed" institutions: "Transforming the concentration camp inmates into servile children, it should be recalled, was accomplished in a matter of months or at most years. The American Negro had been subject to a system designed to destroy ambition, prevent independence, and erode intelligence for the past three and a half centuries. . . . Uncomfortable as we may all find the truth, the truth is that the 'nigger' with which [James] Baldwin is obsessed, the 'Sambo' of Southern folklore, was a reality and to a considerable extent still is" (76–77).

But Elkins is not the only analyst whose explanations are repackaged for popular consumption and political effect. Tocqueville shares Elkins's deterministic view, as does a white liberal historian such as Kenneth Stampp, according to Silberman:

> Liberal historians have gone to great lengths to discover examples of Negro courage, Negro rebelliousness, Negro hatred for slavery—that is to say, all the attributes one would expect to find in those who are "merely white men wearing black skins." But the ghost of "Sambo" cannot be exorcised that easily. Professor Stampp, for example, who has written a major critique of the Southern view of slavery, is forced to concede: "To be sure, there were plenty of opportunities among the Negroes who played the

role assigned to them, acted the clown, and curried the favor of their masters in order to win the maximum rewards within the system." And when the much heralded revolts are examined closely, they turn out to be rather insignificant. Of the two hundred fifty "revolts" which the historian Herbert Aptheker has uncovered, for example, only three are really worthy of the term "revolt." The two best-organized—those led by Vesey and Gabriel—were suppressed quite easily, and the most dramatic, the Nat Turner rebellion, was little more than aimless butchery. The remaining "revolts," even under Aptheker's sympathetic description, are clearly insignificant—little more than outbreaks of local vandalism. (79)

In passages like this Silberman illustrates, more transparently than Butterfield or Bennett, the temptations popularizers face in using experts' arguments and their actual words to buttress simplified and often subtly distorted versions of a historical hypothesis. Here three historians are deployed in apparent support of Silberman's version of one convenient and privileged argument—Elkins's. Aptheker's authority is undercut by the use (secondhand, as a matter of fact) of quotation marks around the key term "revolt." Stampp's argument is slanted by turning a qualification into a major concession, which *The Peculiar Institution* treats far more ambiguously. Most manipulative of all, however, is the way Elkins's ideology and, indeed, his very language are slipped in under the apparent cover of Aptheker's and Stampp's authority. Only expert readers of *Slavery* could be expected to recall Elkins's footnote derogation of his fellow historians, which is pirated in pejorative phrases like "easily suppressed," "aimless butchery," and "local vandalism."[24]

Concealed quotation elsewhere countenances this layman's appropriated and altered explanation. "We need not labor the point," he concludes with equal disingenuousness. "What is essential is neither to rewrite history as some liberals have done nor to pretend that the by-products of a slave system are non-existent" (80). Silberman's ploy in asserting that he (and Elkins) are simply restoring unpleasant "truths" of history is surely as self-serving as Styron's argument at the SHA—"these are the facts. Deal with them." To stick more faithfully to the often ambiguous and even contradictory explanations of Stampp,

Elkins, or Aptheker is evidently impossible for a journalist-social critic determined "to use that history for an understanding of the current 'inferiorities' that *do* exist, and to search for new identities" (80).

The trouble with *Crisis in Black and White*, many black and some white readers of 1964 must have felt, is that blacks, and not whites, bear the chief burden, as Silberman sees it, for finding new identities in mainstream America. Far less space is devoted to European sources of white racism, for example, or to consideration of ways whites must learn to change *their* identities to merge with blacks. Hence Silberman's foray into African history, a section of his social diagnosis based not only on Elkins's *Slavery* but, interestingly enough, also on Bennett's *Before the Mayflower*, is justified to explain the trauma of enslavement, the Middle Passage, and the devastating losses of culture and identity in the New World. Pages are devoted to repeating Elkins's case for cultural deracination under the total institution of North American slavery. Nothing is said about cultural persistence or new cultural adaptations on the part of African slaves or their descendants. Such cultural myopia derives from Silberman's deterministic view that one can read forward and backward from present-day black social "sickness" to antebellum responses to the overwhelming force of slavery and white racist exploitation. Silberman's narrative easily bridges the decades between Emancipation and contemporary Harlem:

> Slavery had emasculated the Negro males, had made them shiftless and irresponsible and promiscuous by preventing them from ever assuming responsibility, negating their role as husband and father, and making them totally dependent on the will of another. There was no stable family structure to offer support to men or women or children in this strange new world. . . . Thus there developed a pattern of drifting from place to place and job to job and woman to woman that has persisted (in lesser degree, of course) to the present day. (94)

An impressive variety of black (and white) voices are selectively quoted to support this bleak picture of black impotence and the lack of culture. Uncle Remus, Charles Francis Adams, W. E. B. Du Bois, Richard Wright, Ralph Ellison, H. L. Mencken are all made to testify in Silberman's court, whose historical verdict is confidently confirmed: "In contrast to European immigrants, who brought rich cultures and long histories with them, the Negro had been completely stripped of his past and severed from any culture save that of the United States" (109). That "the culture of the United States" is a white amalgam goes without saying—for, indeed, Silberman is not really interested in any other cultural dimensions of "the Negro Problem." The remainder of *Crisis in Black and White* is therefore devoted to contemporary social and political problems and solutions. These chapters culminate in an extended discussion of a test case of black self-improvement, the Woodlawn Organization of Chicago, a model for Silberman of concerted action to overcome "welfare colonialism." It is, however, ironic that this singular example of black initiative depended heavily on the leadership—temporary, to be sure—of Saul Alinsky, the white sixties radical and community organizer.

The political commentaries and cultural histories of Butterfield, Bennett, and Silberman did not, of course, monopolize the popular market of early sixties readers incited by events to reacquaint themselves with American history and particularly the antebellum world of slaves and masters. These public historians' roles typify the ways and means by which professional paradigms were transmitted, simplified, and altered, to sizable general readerships, black and white, during the decade after the *Brown* decision. The reprintings and revised editions of these books, like the increased sales and availability of books by Franklin, Stampp, and Elkins and the belated attention paid Aptheker, point to an escalation of public concern. A willingness to connect past and present in new and more inclusive terms and thus to develop, however informally, new demotic historicisms is one plausible conclusion to draw from this examination. How deeply—or, indeed, how widely—popular awareness was affected by these historians is difficult to ascertain, even when one notes that *Crisis in Black and White* had gone into nine reprintings by April 1966 and *Before the Mayflower* appeared in five reprintings or new editions by the end of the decade. The anniversary reissues of *The American Past* (1966) and *From Slavery to Freedom* (1967) and the third edition of *American Negro Slave Revolts* (1970) likewise enlarge the factor of currency without proving impact or influence.

During this period, nevertheless, a dramatic increase in still other models and types of historical messages—each aimed, it often seemed, at more specific audiences—addressed the book-buying public. Street violence and domestic terrors, like the (to some) frightening divisions between white and black America, were some basic circumstances encouraging the proliferation of historical explanations and fragmentation of reading formations. To plot these changes in paradigm formation, popular dissemination, and indoctrination of American youth is the agenda of the next chapter, which questions Silberman's assertion that blacks were stripped of their past and deprived of a distinctive culture.

6

Newer Historical Explanations
Culture as Resistance

In the crucial decade from the late sixties to the late seventies, fresh interpretations of slavery and slave revolts occasioned a more general reevaluation of black history in American cultural consciousness. One major focus of this project and problematic was the historical education of American children—before, during, and after school. In 1979, as we have already noted, Frances FitzGerald reviewed this cultural process in *America Revised*. First published serially in *The New Yorker*, it remains, like John Hersey's *Hiroshima* and Jonathan Schell's *The Fate of the Earth*, a reminder of the public role that elite eastern journal has played in American historical education. Inasmuch as FitzGerald did not, like Silberman, focus particularly upon slavery and its legacy, the present chapter can be considered, in part, an updated extension of her vigorous and widely read critique.

To do so means to locate, once again, Nat Turner at the center of an ongoing cultural controversy. An early and emphatic statement of the black stake in this controversy appeared in *Freedomways*'s second issue in the summer of 1961. The author of "Racist Poison in Schoolbooks" was neither historian nor schoolteacher but a Brooklyn architect and director of the local chapter of the Association for the Study of Negro Life and History. Lowell P. Beveridge, Jr., characterized the contemporary educational situation in uncompromising language: "There is in the United States today a national conspiracy to indoctrinate our children with white supremacist propaganda. This conspiracy operates quite openly; it is condoned by most parents organizations, officially approved by most school boards and . . . subsidized by federal, state, and local governments. . . . I refer to the multi-million dollar textbook publishing industry."[1] His accusation, based on a report from a Brooklyn conference on schoolbooks, is illustrated by a number of popular history texts. From these Beveridge concludes that the average American schoolchild has routinely and for many years received deliberately racist impressions of Negroes and their past. The pattern of interpretation in these textbooks is as follows: "*America was settled by civilized people from Europe, who came here seeking freedom. They were fortunate to have Negroes to do the hard work for them. It is not clear whether or not Negroes were also people, but they were certainly not civilized. They may have come from Africa where there is no civilization*" (164–65). Beveridge constructed this pattern of black experience from four typical school texts, each of which ignored or denied the African origins of American blacks. More dangerously, three of the four also denied that the institution of slavery was evil. None mentions any resistance to slavery. "We also looked in vain for mention of the Negro people in any connection other than slavery during this [antebellum] period" (166).

Beveridge and his Brooklyn conferees specified what new treatments of black American history they believed should be taught. They did not, for instance, insist that textbooks stress only the brutal oppression of slavery.

> Any treatment of the history of the Negro people under slavery in the United States which emphasizes only the evils and suffering would, nevertheless, give an incomplete and negative picture of the role of the Negro people. In spite of, and in many cases because of slavery, the Negro people profoundly influenced American history. The existence of suppression by force implies resistance to force. And indeed the Negro people compiled a record rare in all history for heroic resistance to bondage and ended by supplying the edge of power necessary for the victory of Union arms in the Civil War.
>
> More than 300 slave revolts, led by such daring men as Nat Turner, Denmark Vesey and Gabriel Prosser, kept the slaveholders in continual fear during the nearly 250 years of slavery and threatened the foundations of the system. (167)

The myth of the uncivilized or deculturated black is not, they point out, a recent invention. Nor have black historians been lacking to attack such racist myopia. "This work must be continued, improved and expanded," Beveridge declared, "but even if we get to the point where every Negro home contains a well-read library of African and Negro history, we will still be waging a losing campaign if every child of school age in the country must by law go to school and be taught the myths and lies now found in our textbooks" (171). That this situation was neither academic nor insignificant is underlined by his parting advice to *Freedomways*'s readers.

> I suggest that we must consider the proper treatment of Negro history, especially in public education, as a political rather than cultural or educational problem, to be solved by political means. . . . New York City did in fact recently have a book called *New York: Past and Present* published by Noble and Noble especially for use in the city's elementary schools. New York City contains the second largest metropolitan population of Negroes in the world, yet this book contained not a single reference to them in the text and only one picture of a colored person and that was a child playing in the refuse-strewn back yard of a slum building. (172)

Beveridge's 1961 polemic anticipates later arguments over history in the schools, libraries, and homes of black and white Americans. As a challenge to years of silence, stereotypes and scorn, this passionate essay by a concerned citizen provokes questions about all sorts of texts including biographies, picture books, encyclopedias, teachers' guides, and other media whose contents can be surveyed at one key pressure point: the resistance to slavery, both as historical fact and as political symbol of the confrontation between blacks and whites which continued in sixties streets, courtrooms, and prisons. Moreover, the political consequences of protests like Beveridge's are as significant as the silences that provoked them; as FitzGerald pointedly observes: "As late as 1964, *New York: Past and Present* made only fleeting references to blacks. Two years later another Noble & Noble book, *The New York Story*, included five chapters on blacks" (40).

Pre-Sixties Textbooks and Other Messages to the Young

Since the thirties has already proved a fertile staging period for literary and historical articulations of these loaded issues, the testing of Beveridge's accusations might suitably begin with a backward glance at two textbooks of this vintage—one for elementary schoolchildren, the other aimed at older students. The copy of *America—Today and Yesterday* (1937) that I picked from an education library shelf was in 1941 the property of the board of education of Mt. Vernon, New York.[2] Its authors, Homer Aker, Eugene Hilton, and Varza Aker, were schoolteachers and administrators in California and Utah. Their text exhibits precisely the racial and regional stereotypes Beveridge resents nearly twenty-five years later. For example, they inform fifth- and sixth-grade readers that in the antebellum South "the climate was warm and negro slaves did most of the work" (439); and "Negroes did not suffer from the hot sunshine as did white men, so the slaves were useful to the Southerners. Naturally they did not wish to free them" (441–42). Although slave revolts are nonexistent in this text, the authors carefully point out that "the condition of the slave depended on his master. . . . The slaves of a good master were usually well-fed, well-housed, and well cared for. Those of stern, cruel men were often abused or neglected" (442). But the weight of space and affective language falls on descriptions of good masters and contented slaves. Overseers were sometimes unkind and slave families often broken up, but the predominant picture of life on a plantation is drawn in nostalgic traditional imagery: "The slaves who worked for kind masters had many happy times. On Saturday nights they gathered around big bonfires and sang and danced. The sweet summer air resounded with the strumming of banjos, the music of fiddles, and the melodious tones of gay accordions. Many nights the planter and his family sat on their big white porch and listened to the soft voices of the negroes as they sang the lovely songs of the old plantation" (442). Such passages demonstrate the comforting prosouthern versions of antebellum life that were long dominant in the historical profession and which, two years later, were to reach millions of Americans in the film version of *Gone With the Wind*.

At a higher level of both information and indoctrination stand secondary school and college texts. These, too, have long been lucrative products of the textbook industry. In 1936 appeared one of the most successful of these: William E. Woodward's *A New American History*.[3] Woodward, the popular twenties biographer of George Washington and Ulysses S. Grant, shared most of the cultural assumptions asserted by the Akers and Hilton but expressed them more openly: "American civilization is basically English. . . . We inherit a culture and a speech, and a form of justice, and a way of living, and a code of morals" (vii). Nevertheless, despite his Anglophilia, chapter 5, "Black and White Slaves," includes a spirited defense of American slavery by contrasting it with what he considered the even more cruel practice of white "slavery" in English mines and factories. Though admitting numerous crimes by and against black slaves, Woodward supported southern white "men of sense [who] realized the peril of having a large body of enslaved black people in the heart of white civilization" (81).

> The slave system, as it developed in the first half of the century, was an economic absurdity—the festering relic of a primitive and patriarchal society grafted onto a civilization of money and machines. It did incalculable harm to the white people of the South, and benefited nobody but the negro, in that it served as a vast training school for African savages. Though the regime of the slave plantations was strict it was, on the whole, a kindly one by comparison with what the imported slave had experienced in his own land. It taught him discipline, cleanliness, and a concept of moral standards. (412)

By such channels as *A New American History* did the decades-old explanations of Phillips and his school continue to reach American students in the late thirties and forties. Yet Phillips himself dealt openly with slave resistance, a topic Woodward here ignored. Although few white students—clearly this text's intended audiences—might realize what was missing, some teachers might have been better able to point out the absence of figures like Nat Turner in this "official" white account. Indeed, a few could perhaps mention to their classes the unintended irony of Woodward's comment about the angel who brought Joseph Smith the original inspiration for the Mormon religion: "It is well known that angels seldom call on people. According to Joseph Smith, a seventeen-year-old farm hand living in the western part of New York State, an angel dropped in to see him and chat awhile on the night of Sept. 21, 1823" (421). No mention, however, appears of divine messengers arriving a few years later to visit a black farmhand in Southampton County, Virginia.

FitzGerald provides ample evidence to suggest that textbooks such as *America—Today and Yesterday* and *A New American History* often enjoyed a long shelf-life, and so they should not be too quickly dismissed from sixties culture as irrelevant relics. Moreover, the fears and accusations of Beveridge and Ralph Ellison are sustained by recognition of the entrenched authority of the textbook publishing industry and its educational and political clients in American communities. Until the sixties—and only then in certain cities like Detroit or New York—black American teachers, parents, and students remained disadvantaged in challenging the practices by which white racial explanations of the past were disseminated as the truth. Hence in surveying this cultural historiography, attention should be focused on the activities and achievements of writers and teachers who used bookstores and libraries rather than required texts in classrooms as avenues to the moral imaginations of the young.

It was far simpler, though still not easy, for Arna Bontemps, for example, to write *The Story of the Negro: A Borzoi Book for Young People* and have it published by Knopf in 1948, the year after Knopf issued Franklin's *From Slavery to Freedom*. To be sure, a formidable network of superintendence, including the American Children's Library Association and the *Hornbook* prizes and endorsements, existed to monitor the fate of Bontemps's book. Its author, too, had painful memories of other kinds of community pressure, some of which he relates in his introduction to *Black Thunder*. In the mid-thirties, fearful Alabama black school authorities ordered him to burn his personal library of "race conscious and provocative" books like *The Souls of Black Folk* as the price of retaining his teaching position (xiii–xiv).

The Story of the Negro would probably have been consigned to those flames had it then existed. In the safer northern milieu of postwar America, his voice could and did carry a sharper edge and message for young readers. The pertinent section of the story is "Freedom is a Powerful Word." Here Bontemps speaks directly about slavery as a two-way experience: "What every slave wanted of course, was freedom. If you argue that a master may punish a slave in order to subdue him, you must grant that the slave has the right to turn on his master in an effort to win his freedom."[4] There follow seven or eight pages of sometimes graphic description of slaves turning on their masters. Again, Prosser, Vesey, and Turner are exemplars in planning or executing what the author insists was legitimate violent resistance. Bontemps's language (by contrast with that of *America—Today and Yesterday*) makes few concessions to his young readers' presumed skills or intelligence, nor does he sidestep unpleasant realities and ambiguities. After describing vividly the abortive attempts of Gabriel and Denmark Vesey, he devotes several pages to the era's major challenge by Nat Turner.

> All his life this thirty-one-year-old slave had believed that he was born for something special. He claimed he had seen drops of blood on the corn in the field, and, on the leaves in the woods, letters and numbers and the shapes of men. . . . When an eclipse of the sun occurred in February of 1831, Nat Turner took this for the sign that had been promised to him and rose up to prepare himself to slay his enemies with their own weapons. . . .
>
> The attacks started with a crusading fervor and at first seemed to go according to plan. The first backset occurred at a Dr. Blunt's house, where the slaves rose up and defended the master to whom they were devoted instead of joining the rebellion. This delayed the attackers and gave time for an alarm to spread. . . .
>
> But they didn't get together as planned. The militia was aroused and began to comb the countryside. Volunteer companies were sent out from Richmond, Petersburg, Norfolk, and other cities. Soon the odds against Nat Turner and his broken ranks were overwhelming. They did not meet again that night nor on any night that followed until they were reunited on the gallows. (115)

Describing Turner's capture, Bontemps shows a historian's restraint while frankly celebrating a black hero and martyr. "Nat himself was the last to be captured," he concludes the account. "It took more than two months to root him out, and even then there was a gleam in his eye. His strange half-Biblical confession shows that his longing for freedom was still as strong as ever. That was a thing that wouldn't die, no matter how many rebellions were crushed or how many slaves perished" (115).

New and Other Teaching Tools and Texts: Toward Dormon and Jones, *The Afro-American Experience*

The Story of the Negro offered one model to later writers willing to reconfigure American history narratives for young readers, black and white. In fact, its relatively sophisticated style and high reader expectations made Bontemps suitable for older readers as well. Acquainting schoolchildren *and* adults of all races with the multiracial nature of their common pasts became a prime project for many amateur and even professional historians, especially those familiar at firsthand with urban education realities. Assisting these innovators were journalists like Fred Powledge who, in 1967, published *To Change a Child*.[5] Aimed at teachers, parents, and citizens rather than directly at schoolchildren, Powledge's report publicized the pioneer work of demonstration programs for so-called "disadvantaged" youngsters going on in Harlem's P.S. 175 and elsewhere across the nation. Innovative experiments capitalizing on children's "heightened curiosity and initiative" (vi) occurred in kindergarten settings where the subject of black history was normally inappropriate. For older students, too, the enterprise even more directly encouraged independent reading of relatively advanced books, which their teachers were taught to introduce. Part of the new social studies program thus involved "teacher training in Negro history and the problems of modern-day ghetto life" (74). Recommended textbooks were *Manchild in the Promised Land* by Claude Brown and *Crisis in Black and White* by Charles Silberman. At the same time, programs encouraged parents themselves to become historically sensitive about black history. In the anteroom of the kindergarten area, for example, "were a table and chair and reading material for visiting parents. On the table there were copies of *Story of the Negro* by Arna Bontemps; *Go Tell It On the Mountain* by James Baldwin; *Strength to Love* by Martin Luther King, Jr., and issues of *Ebony* and *Women's Day*" (52).

In the following year, Powledge's publisher, Quadrangle Books of Chicago, published William L. Katz's *Teacher's Guide to American Negro History*. This work provided classroom teachers with outlines, dates, bibliographies, and even illustrations (like the one of Nat Turner's capture) bringing them up to date on controversial topics like slavery and slave insurrections. That same year (during which the Nat Turner controversy raged in the popular and academic press), Parents Magazine Press entered the field with an ambitious volume, *Chronicles of Negro Protest: A Background Book for Young People*. "We have not been honest with ourselves," the historian C. Eric Lincoln wrote in the anthology's introduction. "What is infinitely more tragic, as parents and as teachers, we have not been honest with our youth. We have sought to avoid the implications of our history by avoiding the facts of our history."⁶ As a first step, *Chronicles* reprinted, among forty-two key documents in black American history, a sizable excerpt from Gray's *Confessions*. By way of introductory commentary on this text, young readers were told some plain truths that many college-level textbooks still sidestepped: "Turner's confession, as made to a lawyer named T. R. Gray, follows below. The calmness and composure of his manner as he details how he and his band killed ten men, fourteen women, and thirty-five children reveal with shocking clarity the overpowering determination of one black man to achieve freedom."⁷ Indeed, Chambers's anthology—aimed ostensibly at older children and teenagers—was at least as explicit and detailed as more adult-oriented collections of black history documents, which had, by 1968, also made Gray's *Confessions* familiar to wider audiences.⁸

Indeed, Gray's account was recognized as an essential source for teaching young and old how to reconstruct their own versions of Nat Turner in still another sixties teaching tool—the casebook. Two of the most widely available casebooks appeared in 1971, one designed for and by young inexperienced historians, the other intended for college classrooms. Like other accounts or collections intended for adolescents (or even children), *The Nat Turner Rebellion: The Historical Event and the Modern Controversy* is a sophisticated teaching tool. John Duff and Peter Mitchell, its editors, designed the book for and with the help of "a group of students, mostly black, enrolled in an introductory course in American history at Seton Hall in the fall of 1968 under the auspices of the State of New Jersey's Equal Opportunity Program."⁹ These nontraditional students were so little condescended to that they were expected to read and assess Gray's *Confessions* and other contemporary sources and later historical treatments, Hayden's "Ballad of Nat Turner," and no fewer than eleven selections from the still-bubbling controversy over Styron's novel. Duff and Mitchell shrewdly assessed the social situation in which their own and other students were invited to participate:

> That Nat Turner and his Rebellion have not been well known is only partly due to the neglect of black history. It also has something to do with the nature of the event. Until recently, any lengthy discussion of the Rebellion had been avoided, perhaps be-

cause such a "blood-thirsty" legacy might prove embarrassing at a time when co-operation between blacks and whites was deemed essential to most Negro organizations. . . .

This atmosphere has changed. Black nationalism and black militancy have taken hold of the Negro Revolution; a newer generation of black historians looks for different answers in the past and for them the interpretation of the Turner revolt (and of slavery itself) has assumed a crucial importance. For us, Turner's revolt is not just a major event in the history of black Americans; its historiography and the questions raised by Styron's impressionistic account illuminate the function of written history and its relationship to the contemporary crisis in American race relations. (vii–viii)

Eric Foner, too, in his *Nat Turner*, assents to the same political rationale.[10] But his collection, in which Gray's *Confessions* is also a central document, is more narrowly historiographical. A college-level casebook, this more traditional treatment seems to reflect a compromise between two sides of Foner himself: a radical white editor's sympathies; and a conventional historian's teaching experiences at Columbia University. Nevertheless, both Foner and Duff and Mitchell represent the late-sixties awareness by younger historians that conventional textbook instruction could no longer meet the demand for fuller, franker discussions of racial violence in the American past. "The most widely used text in Negro history," Duff and Mitchell point out, "John Hope Franklin's *From Slavery to Freedom*, devotes only a few lines to Turner as if to reassure the white majority that Turner was not typical of the Negro in the United States" (vii).

From this survey of new modes and models of black history we can profitably return to Beveridge's denunciation of "poisonous" history textbooks. Two widely adopted sixties college texts, both by respected older white historians, provide plausible contrasts to the thirties textbooks mentioned above. The larger of the two, *The Oxford History of the American People*, appeared in 1965 under the distinguished name of Harvard historian Samuel Eliot Morison.[11] Bracketing Morison's 1122-page tome were the first and second editions (in 1964 and 1973) of a rival text, *The Structure of American History*.[12] This work was created by a trio of leading experts, Richard Hofstadter of Columbia, William Miller (an independent writer), and Daniel Aaron of Smith College. Since this practice of collaborative authorship of history textbooks was firmly in place in 1965, Morison devoted part of his preface to reassuring academic and general audiences that a number of experts in specific fields of American history assisted him. However, no authority on either southern or black history is thanked.

Although Morison's ironic and gentlemanly style lends itself to ambiguity, there is no mistaking this Boston Brahmin's ingrained sympathy for the white southern aristocrat, "the human thoroughbred of the plantation regime" (501). Nonetheless, in the chapter "The Southern States, 1820–1850," he addresses squarely the question of the day:

> What did the Negro himself think of this system? Here we have inferences that are poles apart. On the one hand (as stated by Jefferson Davis in his reply to Lincoln's Emancipation Proclamation) these "several millions of human beings of an inferior race" were "peaceful and contented laborers in their sphere." The pampered domestic servant, the happy, care-free, banjo-playing "darky," theme of countless post–Civil War novels, were all that many upper-class travelers saw of the South's "peculiar institution," as her statesmen liked to call it. On the other hand, it is the fashion of Negro intellectuals to describe their forebears as the most oppressed and exploited labor force in modern history, held down by fear and force, constantly striving for escape from slavery. It has often been said that the Negro understands the white man much better than the other way around; but it is also possible that the colored intellectual of the 1960s knows less about the plantation Negro of the 1840s than did many white masters of that era. (505)

Not many contemporary readers, it may be assumed, missed the intentional irony (or at least the deliberately old-fashioned practice) of his phrase "the colored intellectual." Suspicions are strengthened when Morison, like Elkins and others, focuses almost exclusively on southern ideas and ideology. Thus although he mentions Frederick Douglass and Booker T. Washington as "talented or intellectual Negro slaves" (505) he ignores all other nineteenth-century black ideologues like Walker, Garnet, or Delany. Ideology in action is a somewhat different matter. Denmark Vesey and Nat Turner receive careful though brief treatment: "A very serious insurrection took place in tidewater Virginia in 1831. A pious slave named Nat Turner enlisted a number of others who ran wild in August and killed 57 whites before they were rounded up, with the help of regular troops from Fortress Monroe and sailors from the navy. Between 40 and 100 Negroes were killed, and Turner was hanged. This outbreak was blamed by Southern opinion on William Lloyd Garrison's new abolitionist newspaper, *The Liberator*, although there is not the slightest evidence that even one copy of it had reached any Southern Negro" (508). He concludes by quoting, as Aptheker had done, from the southern lady's eloquent letter to the Boston mayor describing the South as a "smothered volcano" (509). Unlike many other contemporary textbooks, however, Morison ends by mentioning a later abortive uprising in Maryland in support of his final judgment: "However docile the majority of slaves may have been, unrest was so widespread as to keep the master class in a constant state of apprehension" (510).

Though written by three far more liberal scholars than Admiral Morison, *The Structure of American History* betrays both the traditional and revisionist value judgments expected of up-to-date history textbooks during this conflicted era. In their 1973 revision, for example, the authors, after noting the ten years of momentous change in history and historiography since their first edition, reassert their aim to help readers "discover in the past the sources of strength in the American experience on which many earlier generations, like our own, have gravely trespassed, and yet from which new generations have drawn fresh inspiration and purpose" (vii). Chapter 8, "Two Nations: North and South," is the narrative setting in which Nat Turner's exemplary experiences of slavery are recounted. Though their strategy (inevitable, perhaps, in all commercial textbook productions) is to balance regional, racial, and ideological perspectives, in this case the result is demonstrably different from Morison's: "Abolitionists sometimes exaggerated the brutalities of slavery, yet documented evidence abounds, were it needed, to lay to rest claims that 'fetters on black skins don't chafe.' Thousands of slaves stood sunk in unalleviated depression and despair. Others, to escape forced labor, would mutilate themselves, feign sickness and stupidity, devise many other stratagems, and sometimes openly rebel" (138–39). Turner's act of resistance is the chief but not sole instance of open warfare. "Horrible and barbarous massacres" are mentioned far back in the colonial period, but

> By far the most sensational nineteenth century slave revolt was that engineered by the black Virginia preacher Nat Turner, in 1831, with the intention of killing every white person in Southampton County. Believing himself divinely appointed, Turner led a two-day rampage that ended with the death of fifty-seven whites and about a hundred blacks. Tracked down after a desperate manhunt, Turner and twenty followers were taken and executed.
> Turner's was the last major slave revolt. The reports of suppression and bloody reprisals carried a disheartening message across the black South, while, with the spread of abolitionist propaganda after 1830, the white South mobilized its protective forces. (139)

As a crucial instance of extreme responses, the Southampton slave revolt is carefully presented as a three-way transaction among the black South, the white South, and northern abolitionists. In this confrontation, as cultural as it was economic and political, religion played a central role. To Hofstadter and his colleagues, a key factor was the "Great Revival" that "spread across the North, from which the temperance crusade and abolitionism itself took fire.... To many Northerners newly admitted to the 'mighty Baptism of the Holy Spirit,' no greater sin could be found in Christendom than pride of pigment, the enslavement of one Christian brother by another. To many southerners, the word of the Lord placed the black sons of Ham in everlasting bondage. Fundamentalism in religion reinforced the slave foundation of southern life and the sorry fate of 'Jim Crow'" (139). However, apart from the vague phrase "believing himself divinely appointed," Nat Turner's participation in this religious ferment linking and dividing Americans is ignored. To be sure, Hofstadter and his fellows' narrative is one-third the length of Morison's. Yet like his, their sources for this chapter are drawn (with the single exception of one Franklin article) exclusively from white historians' work on slavery. By 1973, at least, these sympathetic historians might have consulted some major black discussions of religion and slavery such as Vincent Harding's, as well as important contributions by Eugene Genovese in this area. In their absence, *The*

Structure of American History testifies to the liberal aspirations of its respected authors but also to the reality of lag, myopia, and racial divisions that persisted among historians and the textbook industry even in 1973.

If the early seventies found many students still learning from white-oriented, white-written history texts like Morison's or Hofstadter/Miller/Aaron's, the situation for some others had more clearly begun to change. One instance of a more inclusive cultural context within which to encounter new interpretations of slavery and slave resistance is a 1974 textbook, *The Afro-American Experience: A Cultural History through Emancipation*, written by two younger black historians, James H. Dormon and Robert R. Jones.[13] Theirs was one contribution from the relatively few black academic historians beginning to compete among a much larger cadre of predominantly white professionals for control of textbooks on black American history. In this role, Dormon and Jones first saw themselves fighting against a more immediate foe—the comprehensive neglect of the subject that was characteristic of most American historiography before the 1950s. Previous "establishment historians," they asserted in the preface, "were neither ready nor able to rethink America's past and give the black experience its proper place and perspective" (v). Now that the public situation has begun to change, the black studies movement has begun to make available much new work, some of questionable standing but some of unimpeachable quality. "As is usually the case, however, the new original, provocative scholarship of the past decade has not yet filtered down to popular publications or to the history and social studies textbooks used in American schools." *The Afro-American Experience* sought to rectify that situation in "a readily available, brief volume" (vi).

Unlike virtually all competing texts, Dormon and Jones's is not only black-written and black-oriented but radically cultural in perspective: "Whenever possible we have used primary materials from black sources in order to evoke black ideas, feelings, and sensibilities, and to emphasize that in the history of Afro-America, black people themselves were the active historical ingredients" (vii). Furthermore, like Duff and Mitchell, they recognize contributions from young black students:

> We owe most to those who have made Afro-American history and culture a viable and challenging field of study. . . . We refer

to those countless hundreds of people, mostly young and mostly black, who have determined to create an atmosphere in the United States in which black people may live in dignity, comfort, and pride in their heritage[;] these history-makers have fought on many fronts: in courthouses and state houses, in the streets, on buses and trains, in schools and churches and, often enough, in jail. They have made an ongoing revolution [and] this book is dedicated to them. (vii–viii)

In light of culture-based studies of black history, by John Blassingame and others, already in print by 1974 and filtered for popular consumption, *The Afro-American Experience* is, by admission and design, unoriginal. What is novel, however, for a school text is its anthropological stance. Black culture is presented as a complex historical product of limited acculturation to the main activities, institutions, and values of the dominant Euro-American culture. Of all the modalities slaves encountered, were excluded from, and recast—the English language, literacy, family and gender roles, business enterprises, and the democratic ideals of the American Revolution—the most important for synthesis and survival was the Christian religion. Unlike previous historians such as Stampp and Franklin, however, Dormon and Jones repudiate the cool secular perspective that emphasizes primitive, escapist, and emotional characteristics and functions of the black church. They repeat with approval Paul Radin's insight: "The antebellum Negro was not converted to God. He converted God to himself" (198). The God of the black community was worshipped not by separate individuals so much as in collective performance of rituals, songs, sermons: "All blacks shared in the black sub-culture," they assert, though slaves on large plantations were the most community-influenced because opportunities existed "to develop their own life-styles, their own life patterns, their own Afro-American subculture utilizing elements of both the African and white cultural traditions[;] it was essentially a new cultural system adapted to the needs of Afro-Americans and to the peculiar circumstances in which they lived in the United States" (187). Though slaves' sense of community varied widely—house servants often living separate, more white-oriented lives, with consequent class divisions and betrayals—"the operation of the slaves' self-generated value system tended to encourage resistance to slavery and made the task of slaveholders infinitely more difficult. It made possible a situation in which thousands of slaves all over the South were able to escape temporarily from their plantations for periods varying from a few hours up to several years" (196).

Slave revolts were a natural but extreme form of escape. Dormon and Jones devote more space to these inevitable expressions of black culture than most other textbook authors since Aptheker. Their treatment relies also on a more extensive range of sources than any white writer of school or college texts. Their point of departure is to distinguish carefully among earlier historians' definitions of revolt or insurrection by Aptheker, Elkins, Carl Degler, and Blassingame. Throughout, their treatment repudiates all explanations, white or black, which deny purpose, planning, or political significance to events like the Southampton slave revolt.

> The slave revolts were not the purposeless and nihilistic thrashing about of a psychotic people; they were the desperate but reasoned actions of those who had determined that they must strike out against slavery even if failure meant certain death. The slave revolts were the first radical blows for black freedom. As such, they helped to widen the existing cracks in the institution of slavery and they bequeathed to later generations of Afro-Americans a tradition of heroic resistance, hope, and determination, a tradition passed down in folklore and song:
>> And your name mought be Caesure sure,
>> And got you cannon can shoot a mile or more,
>> But you can't keep the world from moverin' round
>> Nor Nat Turner from gaining ground. (211)

As "the most famous slave insurrection in United States history and the one which had the greatest impact on the Afro-American experience" (213), Nat Turner's is also the one in which leader, participants, and a religion-based community interacted most demonstrably. Gray is heavily drawn upon to underline Turner's early experience of a divine calling, his family's and fellows' expectations that he was destined to be a prophet, and his adult visions and other encounters with the Holy Spirit. The question of a planned revolt is resolved by stressing the fact that "the rebels were headed for the county seat, Jerusalem (a name with striking appropriateness in light of Turner's Messianic self-image).

Ultimately the insurrectionist force numbered around 70, attracted not only by the idea of striking a blow for freedom but also by their faith in Turner as a religious leader. . . . 'they believed and said' Turner noted, 'that my wisdom came from God'" (214). In this retelling, therefore, no use is made of the common phrase "religious fanatic."

Dormon and Jones's description of the bloody course and aftermath of the revolt is scarcely longer than that of its origins. Nor are any doubts or weaknesses admitted regarding Turner's motivation or personal behavior. Like other contemporary historians, these authors ignore questions of who axed whom or whether Turner was wracked by doubt. Never do they mention Margaret Whitehead's name. The attention of historians (and especially textbook authors), whether white or black, is focused on larger and often different issues than those engaging the imagination of William Styron. (Indeed, except in Duff and Mitchell's casebook and Henry Tragle's *The Southampton Slave Revolt*, Styron's name is conspicuously absent from post-1968 historical accounts.) Dormon and Jones emphasize to the end Turner's and his community's short-lived but deeply rooted act of brave resistance and self-sacrifice.

> The insurrectionists never reached Jerusalem (now Courtland, Virginia). On Monday afternoon they were defeated in a short engagement at Parker's field, three miles from Jerusalem, and after a final skirmish the next morning, the revolt was over. . . . From the time of his capture to the moment of execution, he maintained a "calm deliberate composure." He freely admitted his part in the insurrection, but he never intimated feeling the slightest guilt or remorse for his actions. He had taken up Christ's yoke to "fight against the Serpent," he said, because the Spirit had informed him that "the time was fast approaching when the first should be last and the last should be first." Queried as to whether he did not now find himself mistaken, he replied, "Was not Christ crucified?" (214–15)

Turner's significance for subsequent generations of blacks, therefore, is larger than simply that of rebel and martyr. For these historians and perhaps to their youthful, mostly black audiences, Nat Turner is a model of the righteous man in his culture. "Because Afro-American slaves retained a positive self-image and continued to see themselves as a 'moral people' they were able not only to survive in slavery, but to transcend the institution that bound them, bequeathing to their posterity and to the world a unique example of survival and creativity in the face of extreme adversity. They 'made it'" (216).

Culture as Resistance in Seventies Histories: John Blassingame, Eugene Genovese, Lawrence Levine

The Afro-American Experience, though perhaps not a widely influential textbook in its day, marks a symbolic if not literal turning point in the demotic and educational dissemination of new historical interpretations spawned during a decade and more of social ferment and civil unrest. It represents one of several attempts by younger historians, black and white, to relay to young or unsophisticated audiences the fundamental shift taking place in American history during the late sixties and early seventies. James E. Olsen has subsequently analyzed this historiographical move away from the more deterministic explanations of Frazier, Elkins, and Stampp: "The existence of a mature slave culture was hardly a consideration at all," he writes of these older authors, "the liberal revisionists could not see beyond the limits of white society, as if slaves existed only in terms of their relationships with white masters. But late in the 1950s and throughout the 1960s and 1970s, the civil rights movement paved the way for a new understanding of the slave personality, the slave family, and Black culture." The result, he continues, was "a more sensitive, integrated portrait of slave life. Those like John Hope Franklin, Eugene Genovese, Peter H. Wood, Edmund Morgan, Leon F. Litwack, John Blassingame, Leslie Owens, Gerald Mullin, George Rawick, Herbert Gutman, Robert Fogel, Stanley Engerman and Lawrence Levine accepted Black culture on its own terms rather than viewing it exclusively as a white derivative."[14]

Olsen's approbation of these seventies historians underscores the accuracy of Elkins's wry acknowledgment that "by the end of 1974 it was apparent that another area—black culture—had come to predominate over all other concerns in the study of American slavery."[15] Part of Olsen's sympathetic study of black cultural tradition involved a necessary problematic: the degree to which African and Afro-American cultures or subcultures were and are unique and in what respects they came to share cultural patterns with southern white Americans. Both

Peter Wood's *Black Majority* (1974) and Gerald Mullin's *Flight and Rebellion* (1972) demonstrate that, in eighteenth-century Virginia and South Carolina respectively, cultural synthesis by bondsmen and acculturation in the interest of profitability by slaveowners were processes causally linked to slave resistance.[16] Wood's analysis of the Stono Rebellion of 1739—the most serious and perhaps most often ignored slave insurrection before 1800—affords concrete evidence and suggests analogies both to the case of Nat Turner and with larger aspects of black slave culture as it developed independent forms in the nineteenth century.

The cultural history probably reaching the broadest readership during this period of reorientation was John Blassingame's *The Slave Community* (1972). Issued by Oxford University Press, the modestly sized, clearly written, plentifully illustrated paperback edition was speedily and widely adopted for use in college and high school classrooms. As the preface acknowledges, its young, black, Georgia-born author and Yale historian stood in the direct descent of older historians (C. Vann Woodward, David Brion Davis, Edmund Morgan, and John Hope Franklin) from many of whose interpretations he tactfully but unmistakably departed. As a synthesis of new interpretations and a general treatment, *The Slave Community* was less original than the more narrowly focused studies by Wood, Mullin, Genovese, Gutman, and Levine. Arguably, this limitation actually gave Blassingame's contribution greater social range and impact. In addition, specific features of his account overcame intellectual, ideological, and ultimately racial barriers between historians shaken but not demolished during the preceding decade.

Nat Turner's name and cultural significance are linked to each of Blassingame's reinterpretations. In discussing African survivals during the acculturation process, for instance, Blassingame uses his favorite historical source—slave narratives—for evidence of early slave resistance and instances of cultural persistence. Thus Blassingame's subsequent use of Gray's *Confessions*, with its reference to African roots, family and community support, and messianic martyrdom, retains a cultural plausibility not undercut by the fact (left undiscussed) of its white authorship. Furthermore, in *The Slave Community*'s four central topics—slave culture, slave family life, "runaways and rebels," and slave personality types—the weight of historical documentation supports an inevitable conclusion: Nat Turner, though an extraordinary individual, was representative of the complex and vital culture in the slave quarters of nineteenth-century Virginia. Social cohesion and support, therefore, are implicit in Blassingame's carefully worded (and, compared to Aptheker and Bennett, narrower) definition of a slave revolt: "Consigning conspiracies to the general category of 'resistance,' a revolt is defined as a concerted action by a group of slaves with the settled purpose of and actual destruction of the lives and property of local whites. In addition, the activities must have been recognized as an insurrection by the public officials who called out the armed forces of the locale to destroy the rebels. Applying this rigid definition, there were at least nine slave revolts in America between 1691 and 1865. Although most of the large-scale conspiracies occurred in cities, most of the actual rebellions took place in plantation counties."[17] Both in his four-page retelling of the Nat Turner revolt and his concluding comments, Blassingame treads a careful path between celebration of a uniquely heroic figure and a socially deterministic explanation of man and event.

Blassingame's willingness to generalize as an interdisciplinary social scientist, not just as an archival researcher, gives Nat Turner another kind of immortality and representativeness in *The Slave Community*. In the work's most original contribution, its discussion of slave personality types, he draws upon a variety of social psychologists for theories to order the concrete evidence of slave behavior patterns found in slave autobiographies, plantation management manuals, and other historical sources. The resulting amalgam creates a typology of slave personalities radically different from and more complex than models advanced by Elkins and other previous historians. Several typical stances or behavior patterns are identified in the records as clarified by twentieth-century studies of identity and role by Erving Goffman, Peter Blau, and others: "Some slaves were compelled to shape their behavior so completely to the white man's moods that they became Sambos," Blassingame admits (200). Nevertheless, "the important fact which emerges from the black autobiographies is that the master-slave relationship was not the only factor that determined the slave's behavior" (214). Group solidarity gave a measure of support to a broad range of individual responses to bondage and white racism: "Some slaves were always docile; others were docile most of the time and rebellious at other times. Likewise, some resisted bondage throughout their lives in various ways, while others, generally docile, might be rebellious only once. In other words, the slave was no different in most ways from most men. The slave range of personality types existed in the quarters as in the mansion" (213).

Attention to actual testimony by both slaves and whites leads Blassingame to identify three personality types that were at the same time literary stereotypes and plantation roles. In addition to Sambo (the white cultural construct mixing features of Uncle Remus, Jim Crow, and Uncle Tom), white writers projected—and history records actual instances of—two other typical slave personalities, Jack and Nat. Thus Blassingame connects literary imaginations and historical sources with social psychology to sharpen and reorient previous explanations of the way culture and personality interacted in specific historical slave communities. While Sambo is a familiar description not notably thickened by Blassingame's discussion, Jack and Nat represent fresher constructs.

> The one rarely seen in literature, Jack, worked faithfully as long as he was well-treated. Sometimes sullen and uncooperative, he generally refused to be driven beyond the pace he had set for himself. Conscious of his identity with other slaves, he cooperated with them to resist the white man's oppression. Rationally analysing the white man's overwhelming physical power, Jack either avoided contact with him or was deferential in his presence. Since he did not identify with his master and could not always keep up the façade of deference, he was occasionally flogged for insubordination. Although often proud, stubborn, and conscious of the wrongs he suffered, Jack tried to repress his anger. His patience was, however, not unlimited. (133–34)

The third figure in Blassingame's refined typology, Nat is only approximately faithful to southern white experiences, based more on fear of the real Nat Turner than on reality. "Nat was the rebel who rivaled Sambo in the universality and continuity of his literary image," he observes of this fictional creation whose lineaments also appeared in runaway announcements, 1831 newspaper accounts of the revolt, and later historical explanations.

> Revengeful, bloodthirsty, cunning, treacherous, and savage, Nat was the incorrigible runaway, the poisoner of white men, the rav-

ager of white women who defied all the rules of plantation society. Subdued and punished only when overcome by superior numbers or firepower, Nat retaliated when attacked by whites, led guerilla activities of maroons against isolated plantations, killed overseers and planters, or burned plantation buildings when he was abused. Like Jack, Nat's customary obedience often hid his true feelings, self-concept, unquenchable thirst for freedom, hatred of whites, discontent, and manhood, until he violently demonstrated these traits. (134)

Blassingame argues that it was not Sambo or the hazier presence of Jack who actually dominated southern white consciousness. The rebel was the fearsome cause and antitype of the docile loyal bondsman. As the historian points out, "another of the important reasons for the pervasiveness of the Sambo stereotype was the desire of whites to relieve themselves of the anxiety of thinking about slaves as men. In this regard, Nat, the actual and potential rebel, stands at the core of white perceptions of the slave. With Nat perennially in the wings, the creation of Sambo was almost mandatory for the Southerner's emotional security" (139). Given this psychological source in whites' pervasive fear and anxiety, both Sambo and Nat were misleading representations: "For various reasons, often having more to do with whites than blacks, antebellum whites apparently focused on two extreme forms of slave behavior—childlike docility and rebellion—in formulating the Nat and Sambo stereotypes. Both stereotypes were probably blown out of proportion to their relationship to the actual behavior of most slaves. . . . Perhaps the only thing that the white man's stereotypes of the slave as Sambo, Jack, and Nat does is to indicate the range of personality types in the quarters" (143–44).

When Blassingame turns from psychosocial typologies to retelling the Southampton slave revolt, the historical Nat Turner is presented as "the arch rebel" (127) who embodied many of the emotional and cultural forces separating white southern society from the slave community, until violence suddenly revealed their intimate interconnections. Though Turner's intelligence, literacy and some religious training brought him into intimate contact with the master's world, the social and spiritual roots of his rebellion lay in the slave quarters. Hence

Blassingame's account, based principally on Gray as filtered through a white account by F. Roy Johnson, *The Nat Turner Slave Insurrection* (1966), stresses family and community belief in the religious justification of Turner's leadership and bloody deeds.[18] Yet there are uniquely personal ingredients as well in this intercommunity conflict. Running away and then returning to the plantation after thirty days, an illness "as the result of anxiety" (129) that postponed the revolt, failure in his first attempt with a dull light sword to kill Joseph Travis, the murder of Margaret Whitehead "by a blow on the head, with a fence rail" (129)—these are details from Gray's *Confessions* that particularize man and event. They hint that Blassingame, a historian especially aware of literary history, has Styron's book as well as earlier southern novels and romances in mind. Specific historical images of this "short, coal-black man [who was] fearless, honest, temperate, religious, and extremely intelligent" (130) are repeated from Gray in order to re-embed them in a twentieth-century interpretation. This seventies explanation, while acknowledging Gray's propagandistic appeal through rhetoric and imagery to his fearful white readers of 1831 and 1832, also suggests Nat Turner's deliberate manipulation, by declaration and gesture, of potential liberators and fellow slaves. The complex message and double role are deduced from Gray's text and contemporary illustrations. Two familiar examples of these are represented amid the text of chapter 4, "Runaways and Rebels": Nat Turner in the swamp with his five original followers stands for all "conspirators," and the picture of Nat surrendering to Benjamin Phipps represents the "Capture" of the particular rebel whose name became archetypal in the aftermath of the most destructive of all slave revolts.

To seventies readers, *The Slave Community* offered a carefully balanced synthesis of recent research. It also represents a carefully black reinterpretation of previous explanations by Phillips, Stampp, and Elkins, as well as of history textbook writers such as Morison and Hofstadter/Miller/Aaron. To be sure, Blassingame's typical tactic is not to confront directly his white and black predecessors. Yet his amalgam of social-psychological theories about identity formation and role-playing, literary images from white novels and black autobiographies, and fresh historical insights from neglected sources such as plantation management manuals provides an early demonstration of the interdisciplinary imperatives of the new cultural history that flowered during the next decade. More particularly, Blassingame moved Nat Turner from the margins of slavery to the very center of the peculiar institution.

Although Eugene Genovese did not participate fully in this shift, his *Roll, Jordan, Roll* (1972) amplified previous analyses of slave culture, especially of black religious and family life. His Nat Turner was not, however, firmly enmeshed in this cultural complex and it is revealing that book 4, in which slave revolts are treated, comes at the close of his long discussion, not in the center as in *The Slave Community*. More revealing still is Genovese's continuing disbelief in American slave revolts as politically meaningful acts—the position he held during the 1967–68 stage of the controversy. Turner's adoption, for instance, of "a messianic stance . . . among a people not prone to following messiahs" is asserted as a prime reason for the failure of his insurrection: "The slaves of the Old South could not readily throw up a Toussaint—a revolutionary of measured temperament, scorning fanaticism, coolly studying his terrain, alternating compromise with intransigence. . . . Nat Turner, on the other hand, foreshadowed his white counterpart, John Brown—fanatic, millenarian, and possibly mad."[19] How little Genovese had budged from earlier arguments with Vincent Harding is indicated by the concluding remarks in *Roll, Jordan, Roll:* "Songs and stories about Gabriel Prosser and Nat Turner did exist, and some tradition had passed down to the present in localities like Southampton County, Virginia. But as the slave narratives suggest, southern slaves as a whole knew little about the great slave rebels. No powerful tradition emerged, perhaps simply because the revolts never achieved appropriate size or duration. But the rebels did their best, and weak as their effort was, it was a great deal better than nothing" (597).

Other historians, however, more cultural and psychological than economic and political in outlook than Genovese, adduced evidence to qualify if not demolish this conclusion—whose magisterial tone sounds almost as condescending as some of his *New York Review of Books* proclamations of 1968. Among the most perceptive and influential of culture-as-resistance historians was Lawrence W. Levine, whose *Black Culture and Black Consciousness* (1977) was hailed by both white and black critics as a tour de force of cross-racial scholarship. A mainstay of his interpretation is the concept of the sacredness of black consciousness under slavery: "No one has better captured the sacred code of

Nat Turner's 1831 rebellion than Turner himself," Levine observes of Gray's *Confessions*. "Though Turner had contempt for conjuring and never directly practiced its arts, his revelations, his portents, his signs, his sense of the supernatural, and his power flowed organically from the slaves' sacred world in which magic and Christianity were integral ingredients. If Denmark Vesey, Gullah Jack, and Nat Turner were not typical products of the slaves' sacred universe, neither were they alien to it. Their actions and beliefs outline in exaggerated relief a truth which emerges from the bulk of evidence relating to slave culture: that the religion and folk beliefs of the slaves provided them with crucial alternative standards and possibilities."[20] To Levine, the emphasis of a Genovese upon military and political considerations and constraints in measuring the significance of slave revolts is much too narrow and simplistic. Historical and social truths in the case of Nat Turner are more subtle, if not completely contrary. Granted, a viable culture did not automatically mean liberation:

> The slaves, after all, remained slaves, the whites remained masters, and the harsh, exploitative history of the Peculiar Institution continued. If our sole criterion of judgment is physical freedom, then the slaves' sacred folk beliefs had a very limited effect, though they unquestionably encouraged some slaves to escape. If we extend the criterion to material well-being, the effects are greater.... If we extend it yet further into the more speculative but crucial area of the slaves' psychic and emotional state, the results are more positive still. The slaves' expressive arts and sacred beliefs were more than merely a series of outlets or strategies; they were instruments of life, of sanity, of health, and of self-respect. Slave music, slave religion, slave folk beliefs—the entire sacred world of the black slaves—created the necessary space between the slaves and their owners and were the means of preventing legal slavery from becoming spiritual slavery.[21]

Passages like this epitomize the distance some American historical explanations in this conflicted arena had come in the two decades since Stampp's *The Peculiar Institution*. Here in a spiritual and cultural space Levine carefully exposes to view, Nat Turner was located as a man able to imagine and then act out the dreams—and nightmares—of his fellows, some of whom followed him along the roads of Southampton, while others suffered his fate whether or not they rose in support of Old Prophet Nat.

Styron Returns to the Debate:
Peter Rose, Henry I. Tragle, Stephen Oates

Blassingame's and Levine's books represent early and later articulations of seventies reappraisals of black history and culture, centering often on Nat Turner and antebellum resistance to slavery. Though expressing continuities as well as innovations, neither historian (even Blassingame, with his sympathetic attention to fiction as historical source) referred directly to Styron and the controversy of the late sixties that, directly and indirectly, stimulated these new explanations. Only in Genovese's *Roll, Jordan, Roll* is the Virginia novelist mentioned. Thus though we can observe some racial and professional barriers falling as the black culture paradigm gains currency, the same opening-up of two-way traffic between novelists and historians is not notably present.

Yet there are two early-seventies histories and a mid-decade biography that belie this generalization. They return or continue Styron's *The Confessions of Nat Turner* as public and professional participant. Although neither collection (for both are anthologies, not monographs or textbooks) reached the same general readers as Blassingame (and perhaps Genovese and Levine), each kept Nat Turner's past and present significance alive for students of history, literature, and culture—as did, for a more general audience, the biography. These new summaries of novel and familiar explanations provide a convenient and symbolic finale to this survey of texts, networks, and occasions through which the return of Nat Turner continued during the seventies.

The title of the earlier of the two collections, Peter I. Rose's *Old Memories, New Moods* (1970), captures well the continuities between sixties and seventies issues and between nineteenth- and twentieth-century priorities. Rose, no historian, was a white Smith College sociologist long interested in racial and ethnic relations. *Old Memories, New Moods* links the two cultural problems preoccupying nearly all authors we have here discussed: black protest and the quest for community. Significantly, Rose approaches contemporary black protest from a single historical question: Who was Nat Turner? Black power and issues of black identity, then, arise implicitly from the test case of the rebellious slave who is listed as a contributor to this otherwise twentieth-century debate. "Nat Turner" symbolically and literally takes his place in a dialogue among white and black social scientists, historians, literary scholars, and another dead black leader, Martin Luther King, Jr. In this broad cultural confrontation are included writers already familiar to us: Lerone Bennett, Jr., Eugene D. Genovese, C. Eric Lincoln, August Meier and Elliot Rudwick, Gerald Mullin, George Plimpton (and with him, William Styron), Alvin Poussaint, and Mike Thelwell. Turner (through Gray) addresses his posterity through still another reprinting of *The Confessions of Nat Turner*. For his own part, Rose has assembled a conventionally academic spectrum of viewpoints. Observing that "few topics are more timely, or more controversial, than that brought out by the publication of William Styron's historical novel *The Confessions of Nat Turner*,"[22] Rose attempts to replay the controversy in this 1970 interdisciplinary and interracial arena.

The result is less than satisfactory, however. Styron himself appears only in his prepublication interview with George Plimpton where he repeats his notorious reply to the question about research: "What there is to know about Nat Turner can be learned in a single day's reading" (97). Historians from the sixties are also present to challenge and correct, but Rose arranges for them to address other aspects of slave resistance and revolt than those provoked by Styron. The editor's historical naïveté, moreover, is displayed by his introductory comment on Gray's *Confessions:* "Unlike Gabriel's Rebellion, Nat Turner's Revolt was not well documented. Yet of the bits and pieces of information still extant, one is most remarkable, Nat's own Confession" (74). Neither Genovese nor Mullin corrects this outdated historiographical assertion, which sounds suspiciously as if issuing from Styron's lips. Hence Rose's liberal-minded symposium, like certain sixties anthologies and casebooks that preceded it, represents a mélange of disparate viewpoints rather than a coherent discussion in answer to the question, Who was Nat Turner?

In the other historical source book that appeared the year following *Old Memories, New Moods*, Rose might have found the historian he needed to address Styron's pronouncements and contribute concretely to a more focused history-and-literature reprise. Henry I. Tragle, editor and contributor to *The Southampton Slave Revolt of 1831: A Compilation of Source Material* (1971), was, in fact, a near neighbor of Rose's and the recent author of an essay in the *Massachusetts Review*, "Styron and His Sources."[23] Tragle's twin objectives are to set the record straight on available contemporary sources of information about Nat Turner and to challenge Styron's historicism and claims as a historical novelist: "One wonders why such critics [including C. Vann Woodward] have not more persistently questioned Styron's bland omniscience with regard to *all* the historical sources which bear on the event. Many historians, meanwhile, have been willing to accept Styron's claim of historical authenticity" (398). Tragle's research, including successive journeys to Southampton County to interview residents, has turned up three hundred pages of documentation, including contemporary newspaper accounts, verbatim trial records, state correspondence, and related documents. Then, in silent agreement perhaps with Barbara Herrnstein Smith and Tony Bennett, he reprints a generous selection of retellings (thirteen in all) of the revolt, from 1831 to 1970, by both white and black authors. This selection of relevant evidence (80,000 words from Virginia newspapers alone) supports Tragle's strenuous refutation of Styron's often-repeated position that he "had mastered the historical material relevant to the setting and the time of his book" (398–99). To a historian, he argues, it was simply irresponsible for a novelist to announce that "I had already been reliably informed . . . that [the Southampton Court records] would prove unrewarding" (399), and to add "there were a few little newspaper clippings of the time, all of them seemingly sort of halfway informed and hysterical and probably not very reliable" (399). Referring to Styron's author's note, Tragle exclaimed indignantly:

> How is it possible, if one seeks to ascertain the *known* facts about an event and to understand the true nature of the time and place in which it happened, to dismiss contemporary day-to-day accounts as "halfway informed and hysterical"? Is it not a part of the role of one who takes on the task of writing a "meditation on history" to sift the chaff for the grains of wheat which might be there? . . .
>
> The patient reader can learn a great deal from these old papers. Perhaps not very much about Nat himself, but at least about the

place and the time in which he acted, and about those who in turn re-acted to what he did. (400)

To those who would accuse him of applying inappropriate historiographical criteria to a fiction writer, Tragle replies: "Styron has insisted that he 'rarely departed from the *known* facts' when there were such facts available, but that he allowed himself 'the utmost freedom of imagination in reconstructing events.' No one can object to the artist's right to do this: in fact it should be insisted upon. But the groundswell of indignation raised by this novel, and particularly by Styron's characterization of Nat Turner himself, very properly raise questions about the line which separates freedom in the reconstruction of events when facts were lacking from deliberate distortion of *known* facts" (409). One "known fact" Styron is responsible for, Tragle believes, is found in a letter in the Richmond *Constitutional Whig* of September 17, 1831. It was written by a Southampton resident who, on grounds Tragle carefully explores, may well have been Thomas R. Gray. "He likewise pretended to have conversations with the Holy Spirit, and was assured by it that he was invulnerable," wrote this unidentified correspondent, adding, "'Tis true that Nat for some time had thought closely on this subject—for I have in my possession some papers given up by his wife, under the lash—they are filled with hieroglyphical characters, conveying no definite meaning" (407). In the same letter is additional information about the fight at Dr. Samuel Blunt's house which, the correspondent avers, corroborates "in a slight degree my opinion that the insurrection was not general," that "the slaves of Dr. Blunt, many in number, joined heart and hand in the defense of their master" (408). Styron might have thought twice about moving the fight, apparently unnecessarily, to Major Ridley's had he known this "fact." Tragle's demand for historical awareness—if not complete accuracy—on Styron's part thus conjoins two "controversial questions that have raged around Styron's book: Was Nat Turner married? Did some slaves join their masters in fighting against Nat Turner and his band?" (408).

These are instances—by no means isolated ones in a fat volume—of fact-finding as fault-finding. Tragle nevertheless insists such interrogations of method and motive have both literary and historical relevance to the heart of Styron's novel: its characterization of the protagonist in his relations to whites, especially white women as well as Thomas R.

Gray. More peripheral, Tragle believes, but also indicative of a narrowly white, ahistorical, and psychological bias is Styron's fact-finding expedition to Southampton with its dubious methods and faulty results. Two details in "This Quiet Dust" become particularly ironic. The first is that Styron's whirlwind tour of the county produced the impression that Nat Turner's name and historical significance had all but disappeared from the memories of local residents. On the contrary, Tragle's own series of visits and interviews with over sixty individuals produced a number of natives like Percy Claud and Herbert Turner, both black, who readily shared their family knowledge of Turner and the revolt.

The second ironic detail is more personal. According to his own research, Tragle denies Styron's claim to have found the actual Whitehead farmhouse where Margaret died and on whose porch one of his more poignant meditations of 1964 took place: "The Whitehead House (known locally as the Sykes place) is still standing. It is situated three-quarters of a mile south of the junction of County Roads 665 and 667, but is so screened by trees that it is impossible to see it from either road at any season of the year. A discussion with the County Sheriff in February 1969 confirmed that this was not the house which Styron visited" (414). Though merely a minor mistake, this detail suggests how differently one novelist and one historian can feel about "'facts' that are there—old buildings, features of the landscape, and the little stories people have to tell" (414). As the historical novelist Fred Chappell observed about this time, "it is not possible for fiction and history to share the same events. They may be called by the same names, but they are not identical. They are, however, metaphorically congruent."[24]

Tragle's compilation, when compared with the more general studies that succeeded it, is narrowly focused upon historical sources, communication networks, and previous accounts of one slave revolt. Both *Old Memories, New Moods* and *The Southampton Slave Revolt of 1831* fail to examine broadly cultural aspects of this event and its leader's life—because neither author chose to do so. Only in Tragle's careful attention to rural culture, as reflected in buildings, the Virginia landscape, and old folks (black and white) talking one's ear off about something that happened there a long time ago, do we sense this historian's awareness of and sympathy for the rich social milieu out of which Nat Turner's revolt must have emerged and in which it remains a significant event. But if cultural history is not Tragle's approach and prime contribution to continuing seventies disputes over slave resistance and slave culture, his careful sifting of historical chaff and his collection of more than a few kernels remain permanently valuable. Tragle's legacy, therefore, may be detected in the work of other historians.

One of these, like Rose and Tragle a resident of the Connecticut River valley, is Stephen B. Oates. Another participant in the Nat Turner controversy in the late sixties, Oates published in 1975 *The Fires of Jubilee: Nat Turner's Fierce Rebellion*. As both academic historian and popular biographer, Oates clearly intended his brief paperback account for the general reader: "I have attempted to bring the historical Turner alive in the context of his time, to re-create him and his world with common sense and human compassion—and to do so on the basis of meticulous research in all available records and a thorough retracing of Nat's insurrection in Southampton County itself."[25] So runs the author's foreword. Its promise is confirmed and chief debt paid in the reference notes. There Oates writes: "Of the published sources and books about the rebellion, by far the most valuable is Henry Irving Tragle (ed.), *The Southampton Slave Revolt of 1831* (Amherst, Mass. 1971), a collection of documents about virtually all aspects of the Turner story" (178). *The Fires of Jubilee* reflects the author's care in enacting his role as channel of primary historical research done not only by Tragle but his predecessors, including Aptheker, Stampp, and Vincent Harding. There is also a single reference to Styron's *The Confessions of Nat Turner*.[26]

The timing of Oates's book and the appearance two years later of Levine's *Black Culture, Black Consciousness* are symbolic if not coordinated events in the revisionist historiography I have here sketched. These works by two sympathetic white historians bracket the American Bicentennial, a moment and public occasion of heightened historical awareness. Like other works by Blassingame and Genovese, they signal a significant elevation of attention by both whites and blacks to the phenomenon historians had wrestled with over the past decade and a half. That Nat Turner and his legacy would continue to attract scholars and general readers alerted by the Bicentennial to dark corners of history is further suggested by a project begun during these fertile years but not completed until 1980. Vincent Harding's *The Other American Revolution*, though its title bespeaks seventies concerns and celebrations, is a black contribution to be considered as I turn, by way of conclusion, to still further versions of Nat Turner's cultural history.

7 Echoes in the Eighties

Any cultural debate like the one reconstructed in this book, involving the social uses of history and historical literature, has a probable beginning but no clear-cut conclusion. Given these charged topics, new imaginations are sure to be periodically fired to retell already retold narratives. Whether or not new historical data are discovered—not notably the case with the Southampton slave revolt or the life of its leader—changing circumstances inevitably occasion different answers to existing questions. New disputants will also alter the agendas of their predecessors. The "anxiety of influence" affects historians as well as poets and novelists. Each of these platitudes about the processes of cultural history is exemplified in the Nat Turner controversy, as can be documented by a parting look at the historiography and imaginative literature of slave revolts in the eighties.

The unsurprising conclusion to emerge from these later writings is that the debate over Nat Turner and slave revolts persists but without the sixties ardor and acrimony. A secondary hypothesis, scarcely less unsurprising, is that some of the ideological intensity of former expressions and occasions is maintained by a few major actors whose temperaments and commitments (as we have reason to suspect) seem to preclude fundamental rethinking or retreat. Representative of this small but articulate band of defenders are—in descending order, perhaps, of determination—William Styron, Vincent Harding, and Eugene Genovese. Moreover, among younger writers attracted to the subject of slave resistance and violence are more blacks and women. Thus the ensuing survey of recent retellings and new explanations begins with four exemplary restatements: Harding's two popular histories *The Other American Revolution* (1980) and *There Is a River: The Black Struggle for Freedom in America* (1981); Genovese's *From Rebellion to Revolution: Afro-American Slave Revolts in the Making of the Modern World*

(1979); and Styron's *This Quiet Dust and Other Writings* (1982). It proceeds, after brief considerations of representative contributions by younger historians and textbook writers, to a concluding look at two powerful pieces of recent black fiction, David Bradley's *The Chaneysville Incident* (1981) and the even more pointed counterstatement by a black woman artist and amateur historian, Sherley Anne Williams's *Dessa Rose* (1986).

Present-day readers should require no extensive summary of the social, political, and cultural changes and challenges that have occurred since the Bicentennial. Some of these shifts are alluded to in the eighties texts; others are implicit but important preconditions affecting the texts' expression and reception. Among the most pertinent changes in American public life through the eighties are the close of the Vietnam conflict with its (bitterly) ironic lesson to America as a neocolonialist power; decreasing attention to civil rights agitation and legislation; the relative absence of major urban riots (Miami excepted), with violence imploding as internal crime (often drug-related) rather than as national reminders of continuing oppression, racism, and class divisions; the increase of political power among middle-class urban blacks as black mayors, legislators, and school-board members exert greater influence over issues such as the politicization of history in textbooks, monuments, and holidays; the fading from acute public consciousness of sixties threats to white complacency like the Black Panthers, the Nation of Islam, and aggressive black nationalism—a shift best symbolized, perhaps, by Eldridge Cleaver's return as a born-again Christian; a decline in political assassinations; and the entry of black preachers into national politics, represented by the shift in mass media images of Malcolm X, Martin Luther King, Jr., and Jesse Jackson.

These and other circumstances help create a cultural milieu quite different from that of the sixties. The yeasty ferment amid which Styron and the ten black writers spoke and wrote has been aptly characterized by Fredric Jameson as "an immense freeing or unbinding of social energies, a prodigious release of untheorized new forces: the ethnic forces of black and 'minority' or third world movements everywhere, regionalisms, the development of new and militant bearers of 'surplus consciousness' in the student and women's movements, as well as in a host of struggles of other kinds."[1] The era of Carter, Reagan, and Bush has not, it seems to me, extended or re-created conditions within which much "surplus consciousness" flows into the channels of American and black American history-making examined in these pages.

Nevertheless, despite much evidence of social retrenchment and hardening of racial lines, an altered cultural climate does persist in which black energies of creation and re-creation combine with white to search for a common history and historiography. Within the select (but perhaps expanding) subset of Americans who take history seriously, some basic shifts of consciousness can be descried. Encouraging such changes in the later seventies and early eighties were several converging developments. One of these is the institutionalization of black studies in hundreds of universities, colleges, and schools, where the month of February as Black History Month is now a calendar fixture. Concurrently, black American literature and history have become respected academic subjects and scholarly specialties. Such courses in secondary and higher institutions have, moreover, attracted increasing proportions (if not numbers) of white students, just as the cadre of historians and literary scholars includes both whites and blacks writing about (and, for whites, occasionally teaching) the black experience. Finally, there are theorists who, in the allied disciplines of history, literary criticism, culture studies, linguistics, and philosophy, continue to study the overlapping traditions and functions of history and literature—literature as history, history as literature.

Beyond these often elite and circumscribed circles lies the whole terrain of American popular culture and the growing number of enthusiasts and scholars studying its many manifestations. One epochal event in this arena of particular importance to the return of Nat Turner was identified early by the playwright Amiri Baraka and the historian Vincent Harding—the TV version in February 1978 of Alex Haley's *Roots*, a series that drew an audience in excess of, by some estimates, 80 million viewers. At this moment a radicalized and embittered Baraka was about to publish *The Motion of History and Other Plays* (1978). His title play "sets itself the task of exposing the treachery and sham, but also of telling a part of the nation's history through its recurrent rebellions. (This was one of the grave defects of the TV *Roots*, that it made only weak and confused reference to the slave rebellions, inferring that most slaves could buy their way to freedom. Also the whole history of slavery was told through the lives of the house servants and petty bourgeoisie-to-be, not the field slaves who were, and are, the majority!)"[2] Unfortunately, Baraka's later drama packs little of the impact of his earlier *Dutchman* or *The Slave Ship;* rather, it often sounds like a wooden proletarian pageant and signals no significant artistic advance over Edmonds's *Nat Turner* or Duberman's *In White America.*

Following publication of *Ten Black Writers Respond*, Harding, another seventies radicalized black intellectual, moved from the bourgeois safety of Spelman College to help establish, as part of the Martin Luther King, Jr., Memorial Center in Atlanta, the Institute of the Black World, an independent research center whose aim was to reach the black masses as well as the educated elite. At the same time he began what was eventually to become *There Is a River: The Black Struggle for Freedom in America*. In part, this work was a reply to Genovese's challenge to him and other black authors to write their own versions of slavery and slave resistance. At the same time, black cultural leaders in several cities sought new channels for educating American publics through black versions of black experience. "Early in the seventies," Harding wrote in the preface to *The Other American Revolution*, "at the height of the recurring battle for hegemony over the interpretation of the history and the future of black people in America, many local community groups began to organize to challenge the mass media outlets, especially television stations."[3] One result came in 1973 when WMAL in Washington, D.C., agreed to air a new series, for the upcoming Bicentennial, on black history and culture. Harding scripted the series by adapting portions of his work in progress. However, the series was jettisoned because of what Harding later interpreted as a mainline response to the building publicity campaign for the *Roots* series: "Many persons in the television industry apparently assumed that *that* would be the medium's big black history thing for the rest of the decade," he wrote. Harding ultimately used his script in audio tapes and serialized segments in the magazine *Black World-View*. Finally, in 1980, *The Other American Revolution* appeared as a belated black Bicentennial statement. Jointly published by the Center for Afro-American Studies at UCLA and the Institute of the Black World, the book's imprimaturs signaled the easier relationship between academic institutions and Harding's previously separatist enterprise. Its argument was plainly addressed to black readers but also to all others suspicious of the Bicentennial's smugly celebratory spirit. The black battle for liberation and justice, he declares, continues as "the longest, unbroken, active struggle for freedom ever carried out in the annals of American history" (xv).

Nat Turner is a key actor in this centuries-long movement. He becomes, therefore, the subject of a separate chapter whose title echoes Baraka: "Slay My Enemies with Their Own Weapons": "Nat Turner's status was clear. His break with the slave system, his open challenge to its power, his audacious attempt to organize his fellow captives to seek a new kingdom of justice—these were all unambiguous elements of the other American revolution" (37). The adjective "unambiguous" sounds like a dig at William Styron and his version of slave motivations, but is also a reference to historians who still inscribed this rebel as an unrepresentative slave, privileged and impelled by private aspirations. Instead, "Nat Turner was a product of the deepest inner life of the black community" (33). Each distinctive feature of the Prophet's biography, and particularly his religious participation and leadership, bespeaks an unexceptional slave. The revolt, flatly termed a brief "war on a Christian basis" (35), was admittedly less extensively planned than Prosser's or Vesey's conspiracies. "Perhaps he was far more convinced of direct intervention than they," Harding explains. But for a variety of reasons that Harding does not explore, the rebels never reached Jerusalem. Instead, Turner's fate and opportunity for influence and immortality came on the gallows and, later, at the hands of Thomas R. Gray.

However, Gray's *Confessions* is not the sole evidence and instrument of the rebel's prophetic presence in American culture. Harding reports still another variant of the black folksong celebrating Old Prophet Nat:

> You might be Carroll from Carrollton
> Arrive here night afo' Lawd made creation
> But you can't keep the World from movering round
> And not turn her back from the gaining ground.

In these lyrics, Harding finds a proper instance of mystery and ambiguity in the life of Nat Turner. For "only when that last ambiguous line was repeated again and again in the chorus might it become clear that 'not turn her' was Old Prophet Nat in disguise, alive on the lips of his people. Even in song, the struggle continued" (36).

Harding's own role continued, too, the following year, in *There Is a River*. The first of a projected two-volume history, the new book was not intended to challenge Franklin's *From Slavery to Freedom;* it is not "another general survey history of black people in the United States" but rather "the first published attempt to provide a comprehensive and organic historical survey of the black movement towards freedom, of our search and struggle for justice, equality and self-determination in the United States."[4] Harding sees himself working within a broad tradition of black authors including W. E. B. Du Bois, C. L. R. James, Lerone Bennett, Lorraine Hansberry, Langston Hughes, and Robert Brisbane. More revealing still than this impressive lineage is Harding's major model and hero, for the spirit of Martin King and his goal to "redeem the soul of America" explicitly preside over *There Is a River*.

Because the moral fervor and something of the rhetorical style of a King or Malcolm X infuse this eighties work, Harding recognizes that neither his theme nor treatment will please many professional colleagues. But to fellow historians with their current (and often exclusive) preoccupation with racism and capitalism as key factors in the history of all black oppression and liberation Harding asserts the "renewed urgency to emphasize the role of religion and spirituality in our freedom struggle" (xxiii). This is, he confesses, a deeply personal imperative as well. "Having been raised in a tightly knit, Bible-centered black church community in Harlem" (xiii), he recalls several formative experiences in his own "unorthodox pilgrimage." During the early sixties, Harding and his wife moved South where (with two white fellow historians at Spelman, Howard Zinn and Staughton Lynd) he became deeply involved in the civil rights struggle. In 1968 he stood vigil over the body of King as it lay "available to that steady stream of ordinary black men and women who came in from the darkness of the early morning to bid their last farewell to the dreamer" (xvii). Flooded with outrage, Harding began to assemble a nucleus of black scholars and artists in the Institute of the Black World. This talented intellectual network constituted a seventies version of the ten black writers and included Lerone Bennett, Stephen Henderson, A. B. Spellman, William Strickland, and Council S. Taylor. Here Harding pursued his historical study of black radicalism. Yet, though avoiding white and white-sponsored institutions, the one-time Mennonite pastor retained the same stubborn belief in American progress long shared with King.

This persistent Christian faith in the transcendent implications of history in part redeems bittersweet memories of the sixties and becomes the rationale for this people's history. Harding's introductory peroration powerfully voices that wry optimism.

> Indeed, as a result of the history I have explored, I am foolish enough to identify the decade of the 1980s as a time of hope. In the face of all the predictions and signs of breakdown and great danger that I see and hear all around me, I hear and see more as well. . . . I sense a time of tremendous opportunity, not an easy time, but a period of great possibilities. I think it is especially significant that when this decade ends we will have come to another Bicentennial, this time the anniversary of the nation's Constitution. . . . From the perspective of the black river, considering the struggles of women, Native Americans, Hispanics, and many others, we can now understand that the first constitutional creation of the American nation was more like a poorly attended dress rehearsal, with most of the rightful and necessary performers and creators barred from the stage. Women were locked in homes, black people held in thrall in both South and North, Native Americans harassed, destroyed, and driven from their land, and poor people of every hue taught to let their propertied "betters" make the crucial public decisions for them. (xxv)

These inspirational accents, though tinged for some with an outdated SCLC hopefulness, echo throughout *There Is a River*. The ideology and historicism behind that prophetic voice likewise determine the choice and arrangement of subjects. Thus Nat Turner, who had his own short chapter in the preceding narrative, is here treated in tandem with David Walker in a chapter entitled "Symptoms of Liberty and Blackhead Signposts." (The term "blackhead signposts" refers, of course, to the severed heads of slaughtered slaves and rebels displayed along southern highways and fences.) The pair of men represent the radical black tradition in action—one speaking the Word through the *Appeal* "as a kind of angry black pastor to white America" (92), the other, a real pastor, acting out righteous retribution and then testifying through an amanuensis. Actual contact between the two was unnecessary, he asserts, "for Nat Turner had long been convinced that the God of Walker's *Appeal* had always been in Southampton" (94). The rhetoric of the "angry black pastor" and ex-college historian is typically reflected in Harding's succinct retelling of the revolt's progress:

> At the height of the advance, there were apparently some sixty men in Nat Turner's company, including several described as "free." Together, in a breathlessly brief period of solidarity, they were marching to Jerusalem, Virginia, and their leader was now "General Nat." Once again a captive black prophet, wresting the religion of white America out of its hands, had transformed it and had in turn been utterly changed. Now, as an insurrectionary commander carrying out the sanguinary vengeance of a just God, Nat Turner took up the spirit of David Walker's *Appeal* and burned its message into the dark and bloody ground of Virginia, streaking the black river with blood. (95)

Harding here wrests the language and methodology of conventional historians like Franklin, Elkins, and Genovese, transforming diction and details from the records into frankly sermonic prose. Nonetheless, in the passages that follow, he continues to recognize the scholarly limits within which inspirational narrative must operate. Black oral traditions, rumors, fears, and premonitions are less tangible factors in and sources for the story Harding retells. But in the chapter's footnotes he takes greater pains than the general reader might expect or require to document the discourse. Regarding the original *Confessions* he offers a retrospective evaluation: "I suspect there is much truth in the *Confession*, that Gray inserts himself more than is helpful, and that Turner conceals a good deal" (352). In addition to Tragle, Oates, and Aptheker, Harding also pays respectful attention to Genovese's *Roll, Jordan, Roll* and *From Rebellion to Revolution*. But there is no attempt here to invoke other interpretations (particularly by black scholars like Blassingame and Leslie Owens) that link Turner to black culture in broader terms than black religion. Hence the 1986 judgment of Meier and Rudwick seems well taken: "Indeed, the discussion of slave protest in his major opus, *There Is a River* (1981), has a decidedly old-fashioned air. Despite Harding's emphasis on the messianic content of slave religion, his presentation in this volume owes a good deal to the anti-Phillips genre of history-writing in the 1930s and 1940s, and nothing at all to the resistance through culture arguments that loomed so prominently in the 1970s. Instead, it was [Sterling] Stuckey who, in his essay, 'Through the Prism of Folklore: The Black Ethos in Slavery,' more explicitly developed the thesis that the slaves fashioned 'a life style and set of values—an ethos—which prevented them from being imprisoned altogether by the definitions which the larger society sought to impose.'"[5]

Harding's tip of the hat, like Meier and Rudwick's reference to the larger society in tension with black slave culture, draws attention to recent work by Harding's antagonist of November 1968. Genovese's *From Rebellion to Revolution*, though not quite as long in gestation as Harding's popular, black-oriented works, shares certain arguments with both books. It also reflects even more clearly changes in historical explanations advanced in the seventies. Nevertheless, its treatment of black culture, and of slave religion in particular, is cursory inasmuch as *From Rebellion to Revolution* rests on detailed discussions of those topics already deployed in *Roll, Jordan, Roll*, to which it is the promised sequel.

As such, Genovese's latest thinking reflects in its basic aims and assumptions his continued allegiance to economic and political explanations of North American slavery and slave resistance and his insistence on subordinating regional and local to hemispheric and world explanations. That these lead him along quite different lines of investigation and argument from Harding is clear from the brief book's opening remarks. (These are, indeed, *remarks*, as this work originated as the Walter Lynwood Fleming Lectures in Southern History at Louisiana State University.) Genovese declares that slave rebellions in the New World must be seen as radical expressions of a two-centuries-long worldwide struggle, beginning in the age of democratic revolutions, both within and ultimately against bourgeois capitalism and polity. These revolutions, of which Toussaint L'Ouverture's in Haiti was a crucial instance, challenged the dominant liberal bourgeois ideals of western societies— individual freedom, equality, and democracy. At the same time, slave revolts prefigured the socialist challenge to capitalism occurring in twentieth-century societies of the nonwestern world. Slave revolts are, therefore, doubly significant to all American historians.

Nevertheless, insurrections in North America proved less significant as effective actions against capitalism than as early harbingers of protosocialist protest. Hence their long-term importance in the world process of modern history must be set against their relative infrequency and low intensity in the Old South. Genovese now acknowledges that there were not three but seven significant North American revolts and conspiracies. Genovese also argues that this small number with its marginal political importance does *not* imply slave docility or infantilization: "Nothing could be more naive—or arrogant—than to ask why a Nat Turner did not appear on every plantation in the South, as if, from the comfort of our living rooms, we have a right to tell others, and retrospectively at that, when, how, and why to risk their lives and those of their loved ones. As the odds and circumstances become clearer, there is less difficulty in understanding the apparent infrequency of slave revolts throughout history and less difficulty in appreciating the extent of the rebels' courage and resourcefulness and the magnitude of their impact on world history."[6]

Nevertheless, Genovese remains convinced of the accuracy of his earlier argument in *Roll, Jordan, Roll*. American slave revolts, in their modern and world-stage forms, emerged after the cessation of the slave trade and must be seen as responses to the generally improving living conditions slaves experienced under necessarily more enlightened southern paternalism. As one factor accounting for the low incidence of nineteenth-century revolts, paternalism—"that is, the development of a sense of reciprocal rights and duties between masters and slaves—implied considerable living space within which the slaves could create stable families, develop a rich spiritual community, and attain a measure of physical comfort" (6). This "space" meant that, though southern slaves never accepted slavery, they did come to recognize the realistic chances for successful revolts and chose "forms of resistance appropriate to their survival as a people even as slaves" (6). Black slave religion played a key role in this rational policy of selective resistance.

> Their Christianity served as a bulwark against the dehumanization inherent in slavery. But increasingly, black preachers understood, especially after the failure of Gabriel Prosser, Denmark Vesey, and Nat Turner, that revolt would be suicidal, and, therefore, with a few important exceptions, they counseled a defensive strategy of survival. Thus, the social context of black religion became circumscribed by wider political realities, which it then reinforced. . . . [Hence] the development of black Christianity did

not arise mechanically from the failure of slave revolts; nor can the failure of slave revolts be attributed to black Christianity. Each arose within the totality of social relations, and steadily reinforced the other. (7)

This argument, like Genovese's early writings including his 1968 exchanges with Harding in *The New York Review of Books*, still does not address the full social and psychological significance of slave revolts (no matter how few or militarily unsuccessful) for both slaves and their descendants in twentieth-century tenant farms and ghettos. Nor does it explain Nat Turner. Genovese, finessing explanation of the religious and psychological elements in specific slave insurrections but unwilling to dismiss Turner and his predecessors as he had once done, still seeks a rational secular explanation of such events. Again, this becomes possible only by taking the comparative, hemispheric, and long-term perspective originally used to justify his admiration for Styron's novel: "General risings of thousands, such as those in Jamaica, Demerara, and Saint-Dominique, or even of hundreds such as those in many countries, remained a possibility, which, however slim, rendered the hopes of a Gabriel Prosser, a Denmark Vesey, or a Nat Turner rational. Turner did not succeed in raising the countryside *en masse*, but he might have, had he sustained his pilot effort even for a few weeks or escaped to forge a guerilla base in the interior" (8).

In comments such as this one, which takes such a broad view that a geographical detail like the Dismal Swamp is never mentioned, Genovese exhibits his continuing preference for Caribbean or South American uprisings. Even the early Latin American insurrections, with their separatist aim of restoring African communal life rather than challenging the slave system itself, are treated more fully than Nat Turner's holy war. Thus "the Christmas rising in Jamaica in 1831 [a scant four months after Southampton] laid bare the new quality of the nineteenth-century slave revolts. . . . Large numbers of Jamaican slaves participated in some of its activity even if not the most militant or dramatic. The setting contained familiar elements. Blacks outnumbered whites about ten to one; the island had a tradition of revolt and maroon war; the planters were fighting a desperate battle against abolitionists in England; and the slaves threw up leaders from their most privileged strata" (102). By contrast, the Southampton County revolt and Nat Turner were beaten before they began. Genovese develops in some detail the implicit superiority of Sam Sharpe, the black Baptist slave leader from Montego Bay, over his Virginia counterpart. Not only did the Jamaican revolt "not raise millenialist slogans or take on the features of a holy war" (103), but even Nat Turner's audacity in killing white men, women, and children, did not go as far as Caribbean violence: "Since the first rule of such desperate warfare is to proceed as rapidly as possible before the more powerful enemy can regroup, compassion for women and children equaled a death warrant for the compassionate. That 'bloodthirsty' Nat Turner ruined himself not by his executions but by precisely such compassion" (105). However, Genovese offers no evidence of crippling Christian mercy in the records of the Southampton revolt. Rather, he seems to continue to argue from the general to the particular instance, pointing out that slave and peasant revolts throughout history—and perhaps especially in the New World—have been marked by fewer atrocities, murders, and rapes than were visited upon the low-born rebels by revengeful masters. Genovese is on safer ground, therefore, when he instances the typical experiences of Southampton blacks in the revolt's aftermath: "The slaveholders, shocked by the evidence that the slaves had killed a few whites—so few in fact in the United States that Nat Turner's fifty or so victims seemed beyond belief—or that they had had the audacity to contemplate doing so, responded by showing just how much more civilized they were than their degraded slaves. . . . They lynched, burned alive, tortured, and dismembered suspected slaves, many of whom they later admitted had been innocent" (106).

From Rebellion to Revolution marks, therefore, a qualified change in Eugene Genovese's previously negative assessment of the political significance of American slave revolts. Though still suspicious of messianic religion and other manifestations of "irrationalism and fanaticism"—"even when these elements have paradoxically often proven necessary to stimulate revolutionary voluntarism" (122)—he now acknowledges that even the few and apparently unsuccessful southern uprisings not only "contributed significantly to the shaping of the Age of Revolution" (110) but aided later in the nineteenth century to support abolitionist and meliorationist endeavors; "in the United States, as C. L. R. James has noted, Nat Turner made Garrison a household word" (112). For such short-term results to become long-term accomplishments, however, a modern revolutionary ethos had to emerge, involving

> the gradual transfer of allegiance from the prophetic leader to the party, the movement, or the nation [narrowing] the possibilities for acquiring blind loyalty. And for these very reasons the secularization of revolutionary ideology has vastly improved the chances of victory. Stripped of the requirements of prophetic specificity and of the myth of the divinely chosen leader, the party can much more readily prepare the masses for tactical retreats and compromises and for the acceptance of defeat and even disaster while it regroups in protracted war. (123)

Yet this secular ideologue is also a historian respectful of his sources. In the case of Nat Turner and other rebels, these are cited in the extended bibliographical essay that replaces footnotes in this book of lectures. His decided preference for "rational" anticlerical politics must come to terms with evidence of Christianity's political usefulness to slaves themselves: "The slaves' Christianity sang of freedom and deliverance and blended easily into the political message of the Revolutionary War. The religion of the slaves, at least during the nineteenth century, normally eschewed calls to insurrection and took the path of long-term survival in a world of hopeless odds, but its essentially militant core could be turned into revolutionary channels at given moments. Thus, the message of the Revolution, in the hands of a Gabriel Prosser, a Denmark Vesey, or a Nat Turner, could be made to reinforce rather than challenge the religious spirit of the people" (130).

These three historical explanations by the black and the white historian usher in the eighties and exemplify the persistence of the powerful cultural and social forces that influenced sixties events and expressions. One force represented by Vincent Harding was (and remains) the religious convictions of black and white Christians and other religiously inspired activists. For this audience—many of whom like the historian himself were then entering their fifties—Harding's books attempted a tricky task of cultural work. Both author and audiences would recall the late-sixties erosion of support, within the black and civil rights communities, for Martin Luther King's ideology of nonviolence. In *The Motion of History* Amiri Baraka voiced the depth of his radical alienation from

King's policy: "Is the Act as legitimate as the Word? (A question that could only be asked in a bourgeois society, it is so absurd.) Now we know the act is *more* legitimate, it is principal!" (12). Harding's joining together of Walker and Turner in *There Is a River* represents a passionate yet qualified reply to Baraka and other zealots of the act. The black river of history contains *two* intermingled currents. The angry voices of the black pastors of the past outweigh but do not dilute the equally religiously inspired violent deeds of a Nat Turner or a John Brown. Moreover, black revolutionists of the scythe and sword, Harding reminds his readers, have relied on the word of historians, autobiographers, and other testifiers to transmit the example of their bloody deeds to future generations of resisters. Though King's name is not evoked to condone righteous acts of vengeance, Harding's intention throughout his two people's histories is to demonstrate both religiously sanctioned modes of belief and behavior and thus to show black Christianity's dual role in the black vision of a better America. His image of history as a river of black lives and red deeds implies nature's force behind the eventual triumph of the soul of black people.

If Harding's eighties explanations of Nat Turner are principally addressed to and on behalf of black readers and listeners, Genovese's *From Rebellion to Revolution* is just as plausibly addressed to a wider, secular, and essentially white audience of fellow historians and their educated allies. These recipients can be imagined as those in the lecture hall at LSU who heard the 1973 versions of these chapters. Though other evidence is lacking, the occasion shows similarities yet also striking differences from a previous Louisiana academic occasion—the SHA session in 1968, which took place ninety miles to the south of Baton Rouge. How many blacks were seated among the historians, students, and townspeople present at the Fleming lectures is not known to me, yet Genovese's preface and bibliographical essay suggest a chiefly white conclave and discourse. On the other hand, Genovese's former magisterial tone, in lecturing black readers about Styron's novel and historians of its subject, is largely absent from this later work. Indeed, his working-class vehemence in specifying acts of brutal repression (by patricians and poorer whites) of slave revolts like Turner's suggests a not-so-buried desire to hold genteel white soles/souls to the fire of guilty class consciousness. In the same vein, his outspoken admiration for the flexible, politically productive strategies of a Toussaint or

Sam Sharpe—approaches that he claims had long-term consequences in the class struggles of the following centuries—may be read as inspirational messages to socialist and other leftist readers discouraged by the "counterrevolutionary" ethos of the Reagan era. As he once argued for a hardheaded look at religiously inspired leaders and insurrections, so now Genovese implicitly repudiates Harding's post-SNCC historicism in favor, for example, of Martin Kilson's structural modeling of slave revolts.[7] Thus *From Rebellion to Revolution*, though drastically different in ideology, tone, and sense of audience from *There Is a River*, serves a similar consolatory function for survivors of the sixties and their beleaguered or discouraged ranks of eighties followers.

Styron's Last(?) Stand

If these speculations about two major historian-participants in the past debate suggest some significant changes as well as even stronger continuities, the same mixture is scarcely evident with the novelist once at the center of the sixties event. William Styron's afterthoughts, to be sure, are not expressed in full-length form. *Sophie's Choice* (1979), his next novel after *The Confessions of Nat Turner*, echoes its predecessor only in certain respects. It addresses an even more daunting historical subject, one possibly evoked (and complicated) by Elkins-inspired reflections on parallels between slave plantations and German concentration camps. It mixes sex, violence, racism, and autobiography in somewhat similar and characteristic proportions. But *Sophie's Choice* provoked only a relatively minor furor from Holocaust survivors and what opposition did arise did not prevent the appearance of a highly successful Hollywood movie version. In any event, Styron did not take deep umbrage at critics of this work.

The evidence for Styron's (by comparison) unyielding tenacity in debate rests, instead, upon two other sources: the nearly one hundred interviews from which James L. W. West III selected his *Conversations With William Styron* (1986) and Styron's introduction to the section entitled "South" in *This Quiet Dust and Other Writings*. Since the second piece sums up the novelist's retrospective estimate of the controversy in a volume of carefully selected essays and reviews, it should properly receive attention here. Styron's well-known weakness for interviews, occasions on which he frequently repeats himself and makes ill-advised, off-the-cuff comments, should not be allowed to divert attention from the 1982 introduction, his most thoughtful meditation to date.

This five-page commentary is surely one of the more arresting documents of the Nat Turner controversy. Subjecting it to cultural analysis runs the risk of fitting, all too uncomfortably, Styron's expectations of his molesters and carping critics. We have already heard him say, "It is beneath a writer's dignity to discuss his critics in print," and this introductory comment continues in the same disingenuous vein:

> There is, I am sure, hardly a writer of any merit who does not find the impulse nearly irresistible to reply to some of those who have molested him—more often than not, professors of English who are themselves authors of fiction of undisputed harmlessness. . . . Although one should never respond to criticism in general, I think I can make an exception for myself in the case of *The Confessions of Nat Turner*. . . . I have no intention of opening old wounds (especially my own) by taking up the fight again and contriving a defensive reply to those antagonists of the 1960s. But the controversy over *The Confessions of Nat Turner* was a fascinating one, and now—fifteen years later—the advantage of hindsight has enabled me to indulge in some useful reflections.[8]

How useful or undefensive Styron's hindsight proves should not be difficult for readers of this history to estimate. Virtually every sentence and paragraph of this "confession" recalls an argument, text, or occasion from the past. Each statement seethes again with emotion and social resonance. As a considered meditation, the introduction recapitulates in personal terms many fundamental issues of the public discussions: the rights and duties of this (or any other) novelist as amateur historian; the familiarity or ignorance Americans shared about Nat Turner before 1967; the animus behind the attacks by black critics and historians and the notable exceptions to such hysterical responses; the actual extent of available sources on the Nat Turner revolt and Styron's use or ignorance thereof; the limits of white sympathy and understanding of black experience, past or present; and, finally, what Styron calls "the bustling cottage industry which *The Confessions of Nat Turner* spawned during the subsequent years" (6).

Though baseless charges of racism, distortion, and other "derelictions laid against me by blacks everywhere" have, he insists, been largely shrugged off, what sticks "most undislodgeably" in this proud writer's craw is the accusation that his book maligned a hero "universally known and revered throughout the black world in America" (4). Still defending his nonprofessional status as a historian and his importance as rediscoverer, Styron stubbornly insists that Turner was, in fact, a figure not widely known in the sixties black community. This old opinion is supported by subsequent approval from recent acquaintances, "two well-educated, worldly" black doctors, both Ivy League graduates, who once admitted to him "without any apparent embarrassment that neither of them had ever heard of Nat Turner in their lives" (4). Even more to the point was the skimpy ("and when not skimpy, unreliable") information in history books regarding Nat Turner; "with a single exception," he now declares, "there had been no substantial work on Nat Turner which could be said to be the product of a professional historian" (4). It is, he remains convinced, simply a fiction that this black slave "was a vital figure in black consciousness before 1967, studied and explicated by black scholars" (4). Responding to an accusation by Vincent Harding—"one of the more intelligent of my ten black respondents"—that he "ignored the work of black historians by taking credit for resurrecting a black hero," Styron retorts: "When were writers of historical novels obligated in any way to acknowledge the work of historians?":

> Claiming no credit really, even now, I still have to insist that prior to my own work there was no important study by any reputable scholar, black or white, with the sole exception of that of a white man, Herbert Aptheker, the Communist party theoretician, who covered the rebellion at some length in his *American Negro Slave Revolts*. (As if I didn't have enough trouble with the blacks, Aptheker became one of my fiercest adversaries and during that period denounced me both publicly and in print. Strange how the passing of time engenders charity. I bear no ill will against Aptheker and keep trying to remember—as it might behoove us all to do—that in the horrible dark night of racism at its worst in America, the 1930s, the Communists were among the few friends black people had.) (4–5)

Regardless of his disputed role in the return of Nat Turner, Styron remains unambiguously confident and proud of his novel as a cultural phenomenon. Importance, however, did not bring admiration: "While, of course, many works of science or history or literature have elicited symposiumlike responses in the form of other books, *Nat Turner* was the first *novel* in the long annals of American publishing to evoke such an immediate, entirely hostile attack. There was no pretense of balance here, no observance of the gentlemanly rules of polemics or the usual admixture of pros and cons and the attempts to reconcile the bad and good" (5). Styron's memory of an "entirely hostile" reception is at best inaccurate, as signaled by his own account of the controversy in the press. Clearly taking *Ten Black Writers Respond* as target and model, he recalls the situation thus:

> Justifying their lopsided animus by way of the dual complaint that my book had received unqualified praise in the white press (which was hardly true; it got some very poor reactions, among them a glibly contemptuous review on the front page of the *New York Times Book Review*) and that no black person had been invited to review it (again untrue; it was reviewed very favorably on the front page of the *Chicago Sunday Tribune* book section by John Hope Franklin, one of the country's most distinguished historians), the ten black writers let go an all-out assault. It contained such pitiless indictments of my artistry, my historical and social responsibility, my ethical stance ("morally senile" was the most memorable quote), and even my probable sexual inclinations, that the savagery was at first truly impossible to comprehend. . . . Gradually it sank in that I was being subjected not even to discussable criticism but to the most intractable kind of hysteria—understandable perhaps, though no less ugly for being part of the chaotic racial politics of 1968. (5)

Styron's remembered responses indicate the still-anguished feelings of a white liberal southerner suffering unjustified attack from supposed friends: "Of course, I fretted and brooded a bit. No Southerner who had fought as hard as I had to free himself of the last clutches of the racial bugaboo wants to hear himself called 'an unreconstructed white racist.' Nonetheless, though many of my friends were horrified, I rather surprised myself by the equanimity with which I took this onslaught. (I had even begun to receive phone calls and mail heavy with threat.) Perhaps I simply knew, beleaguered as I was, that help was on the way" (5–6). Help first came not from the *New York Times* daily book critic who had accorded the *Confessions of Nat Turner* very favorable treatment but later had the temerity also to accord the ten black writers equal attention, in Styron's words, "treating their charges with gravity and respect and leaving the impression that I might be every bit the honky trickster I was accused of being" (6). Instead, justification came from two impeccably respected historians, both white: Martin Duberman and Eugene Genovese. The latter's *New York Review of Books* counterattack, "a beautifully crafted essay, which point by point dealt inflexibly with all my alleged crimes, not only disposed of the case once and for all but did it with such lofty outrage that the effect was like that of catharsis" (6). (It is an uncanny instance of déjà vu in this cultural event to note how closely in tone and language this description of Genovese's review of *Ten Black Writers Respond* echoes Ossie Davis's review of the same collection in *Freedomways*.)

Styron's final reflection rises above such remembered occasions of acrimony and assistance to reach the austere level of generalization about the abiding issues. These are precipitated by some lower-level comments on recent products of the *Nat Turner* "cottage industry" of books, essays, and anthologies. "Each of these writers had plainly worried about my *Nat Turner* a lot" (6–7), he recalls, and notes that a continuing bone of contention is the documentation of his historical/fictional insights. Without mentioning Tragle's *Southampton Slave Revolt of 1831* by name, he acknowledges: "[T]hat I did ignore or even willfully avoid certain information which may have been available to me is true. Also, had I been entirely meticulous, I should not have implied—as I implied in this volume's first essay, 'This Quiet Dust'— that I examined every source of fact and data. There obviously existed material which, had I been something more of a scrounger, I might not have wanted to skip. However, I don't see much importance in all this" (7). What remains of decisive importance, Styron concludes, is his and every artist's right to treat historical records freely and thereby "to provide historians with a touchstone to measure their own notions of accuracy by" (7). Then he restates a deep conviction:

There are few historians who appear capable of understanding that a historical novel is in actual flight from facts and the restrictions of pure data, and that the better the novel is—so long as it does not seriously compromise the historical record—the less likely it will show itself to be cluttered by the detritus of fact. About Nat Turner—of whose departed flesh-and-blood self so little is known, or ever will be known—I cared to discover only so much as my instinct as a novelist told me to care. In any case, I am pleased that *Nat Turner* has survived so well, and that it is now even being read, occasionally, by some intrepid black person of independent mind. Since the book invites the reader, black or white, merely to partake in an imagined vision within a vision, and claims for itself the quality of being "a meditation on history"—not the revealed truth—there should be nothing in it to fear or hate. (7–8)

In light of such frank feelings, lasting in some instances with undiminished intensity for fifteen years, it is difficult to determine precisely what cultural work Styron is performing here for a spectrum of readers. Unlike the 1967 novel or the 1965 *Harper's* essay, this introduction does not stand on its own as a fresh imaginative or ideological expression. Rather more than is the case with *There Is a River* or *From Rebellion to Revolution*, Styron's words point *inward* to the writer's disturbed consciousness and are addressed primarily *backward* to earlier readers and admirers who come here as survivors and rememberers of sixties events and emotions. That the introduction does not face *forward* inviting younger readers to adopt new and appropriate attitudes toward the course of history is perhaps inevitable, given its location in a retrospective collection of unrevised essays, reviews, and profiles. "Unrevised" is a key term, too, suggesting not only Styron's desire to speak for and about himself in accents little changed from previous declarations, but also to console and confirm a segment of his public in commonly held opinions. We might reconstruct these implied readers as a band of devoted followers. Individuals of a certain age (perhaps the same as or a bit older than Harding or Genovese), they are, arguably, predominantly white despite Styron's desire for fair-minded black readers. Their present politics might conceivably reflect the common disappointments of (ex-)liberals whose dreams of interracial cooperation have given way to resignation (or even reactionary secret satisfaction) over the tamer stalemates and persisting divisions in eighties society. More specifically, these faithful remain wedded to literature—not history—as a middle-class pastime and valued white cultural institution. Thus Styron does not expect them to be better acquainted with American history or black fiction than were his original readers of 1967 and 1968. He appears to expect and appreciate readers who have not read or thought widely about issues that once excited them and others during the exciting days of the controversy.

Admittedly, these are speculations supported chiefly by internal evidence from the author's own text, conceived rhetorically as an appeal for certain kinds of indulgent readers. In these terms, Styron's introduction fits blueprints for treating all discourse as cultural work. Whether as historical narrative, social commentary, or imaginative reconstruction, prose writing as social communication speaks, first, *for* a particular individual and for an immediate or self-declared body of peers and fellow believers. It speaks also *to* a wider potential audience who may derive pleasure and profit from assenting—provisionally, at least—to the tribal values and attitudes expressed. In this case, we are on increasingly slippery footing as we try to imagine moving outward from William Styron to the wider (and hazier) social circles around the author in the aura of his emotional involvement with his text.

Madison Avenue Plays Catch-Up:
America Revised in Eighties Textbooks

As changing historical explanations are codified in eighties historiographies such as Meier and Rudwick's and Novick's, so the social production of school textbooks and other authorized explanations for the young finds its premiere historiographer in Frances FitzGerald. *America Revised*, though a lively historical/cultural critique of 1979, cannot, of course, guide one through the following decade. Nonetheless, FitzGerald opens the door to the future when she points out in her witty preface, through the ironic comments of a fictionalized informant from within the Madison Avenue publishing world, that time lags are inevitable in this commercial sector of the dominant culture's communications network: "The reactions of the textbook industry aren't all that fast. It takes five years or more to get a book out, start to finish, so back in the mid-sixties we were really caught. All we had was George Washington Carver in the plates. . . . A bit thin, those books. You can only take so much of peanuts!" (3). Recalling hasty attempts to catch up with new versions of a more inclusive history and to meet the public's "chorus of protests against the white, male, middle-class orientation of the texts" (3), he recalls a time "marked not just by the canonization of George Washington Carver but by the drypointing of white middle-class faces and the hasty appendage of chapters about the Civil Rights Movement or, a year later, The Black Revolution" (3). Black quickly replaced green ("stuff about ecology") as the going topic, only to be threatened in turn by the later demand for historical and sociological explanations of alcohol and drugs. "Some companies have gone out of business trying to keep up" (4), he concludes.

FitzGerald's summary chapter, like its predecessors, does not pursue the question of Carver, nor does it mention Nat Turner. Nevertheless, the question of time lags sets the stage for a look at eighties messages to see if, how, and when the black "fad" persists and how the turn is made from peanuts to slave revolts. FitzGerald helps this extrapolation by offering a general ideological framework for considering such transmissions or explaining their absence. She posits three competing social-ideological groups of historians, each working under common superintendents, each addressing common audiences. The dominant force in sixties textbook writing and teaching, she finds, were advocates of the progressive or liberal tradition, increasingly inclusive in their treatment of social and political behavior and hence alert to the sixties protests mentioned above. Pitted against them, in the last years of the decade and on into the seventies, were back-to-basics educators. Their response, she argues, was

> conservative, pessimistic, nostalgic, it seems to be some kind of quest for certainty in an uncertain world. The argument itself [favoring reading and writing, drill and rote learning, key cultural information] is not racist or anti-democratic, but it always seems to appear in the wake of efforts to democratize the school system, and its proponents always insist on the importance of maintaining middle-class standards and values. . . . In its distrust of experi-

mentalism and its glorification of the past, it is the opposite of what might be called the progressive temperament. At bottom it is not conservative but fundamentalist, for its proponents, too, have no interest in history and no sense that the whole culture is worth preserving. (207)

These progressive and fundamentalist antagonists are joined on the battlefield mapped in *America Revised* by a third cultural force and historical tradition. These are the mandarins, professional historians who, whether or not dedicated to preserving the "whole culture," are deeply interested in history and committed to helping maintain its "official" status (Ellison's term, not FitzGerald's). This group, she believes, is composed of "temperamental agnostics who believe nonetheless in meritocracy, in the power of the intellect, and in the value of science and the cultural tradition" (198–99). Combatting, on the one hand, the ahistorical iconoclasm of many sixties radicals and romantics, and on the other, equally opposed to fundamentalists' insistence upon indoctrination of facts and narrow ideological values, the mandarins are often involved in the production of school texts. Indeed, one publishing strategy developed since World War II to meet the competition and confusion of a rapidly changing marketplace is the multiauthor history survey. By bringing together a team of historians, ostensibly headed (or fronted) by a famous mandarin but including two or three others representing classroom teachers, administrators, and even psychologists or other social scientists, publishing companies seek to assemble and guarantee products that will keep American history up to date while placating contesting groups of potential buyers and users.

Ultimately, of course, these customers include American schoolchildren themselves. But examination of eighties textbooks suggests that their producers still heed influential others—teachers, school administrators, state and local officials, parents, politicians, and the clergy—sooner than they do schoolchildren. Hence FitzGerald believes high school and junior high textbooks—books such as *America: The Glorious Republic; America's Heritage; American Spirit: A History of the United States*, or a number of their competitors—accurately reflect the dominant attitudes and values of American adults. Much important cultural work is, indeed, performed in the profusely illustrated pages of these fat books. Though specific titles are often absent from

FitzGerald's analysis, their messages (verbal and visual) reflect fairly current thinking by certain groups as well as older or recently displaced attitudes held by other groups.

Instead of dissecting this corpus of cultural evidence and comparing its varieties with messages previously identified in older textbooks, we should note a few features shared generally by eighties American history surveys. I have examined eleven examples, chosen from the shelves of the University of Iowa's College of Education library, nine published during the eighties, one from 1979, and one 1965 volume for contrast.[9] First, all volumes in this random sample of currently adopted texts provide extensive treatment (running sometimes to more than twenty-five pages) of slavery and slave resistance. This coverage appears in at least two separate sections: one on slavery as an economic and social system and another on abolitionism, white and black. Moreover, retrospective references to slaves like Nat Turner and Frederick Douglass also often appear in later chapters on the civil rights movement of the 1950s and 1960s. In these textbooks, violent slave resistance is explicitly mentioned and Nat Turner's name is cited, often more than once, in each account. Furthermore, among the illustrations in five of these texts is one of Nat Turner in the swamp or showing the capture of Nat Turner. In several cases, Nat Turner's picture heads the chapter on slavery and competes there for students' initial attention with more sumptuously colored reproductions of paintings of slaves by white artists Eyre Crowe and Eastman Johnson. Most of these textbooks, moreover, draw specific attention to slave revolts in their accompanying list of questions for class discussion.

If we suppose that time lags occurred in the production of all these representative texts, it is slightly paradoxical that the earliest work from this group provides the fullest and most up-to-date treatment of slavery and slave violence. *The American Experience: A Study of Themes and Issues in American History* appeared in 1979, and its stable of authors included Robert F. Madgic, Stanley S. Seaberg, Fred H. Stopsky, and Robin W. Winks. As a noted Yale historian, Winks fits the mandarin role in this group. To them, slavery remained a complex and vital issue in American history, and they challenged younger readers to approach it from several perspectives. Of the twenty-six pages on "Slavery: A Question of Social Conscience," four are devoted to "The Black Man's Reactions to Slavery." Each response—acquiescence, agitation, and rebellion—is examined in light of black experiences and illustrated (where possible) by actual slaves' words. Unlike most other treatments published in the eighties, *The American Experience* does not emphasize Nat Turner over other manifestations of violent slave reaction. The authors were concerned to suggest diversity and range rather than any single dramatic episode and actor: "These differences in Negro responses to slavery helped create ambivalent attitudes toward slaves in the minds of whites. Supporters of slavery argued that slaves were satisfied with their position, as the docility of so many of them seemed to show. But there were always men like Frederick Douglass, Gabriel, Nat Turner to remind whites that the supposed docility of the slaves was often unwilling submission to a system that the slave would seek to change as soon as he had the opportunity" (90). To picture ambivalent as well as violent reactions, *The American Experience* contains two contrasting illustrations, an early nineteenth-century watercolor of slaves dancing and playing musical instruments of African origin and Nat Turner captured by Benjamin Phipps, here identified as "the only known picture of Nat Turner" (91).

Of greater importance, in fact, than Nat Turner's revolt itself are the wider implications and revelations of American slaves' actions and reactions. Slavery in Latin America receives several pages of comparative description, with Haiti and Toussaint L'Ouverture as signal factors. Even more revealing of the authors' willingness to expose student-readers to still-current issues surrounding slavery and black violence is the section titled "A Bitter Heritage." Here Daniel P. Moynihan's controversial report is followed by a counterattack by William Ryan and both are set in historical perspective by a surprisingly detailed discussion of Stanley Elkins's theories of deculturization, Sambo, and the concentration camp analogy: "Because so many historical and psychological factors are involved, no single explanation can completely answer the questions of why blacks have not found full acceptance in American society and why their lives have followed certain patterns. Nonetheless, the thoughts of Daniel Moynihan, Stanley Elkins, and other historians and sociologists suggest new approaches to old problems and point up the difficulties faced by negroes in this country" (104). In "Questions and Suggestions for Class Discussion and Further Reading" Madgic and his team suggest first addressing the question, What current issue most resembles slavery in the sense of awakening the nation's social conscience? (106). After considering the range of other issues involved, the authors finally offer a sophisticated series of additional readings. These histories, novels, autobiographies, and travel accounts are perhaps more likely to be sampled by teachers than by students. Nevertheless, both groups are reminded of pertinent works by Harriet Beecher Stowe, F. L. Olmsted, Herman Melville, Kenneth Stampp, Stanley Elkins, William Styron, and Martin Duberman. The only black author on their list is Arna Bontemps.

By virtue of its focus on selected themes and issues and the generous space devoted to slavery and race, *The American Experience* might be thought atypical of recent history surveys used in American schools. However, the later textbooks do not significantly diverge from the interpretations and emphases of Madgic, Seaberg, Stopsky, and Winks. Most discussions are briefer and many more factually oriented. For instance, John Garraty's *American History* (1986) concludes by asking its young readers: "when Nat Turner rebelled, what bloody fate befell Virginia's Southampton County?" The answer appears in blue italics: "He and his followers murdered 57 people." The white bias here displayed is not widely shared. Margaret Stimmann Branson's *America's Heritage* (1982), for instance, points out that "before troops stopped the rebellion, 59 white people and more than 100 slaves were killed" (279).

Furthermore, several of these textbooks go further than *The American Experience* in treating the private experiences and cultural life of slaves. Daniel J. Boorstin, Brooks M. Kelley, and Ruth F. Boorstin's *A History of the United States* (1986) devotes a separate section to "A World of Their Own" in which marriage, religion, singing, and dance are discussed: "Even under the most dreadful oppression [slaves] created a life for themselves" (226). William Jay Jacobs and his collaborators in *America's Story* (1988) go a step beyond in their chapter 14, "Cotton Shapes Southern Life, 1815–1846." There, a separate section entitled "Slaves Develop a Unique Culture" instances Christianity, the spirituals, and extended as well as nuclear families as components of "the rich culture of their own" (334) cultivated by slaves. "Slaves showed their desire for freedom in their actions as well as their culture," they continue. "Some slaves ran away. . . . Often desperate slaves planned to rebel against the slaveowners. About 200 slave rebellions took place during the years that slavery existed in the United States. These events seldom won freedom for the slaves involved, but they showed that slaves did not meekly accept slavery. A Virginia slave named Nat Turner led one of the bloodiest of the slave rebellions" (336–37).

It seems plausible to assert, then, that by the 1980s American history surveys used in high schools routinely incorporated basic facts and interpretations of slave resistance already in circulation in professional circles. At the least, the pockets of silence that once kept Nat Turner's name from textbook pages and indexes and his face from illustrations had disappeared. Nor do we find—in these texts, anyway—many striking instances of careless or loaded phrases used earlier to characterize Nat Turner's revolt as "senseless slaughter" or "running amok." Perhaps the clearest instance of a volte-face is that of Clarence L. Ver Steeg of Northwestern University. In 1965, Harper and Row issued his *The Story of Our Country*. Like the 1937 schoolbook by the Akers and Hilton cited earlier, this textbook makes no mention of Nat Turner or slave revolts. In 1982, at the instigation of Follett Publishing Company, Ver Steeg repeated his performance. This time, his *American Spirit: A History of the United States* devotes seven pages to the antislavery movement and a chapter on slavery and slave resistance. His summary of the Southampton slave revolt omits little that appears in other eighties textbooks. In fact, Ver Steeg's list of questions for his young readers is one of the most specific:

1. Name four ways slaves protested their condition.
2. Which form of protest did the southerners fear the most?
3. What were the effects of Nat Turner's revolt on southern whites? (342)

Where he falls short of others' treatments, however, is in scanting slave culture as a mode of resistance. Slave families exist only to be broken up and nothing is said of religion, music, folklore, or other institutions and activities.

As major publishing houses of the nation and their cadres of expert textbook writers began to redress for high school students earlier treatments and oversights, some more modest but suggestive steps were taken to reach still younger readers. Illustrated children's books, such as Ruth Wilson's *Our Blood and Tears: Black Freedom Fighters* (1972), remained in circulation and, if not widely used in elementary schools, were available in libraries.[10] Also available was at least one filmstrip for classroom teachers and librarians. A segment of the Encyclopedia

Britannica Education Corporation's 1969 series "Chains of Slavery—1800–1865" is devoted to "Nat Turner's Rebellion."[11] Wilson, a black fifth-grade teacher in Harlem, makes Nat Turner the representative hero of her chapter entitled "The Age of Violence." Concluding nearly sixty pages on his life and death, she carefully informs youthful readers of this "American history as blacks lived it." After citing Gray's *Confessions* as "the main source of information on the black leader and his deeds" (115), she adds noncommittally, "a few years ago a fictionalized version of Turner's life was published by William Styron under the same title" (115). The Encyclopedia Britannica filmstrip concludes in more orthodox textbook fashion by asking young viewers what immediate effects Nat Turner's rebellion had on the condition and treatment of slaves and what were its long-range effects. These educators also challenged young viewers to ponder Stampp's assertion that Nat Turner had an impact on the South as great as John C. Calhoun or Jefferson Davis.[12]

To these sixties and seventies materials for fifth or sixth graders was added at least one new medium of historical indoctrination in the eighties. *Black History for Beginners* (1984), a production of Writers and Readers Documentary Comic Books written and illustrated by two black women, Denise Dennis and Susan Willmarth, is a comic book meant for children just starting to read and use textbooks at school. The authors carefully define "black history" for this emerging audience. It is "the American history that was omitted from your textbooks" and the point is driven home by an illustration of a black cowboy with a rifle.[13] Slavery and slave resistance are treated at length and (for some adults at least) in surprisingly sophisticated historical detail. As with some textbook writers for older students, Dennis and Willmarth place the picture of Nat Turner's capture at the head of the slavery section. "Revolt for Freedom" shows and/or tells the actions of Gabriel Prosser, Denmark Vesey, Nat Turner, Frederick Douglass, and David Walker. Turner receives chief billing, his huge hand dominating the page where his God-inspired "bloody revolt" is retold.

New Voices and Some Old Views: Bertram Wyatt-Brown and Sterling Stuckey

The textbook and children's book writers mentioned above are almost exclusively engaged in relaying information and interpretations generated in the preceding two decades. That, after all, is the ideal as well as practical function of popular or public historians. That, too, was the perhaps inevitable consequence of the waves of sixties publicity still bringing to eighties ears a renewed and wider discussion of slavery, violence, and race. That Styron's novel played a part in this cultural flow is suggested not only by the reprinting of "This Quiet Dust" in 1982 but also by his name and book's reappearance in several eighties retellings aimed at American youth. Thus though the authors and teams involved were, by and large, not active in the earlier controversy, their explanations connect backward to previous issues and interpretations rather than sidewards to current explanations centered in different writing formations of the eighties. Identifying *very* pressing contemporary concerns usually involves risks—ideological and commercial—which textbook authors are probably counseled to avoid. Whether progressive, fundamentalist, or mandarin in sympathy and outlook, the public historian operates (more or less comfortably) as conduit of, at best, slightly outdated data, paradigms, and concepts. Thus even as we note the appearance at mid-decade of a younger black historiographer like James C. Morgan, we find his *Slavery in the United States: Four Views* (1985) to be a critique of older, exclusively white historians.[14]

Nevertheless, fresh interpretations of this contested portion of the antebellum past and its relevance to the present did appear concurrently with the textbooks by Madgic, Jacobs, Boorstin and their associates. Two of these represent additions to and substantial redirections of the inherited debate over slave rebellions. The earlier, Bertram Wyatt-Brown's *Southern Honor: Ethics and Behavior in the Old South* (1982) has already proved the more controversial, while the newer book, Sterling Stuckey's *Slave Culture: Nationalist Theory and the Foundations of Black America* (1987), represents a more direct extension of the attitudes and approaches of the sixties and seventies.

Southern Honor treats Nat Turner and other nineteenth-century rebels under the heading "Policing Slave Society: Insurrectionary Scares." For Wyatt-Brown, cultural analysis centers on the white system of social control and its members' notions of right actions; "I have not placed slavery at the center of Southern concern," he warns readers.[15] When he examines ways that southern white codes of honorable conduct affected slaves, his attention falls upon the "imaginary" realm of plots, rumors, and conspiracies rather than actual armed revolts:

> The issue here is not to decide once and for all whether insurrectionary panics were based upon authentic black conspiracies. The topic cannot be wholly set aside, but it is less relevant to the purposes at hand than the use whites made of such affairs, real or imagined. For instance, there is no question that Nat Turner's bloody trail across Southampton County, Virginia, in 1831 was not a figment of popular hysteria. Outside that southeastern corner of the state, however, scores and possibly hundreds of slaves were whipped, maimed and killed by one form of justice or another, innocent though all of them were in complicity in the lonely undertaking of Turner and his small band of religiously guided associates. (403)

The discussion that ensues deliberately marginalizes Turner and others, downplays persistent dread of revolt among the master class, and stresses the impotence of innocent, usually unresisting blacks. Wyatt-Brown also sidesteps recent histories of slave resistance in the South. One chief trend in these accounts, as we have noted in these pages, is to confirm many of Aptheker's original arguments about the frequency and importance of slave revolts. A concurrent move is likewise discounted: to connect slave violence to other kinds of resistance and to ground all such slave behavior in an effective margin of cultural autonomy of slave communities. Such realities are presumed irrelevant to the white male honor code:

> Obedience and even the semblance of affection were the first requirements of slave conduct; impudence was thought a prelude to insurgency. The method of testing these attributes in a public way was to create what one social scientist has called "degradation ceremonies," a term that has lately been applied to the corporal styles of early American legal punishment. By this means the black rebel became a visible and punishable sacrificial

victim. He was the archetypal reverse image of the self-effacing "uncle" that whites like to think was the ideal servant. Whatever the malefactor's former character might have been, he was thereafter the personification of unreliability, disorder, and nameless horror. (406)

What followed was a patterned ritual behavior. Rumor and hysteria were used to reverse apathy and arouse whites to violent reactions, often to wholly imaginary dangers. Black informers beforehand and slave testifiers at ensuing trials divided the slave community and defused immediate danger: "Perhaps the repression of potential revolt was really aimed at achieving just this: the outward appearance of black submissiveness and the restored sense of security arising from white consensus. In addition, the process of repression served to break up any motions toward black unity under a body of leaders like Nat Turner and potentially dangerous figures like Billy, whose self-possession had been interpreted as an unmistakable sign of incorrigibility and 'impudence'" (412).

Insurrectionary scares, then, under Wyatt-Brown's sidelong scrutiny, are best understood not as "authentic warfare between the races" (425) but as occasions of intrawhite community spasms of horror and pride. They produced what they were designed to achieve: brutal conformity to white male notions of honor which, among other psychic supports, rested on the passivity of white women and the inferiority and impotence of blacks. Previous historical explanations emphasizing the antebellum South as a transactional bicultural society with slaves possessing some real power over events leading to the Civil War—this tradition Wyatt-Brown virtually ignores. For his thesis, slave culture per se simply does not matter. Furthermore, the role of Christianity, both white or black, is neglected in this psychosocial interpretation, as John Blassingame has pointed out.[16] The course of actual slave revolts like Prosser's or Turner's does not need to be examined in detail, although Wyatt-Brown's use of David Hackett-Fischer's "braided narrative" (xiv) allows him to devote several pages to the case of Will, an innocent slave caught in the 1802 Virginia slave plot:

> An anthropologist examining the insurrectionary phenomenon might well conclude that the purpose of the exercise was the restoration of order through the venting of society's worst fears. By

proclaiming that catastrophe was about to descend, the whites rallied to the banner of white supremacy and sought out victims over whom they could unmistakably triumph. Indeed, the chief result of the scares was the prevention of insurrections. By primitive but effective means, the frenzy reestablished proper race relationships, as whites defined them. In a sense, even the genuine cases of rebellion achieved this end, none being more helpful than Nat Turner's. (431–32)

For many of Wyatt-Brown's readers, his overreliance on ahistorical anthropological models—reminiscent of Elkins's ambitious use of social science concepts a generation earlier—joins disturbingly a sometimes cavalier inattention to disconfirming circumstances. The result creates a skewed picture of the world masters and slaves jointly inhabited. Moreover, the tempo of southern white, northern, and southern black relationships in the decades leading to secession is defined in *Southern Honor* very differently than in many previous accounts. Historians, black and white, may, for example, question this concluding image of nineteenth-century southern life in chapter 15:

> Soon enough, as the Virginia experience between 1800 and 1802 suggested, the same old problems reappeared: quarrels on the muster field, sloppy patrol rounds, broken or misplaced firearms, and other signs of mischief and public lassitude that critics had thought the recent emergency would permanently cure. A resurgence of black encroachments on white regulations (inattentiveness, tavern-going, wearing of fancy clothes, Saturday afternoon horseplay in the village square), increases in masters' largess (indiscriminate pass privileges, unsupervised black church worship), and new symptoms of economic and political woes set the stage for the next panic. Then as the cycle began again the rich and poor, the townsman and countryman, the soldier and civilian, the drunk and sober rallied to the racial banner. (434)

In this all-too-predictable cycle, deviants—whether Nat Turner and his band or John Hartwell Cocke and similar-minded moderate slaveowners—serve chiefly to redefine norms of "acceptable" behavior. They do not effectually change the pace of events or the agenda of issues both within or beyond the South. The Virginia legislative session of

1831–32, the texts and cumulative impact of Gray's *Confessions* and Garrison's *The Liberator*, and the sheer number of plots and uprisings cited by Aptheker and others, are items, among others, of public and cultural history not readily contained by Wyatt-Brown's psychological-anthropological model. To be sure, the author of *Southern Honor* promises readers a sequel that, in Blassingame's words, will examine the "penetration of the slave into the white's psyche."[17] Lacking that amplification, however, present-day readers may conclude that, although this work has been favorably compared to W. J. Cash's *The Mind of the South*, it likewise resembles some other works of eighties scholarship on the South, including Daniel Singal's *The War Within* (1982) and culminating, in 1989, with the *Encyclopedia of Southern Culture*.[18] Of that monumental compendium Howell Raines observed in the *New York Times Book Review:* "the fact that this book is more comfortable with the Civil War than with the civil rights era demonstrates that Southern scholars have not fully assimilated the experience of the past 25 years or learned to honor black achievement with the ease with which they laud something like the cavalry tactics of Gen. Nathan Bedford Forrest. This book—like the South, like the nation as a whole—suffers from having its vision blinkered along racial, gender and generational lines."[19] In a 1989 roundtable discussion in the *Journal of American History* on "What Has Changed and Not Changed in American Historical Practice?," David Levering Lewis remarks on Singal's view of southern thought and culture as fundamentally split into white and black traditions and texts. Of *The War Within* Lewis wryly quotes Singal's excuse for racial exclusion: "An important study remains to be written on black culture and thought in the South, but the task will involve the use of *sources quite different* from those employed for the present book." Lewis adds "In Singal's South, obviously the sociology of Charles S. Johnson, the history of Alruthers A. Taylor, and the poetry of Sterling Brown have no place beside the sociology of Howard Odum, the history of Broadus Mitchell, or the poetry of Donald Davidson because of what he sees as their incommensurability."[20] "Without comparison and integration," he points out, historians surrender, willingly or not, to the "separate equality school," by which "African-American topics" remain inaccurately isolated: "Class, but not *classes*, Race, rather than racial components, have too much prevailed."[21]

A second and very differently slanted return to the braided topic of slave resistance and slave culture is by a one-time participant in the Nat Turner controversy, Sterling Stuckey. Along with Vincent Harding, he was one of the younger black historians to take on, and eventually help reeducate, Eugene Genovese. Stuckey, however, though making a seminal contribution to sixties discourse in his essay "Through the Prism of Folklore: The Black Ethos in Slavery," did not achieve a full-length articulation of his position until 1987 when *Slave Culture: Nationalist Theory and the Foundations of Black America* appeared. In one important respect like Wyatt-Brown, Stuckey struck out in a new direction instead of retracing earlier arguments by fellow black historians Blassingame and Owens.

Also like Wyatt-Brown, anthropology played a major role in opening Stuckey's eyes. A fresh vision of the slave culture which produced rebels like Gabriel, Vesey, and Turner emerged from Stuckey's immersion in anthropological records of West Africa and personal insights picked up from foreign-born black scholars living in the United States who argue that "the American Negro is basically African in culture."[22] At the center of the slave culture developed in the American South were its African roots. These were, moreover, socially and symbolically represented by a particularly significant African ritual, the ring shout. This rite cemented black group solidarity in some ways parallel to the role played by "degradation ceremonies" in Wyatt-Brown's version of white southern culture. Widely shared across regional, linguistic, and tribal barriers, the ring shout helped bind an oppressed and disparate folk into a protonation. It helped forge the black will to *be* a nation. Stuckey further argues that this North American process in the nineteenth century anticipated twentieth-century developments on the African continent whereby to achieve nationhood Africans had to detribalize. Here another parallel—this time to Genovese's *From Rebellion to Revolution*—suggests itself: nineteenth-century revolts are of global importance in showing the way for later anticolonialist revolutions of the present century.

If indeed "the ring in which Africans danced and sang is the key to understanding the means by which they achieved oneness in America" (12), then the historical issue of slave rebellions as cultural acts is, theoretically, at least, simplified. The main questions become: do records reveal that African roots and rituals played a part in the conspiracies and insurrections by which some slaves mounted organized resistance to oppression and deculturalization? If such rituals were chiefly artistic and religious (that is, "sacred") enactments of a shared spiritual life, might they also prove effective in secular, even quasi-military ways? Did fundamentals of African social faith infusing American slave culture have anything to do with specific revolts? In the case of the Southampton slave revolt, for example, was Nat Turner as religious leader a Virginia-born version of the "priest-king" who enjoyed status and power in black Africa?

Stuckey's immediate answer to such queries is to displace attention from Nat Turner to his pair of famous predecessors. The historian's first document is, significantly, Arna Bontemps's *Black Thunder*. He reminds readers of the novelist's vivid depiction of the burial ceremony following the brutal killing of old Bundy:

> They were burying old Bundy in the low field by the swamp. They were throwing themselves on the ground and wailing savagely. (The Negroes remembered Africa in 1800) . . . Roast a hog and put it on his grave. Down, down. How them victuals suit you, Bundy? How you like what we brung you? . . .
>
> They had raised a song without words. They were kneeling with their faces to the sun. Their hands were in the air, the fingers apart, and they bowed and rose together as they sang. Up came the song like a wave, and down went their faces in the dirt . . . at the place where the two worlds met. (42–43)

By this move Stuckey declares literary documents to be historical sources. He also underlines a fact that should now be apparent to readers of an earlier chapter of this book: Bontemps's grasp in the thirties of African-American culture as a matrix of slave resistance long preceded historical explanations of slave culture in the seventies. Nevertheless, Stuckey does not pursue the issue with an extended look at Gabriel Prosser's revolt; even Bontemps's further references to African roots in *Black Thunder* are left unmentioned.

Instead, he proceeds to a full—and, for his thesis, more profitable and plausible—discussion of the cultural climate out of which Denmark Vesey's Charleston conspiracy of 1822 emerged. Stuckey aligns himself with fellow historians (Robert Starobin, Gerald Mullin, William Freehling) who emphasize the presence of African-born participants in this event and the leader's fusion of Christian and African beliefs into an ideology of rebellion.[23] Denmark Vesey thus takes his place in the succession of black American artificers of a nationalist tradition, which extends to David Walker, Henry Highland Garnet, W. E. B. Du Bois, and Paul Robeson: "In the Vesey conspiracy the very process by which Africans were being transformed into a single people is revealed" (47). Stuckey argues, therefore, that slave rebels were neither necessarily men with the greatest exposure to white culture nor even basically "American" and "Christian" in outlook: "On the contrary, the most acculturated slaves, like slaves generally, appropriated values from the larger environment and relied on African values that pointed the way to creative solutions to a variety of problems, cultural and political. To find, for example, some aspects of Christianity extremely useful and satisfying did not mean—certainly not for most slaves or for most slave preachers—that they ceased to be African anymore than those blacks who embraced aspects of Christianity in Africa ceased to be African" (48).

Vesey is, therefore, seminal and prophetic. He and his large-scale conspiracy epitomized the presence and power of the impulse toward autonomy and independence, by violent means when necessary. Africa, Gulla Jack, the newly formed black Methodist African Church near Charleston, and the principles of the Declaration of Independence were, therefore, all components of this segment of slave culture in the posture of rebellion. They were all imminent in the protonationalist hymn "Hail! all hail! ye Afric clan," which was first sung off the coast of Charleston in 1816. The rebels' persistence to the end was demonstrated by the silent African composure with which (like Gabriel Prosser) Vesey, Gulla Jack, Mingo, and other black leaders went to the gallows. Part of the explanation for the brutal suppression of this plot—35 people hanged; 31 pardoned but deported; more than 40 sent to Africa or the West Indies—lay in white Christian fears of the African dimension of this "barbarous," savage event.

Such prophetic features were largely absent from the Southampton slave revolt. One reason, therefore, for Stuckey's silence about Nat Turner and his use, for historical purposes, of *Black Thunder* may be suspicions (shared with Bontemps) of the visionary Christian ideology at the center of the 1831 revolt. A common bond between thirties novelist and eighties historian may also explain Stuckey's preference for *Black Thunder* over other records of Gabriel Prosser's conspiracy; Bontemps figures both as prescient historical novelist and modern black nationalist in a lineage that is the proper—and to David Levering Lewis, chauvinist—subject of *Slave Culture*.[24] A further link may also be a shared admiration for stoic, silent leaders of betrayed African-American causes. Unlike Melville's Babo, Lowell's Babu, or Prosser and Vesey, Nat Turner did not go silently. His Christian politics of the Word led him to bequeath his *Confessions* as a twenty-page testament and defense of essentially Old Testament convictions. Turner was, we may suppose, simply too acculturated all around to satisfy these men's historical imaginations.

Bontemps's Legacy:
David Bradley and Sherley Anne Williams

Sterling Stuckey's use of Bontemps, like Wyatt-Brown's use of Faulkner, reaffirms that for many members of this ongoing dialogue novelists *are* historians. "Through metaphor and felicity of language, the novelist's imagination can re-create the way people once thought and acted, so ordering matters toward an ethical veracity that the historian could never achieve" (xi), Wyatt-Brown asserts in *Southern Honor*. Imaginary stories about historical figures and events do, in fact, make as well as modify historical tradition and historiographical innovation. *Black Thunder* returns once again in 1987 to remind historians (and others) of the African elements in Gabriel Prosser's conspiracy as well as to underline the fact that this exemplary novel dramatizes dimensions of an autonomous slave culture delineated fully by historians only thirty or forty years later.

Literary scholars today also recognize similar interconnections. Cultural and disciplinary inclusivity is exemplified by the New Historicism, a methodology and movement whose roots go back at least to the first issues of *New Literary History*.[25] The eighties have been marked by other stirrings as well. In 1987, for instance, the English Institute, an elite and innovative institution of fashionable literary criticism, devoted a session to "Slavery and the Literary Imagination." Two years later, a collection of essays recorded the event and the literary appropriations of slave history, which its participants explored. In one of the most penetrating analyses, Hazel V. Carby discusses "The Historical Novel of Slavery." Without mentioning Styron but instead concentrating upon black writers who, like Bontemps, have used slave narratives and other black historical sources, she points out that "in formal terms a narrative of slavery has three conventional conclusions: escape, emancipation, and death."[26] Margaret Walker's *Jubilee* and Ishmael Reed's *Flight to Canada* variously treat emancipation as a crucial (though often ironic) black experience. Escape (and, by implication in the epilogue, emancipation) is the dramatic solution in Sherley Anne Williams's *Dessa Rose*, while death as imposed or secretly desired destination is the speculative subject of David Bradley's *The Chaneysville Incident*. In Carby's discussion, Bradley's artistic lineage is traced back to Bontemps. Unfortunately, her essay's scope and enthusiasm for *Black Thunder* leave no room for exploring Bradley's disturbingly powerful narrative from other perspectives or mentioning *Dessa Rose* as a purposeful black feminist reply to Styron's novel. Both eighties historical novels, in fact, carry strong echoes of the sixties in their re-creations of the black past of slavery and resistance to it.

Bradley's relationships to Styron, though less openly acknowledged than Williams's, provide revealing signposts along the way into his vision of both free black and slave culture. *The Chaneysville Incident*, to begin with, is explicitly a meditation on history. Its protagonist, John Washington, is a young black historian drawn in 1979 to reenter the past of his free antebellum family and its native town with its strategic location in south-central Pennsylvania. Bedford County is historically and imaginatively linked by several details to Southampton County, Virginia. One tie is Judith Powell, Washington's white lover, a descendant of FFVs who once owned slaves and pursued them northward when they ran away. In fact, the southern end of Bedford County contains a Southampton Township: "a little piece of the South down there. It started out being Virginia."[27] Today it remains a hotbed of KKK members and virulent racists. There occurred the incident around which the dramatic and psychological action revolves: "that story of a dozen slaves who had come north on the Underground Railroad, fleeing whatever horrors behind them, and who had got lost just north of the Mason-Dixon Line, somewhere in the lower reaches of the County, and who, when they could no longer elude the men who trailed them with dogs and horses and ropes and chains, had begged to be killed rather than be taken back to bondage" (64).

Washington becomes obsessed by the need to track down the elusive facts and implications of this obscure historical event. He discovers several chains binding him to that band of slaves who died on the snowy hillside above Chaneysville in December 1859. The desperately brave act of self-destruction has its roots and reverberations in his own family and soul. For the historical records assembled in his father's attic point to C. K. Washington, John's great-grandfather, as the ex-slave from Philadelphia who, having carried on a successful campaign to guide large groups of slaves along the Underground Railroad, finally arrives a few minutes too late to lead this band to safety. It is his revolver which, one by one, kills the slaves as they sing "And before I'll be a slave, I'll be buried in my grave"—and he then turns the weapon on himself. The descendant reimagines himself back into that past for another, equally pointed reason: His father, Moses Washington, killed himself almost a century later on the same spot where thirteen small grave-markers memorialize the group immolation. Was the 1958 act a fitting response to the full meaning of their ancestor's life and death? A further irony of history is the possibility that Judith's Powell ancestors were involved in this very slavehunt. Thus slavery and racism, ancient resistance and present-day hatreds and loves between the races, the fierce will of blacks to survive, and the equally strong attraction some felt to return through death to "mother Africa," together with the necessary union of historical fact and leaps of fictional intuition that make explanations of these issues plausible and powerful—these are all shared concerns connecting Bradley to Styron and, of course, to other historical novelists as well. Grasping these texts and authors together in their separate but overlapping transactions with various audiences lends weight to Barbara Foley's contention that, just as black history provides essential materials and models for all sorts of historically conscious American readers, so, too, must the category "black literature" come to include both black and white writers and texts.[28]

Nevertheless, *The Chaneysville Incident* cannot be read simply as a not-so-secret successor to *The Confessions of Nat Turner* or *Black Thunder*. It is much more than a displacement northward and into later historical moments of themes expressed in 1967 or 1936. For one thing, Bradley commenced writing this, his first (but, in order of publication, second) novel in 1970, in the aura of the Nat Turner controversy. But the eleven-year task of research and writing was also done as historians like Blassingame, Stuckey, and Levine were articulating their various slave-culture-as-resistance arguments. Although specific details suggest his awareness of Styron's story as anti-text, Bradley's general treatment of black culture, past and present, and especially the African undercurrents in modern black consciousness, indicates a sophisticated familiarity with contemporary historiographical developments. In several places both streams of influence converge. Thus one slave in the band came from a plantation on the Nottaway River, thus thickening the Southampton connection. Furthermore, Nat Turner's name is invoked when C. K. Washington as a younger man and escaped slave attends the first National Negro Convention of 1831. There he casts a decisive *nay* vote defeating the passionately worded resolution of Henry Highland Garnet approving the violent resistance of Denmark Vesey and Nat Turner: "You cannot be more oppressed than you have been—you cannot suffer greater casualties than you have already. Rather die free men than live to be slaves" (363). John Washington reconstructs his ancestor's opposition to slave insurrection as "a stupid idea" (365). A far more effective way to bring down slavery, he believed, was to help significant numbers of female slaves and children escape: "Steal the slaves, and the planter had no way to repay his loans, and the bankers had nothing to foreclose on, either. Six billion dollars, and every dollar's worth had a pair of feet" (370). That C. K. Washington's economic analysis was no less brave—and ultimately no less violent—a response to slavery is demonstrated by his willingness to die alongside the runaways.

Bradley's protagonist, this passionate historian, is in several basic respects an autobiographical projection, although Washington's fictional family tree contains historical figures as well as archetypes of black middle-class northerners. "The Town" is clearly Bedford, Pennsylvania, where Bradley's father was for many years pastor of the AME Zion Church and his mother an amateur historian of the county's black communities. She is the one who rediscovered the evidence of the Chaneysville incident. Washington's obsession to go beyond the mountain of facts in order "to discern the shape that they filled in" (152) expresses the author's own decade-long struggle to give this historical and family drama its proper imaginative form. "I tried at first to write it as nonfiction, as history," Bradley recalled, "but that didn't work. History, after all, is pretty dry."[29] Finally he combined history, autobiography, and artistic imagination in a narrative of multiple perspectives—legendary, mythic, political, folkloric, philosophical.

Focusing these concerns is the fictional question of imagining plausible historical explanations for two Washington ancestors' deliberate choice of death. The drama takes place in John Washington's head; hence the narrative contains large sections of historical description and anguished reflection. C.K.'s death is simpler to account for than Moses Washington's. Yet perhaps for this reason John's father's suicide on the Chaneysville grave-markers is more meaningful to his historian son. For the father, a fiercely independent moonshiner, has left an attic full of county documents which the son must confront and arrange into an explanatory pattern. Inseparable from this analytical/archival task are the attitudes toward history itself (and especially black American history) shared by C.K., Moses, and John. The present-day historian concludes that this Pennsylvania place has for centuries exuded an atmosphere of hate emanating from slavery times. "This place stinks," he tells Judith, who cannot understand how John can both love and hate her at the same time. "It makes me choke. It's not the people; it's not the mountains; it's not anything in particular. It's just a stench, like somebody buried something, only they didn't bury it quite deep enough, and it's somewhere stinking up the world" (288). That stench is history itself, "the awful odor of eternal misery" (223). Because black Americans live with the stench always in their nostrils, John Washington, the university-trained Philadelphia historian, becomes convinced of his ancestors' belief in ancient African thinking about life, death, and the afterlife: "And if the African belief is true, then somewhere here with us, in the very air we breathe, all that whipping and chaining and raping and starving and branding and maiming and castrating and lynching and murdering—*all* of it—is still going on" (222). Indeed, John Washington can, when he allows himself, hear the sounds of that ancient tragedy coming over the telephone wires—for example, after his mother or his lover have hung up. A primitive African awareness of the spirit world of unforgotten and unforgivable suffering has turned this modern black intellectual into a historian who hates.

"Oh," she said. "Is that what being a historian means—hating for things that don't mean anything anymore?"

"No," I said. "No, it means hating for things that still mean something. And trying to understand what it is they mean, so you can hate the right things for the right reasons." (287)

As Judith only partially grasps, Washington is an archetypal black man who is plunged through family and local history down to a bedrock vision of human corruption, bigotry, greed, and ignorance. The brute presence of history itself is, therefore, typified by Judith's experience of first visiting John's black neighborhood in the town. "So you walked up the Hill," John interprets her arrival. "Now, I don't know what you saw, because I don't know which way your head was turned. But I know what you smelled. You smelled old rotting timbers in those falling-down houses, and you smelled a little sweet-sour smell from something that had died in the weeds, and you smelled pinewood smoke, and you smelled gassy smoke from coal and you smelled fresh earth from the graveyard. And you smelled the stink from the outhouses. . . . Not just the ones now; you smelled maybe a century and a half's worth of outhouses. You smelled a hundred and fifty years' worth of . . . shit" (289–90). Digesting this black version of past and present reality had turned John Washington into a misogynist as well as an obsessed devotee of history. Communicating his vision to Judith, it becomes clear that while her white head will never turn in enough directions to discover the full truth, his black head (eyes, nose, and hunter's instincts) has become fixated upon the dirty corners of the historical landscape. Hence the novel's enigmatic conclusion, in which John sends Judith back down the Hill and builds a small pyre of "the books and pamphlets and diaries and maps" (450) from which his picture of antebellum and contemporary violence has been painfully reconstructed. Whether Washington will immolate himself along with the dirty history of Bedford County remains the last question Bradley drops on the reader's plate.

Even from this truncated account of Bradley's historicism and fictional imagination working together, we can reconstruct some of the cultural business transacted between this author and likely readers of *The Chaneysville Incident*. His audiences (in sizable numbers) must have felt both moved and perplexed by the cold heat and bitter love emanating from the educated middle-class black ethos of the two Washingtons. Such conflicted emotions, anchored in and infused by historical consciousness, resemble but also differ from the mixed passions of Styron's protagonist and the equally conflicted feelings of many of

Styron's readers fifteen years before. In different historical and social domains, John Washington and Styron's Nat Turner are meditative rebels against a white world intimately known and to which they are deeply drawn. Washington's reconstruction of the black past, which obliquely incorporates Nat Turner and his revolt, speaks particularly to the emotional and ideological conflicts of post-sixties northern blacks who, like all black Americans, smell the stench of suffering off the pages of history but have familial and ideological reasons for fearing or repudiating violent resistance. Indeed, Bradley confronts all Americans with the moral and existential implications of the three historical choices Hazel Carby asserts all slave narratives implicitly contain. If escape and emancipation offer, to later generations, the hope of interracial reconciliation and love, then the relationship of John Washington and Judith Powell is an ambiguous and only guardedly hopeful commentary on sixties diatribes and testaments such as Cleaver's *Soul on Ice* and Herndon's *Sex and Race in America*. No more consoling is the picture and appeal of male enclaves, black and white, in *The Chaneysville Incident*. The sexist as well as racist tensions in several sectors of American society are dramatized here in male cultural rituals of hunting, drinking, storytelling, and burying the dead. Bradley's success in evoking the male world of black moonshiners, hunters, and athletes, one based in part on near-brutal misogyny, creates another ambiguous cultural message. In any case, both male and female readers confront the presence of self-inflicted death as the third choice Bradley's story poses as a perennial solution to the contradictions of history, interracial heterosexual love, and black male bonding. That *The Chaneysville Incident* does not explicitly endorse this suicidal response to American life but leaves open a possible future for John and Judith may help to explain the popularity of this novel which quickly became a Book-of-the-Month Club selection and won the PEN/Faulkner Award for 1981. Yet its power to affront female readers and console male ones must not be discounted either. After all, *The Chaneysville Incident* was also a selection of the Playboy Book Club. Moreover, the book's ensuing fame earned its author inclusion in *Esquire*'s heavily male pantheon of talented younger writers invited to contribute to "50 Who Made a Difference—A Celebration of American Originals," in December 1983.[30]

A sometimes overwhelming recognition of death—either as murder, rebellion, or suicide—as an appropriate black response to personal and racial history is, of course, shared by many black writers. This third choice emanating from the slave past is seen by female as well as male authors living and writing in the aura of sixties violence and cultural controversy. It surfaces, for example, in the first volume of Maya Angelou's serial autobiography, *I Know Why the Caged Bird Sings* (1970). The book hardly represents an extended reply to white assertions (like Genovese's) that blacks have historically lacked a political tradition in which Nat Turner's name has been treasured and passed on from generation to generation. Yet redefinitions of what *is* "political" in women's writing occur repeatedly in *Caged Bird*, and nowhere more vividly than in the Stamps school graduation scene. As twelve-year-old Maya sits in silent anguish listening to the racist white school administrator lecture her classmates about their proper fates as "maids and farmers, handymen and washerwomen," her young imagination turns to history and destruction: "Then I wished that Gabriel Prosser and Nat Turner had killed all whitefolks in their beds and that Abraham Lincoln had been assassinated before the signing of the Emancipation Proclamation, and that Harriet Tubman had been killed by that blow on her head and Christopher Columbus had drowned in the *Santa María*."[31] To be silenced by the brutal finality of history, whether as resistance or victimization, leaves young Maya yearning for extinction just as much as John Washington.

> We should all be dead. I thought I should like to see us all dead, one on top of the other. A pyramid of flesh with the whitefolks on the bottom, as the broad base, then the Indians with their silly tomahawks and teepees and wigwams and treaties, the Negroes with their mops and recipes and cotton sacks and spirituals sticking out of their mouths. The Dutch children should all stumble in their wooden shoes and break their necks. The French should choke to death on the Louisiana Purchase (1803) while silkworms ate all the Chinese with their stupid pigtails. As a species, we were an abomination. All of us. (153)

Such bitter memories (or vivid reimaginings) of a black twelve-year-old schoolgirl in Arkansas resonate prophetically with Bradley's protagonist's thoughts of destruction and self-destruction. They also underline a common characteristic of much twentieth-century black writing from Bontemps to his seventies and eighties descendants. Children are both subject and (sometimes) audience in black historical narratives, which are occasionally violently realistic. This practice is pertinently exemplified by another black woman writer. Alice Childress's *A Hero Ain't Nothin' but a Sandwich* (1973) is a novel (ostensibly for teenagers) about a thirteen-year-old heroin addict (or near-addict), Benjie Johnson. Far less sophisticated a dreamer than the young Maya Angelou, Benjie does not imagine the return of Gabriel Prosser or Nat Turner. But he is bombarded in his Harlem world by adult voices reminding him and his readers of the presence of a black past as a source of strength and resistance to the poverty, drugs, racism, divorce, bad schools, and spiritual isolation of the contemporary ghetto. Nigeria Green, for example, is Benjie's idealistic but exasperated history teacher whose black nationalist slogans cover the classroom walls. His thoughts, too, are replete with violent imagery. As he recalls his own family's black cultural roots, he cries out, "misery was almost sweet, plenty of finger-poppin and dancin—in between folks bein killed, chased, shot at, segregated. I finger-popped along with the rest and ate my share of souse and sweet potato pie. But I had me a plan, Nigeria Greene was gonna be the Black Messiah of the classroom, gonna light the way with Blackness. I try to do it. I try, like Nat Turner said, 'because it pleases me to try.'"[32] If Nigeria Greene is meant at moments to sound slightly absurd to Childress's youthful readers, these final words carry an unmistakable import: he, too, is a spiritual relative of John Washington. Even more dire are the words of the "Street Corner Speaker" whose jeremiad all but closes *Hero*. Looking down from his stepladder on the hurrying Harlem crowds, the streetcorner preacher denounces his brothers and sisters:

DIG HOW TO KILL NIGGA WITHOUT FIRING A GUN! Teach him to kill hisself! Look at em walking to the detox center where they can get a little taste-a something else to ease off skag. Go to hell, man! You can't get angry, cause you *numb*, can't feel a-tall. Walk on, man, damn your coward soul! I gave yall my life . . . now I'm standin before you, a money less, broke down son a Nat Turner. . . . I got nothin left but breath in my body . . . here it go . . . all I got left to offer the race . . . breath, breath . . . Freeeeeeedom now! Freeeeeeeeeeeeeedom now! (122–23)

Though younger audiences of *A Hero Ain't Nothin' but a Sandwich* might miss the implication of "I gave yall my life" as historical signpost pointing to Ol' Prophet Nat, surely the irony is complete as the "broke down son a Nat Turner" shouts his despairing call to freedom at the heedless multitudes of the modern metropolis. In Childress's imagination these death-seeking victims are nodding their way to oblivion unconsoled by history or any African belief in the afterlife of liberated black souls. A somber and adult message, indeed, for junior readers, and Childress's decision to treat the young in this fashion is characteristic of other black writers of children's books, including Arna Bontemps.

If Maya Angelou and Alice Childress indeed stand on the margins of the Nat Turner controversy, their seventies location as black artists and amateur historians suggest the limits and waning importance of events kept alive in these women's writings only by glancing references. If so, the most recent transmogrification of Nat Turner in eighties fiction demands celebration and closer examination as a possible rebirth and redirection of interest. Even as isolated and privately motivated expression, however, Sherley Anne Williams's *Dessa Rose* marks a significant event in the modern literature of slavery, historical and fictional. It is the first major text written by a woman that is explicitly linked to the paradigmatic episode we have been tracing. More particularly, *Dessa Rose* is self-consciously a meditation on, as well as dramatic reenactment of, the slave past through the twin perspectives of feminist history and black literature.[33] In fact, this story of slave revolt and escape is centered in the black heroine's self, voice, and community, and thus goes beyond *The Chaneysville Incident* in exploring common issues of violence and suffering, love and hate, entrapment and evasion, race and gender.

As Williams's author's note flatly announces, this slave woman's story is both historically grounded and imaginatively structured as a retort to Styron's *The Confessions of Nat Turner*, "a certain critically acclaimed novel of the early seventies [sic] that travestied the as-told-to memoir of slave revolt leader Nat Turner."[34] Williams's counternarrative is sounder history and more faithfully imagined fiction than Styron's, she suggests, even though it represents a merger of two separate historical incidents. One was a slave coffle uprising in Kentucky in 1829, as reported in Aptheker's *American Negro Slave Revolts* and repeated more recently by Angela Davis.[35] In that revolt, a pregnant black woman played a violent and leading role. The second, even less noticed bit of women's history (also cited in Aptheker) was the action of a white woman on an isolated North Carolina farm who in 1830 broke with southern racial tradition by harboring runaway slaves.[36] "How sad, I thought, that these two women never met" (5), Williams observes. In *Dessa Rose* their bare-bones histories are united and fleshed out in a narrative combining the Afro-American tradition of storytelling, authentic historical data, and an ironic imitation of Styron's and Gray's roles as white scribe-interpreters of black experience. "I loved history as a child," Williams explains, "until some clear-eyed young Negro pointed out, quite rightly, that there was no place in the American past I could go and be free" (5–6). Years later, the novelist-as-historian carves out this free space in the slave past for herself and for other blacks, women, and all Americans. In the process, Williams revitalizes Ralph Ellison's remark at the SHA cited in Chapter 1: "through our Negro American oral tradition . . . these reminders of the past as *Negroes* recalled it found existence and were passed along. Historical figures continued to live in stories of and theories about the human and social dynamics of slavery. . . . Assertions of freedom and revolt were recalled along with triumphs of labor in the fields and on the dance floor; feats of eating and drinking and of fornication, of religious conversion and physical endurance, and of artistic and athletic achievements" (68–69).

Dessa Rose's retrospective account of her girlhood as field hand, she-devil in the uprising, teenage mother, and ladies maid in an escape adventure is related mostly in her own vernacular voice. This autobiographical presence is, however, interrupted, in the early chapters, by the condescending voice of Adam Nehemiah, a white man writing a study of slaves, to be entitled, *The Roots of Rebellion in the Slave Population and Some Means of Eradicating Them*. (*Roots*, as it is subsequently referred to, not only echoes and undercuts Gray's and Styron's accounts but implicitly calls Alex Haley's "faction" into question as well.) However, as the narrative of violence and escape draws to its picaresque climax, the presence of a third storyteller is acknowledged. This is a young relative, educated and living several generations later in Dessa Rose's family, somewhere west of Council Bluffs, Iowa.

(Williams lives and teaches in San Diego.) "I hope I live for my people like they do for me," the old ex-slave exclaims at the end, "so sharp sometime I can't believe it's all in my mind. And my mind wanders. This is why I have it wrote down, why I have the child say it back" (236). The "child," as contemporary black scribe, has lent her voice, vocabulary, and imagination to the illiterate slave, Dessa, and to her fellow rebels from the slave coffle, Nathan and Harker. She speaks also for and through Miz Rufel, the white mistress of The Glens, who represents the sympathetic white farmwife lifted from Aptheker's page. Miz Rufel becomes a willing confederate in the slaves' plot to escape west by pretending to be their mistress traveling along Alabama rivers to join her husband. In this trickster plot, hers is an ironic reminder of Benito Cereno's role in Melville's shipboard charade and Lowell's modern drama. These Alabama adventures are also an ironic commentary on two other male texts about slavery—Bradley's contemporary version of the historical Underground Railroad and, at further remove, Mark Twain's nineteenth-century vision of Huck and Jim escaping down a larger western river.

This mélange of narrative modes and male countertexts places *Dessa Rose* securely yet obliquely within American literary tradition. Williams's novel stands halfway between the first-person, pseudo-autobiographical texts of Mark Twain, Styron, and Bradley and the multiple perspective of Bontemps's more public historical fiction. *Black Thunder* is perhaps less susceptible to parodic retelling here as women's history than the others. Nevertheless, Williams reexamines through a woman's eyes virtually all the historical themes and conflicts repeated in previous narratives of slave resistance and escape from Douglass's *Narrative* to Bradley's 1981 novel. Against the dominant culture's cruel pressures of slavery, oppression, and violence, Dessa Rose and her allies oppose their individual wills expressed as heterosexual love, the racial solidarity of suffering, the speech, songs, and work rituals of the slave quarters, and the oppressed's skills at lying, masking, and role-playing. What's notably absent, however, from this version of the slave past is the support of black religion, a cultural resource virtually ignored in *Dessa Rose* as it is in *The Chaneysville Incident*. In its place as an ideology usually dividing but occasionally uniting blacks and whites is a sharper, secular belief and justification for slavery and resistance to it. Dessa's first lover, Kaine, is killed by a blow from the master's shovel for precisely the same reason Dessa later helps kill the white slave traders. "I kill white mens," she tells Nehemiah, "I kill white mens cause the same reason Masa kill Kaine. Cause I can" (20). "Cause I can" also explains the surprising act of Miz Rufel in breastfeeding Dessa's tiny black baby. When the white mistress and black runaway first come to know each other, the curious white woman asks Dessa's name.

> "Dessa. Dessa Rose, ma'am," she said in a raspy voice.
> Rufel was somewhat taken aback; she had not expected the wench to answer so readily. "Why's you run away?"
> The darky kept her eyes downcast and plucked nervously at the coverlet. "Cause, cause I didn't want my baby slaved," she said finally in a rush and still without looking at Rufel.
> Rufel looked at the baby, seeing in him the pickaninnies at Mobile. And that's what he'd look like, too, if I put you all out of here, she thought pettishly. "I mean, why your mistress use you so?"
> "Cause she can," the wench said on a long shuddering breath as she turned her face away. (139)

The lived ideology of "Cause I can" eventually liberates Dessa Rose and her friends and lovers in the slave community. It also liberates Miz Rufel. For in her encounters with this group of resolute escapees the young white woman gradually overcomes her Charleston background of aristocratic racism. Not only does she, almost instinctively, nurse Dessa's baby and sleep in the same bed with them, but she also falls deeply in love with Nathan. The sight of her milkwhite body intertwined with Nathan's black body shocks Dessa into her most profound and contradictory realizations of racism and reconciliation, of love, lust, and admiration, and of the positive possibilities of existential belief. Love, too, becomes a possibility for all believers in "Cause I can."

Such illumination—liberating but sometimes painful—not only derives from lived experiences of interracial love and women's solidarity but also from the very acts of remembering and retelling the past that have made this narrative itself possible. When first interviewed in jail by Nehemiah about her role in the uprising, she begins to understand herself through the retelling of her own story.

She saw the past as she talked, not as she had lived it but as she had come to understand it. White men existed because they did; master had smashed the banjo because that was the way he was, able to do what he felt like doing. And a nigger could, too. That was what Kaine's act said to her. He had done; he was. She had done also, had as good as killed Master, for wasn't her own punishment worse than death? She had lost Kaine, become a self she scarcely knew, lost to family, to friends. So she talked. She was reconciled to nothing, but the dreams or haunts that had crowded about her in the cellar now walked the sunlit air and allowed her peace at night. (58)

This is an early epiphany in Dessa Rose's oral performance as rewritten by her "child" later in freedom. Yet this insight contrasts strikingly in its clarifying simplicity of "And a nigger could, too. . . . He had done; he was," with the spiritual/sexual meditations of Styron's Nat in another jail. Williams constantly counterpoints the duty of the fictional historian to re-create slavery as living, talking, singing, doing, and suffering recaptured in the always-risky act of writing slavery down. In this scene, Nehemiah's white motives for retelling Dessa Rose's story are to sell books and shore up the institution of slavery. He does this by willful, partly ignorant misrepresentation. His exploitation begins and ends by calling the "black wench" out of her name, by insisting on calling her Odessa, like other whites. Miz Rufel (itself a black nickname for Ruth Elizabeth) also calls blacks out of their names. In turn, Dessa scornfully addresses her as "Miz Ruint" upon discovering her in bed with Nathan. Only at the very close of the novel, as mistress and maid escape the clutches of the pursuing Nehemiah ("Nemi" is *his* misnomer in black mouths) do Miz Rufel and Dessa come to terms with each others' identities.

"My name is Ruth," she say. "Ruth. I ain't your mistress." Like *I'd* been the one putting that on her.

"Well, if it comes to that," I told her, "my name's Dessa, Dessa Rose. Ain't no O to it." I didn't even not think about my tongue. This was the way she was, you see, subject to make you mad just when you was feeling some good towards her. And she was good.

"That's fine with me." . . . I wanted to hug Ruth. I didn't hold nothing against her, not "mistress," not Nathan, not skin. Maybe we couldn't speak but so honest without disagreement, but that didn't change how I feel. (232–33)

This victory of human feelings over misnaming is, in addition, a victory of women, black and white, over slavery and the white male writer Nemi. For his attempts to recapture Dessa constitute a quest subconsciously energized by the fact that, as David Bradley has pointed out, this white man has himself fallen in love with Dessa.[37] His machinations are balked by three women who conspire to keep covered up Dessa's status as a slave with whip-scarred and branded hips. A woman's body is the final battleground, as women defend each other's identity from the incriminating evidence written in Nemi's notebook manuscript. As the pages of *Roots* are scattered over the floor of the Arcopolis jail, Williams's final derisive judgment on white *and* male versions of slavery and slave resistance is delivered: "'Nemi, ain't nothing but some scribbling on here,' sheriff say. 'Can't no one read this.' Miz 'Lady was turning over the papers in her hand. 'And these is blank, sheriff' she say" (232). It is surely no accident that two white readers signal the utter inadequacy of white writing about the institution and experience of slavery.

"This novel, then, is fiction," Williams's author's note concludes, "all the characters, even the country they travel through, while based on fact, are inventions. And what is here is as true as if I myself had lived it. Maybe it is only a metaphor, but I now own a summer in the 19th century." The eighties act of reappropriating history—or a carefully chosen segment thereof—has produced an imaginative illumination of the past shared particularly (but not exclusively) with other women: "I now know that slavery eliminated neither heroism nor love; it provided occasions for their expressions." Moreover, Williams underlines modern women's roles in revitalizing histories such as Aptheker's *American Negro Slave Revolts* when she points out that "the Davis article marked a turning point in my efforts to apprehend that other history" (6).

Dessa Rose, reflecting and refracting bits of earlier works such as *The Chaneysville Incident*, *A Hero Ain't Nothin' but a Sandwich*, and *I Know Why the Caged Bird Sings* is the fullest, most recent demonstration of the historical value of "black literature" for tapping the moral energy generated by revisiting the slave past. Williams's "sense of the real," though triggered originally by her angry denunciation of

Styron's account, contains a recognition not unlike the white novelist's that metaphoric language has the power to communicate "ineffable othernesses" in obscure nineteenth-century lives and actions. Perhaps the current popularity of her and Bradley's stories suggests a greater willingness by general American readers, white and black, male and female, to embrace a broader definition and relevance of black historical literature than was the case when Styron wrote *The Confessions of Nat Turner*.

If sales, reviews, prizes, book club adoptions, and publicity for these —and other—black historical novelists are trustworthy evidence, then we should contrast this changing literary ethos and these reading formations with the apparent persistence of sharper boundaries still separating historians. Many have pointed out the centuries-old dilemma of black writers who, in addition to developing and articulating the concerns of black readers, must also address a perhaps larger body of white readers who are, if not skeptical or hostile, often ill-informed or indifferent. In this complex communication, the black writer's ally has long been historical subject matter with its "informing power of historical fact," as Martin Duberman points out. The force of actual "evidenced" experience in *The Chaneysville Incident* and *Dessa Rose* may well help these stories bridge racial and cultural barriers, while enhancing wider recognition of the powers of black imaginative writing today. If so, it may be that David Levering Lewis is correct in perceiving a somewhat different atmosphere surrounding professional historians and their particular audiences. Though citing several promising instances of an emerging integrationist historiography in recent years, he emphasizes the more pervasive reality—

> that the centrifugal political and social forces at work during the Reagan years have tended to push historians away from the mid-1960s vision of a society greater than the sum of its parts. In one sense, of course, it is perfectly salutary that the past of African Americans and other ethnic minorities, as well as that of women and gays, continues to be more thoroughly and exclusively explored in defense against the demeaning and disintegrative signals emanating from foci of power during the last decade or more, and which (kinder and gentler) promise to continue.[38]

Though Lewis points out that there are several historical explanations (such as Elizabeth Fox-Genovese's *Within the Plantation Household*) that run counter to this separatist tendency, the contrast between literary inclusiveness and historiographical parallelism or pigeonholing may stand as a tentative commentary on these two sectors of eighties elite culture. Additional evidence is suggested by Book-of-the-Month Club and Playboy Book Club selections, *New York Times Book Review* coverage of important bestsellers such as Alice Walker's *The Color Purple* and Toni Morrison's *Beloved* and English Institute, MLA, and ASA programs. It would appear that fiction-reading Americans and their literary and cultural mentors or superintendents are moving toward a more interracial and cross-cultural perspective on antebellum history.

A Coda: Two Microcontroversies

What, then, can be said about present-day reading formations and critical responses to American narratives about the slave world and its rebels? This study of cultural politics opened with Tony Bennett's frank acknowledgment that it is never easy to discover detailed evidence of popular, as opposed to elite, responses—hence the disproportionate reliance throughout these chapters on traditional and often inconclusive inferences of general popularity or neglect. Heavy, perhaps undue weight has been placed on such evidence as the *New York Times Book Review* report for February 1969 that, to date, New American Library's print orders for the mass-produced paperback of Styron's *The Confessions of Nat Turner* totalled 1,544,069.[39] If such data were ambiguous at best in 1969, it may be even shakier evidence today for identifying actual popular responses to Styron's story. How, then, are we to assess the current domain of the book which, more than any other in this controversy, once provoked widespread awareness and clarifying disagreements, helping to bring about the tempestuous return of Nat Turner to public discourse two decades ago?

Two pieces of fragmentary but suggestive evidence may be cited. One front-page story in the *Des Moines Register* carried the headline "Pulitzer Prize-Winning Book Banned by Iowa School Board."[40] The story reported that the school board of Thompson, Iowa, had voted to ban *The Confessions of Nat Turner* from the Thompson High School library after a complaint by the mother of a seventh-grader who had checked the book out for a school project. Highlights from the article provide the following cultural data on some current popular attitudes.

> The book portrays a black preacher who led a slave revolt in Virginia in 1831 and demonstrates the evils of racism. It won the Pulitzer Prize, considered the highest honor that can be bestowed upon a book, in 1968.
> Author William Styron said this is the first time he has heard that the book, published in 1966 [*sic*], has been banned. Styron said Wednesday that the sexual passages in the book are "quite inoffensive" by contemporary standards and are artistically justified. . . .
> In a wry letter about the ban to a friend, Styron wrote: "Now come Mr. and Mrs. Roger Moklestad with their Iowa Gothic wrath. . . . I am devastated. . . . What a bizarre country is this America and its weird ways."
> James Thorsom, a school board member, said the ban, approved by the board 3–2 in March, has not caused a controversy in Thompson.
> "That's part of why no one wants to comment. It's no kind of a controversy at all, but the papers think it is," said Thorsom.
> Bob Bird, the school librarian, says he thinks the ban is wrong.[41]

Although several others agreed with Bird, no one, except the reporter, commented on *The Confessions of Nat Turner* as a once-controversial re-creation of a slave revolt. But next day's *Register* cartoonist lampooned Grant Wood's classic Iowans, the farmer with a pitchfork through a book and wearing a "Ban Books" button on his lapel, his wife holding a cigarette lighter.

The second bit of contemporary history suggests even more pointed responses to Styron's novel. On August 28, 1988, Susan Stamberg's *Sunday Edition* on National Public Radio reported that William Styron had just received the MacDowell Award for Lifetime Achievement as an American author.[42] Remembering 1968, no doubt, Stamberg interviewed two Americans on their reactions to Styron's latest honor. Both recalled *The Confessions of Nat Turner* and its controversial reception. Eric Meyer, a white listener from Boulder, Colorado, observed that

Styron's novel should be required reading in American schools, for he remembered it as affording him his first vicarious experience of slavery. Ruth Farmer, a black woman from Washington, D.C., asserted that a black would never have written such a picture of Nat Turner and if one had done so it wouldn't have been published *or* given a prize.

    This cultural history began with the assumption that the 1968 SHA session on "The Uses of History in Fiction" is a useful model for other discussions and disagreements before and after this symbolic occasion. Such relevance reaches forward even to these two bits of late-eighties evidence of popular reading formations. First, we might note that the Thompson, Iowa, parents appear to be missing the point of the Nat Turner controversy just as blatantly as did certain audience members in New Orleans who seemed willfully to disregard the theories and justifications of Styron and the others on the platform. Only Ellison seemed to anticipate such "misreadings" when he remarked that *"everybody reads now. . . . And everybody is saying: Damn it, tell it like I think it is"* (90). If we add the voices of Jameson and Bennett to the novelist's remark, we must take seriously all responses to this historical/literary phenomenon. In this spirit, is it possible that the Iowans' disapproval of sexual language in *The Confessions of Nat Turner* is a relevant commentary upon the whole sexual dimension of Styron's version of Nat Turner's life and rebellion? Sexuality as an apparently necessary explanation and metaphor for Styron figured in many previous, more "intellectual" and "professional" discussions of the book and historical event. The Thompson school board's seemingly irrelevant action of 1987, justified in terms of language unsuitable for a seventh-grader, suggests that sexuality continues to lead readers and superintendents away from other touchy aspects of Nat Turner's return in this fictional guise. Perhaps Bob Bird, the school librarian, was better aware than his fellow townspeople of these other dimensions highlighted not by blind prejudice but by neglect. Moreover, Styron's feeling "devastated" at another instance of Americans' bizarre insistence on misreading his text can be understood as wry recognition by the novelist that his psychological explanation of man and event continues to serve a dismaying variety of ideological purposes for later generations of readers.

    If these speculations on popular responses are deeply plausible, they help explain the persistent and divisive appeal of Styron's story. Susan

Stamberg's two interviewees return us, for a moment or two, to the climate of 1967–68. Neither, however, mentions sexuality or sexually explicit language as historical data or fictional feature. Indeed, the white Coloradan's pleasure is explicitly rooted in his remembered sense of enlightenment about the experience and institution of slavery. Further, his is an oblique assertion that, although white ignorance, indifference, or hostility persists, this might be mitigated in 1988 by the required reading of *The Confessions of Nat Turner* by American schoolchildren. The Washington woman's indignation, on the other hand, over Styron's continuing eminence in white cultural circles may be linked to previous black disapproval of Styron's (and other whites') ahistorical recourse to sexual motives and behavior to "explain" a slave revolt. Such inferences, backed by remembered remarks by other black writers, may possibly be inferred from oral phrasing like "such a picture of Nat Turner," which a black writer wouldn't have gotten away with.

Two brief and divergent comments on a writer's career, in terms of a more or less sharply remembered treatment of slaves, are not weighty evidence on which to generalize, but their tentative conjunction suggests that, on the basis of mass distribution of ordinary American words and actions, the Nat Turner controversy in some sense continues, reembedded here as emergent or recessive forms of individual and collective transactions. They are evidence of the "living life" of this written text. As "popular" returns of Nat Turner, these are patently minor events in themselves. Yet they point to larger and longer-lasting issues in the culture. Though detached from earlier, meatier texts and more widely publicized occasions, they testify to distinct points on the bigger screen of modern historical consciousness. As clues to eighties awareness, they coexist with *Dessa Rose* and its interracial themes and readerships while they point to those school texts which we have already noted now transmit ampler, more socially and racially inclusive messages to the young than was heretofore the case. That they surface still as conflicts and distinct differences of opinion and emotion attests, finally, to one of the underlying presuppositions of this study. American culture is a construct resting upon the social and historical realities of diversity and pluralism, as well as hegemonic hierarchies and systemic subordinations. Its only unity, in fact, may exist in the tensions and divisions that history records and whose social dynamics and mysterious inner motivations novelists claim as their domain. This view of American culture has been rearticulated by Lionel Trilling, a distinguished critic of elite literature and culture who, as far as I can discover, observed the Nat Turner controversy only from the sidelines:

> Such a division of opinion might seem to bring into question the idea of the unitary nature of culture. Actually, of course, the cogency and usefulness of that idea depend exactly upon its being discovered in a manifest diversity, and, indeed, in the disputes that, in any highly elaborated culture, go on between diverse preferences and opinions. A culture has its being in activity, in its complex response to possibilities, as these are offered by external circumstances or as they are conceived by the culture itself, and perhaps the most characteristic form of its activity is the opposition which one group in the culture offers to another.[43]

Though many will hope and yearn, with David Levering Lewis, for the eventual realization of "the mid-1960s vision of a society greater than the sum of its parts"[44]—an event possibly foreshadowed in certain eighties novels and history books—the goals of a "unitary culture" encouraging "inclusive history" and a proper "black literature" have yet to be widely realized if we take Nat Turner as a test case and exemplary episode.

Notes

1. The Return of Nat Turner in Sixties America

1. *Publisher's Weekly*, July 31, 1967, 53.
2. R. A. Sokolov, "In the Mind of Nat Turner," *Newsweek*, October 16, 1967, 65–69. See also *Christian Science Monitor* (Boston), October 12, 1967, 5; *Charleston News and Courier*, December 31, 1967; *Indianapolis News*, October 21, 1967; *Fresno Bee*, November 12, 1967.
3. *Time*, October 13, 1967, 110.
4. C. Vann Woodward, "Confessions of a Rebel: 1831," *New Republic*, October 7, 1967, 28.
5. Wilfred Sheed, *New York Times Book Review*, October 8, 1967, 1–3; Albert Murray, *New Leader*, December 4, 1967, 18–21; *Blackwood's*, August 1968, 191–92.
6. *William Styron's Nat Turner: Ten Black Writers Respond*, ed. J. H. Clarke (Boston: Beacon Press, 1968).
7. "The Uses of History in Fiction," *Southern Literary Journal* 1 (Spring 1969): 58.
8. *The Confessions of Nat Turner, The Leader of the Late Insurrection in Southampton, Va., As Fully and Voluntarily Made to Thomas R. Gray* (Baltimore, 1831); reprinted here as an appendix.
9. Henry I. Tragle, *The Southampton Slave Revolt of 1831: A Compilation of Source Material* (Amherst: University of Massachusetts Press, 1971).
10. For information on the projected film version of *The Confessions of Nat Turner*, see *Richmond Times-Dispatch*, February 12, 1970, and April 15, 1971.
11. See Clifford Geertz, *The Interpretation of Cultures: Selected Essays* (New York: Basic Books, 1973); Erving Goffman, *The Presentation of Self in Everyday Life* (Garden City, N.Y.: Doubleday, 1959), and *Asylums: Essays on the Social Situations of Mental Patients and Other Inmates* (Garden City, N.Y.: Doubleday, 1961).
12. See especially Kenneth Burke, *Language as Symbolic Action: Essays on Life, Literature, and Method* (Berkeley: University of California Press, 1966) and *The Philosophy of Literary Form: Studies in Symbolic Action* (Berkeley: University of California Press, 1973).
13. Richard H. Brown, "Social Reality as Text: The Analysis of Interactions, Institutions and Politics as Language," paper delivered at Rhetoric of the Human Sciences Symposium, University of Iowa, March 30, 1984. See also Paul

Ricoeur, "The Model of the Text: Meaningful Action Considered as a Text," *Social Research* 38 (Autumn 1971): 529–62.

14. See, on this point, Addison Gayle, Jr., "Cultural Hegemony: The Southern White Writer and American Letters," in *Amistad-I*, J. A. Williams and F. Harris, eds. (New York: Random House, 1970), 3–24.

15. Tony Bennett, "Texts, Readers, Reading Formations," *Bulletin of Midwest Modern Language Association* (Spring 1983): 3–17.

16. See Robert Penn Warren, "William Styron," *Book-of-the-Month-Club News*, October 1967, 6–7.

17. Barbara Herrnstein Smith, "Narrative Versions, Narrative Theories," in *On Narrative*, ed. W. J. T. Mitchell (Chicago: University of Chicago Press, 1981), 213.

18. Fredric Jameson, *The Political Unconscious: Narrative as a Socially Symbolic Act* (Ithaca, N.Y.: Cornell University Press, 1981), 82.

19. Bennett, "Texts, Readers, Reading Formations," 17.

20. See Stanley Kauffman, "Styron's Unwritten Novel," *Hudson Review* 20 (Winter 1967–68): 675–80.

21. Arna Bontemps, *Black Thunder* (New York: Macmillan, 1936; rpt. Boston: Beacon Press, 1968). Future references are to the 1968 edition.

22. See Marc L. Ratner, "Styron's Rebel," *American Quarterly* 21 (Fall 1969): 595–608, and its later text as chap. 5 of *William Styron* (New York: Twayne Publishers, 1972).

23. Fred Chappell, "Six Propositions about Literature and History," *New Literary History* 1 (Spring 1970): 516.

2. William Styron's Meditation on History

1. Frances FitzGerald, *America Revised: History Schoolbooks in the Twentieth Century* (Boston: Little, Brown, 1979), 64. Her quotation concludes: "and then only by virtue of some rather condescending words about Tuskegee and Booker T. Washington."

2. William Styron, "This Quiet Dust," *Harper's*, April 1965, 135; republished in *This Quiet Dust and Other Writings* (New York: Random House, 1982). Subsequent parenthetical citations will be to *Harper's*.

3. *Dictionary of American Biography*, ed. Dumas Malone (New York: Scribner's, 1936), 19: 69–70. Subsequently, at least one early reviewer of Styron's novel, Van Allen Bradley, used this edition of the *DAB* for his summary of Nat Turner's life. See *Memphis Commercial Appeal*, October 15, 1967.

4. For example, William Wells Brown, *The Black Man: His Antecedents, His Genius, and His Achievements* (New York: Thomas Hamilton, 1863); George

NOTES

Washington Williams, *History of the Negro Race in America from 1619 to 1880* (New York: Putnam's, 1882); Carter G. Woodson, *The Negro in Our History* (Washington, D.C.: Associated Publishers, 1922); W. E. B. Du Bois, *The Gift of Black Folk: The Negroes in the Making of America* (Boston: Stratford, 1924), and other titles.

5. Arthur Casciato and James L. W. West, III, "William Styron and the Southampton Insurrection," *American Literature* 52 (January 1981): 568.

6. Olmsted's *A Journey in the Seaboard Slave States* (New York: Dix and Edwards, 1856) may also have led Styron to consult Olmsted's more famous *The Cotton Kingdom: A Traveller's Observations on Cotton and Slavery in the American Slave States* (New York: Mason Brothers, 1861). Casciato and West do not mention *The Cotton Kingdom* but do cite *A Journey* as well as other sources Redding sent Styron, including Samuel Warner's *Authentical and Impartial Narrative of the Tragical Scene Which Was Witnessed in Southampton County* (New York: Warner and West, 1831), and two articles, one by T. W. Higginson, "Nat Turner's Insurrection," *Atlantic Monthly*, August 1861, and the anonymous "The Light Dragoons," *Southern Historical Society Papers*, August 1899.

7. See Tragle, *The Southampton Slave Revolt*, 413. A second highway marker is shown in a photograph in *Newsweek*, October 16, 1967. See Sokolov, "In the Mind of Nat Turner," 65.

8. Tragle, *The Southampton Slave Revolt*, 412–13.

9. James Jones and William Styron, "Two Writers Talk It Over," *Esquire*, July 1963, 57–59.

10. Roy Parker, Jr., *Raleigh News and Observer*, October 29, 1967.

11. William Styron, reviews of *American Negro Slave Revolts* by Herbert Aptheker, *New York Review of Books*, September 26, 1963, 18–19; and *Slave and Citizen: The Negro in the Americas* by Frank Tannenbaum, Special Issue, n.d. 1963, 43. Styron's ambivalence in the early sixties about the frequency of slave revolts is reflected in the Aptheker review: "As a matter of fact, if we can accept Aptheker's evidence—and on the whole his book seems well documented—it would appear that unrest and discontent *were* considerably more widespread than earlier historians would grant" (18). Later, however, he declares that "one does not have to be a white supremacist to note that Aptheker fails almost completely in his attempt to prove the universality of slave rebelliousness" and concludes emphatically "there was only one sustained effective revolt in the entire annals of slavery"—"the cataclysmic uprising of Nat Turner in Virginia in 1831" (19).

12. Robert Canzoneri and Page Stegner, "An Interview with William Styron," *Per/Se* 1, no. 2 (1966): 37–44.

13. *Amsterdam News* (New York), September 2, 1967, 7.

14. See Sokolov, "In the Mind of Nat Turner," 65.

15. *Harper's*, September 1967. The excerpt appeared on pages 51–102.

16. *Directory of Newspapers and Periodicals* (Philadelphia: N. W. Ayer and Sons, 1965), 736. Richard Ohmann includes *Harper's* among the eight most influential periodicals of the sixties and early seventies. The cultural function of these periodicals, he argues, is to serve as "main gatekeepers for new talent and new ideas. . . . The elite, writing in these journals, largely determined which books would be seriously debated and which ones permanently valued, as well as what ideas were kept alive, circulated, discussed." Ohmann, "The Shaping of a Canon: U.S. Fiction, 1960–1975," *Critical Inquiry* 10 (September 1983): 205. Styron is of course listed among the "serious" writers widely canonized by Ohmann's "professional-managerial" class. He figures also as a central focus of sixties cultural conflicts over canonization. "We don't usually notice the power or the conflict, except when some previously weak or silent group seeks a share of the power: for example, when, in the 1960s, American blacks and their supporters insisted that black literature be included in school and college curricula, or when they openly challenged the candidacy of William Styron's *Confessions of Nat Turner* for inclusion in some eventual canon" (199–200).

17. *Life*, October 13, 1967, 51.

18. I quote here from the actual published novel: Styron, *The Confessions of Nat Turner* (New York: Random House, 1967), 382.

19. "The People's Choice," *New York Times Book Review*, February 16, 1969, 26. This issue also included an article, "Black Is Marketable," in which Styron's sales figures are listed alongside those of black novelists and autobiographers.

20. Barbara Herrnstein Smith, *Contingencies of Value: Alternative Perspectives for Critical Theory* (Cambridge: Harvard University Press, 1988), 44–45.

21. See Joan Shelley Rubin, "Self, Culture, and Self-Culture in Modern America: The Early History of the Book-of-the-Month Club," *Journal of American History* 71 (March 1985): 782–806; and Janice Radway, "The Book-of-the-Month Club and the General Reader: On the Uses of Serious Fiction," *Critical Inquiry* 14 (Spring 1988): 516–38.

22. Radway, "The Book-of-the-Month Club and the General Reader," 538.

23. See Elizabeth Long, "Women, Reading, and Cultural Authority: Some Implications of Audience Perspective in Culture Studies," *American Quarterly* 38 (Fall 1986): 591–612.

24. L. O. Mink, "History and Fiction as Modes of Comprehension," *New Literary History* 1 (Spring 1970): 541–58; and "Narrative Forms as Cognitive Instrument," in *The Writing of History*, R. Canary and H. Kozicki, eds. (Madison: University of Wisconsin Press, 1978), 129–49.

25. Styron later explained his phrase thus to C. Vann Woodward and R. W. B. Lewis: "I intend that statement to do two things. One, to literally take

the curse of the phrase 'historical novel' off the book. Also it is a meditation on history in the sense that I hoped to encompass a meditative quality as I wrote." Interview with William Styron, *Yale Alumni Magazine*, November 1967, 52. This aspect of the novel is one of many literary-historical issues engaging the attention of scholars and critics in the more than two decades since the appearance of *The Confessions of Nat Turner*. Since the concerns of this chapter and book are with social production and responses across a wider cultural landscape, I have not directly addressed this rich literature of academic analysis and debate. For guides to the literally hundreds of critical discussions of Styron and his novel see the *MLA Annual Bibliography* from 1967 to the present, and Jackson R. Bryer, "William Styron: A Bibliography" in *The Achievement of William Styron*, ed. K. Morris with I. Malin (Athens: University of Georgia Press, 1981), rev. ed., 299–382.

26. See Appendix for complete text of Gray's *Confessions*. Subsequent citations to this text will refer to Appendix.

27. Styron, *Confessions of Nat Turner*, 23.

28. "Bishop Meade's Amazing Sermon to Slaves" is quoted in Olmsted, *Journey in the Seaboard Slave States*, 131–33. Casciato and West cite this source and point out the few changes Styron made in adapting this source. See Casciato and West, "William Styron and the Southampton Insurrection," 576–77.

29. Eugene D. Genovese, "The Nat Turner Case," *New York Review of Books*, September 12, 1968, 34–37.

30. The rich lady from New Haven thus completes the pattern of "aversive racism" Joel Kovel discusses a few years later in *White Racism: A Psychohistory* (New York: Random House, 1970), especially chap. 8, "The Psychohistory of Racism in the United States," 177–230. Kovel sees avoidance and withdrawal as the second ideal type, preceded historically by "dominative racism" and succeeded by "metaracism," the most abstract and dehumanizing mode of white thought and behavior. Kovel's psychoanalysis of southern dominative racism produces this pertinent comment on slave revolts: "The only check on the development of slaveholding culture could have been from inner control—conscience balanced by morality, or cultural superego. But superego cannot grow if instinctual gratifications are relinquished. This the Southerner was doubly loath to do: first because his life was so immediately enjoyable, so gallant, so virile; and, second, because of the ever-present threat of slave revolts. This menace, the offspring of projected guilt as much as a real potential for black violence, always hung just beyond the horizon of the bright Southern sky" (189).

3. The Public Controversy

1. See *Critical Essays on William Styron*, ed. Arthur D. Casciato and James L. W. West III (Boston: G. K. Hall, 1982), 226–27.

2. See William J. Stuckey, *The Pulitzer Prize Novels: A Critical Backward Look* (Norman: University of Oklahoma Press, 1981), 2d ed., 219–25. See also John Hohenberg, *The Pulitzer Prizes: A History of the Awards in Books, Drama, Music, and Journalism, Based on the Private Files over Six Decades* (New York: Columbia University Press, 1974), 319–20.

3. Quoted in Stuckey, *The Pulitzer Prize Novels*, 250.

4. Ibid., 258.

5. Ibid., 222–23.

6. Gertrude Wilson, "I Spit on the Pulitzer Prize!" *Amsterdam News*, May 18, 1968.

7. Ibid., 17.

8. *Minneapolis Star*, October 10, 1967.

9. *San Francisco Chronicle*, October 9, 1967.

10. *Charleston News and Courier*, December 31, 1967.

11. *Raleigh News and Observer*, October 29, 1967.

12. Wilfred Sheed, *New York Times*, October 8, 1967.

13. Art Buchwald, "Paper Plimpton," *Playboy*, January 1968. "One day I happened to be at Bill Styron's house helping him autograph his book *The Confessions of Nat Turner* when he casually mentioned that George Plimpton was coming up for the weekend" (143).

14. George Plimpton, "A Shared Ordeal—Interviews With William Styron," *New York Times Book Review*, October 8, 1967.

15. Dick Schapp, "Framework for Confessions," *San Francisco Examiner and Chronicle*, October 15, 1967.

16. Woodward and Lewis, interview with William Styron, *Yale Alumni Magazine*, November 1967, 52–58.

17. Woodward, "Confessions of a Rebel, 1831."

18. Shaun O'Connell, "Styron's Nat Turner," *The Nation*, October 16, 1967, 374.

19. "What Really Happened in Newark?" *The Nation*, October 16, 1967, 375.

20. Herbert Aptheker, "A Note on the History," *The Nation*, October 16, 1967, 375.

21. June Meyer, "Spokesmen for the Blacks," *The Nation*, December 4, 1967, 597.

22. The Rahv review, "Through the Midst of Jerusalem," appeared in *New York Review of Books* October 26, 1967, 6–10. Rahv's incriminating and revelatory remark is: "I think only a white Southern writer could have brought

it off. A Northerner would have been too much 'outside' to manage it effectively; and a Negro writer, because of a very complex anxiety not only personal but social and political, would have probably stacked the cards, producing in a mood of unnerving rage and indignation, a melodrama of Saints and sinners. Styron, however, by an act that at once seizes upon his own background and transcends it, maintains throughout his narrative a consistent and highly imaginative realism not only on the objective plane (the economics of Virginia in the 1820s, the social relationships, the ideological defense-mechanisms), but also by recreating the intimate psychology of his characters, the black slaves and the white owners" (6).

23. Sokolov, "In the Mind of Nat Turner," 46.

24. *New Leader*, December 4, 1967, 18–21.

25. John Hope Franklin, *Chicago Sun-Times Book Week*, October 8, 1967.

26. Michael Cooke, "Nat Turner's Revolt," *Yale Review* 57 (Winter 1968): 273–78.

27. See "Recommended Summer Reading," *American Scholar* 37 (Summer 1968): 542–51. In the same issue, Styron is represented in a report on a symposium, "Violence in Literature," held at the New School for Social Research. With specific reference to *The Confessions of Nat Turner*, he remarked, "I think one of the lessons I learned as a writer as I wrote the book [was that] . . . to make violence meaningful . . . I had to withhold it" (485).

28. Benjamin Quarles, *Social Studies* 59 (November 1968): 280.

29. J. H. Clarke, ed., *William Styron's Nat Turner: Ten Black Writers Respond* (Boston: Beacon Press, 1968), 79.

30. Harold Cruse's controversial, no-holds-barred *The Crisis of the Negro Intellectual* (New York: William Morrow, 1967) treats Nat Turner and slave rebellions as examples of American black nationalist rhetoric: "These historical episodes of force and violence in Negro history," he writes, "have become hallowed as prototypical examples of the revolutionary potential in the Negro presence in America. Everyone from Communist whites to nationalist blacks sees in these slave uprisings anything they want to see. . . . But mere rebellions are not revolutions in themselves—especially in America. [The present-day] movement cannot become revolutionary until it articulates objectives which transcend its present aims—racial integration. . . . At least the slaves knew exactly what they wanted—the abolition of the slave system. Today every Negro in or out of the freedom movement knows he wants 'freedom,' but actually not one knows what he *really* wants out of present-day America. Therefore, to hark romantically back to the slave rebellions for the purpose of bolstering present-day revolutionary morale is rather pointless" (350–51). In addition to this general attack, Cruse also picks out John Hendrik Clarke, John O. Killens, and others associated with *Freedomways*, HARYOU, and the Harlem

Writer's Guild for what he derisively typifies as Clarke's "peculiar brand of left-wing-Africanist-integrationism" (338). Little wonder, then, that Cruse was not centrally placed in the Nat Turner controversy or included among the ten black writers. (I thank James C. Hall for urging me to reread Cruse and thereby qualify the argument that Clarke and his colleagues met opposition only from whites and older, more traditional black scholars.)

31. Ossie Davis, "Nat Turner: Hero Reclaimed," *Freedomways* 8 (Summer 1968): 230.

32. Martin B. Duberman, "Historical Fictions," *New York Times Book Review*, August 11, 1968, 1.

33. Herbert Aptheker and William Styron, "Truth and Nat Turner: An Exchange," *The Nation*, April 22, 1968, 543–47.

34. See Lucy Mae Turner, "Family of Nat Turner," *Negro History Bulletin* 18 (1955): 127–32.

35. Clarke, ed., *Ten Black Writers Respond*, 90.

36. Ibid.

37. Eugene D. Genovese, "The Nat Turner Case," 34.

38. Fred Chappell, "Six Propositions about Literature and History," *New Literary History* 1 (Spring 1970): 513.

39. Vincent Harding, "An Exchange on 'Nat Turner,'" *New York Review of Books*, November 7, 1968, 31–33.

40. "Eugene D. Genovese replies," *New York Review of Books*, November 7, 1968, 31–36.

41. Robert Taylor, "The Contentions of William Styron: The Novelist Responds to Critics of 'Nat Turner,'" *Boston Sunday Globe*, April 20, 1969, 6.

42. Quoted in letter from Gabin Stair, director of Beacon Press, to the editor, *Boston Globe*, April 30, 1969, 22.

43. "Genovese replies," 35.

44. Herbert Blau, *The Impossible Theatre: A Manifesto* (New York: Macmillan, 1964), 65.

45. See William Styron, *This Quiet Dust and Other Writings* (New York: Random House, 1982), 3.

46. Clarke, ed., *Ten Black Writers Respond*, 26.

47. Taylor, "The Contentions of William Styron," 12.

4. Other Images, Other Imaginations

1. Ernest Kaiser, "The Failure of William Styron," in *Ten Black Writers Respond*, ed. Clarke (Boston: Beacon Press, 1968), 50–65.

2. Harriet Beecher Stowe, *Dred: A Tale of the Dismal Swamp* (Boston: Phillips, Sampson, 1856); G. P. R. James, *The Old Dominion: or the Southamp-*

ton Massacre (London: T. C. Newby, 1856); Martin Delany, *Blake: The Cabins of America* (1856; repr., Boston: Beacon Press, 1970). Kaiser omits Delany from his survey.

3. Mary Johnston, *Prisoners of Hope: A Tale of Colonial Virginia* (Boston: Houghton Mifflin, 1899); Pauline Bouvé, *The Shadows Before* (1899; repr., Freeport, N.Y.: Books for Libraries Press, 1972).

4. Frances Gaither, *The Red Cock Crows* (New York: Macmillan, 1944); Arna Bontemps, *Black Thunder* (Boston: Beacon Press, 1968); Randolph Edmonds, *Nat Turner*, in *Six Plays for a Negro Theatre* (Boston: Walter H. Baker, 1934); Paul Peters, *Nat Turner*, in Edwin Seaver, ed., *Cross-Section: A Collection of New American Writing* (New York: L. B. Fischer, 1944); Sterling Brown, "Remembering Nat Turner," reprinted in *The Collected Poems of Sterling A. Brown*, ed. M. S. Harper (New York: Harper & Row, 1980), 199–200.

5. Thomas D. Pawley, "Messiah," in "Experimental Productions of a Group of Original Plays" (Ph.D. diss., University of Iowa, 1949).

6. Lloyd T. Delaney, "The White American Psyche—Exploration of Racism," *Freedomways* 8 (Summer 1968): 239–40.

7. Loyle Hairston, "Rescuing Nat Turner from American History," *Freedomways* 8 (Summer 1968): 267.

8. Ibid., 268.

9. William L. Van Deburg, in *Slavery and Race in American Popular Culture* (Madison: University of Wisconsin Press, 1984), briefly discusses Panger's novel as "an improvement over the stereotypical treatment of blacks in white-authored historical fiction" (142–43).

10. Daniel Panger, *Ol' Prophet Nat* (Winston-Salem, N.C.: John F. Blair, 1967), 6.

11. Compare Panger's account with Gray's *Confessions*, Appendix, p. 417.

12. Bontemps, *Black Thunder*, vii.

13. Richard Wright, "A Tale of Folk Courage," *Partisan Review* 3 (April 1936): 31.

14. *Calendar of Virginia State Papers and Other Manuscripts*, 9, January 1, 1799–December 31, 1807 (Richmond, 1892).

15. From the account of an English traveler, Robert Sutcliff, in *Travels in Some Parts of North America* (Philadelphia: Kite, 1812), as quoted in Aptheker, *American Negro Slave Revolts*, 5th ed. (New York: International Publishers, 1983), 223–24.

16. *Calendar of Virginia State Papers*, 9: 153. For another close parallel compare 9: 152 and Bontemps, *Black Thunder*, 86.

17. Winthrop Jordan, *White Over Black: American Attitudes toward the Negro, 1550–1812* (Baltimore: Penguin Books, 1968), 398.

18. See Jane Tompkins, *Sensational Designs: The Cultural Work of Ameri-*

can Fiction, 1790–1860 (New York: Oxford University Press, 1985), esp. chaps. 1 and 7.

19. Ibid., 200.

20. Edmonds, *Six Plays for a Negro Theatre*, 7. For a brief discussion of Edmonds's Nat Turner as a thirties image of the folk hero and martyr, see Darwin T. Turner, "The Negro Dramatist's Image of the Universe 1920–1960," *CLA Journal* 5 (December 1961): 107–8.

21. Seaver, ed., *Cross-Section*, Introduction.

22. Martin Duberman, *In White America: A Documentary Play* (New York: New American Library, 1964), i.

23. Robert Lowell, *The Old Glory* (New York: Farrar, Strauss and Giroux, 1965), xiii. An earlier version of Lowell's play was published in *Show: The Magazine of the Arts*, 4 (August 1964): 82–96. A stage illustration shows Captain Delano emptying his pistol into Babu's body. A broken chain lies on the deck.

24. Amasa Delano, *Narrative of Voyages and Travels in the Northern and Southern Hemispheres* (Boston: E. G. House, 1817; repr., Saddle River, N.J.: Gregg Press, 1970).

25. Robert Lowell, *Imitations* (New York: Farrar, Strauss and Cudahy, 1961), xi.

26. See Allen Guttmann, "The Enduring Innocence of Captain Amasa Delano," *Boston University Studies in English* 5 (Spring 1961): 35–45.

27. Robert Hayden, "The Poet and His Art: A Conversation," in *Collected Prose* (Ann Arbor: University of Michigan Press, 1984), 178.

28. Walter Loewenfels, "The White Literary Syndicate," *Liberator* (March 1970): 8–9.

29. June Jordan, "The Difficult Miracle of Black Poetry in America or Something Like a Sonnet for Phillis Wheatley," in *On Call: Political Essays* (Boston: South End Press, 1985), 97.

30. Ophelia Robinson, "Nat Turner," excerpted in *American Literature by Negro Authors*, ed. Herman Dreer (New York: Macmillan, 1950), 51–52.

31. Sterling Brown, "Remembering Nat Turner," *Crisis* 46 (February 1939): 48.

32. Sterling A. Brown, "Legend," *Collected Poems*, 189.

33. Sterling A. Brown, "Memo: For the Race Orators," *Collected Poems*, 191, 193.

34. Hayden, "The Poet and His Art," 177.

35. Ibid., 178.

36. The text of "The Ballad of Nat Turner" cited here and below is from *Angle of Ascent: New and Selected Poems* (New York: Liveright, 1975), 125–27.

37. Hayden, "The Poet and His Art," 177–78.

38. Ibid., 179–80.

39. Ibid., 178.
40. Ibid., 178–79.
41. "Nat Turner in the Clearing" was first published in *Motive Magazine* 7 (1967): 48.
42. Jerry W. Word, Jr., "An Interview with Alvin Aubert," *Black American Literary Forum* 23 (1989): 419.
43. Lowenfels, "The White Literary Syndicate," 9.
44. Ibid.
45. Tompkins, *Sensational Designs*, 199.
46. Duberman, *In White America*, 179.
47. Hayden White, "Historical Text as Literary Artifact," in *The Writing of History*, R. H. Canary and H. Kozicki, eds. (Madison: University of Wisconsin Press, 1978), 51, 52.

5. New Historical Explanations

1. Gene Wise, "Paradigm Dramas in American Studies: A Cultural and Institutional History of the Movement," *American Quarterly* 31, no. 3 (Bibliographical Issue, 1979): 293–337. See also Wise, *American Historical Explanations: A Strategy for Grounded Inquiry* (Homewood, Ill.: Dorsey Press, 1973).
2. John Hope Franklin, *From Slavery to Freedom: A History of Negro Americans*, 3d ed. (New York: Alfred A. Knopf, 1967), 664.
3. Peter Novick, *That Noble Dream: The "Objectivity Question" and the American Historical Profession* (New York: Cambridge University Press, 1988), 472.
4. See August Meier and Elliott M. Rudwick, *Black History and the Historical Profession, 1915–1980* (Urbana: University of Illinois Press, 1986), 117–18.
5. Ibid., 257, 358.
6. George Rawick, *From Sundown to Sunup: The Making of the Black Community*, vol. 1 of *The American Slave: A Composite Autobiography* (Westport, Conn.: Greenwood Press, 1972).
7. Kenneth M. Stampp, *The Peculiar Institution: Slavery in the Ante-Bellum South* (New York: Knopf, 1956), vii. Subsequent parenthetical citations are to the 1956 Vintage paperback edition.
8. Stampp's footnote (p. 134) cites, in addition to Gray, Drewry, *The Southampton Insurrection;* Aptheker, *American Negro Slave Revolts;* J. C. Carroll, *Slave Insurrections in the United States, 1800–1865* (Boston: Chapman and Grimes, 1938); and Harvey Wish, "American Slave Insurrections before 1861," *Journal of Negro History* 22 (July 1937): 299–320. Stampp also cites contemporary Richmond newspapers and Southampton County court records.

9. Meier and Rudwick, *Black History and the Historical Profession*, 246.

10. David Brion Davis, "Slavery and the Post–World War II Historians," *Daedalus* 3 (Spring 1974), reprinted in *From Homicide to Slavery: Studies in American Culture* (New York: Oxford University Press, 1980), 189.

11. See Meier and Rudwick, *Black History and the Historical Profession*, 292.

12. Ibid., 293.

13. Ibid., 247.

14. Stanley M. Elkins, *Slavery: A Problem in American Institutional and Intellectual Life*, 3d ed. revised (Chicago: University of Chicago Press, 1976).

15. Ann J. Lane, ed., *The Debate Over Slavery: Stanley Elkins and His Critics* (Urbana: University of Illinois Press, 1971).

16. Ibid. See pp. 43–74, 325–78.

17. See, for evidence from the sixties and seventies, Meier and Rudwick, *Black History and the Historical Profession*, 108–9; *New York Review of Books*, September 27, 1963; and David Brion Davis's single reference to Aptheker in *From Homicide to Slavery*, 189.

18. Aptheker, *Nat Turner's Slave Rebellion* (New York: Grove Press, 1968), vi.

19. Kenneth Stampp, "Our Historians and Slavery," *Politics* 1 (March 1944): 58.

20. Aptheker, *American Negro Slave Revolts*, 5th ed. (New York: International Publishers, 1983). Parenthetical references hereafter are to this edition rather than to the Columbia University Press first edition of 1943.

21. Roger Butterfield, *The American Past: A History of the United States from Concord to Hiroshima, 1775–1945* (New York: Simon and Schuster, 1947), v.

22. Lerone Bennett, Jr., *Before the Mayflower: A History of the Negro in America 1619–1962* (Chicago: Johnson Publishing Co., 1962), xi.

23. Charles Silberman, *Crisis in Black and White* (New York: Random House, 1966), 10.

24. Elkins, *Slavery*, 136, quoted above.

6. Newer Historical Explanations

1. *Freedomways* 1, no. 2 (Summer 1961): 163.

2. Homer F. Aker, Eugene Hilton, Varza N. Aker, *America—Today and Yesterday* (San Francisco: Harr Wagner, 1937).

3. William E. Woodward, *A New American History* (New York: Garden City Publishing, 1936).

4. Arna Bontemps, *The Story of the Negro: A Borzoi Book for Young People* (New York: Knopf, 1948), 108.

5. Fred Powledge, *To Change a Child: A Report on the Institute for Developmental Studies* (Chicago: Quadrangle Books), 1968.

6. Bradford Chambers, ed., *Chronicles of Negro Protest: A Background Book for Young People* (Chicago: Parents Magazine Press, 1968), 9.

7. Ibid., 78.

8. See, as instances of both statements, Harvey Wish, ed., *Slavery in the South: First Hand Accounts of the Antebellum American Southland from Northern and Southern Writers, Negroes & Foreign Observers*, vol. 5 of *Encyclopedia Britannica Annals of America* (New York: Farrar Strauss and Company, 1964); and Julius Lester, *To Be a Slave* (New York: Dial Press, 1968).

9. J. B. Duff and P. M. Mitchell, eds., *The Nat Turner Controversy: The Historical Event and the Modern Controversy* (New York: Harper and Row, 1971), vii.

10. Eric Foner, ed., *Nat Turner* (Englewood Cliffs, N.J.: Prentice-Hall, 1971). This was a volume in the publisher's Great Lives Observed series whose announced aim (printed on the title page) was to present "the character and achievement of a great world figure in three perspectives—through his own words, through the opinions of his contemporaries, and through retrospective judgments."

11. Samuel Eliot Morison, *The Oxford History of the American People* (New York: Oxford University Press, 1965).

12. Richard Hofstadter, William Miller, and Daniel Aaron, *The Structure of American History*, 2d ed. (Englewood Cliffs, N.J.: Prentice-Hall, 1973).

13. James H. Dormon and Robert R. Jones, *The Afro-American Experience: A Cultural History Through Emancipation* (New York: Wiley, 1974).

14. James E. Olsen, "Slaves, Psyches, and History," *Journal of Ethnic Studies* 11 (Fall 1983), 101, 102.

15. Elkins, *Slavery*, vii.

16. Peter H. Wood, *Black Majority: Negroes in Colonial South Carolina from 1670 Through the Stono Rebellion* (New York: Alfred A. Knopf, 1974); Gerald Mullin, *Flight and Rebellion: Slave Resistance in Eighteenth-Century Virginia* (New York: Oxford University Press, 1972).

17. John Blassingame, *The Slave Community: Plantation Life in the Antebellum South*, pbk. ed. (New York: Oxford University Press, 1972), 125.

18. See F. Roy Johnson, *The Nat Turner Slave Insurrection* (Murphreesboro, N.C.: Johnson, 1966).

19. Eugene D. Genovese, *Roll, Jordan, Roll: The World the Slaves Made* (New York: Random House, 1972), 594–95.

20. Lawrence W. Levine, *Black Culture and Black Consciousness: Afro-*

American Folk Thought from Slavery to Freedom (New York: Oxford University Press, 1977), 76, 77.

21. Ibid., 80.

22. *Old Memories, New Moods*, vol. 2 of *Americans from Africa*, ed. Peter I. Rose (New York: Atherton Press, 1970), xxv.

23. Henry I. Tragle, "Styron and His Sources," *Massachusetts Review* 1 (Winter 1970): 135–53; republished in Tragle, *The Southampton Slave Revolt*, 398–414. Parenthetical citations are to book publication. See also Tragle's prefatory note in which he apologizes for Styron's presence: "In a work of the present sort Mr. Styron's effort would best be unnoticed, were it not for the aura of historical authenticity with which he has sought to cloak the product of his imagination" (397–98).

24. Fred Chappell, "Six Propositions about Literature and History," 514.

25. Stephen B. Oates, *The Fires of Jubilee: Nat Turner's Fierce Rebellion* (New York: New American Library, 1975), vii.

26. "A sort of 'all-purpose chattel,' as one writer has described him, Nat built the morning fires, hauled water, fed the cows, slopped the hogs" (35).

7. Echoes in the Eighties

1. Fredric Jameson, "Periodizing the Sixties," in *The Sixties Without Apology*, ed. Sohnya Sayres, et al. (Minneapolis: University of Minnesota Press, 1984), 208.

2. Amiri Baraka, *The Motion of History and Other Plays* (New York: William Morrow, 1978), 13.

3. Vincent Harding, *The Other American Revolution* (Los Angeles and Atlanta: Center for Afro-American Studies, UCLA, and Institute for the Black World, 1980), vii–viii.

4. Harding, *There Is a River: The Black Struggle for Freedom in America* (New York: Vintage Books, 1983), xxi.

5. Meier and Rudwick, *Black History and the Historical Profession*, 257. See also Sterling Stuckey, "Slave Resistance as Seen Through Folklore," in *The Black Prism: Perspectives on the Black Experience*, ed. Irene S. Reid (Brooklyn: Faculty Press of Brooklyn College, 1969), 51–60.

6. Eugene Genovese, *From Rebellion to Revolution: Afro-American Slave Revolts in the Making of the Modern World* (Baton Rouge: Louisiana State University Press, 1979), 1.

7. Martin Kilson, "Towards Freedom: An Analysis of Slave Revolts in the U.S.," *Phylon* 25 (Summer 1964): 175–87. Another historian influenced by Kilson's and Genovese's work is Peter Kolchin. In *Unfree Labor: American*

Slavery and Russian Serfdom (Cambridge: Harvard University Press, 1987), Kolchin extends the cross-cultural study of slave resistance by comparing Puyachev's peasant war of 1773–74 to North American revolts such as Nat Turner's. Of the latter he asserts, "these outbreaks were minor affairs that hardly seem to justify the terms *revolt* or *insurrection*. . . . A pervasive *fear* of rebellion certainly engulfed the white South, but the reality was quite different" (253). I thank Waldo E. Martin, Jr., for bringing Kolchin to my attention.

8. Styron, *This Quiet Dust and Other Writings* (New York: Random House, 1982), 3.

9. Henry F. Graff, *America: The Glorious Republic* (Boston: Houghton Mifflin, 1988); Daniel J. Boorstin and Brooks M. Kelley, with Ruth F. Boorstin, *A History of the United States* (Lexington, Mass.: Gunn and Company, 1986); Clarence L. Ver Steeg, *American Spirit: A History of the United States* (Chicago: Follett Publishing Company, 1982); Clarence L. Ver Steeg, *The Story of Our Country* (Evanston, Ill.: Harper and Row, 1965); Margaret Stimman Branson, *America's Heritage* (Lexington, Mass.: Gunn and Company, 1982); William Jay Jacobs, Howard B. Wilder, Robert P. Ludlum, Harriet M. Brown, *America's Story* (Boston: Houghton Mifflin, 1988); Joseph R. Conlin, *Our Land, Our Time: A History of the United States* (San Diego: Coronado Publishing Co., 1987); Lewis P. Todd and Merle Curti, *Rise of the American Nation* (New York: Harcourt Brace Jovanovich, 1982); L. C. Wood, Ralph H. Gabriel, E. L. Biller, *America: Its People and Values* (Orlando, Fla.: Harcourt Brace Jovanovich, 1985); John A. Garraty, *American History* (Orlando, Fla.: Harcourt Brace Jovanovich, 1986); Robert F. Madgic, Stanley S. Seaberg, Fred H. Stopsky, Robin W. Winks, *The American Experience: A Study of Themes and Issues in American History* (Menlo Park, Calif.: Addison-Wesley Publishing Company, 1979).

10. Ruth Wilson, *Our Blood and Tears: Black Freedom Fighters* (New York: Putnam, 1972).

11. "Chains of Slavery—1800–1865" (Chicago: Encyclopedia Britannica Educational Corporation, 1969), ser. 2, Library of Congress filmstrip no. 1862. Consultants included Benjamin Quarles and Sterling Stuckey.

12. Ibid., frames 42, 40.

13. Denise Dennis and Susan Willmarth, *Black History for Beginners* (New York: Writers and Readers Documentary Comic Books, 1984), 8.

14. James C. Morgan, *Slavery in the United States: Four Views* (Jefferson, N.C.: McFarland, 1985).

15. Bertram Wyatt-Brown, *Southern Honor: Ethics and Behavior in the Old South* (New York: Oxford University Press, 1982), xii.

16. John Blassingame, *New Leader*, December 27, 1982, 16–17.

17. Ibid., 17.

18. See Daniel J. Singal, *The War Within: From Victorian to Modernist Thought in the South, 1919–1945* (Chapel Hill: University of North Carolina Press, 1982); Charles Reagan Wilson and William Ferris, eds., *Encyclopedia of Southern Culture* (Chapel Hill: University of North Carolina Press, 1989). An analogous argument about *The History of Southern Literature* (ed. Louis D. Rubin, Jr. [Baton Rouge: Louisiana State University Press, 1985]) is made in my review in *Kenyon Review* 8 (Fall 1986): 125–27.

19. Howell Raines, *New York Times Book Review*, September 17, 1989, 3.

20. David Levering Lewis, "Radical History: Toward Inclusiveness," *Journal of American History* 76 (September 1989): 472.

21. Ibid., 473.

22. Sterling Stuckey, *Slave Culture: Nationalist Theory and the Foundations of Black America* (New York: Oxford University Press, 1987), vii.

23. See Robert S. Starobin, ed., *Denmark Vesey: The Slave Conspiracy of 1822* (Englewood Cliffs, N.J.: Prentice-Hall, 1970); Gerald W. Mullin, *Flight and Rebellion* (New York: Oxford University Press, 1972); William Freehling, *Prelude to Civil War* (New York: Harper and Row, 1965).

24. See Lewis, "Radical History," 474.

25. See, as examples, *New Literary History* 1 (Spring 1970); H. Aram Veeser, ed., *The New Historicism* (New York: Routledge, 1989); and Christopher P. Wilson, "Containing Multitudes: Realism, Historicism, and American Studies," *American Quarterly* 41 (September 1989): 466–95.

26. Hazel V. Carby, "The Historical Novel of Slavery," in *Slavery and the Literary Imagination*, eds. Deborah McDowell and Arnold Rampersad (New York: Columbia University Press, 1989), 139.

27. David Bradley, *The Chaneysville Incident* (New York: Avon Books, 1981), 26.

28. Barbara Foley, "History, Fiction, and the Ground Between: Uses of the Documentary Mode in Black Literature," *PMLA* 95 (May 1980): 389–403. See also her *Telling the Truth: The Theory and Practice of Documentary Fiction* (Ithaca: Cornell University Press, 1986), especially chap. 8, "The Afro-American Documentary Novel."

29. Interview, Patricia Holt, *Publisher's Weekly*, April 10, 1981, 13.

30. *Esquire*, December 1983. Bradley's contribution was "My Hero, Malcolm X."

31. Maya Angelou, *I Know Why the Caged Bird Sings* (New York: Random House, 1970), 152–53. Parenthetical citations are to the 1971 Bantam paperback edition.

32. Alice Childress, *A Hero Ain't Nothin' But a Sandwich* (New York: Coward, 1973). Parenthetical references are to the 1973 Avon paperback edition.

33. See "Meditation on History," in *Midnight Birds*, ed. Mary Helen Wash-

ington (Garden City, N.Y.: Doubleday/Anchor, 1980), 195–248.

34. Sherley Anne Williams, *Dessa Rose* (New York: Morrow, 1986), 5.

35. Aptheker, *American Negro Slave Revolts*, 287–88. See also Angela Davis, "Reflections on Black Women's Roles in the Community of Slaves," *Black Scholar* 3 (December 1971): 3–15.

36. Aptheker, *American Negro Slave Revolts*, 289.

37. David Bradley, review of *Dessa Rose*, *New York Times Book Review*, August 3, 1986, 7.

38. Lewis, "Radical History," 473.

39. *New York Times Book Review*, February 16, 1969, 26.

40. *Des Moines Register*, May 21, 1987.

41. Ibid.

42. Data, and words to this effect, are based on my notes immediately after hearing the broadcast.

43. Lionel Trilling, "What Is Criticism?" in *The Last Decade: Essays and Reviews, 1965–1975*, ed. Diana Trilling (New York: Harcourt Brace Jovanovich, 1979), 88. Guenther Lenz points up some of the elitist contradictions in Trilling's notion of culture-as-dialogue in "American Studies and the Radical Tradition," *Prospects: An Annual of American Cultural Studies* 12 (1987): 21–58, especially 39–40.

44. Lewis, "Radical History," 473.

Appendix

What follows is a reprint of the first edition of Thomas R. Gray's *The Confessions of Nat Turner*. This text was reproduced from an original copy in the Beinecke Library of Yale University.

The Confessions of Nat Turner

The leader of the late insurrection in Southampton, Va. as fully and voluntarily made to Thomas R. Gray, in the prison where he was confined, and acknowledged by him to be such when read before the Court of Southampton; with the certificate, under seal of the Court convened at Jerusalem, Nov. 5, 1831, for his trial.

Also, an authentic account of the whole insurrection, with lists of the Whites who were murdered, and of the Negroes brought before the Court of Southampton, and there sentenced, &c.

Baltimore: Published by Thomas R. Gray.

Lucas & Deaver, print. 1831.

APPENDIX

DISTRICT OF COLUMBIA, TO WIT:

Be it remembered, That on this tenth day of November, Anno Domini, eighteen hundred and thirty-one, Thomas R. Gray of the said District, deposited in this office the title of a book, which is in the words as following:

"The Confessions of Nat Turner, the leader of the late insurrection in Southampton, Virginia, as fully and voluntarily made to Thomas R. Gray, in the prison where he was confined, and acknowledged by him to be such when read before the Court of Southampton; with the certificate, under seal, of the Court convened at Jerusalem, November 5, 1831, for his trial. Also, an authentic account of the whole insurrection, with lists of the whites who were murdered, and of the negroes brought before the Court of Southampton, and there sentenced, &c. the right whereof he claims as proprietor, in conformity with an Act of Congress, entitled "An act to amend the several acts respecting Copy Rights."

> EDMUND J. LEE, Clerk of the District.
>
> In testimony that the above is a true copy, from the record of the District Court for the District of Columbia, I, Edmund I. Lee, the Clerk thereof, have hereunto set my hand and affixed the seal of my office, this 10th day of November, 1831.
>
> EDMUND J. LEE, C. C. C.

TO THE PUBLIC

The late insurrection in Southampton has greatly excited the public mind, and led to a thousand idle, exaggerated and mischievous reports. It is the first instance in our history of an open rebellion of the slaves, and attended with such atrocious circumstances of cruelty and destruction, as could not fail to leave a deep impression, not only upon the minds of the community where this fearful tragedy was wrought, but throughout every portion of our country, in which this population is to be found. Public curiosity has been on the stretch to understand the origin and progress of this dreadful conspiracy, and the motives which influences its diabolical actors. The insurgent slaves had all been destroyed, or apprehended, tried, and executed, (with the exception of the leader,) without revealing any thing at all satisfactory, as to the motives which governed them, or the means by which they expected to accomplish their object. Every thing connected with this sad affair was wrapt in mystery, until Nat Turner, the leader of this ferocious band, whose name has resounded throughout our widely extended empire, was captured. This "great Bandit" was taken by a single individual, in a cave near the residence of his late owner, on Sunday, the thirtieth of October, without attempting to make the slightest resistance, and on the following day safely lodged in the jail of the County. His captor was Benjamin Phipps, armed with a shot gun well charged. Nat's only weapon was a small light sword which he immediately surrendered, and begged that his life might be spared. Since his confinement, by permission of the Jailor, I have had ready access to him, and finding that he was willing to make a full and free confession of the origin, progress and consummation of the insurrectory movements of the slaves of which he was the contriver and head; I determined for the gratification of public curiosity to commit his statements to writing, and publish them, with little or no variation, from his own words. That this is a faithful record of his confessions, the annexed certificate of the County Court of Southampton, will attest. They certainly bear one stamp of truth and sincerity. He makes no attempt (as all the other insurgents who were examined did,) to exculpate himself, but frankly acknowledges his full participation in all the guilt of the transaction. He was not only the contriver of the conspiracy, but gave the first blow towards its execution.

It will thus appear, that whilst every thing upon the surface of society wore a calm and peaceful aspect; whilst not one note of preparation was heard to warn the devoted inhabitants of woe and death, a gloomy fanatic was revolving in the recesses of his own dark, bewildered, and overwrought mind, schemes of indiscriminate massacre to the whites. Schemes too fearfully executed as far as his fiendish band proceeded in their desolating march. No cry for mercy penetrated their flinty bosoms. No acts of remembered kindness made the least impression upon these remorseless murderers. Men, women and children, from hoary age to helpless infancy were involved in the same cruel fate. Never did a band of savages do their work of death more unsparingly. Apprehension for their own personal safety seems to have been the only principle of restraint in the whole course of their bloody proceedings. And it is not the least remarkable feature in this horrid transaction, that a band actuated by such hellish purposes, should have resisted so feebly, when met by the whites in arms. Desperation alone, one would think, might have led to greater efforts. More than twenty of them attacked Dr. Blunt's house on Tuesday morning, a little before daybreak, defended by two men and three boys. They fled precipitately at the first fire; and their future plans of mischief, were entirely disconcerted and broken up. Escaping thence, each individual sought his own safety either in concealment, or by returning home, with the hope that his participation might escape detection, and all were shot down in the course of a few days, or captured and brought to trial and punishment. Nat has survived all his followers, and the gallows will speedily close his career. His own account of the conspiracy is submitted to the public, without comment. It reads an awful, and it is hoped, a useful lesson, as to the operations of a mind like his, endeavoring to grapple with things beyond its reach. How it first became bewildered and confounded, and finally corrupted and led to the conception and perpetration of the most atrocious and heart-rending deeds. It is calculated also to demonstrate the policy of our laws in restraint of this class of our population, and to induce all those entrusted with their execution, as well as our citizens generally, to see that they are strictly and rigidly enforced. Each particular community should look to its own safety, whilst the general guardians of the laws, keep a watchful eye over all. If Nat's statements can be relied on, the insurrection in this county was entirely local, and his designs confided but to a few, and these in his immediate vicinity. It was not instigated by motives of revenge or sudden anger, but the results of long deliberation, and a settled purpose of mind. The offspring of gloomy fanaticism, acting upon materials but too well prepared for such impressions. It will be long remembered in the annals of our country, and many a mother as she presses her infant darling to her bosom, will shudder at the recollection of Nat Turner, and his band of ferocious miscreants.

Believing the following narrative, by removing doubts and conjectures from the public mind which otherwise must have remained, would give general satisfaction, it is respectfully submitted to the public by their ob't serv't,

T. R. GRAY.

Jerusalem, Southampton, Va., Nov. 5, 1831.

We the undersigned, members of the Court convened at Jerusalem, on Saturday, the 5th day of Nov. 1831, for the trial of Nat, *alias* Nat

Turner, a negro slave, late the property of Putnam Moore, deceased, do hereby certify, that the confessions of Nat, to Thomas R. Gray, was read to him in our presence, and that Nat acknowledged the same to be full, free, and voluntary; and that furthermore, when called upon by the presiding Magistrate of the Court, to state if he had any thing to say, why sentence of death should not be passed upon him, replied he had nothing further than he had communicated to Mr. Gray. Given under our hands and seals at Jerusalem, this 5th day of November, 1831.

JEREMIAH COBB, [Seal.]
THOMAS PRETLOW, [Seal.]
JAMES W. PARKER, [Seal.]
CARR BOWERS, [Seal.]
SAMUEL B. HINES, [Seal.]
ORRIS A. BROWNE, [Seal.]

State of Virginia, Southampton County, to wit:
I, James Rochelle, Clerk of the County Court of Southampton in the State of Virginia, do hereby certify, that Jeremiah Cobb, Thomas Pretlow, James W. Parker, Carr Bowers, Samuel B. Hines, and Orris A. Browne, esqr's are acting Justices of the Peace, in and for the County aforesaid, and were members of the Court which convened at Jerusalem, on Saturday the 5th day of November, 1831, for the trial of Nat *alias* Nat Turner, a negro slave, late the property of Putnam Moore, deceased, who was tried and convicted, as an insurgent in the late insurrection in the county of Southampton aforesaid, and that full faith and credit are due, and ought to be given to their acts as Justices of the peace aforesaid.

[Seal.] In testimony whereof, I have hereunto set my hand and caused the seal of the Court aforesaid, to be affixed this 5th day of November, 1831.
JAMES ROCHELLE, C. S. C. C.

CONFESSION

Agreeable to his own appointment, on the evening he was committed to prison, with permission of the jailer, I visited NAT on Tuesday the

APPENDIX

1st November, when, without being questioned at all, he commenced his narrative in the following words:—

SIR,—You have asked me to give a history of the motives which induced me to undertake the late insurrection, as you call it—To do so I must go back to the days of my infancy, and even before I was born. I was thirty-one years of age the 2d of October last, and born the property of Benj. Turner, of this county. In my childhood a circumstance occurred which made an indelible impression on my mind, and laid the ground work of that enthusiasm, which has terminated so fatally to many, both white and black, and for which I am about to atone at the gallows. It is here necessary to relate this circumstance—trifling as it may seem, it was the commencement of that belief which has grown with time, and even now, sir, in this dungeon, helpless and forsaken as I am, I cannot divest myself of. Being at play with other children, when three or four years old, I was telling them something, which my mother overhearing, said it had happened before I was born—I stuck to my story, however, and related somethings which went, in her opinion, to confirm it—others being called on were greatly astonished, knowing that these things had happened, and caused them to say in my hearing, I surely would be a prophet, as the Lord had shewn me things that had happened before my birth. And my father and mother strengthened me in this my first impression, saying in my presence, I was intended for some great purpose, which they had always thought from certain marks on my head and breast—[a parcel of excrescences which I believe are not at all uncommon, particularly among negroes, as I have seen several with the same. In this case he has either cut them off or they have nearly disappeared]—My grand mother, who was very religious, and to whom I was much attached—my master, who belonged to the church, and other religious persons who visited the house, and whom I often saw at prayers, noticing the singularity of my manners, I suppose, and my uncommon intelligence for a child, remarked I had too much sense to be raised, and if I was, I would never be of any service to any one as a slave—To a mind like mine, restless, inquisitive and observant of every thing that was passing, it is easy to suppose that religion was the subject to which it would be directed, and although this subject principally occupied my thoughts—there was nothing that I saw or heard of to which my attention was not directed—The manner in which I learned to read and write, not only had great influence on my own mind, as I acquired it with the most perfect ease, so much so, that I have no recollection whatever of learning the alphabet—but to the astonishment of the family, one day, when a book was shewn me to keep me from crying, I began spelling the names of different objects—this was a source of wonder to all in the neighborhood, particularly the blacks—and this learning was constantly improved at all opportunities—when I got large enough to go to work, while employed, I was reflecting on many things that would present themselves to my imagination, and whenever an opportunity occurred of looking at a book, when the school children were getting their lessons, I would find many things that the fertility of my own imagination had depicted to me before; all my time, not devoted to my master's service, was spent either in prayer, or in making experiments in casting different things in moulds made of earth, in attempting to make paper, gun-powder, and many other experiments, that although I could not perfect, yet convinced me of its practicability if I had the means.* I was not addicted to stealing in my youth, nor have ever been—Yet such was the confidence of the negroes in the neighborhood, even at this early period of my life, in my superior judgment, that they would often carry me with them when they were going on any roguery, to plan for them. Growing up among them, with this confidence in my superior judgment, and when this, in their opinions, was perfected by Divine inspiration, from the circumstances already alluded to in my infancy, and which belief was ever afterwards zealously inculcated by the austerity of my life and manners, which became the subject of remark by white and black.— Having soon discovered to be great, I must appear so, and therefore studiously avoided mixing in society, and wrapped myself in mystery, devoting my time to fasting and prayer—By this time, having arrived to man's estate, and hearing the scriptures commented on at meetings, I was struck with that particular passage which says: "Seek ye the kingdom of Heaven and all things shall be added unto you." I reflected much on this passage, and prayed daily for light on this subject—As I was praying one day at my plough, the spirit spoke to me, saying "Seek ye the kingdom of Heaven and all things shall be added unto you.

*When questioned as to the manner of manufacturing those different articles, he was found well informed on the subject.

Question—what do you mean by the Spirit. Ans. The Spirit that spoke to the prophets in former days—and I was greatly astonished, and for two years prayed continually, whenever my duty would permit—and then again I had the same revelation, which fully confirmed me in the impression that I was ordained for some great purpose in the hands of the Almighty. Several years rolled round, in which many events occurred to strengthen me in this my belief. At this time I reverted in my mind to the remarks made of me in my childhood, and the things that had been shown me—and as it had been said of me in my childhood by those by whom I had been taught to pray, both white and black, and in whom I had the greatest confidence, that I had too much sense to be raised, and if I was, I would never be of any use to any one as a slave. Now finding I had arrived to man's estate, and was a slave, and these revelations being made known to me, I began to direct my attention to this great object, to fulfil the purpose for which, by this time, I felt assured I was intended. Knowing the influence I had obtained over the minds of my fellow servants, (not by the means of conjuring and such like tricks—for to them I always spoke of such things with contempt) but by the communion of the Spirit whose revelations I often communicated to them, and they believed and said my wisdom came from God. I now began to prepare them for my purpose, by telling them something was about to happen that would terminate in fulfilling the great promise that had been made to me—About this time I was placed under an overseer, from whom I ranaway—and after remaining in the woods thirty days, I returned, to the astonishment of the negroes on the plantation, who thought I had made my escape to some other part of the country, as my father had done before. But the reason of my return was, that the Spirit appeared to me and said I had my wishes directed to the things of this world, and not to the kingdom of Heaven, and that I should return to the service of my earthly master—"For he who knoweth his Master's will, and doeth it not, shall be beaten with many stripes, and thus have I chastened you." And the negroes found fault, and murmured against me, saying that if they had my sense they would not serve any master in the world. And about this time I had a vision—and I saw white spirits and black spirits engaged in battle, and the sun was darkened—the thunder rolled in the Heavens, and blood flowed in streams—and I heard a voice saying, "Such is your luck, such you are called to see, and let it come rough or smooth, you must surely bare it." I now withdrew myself as much as my situation would permit, from the intercourse of my fellow servants, for the avowed purpose of serving the Spirit more fully—and it appeared to me, and reminded me of the things it had already shown me, and that it would then reveal to me the knowledge of the elements, the revolution of the planets, the operation of tides, and changes of the seasons. After this revelation in the year 1825, and the knowledge of the elements being made known to me, I sought more than ever to obtain true holiness before the great day of judgment should appear, and then I began to receive the true knowledge of faith. And from the first steps of righteousness until the last, was I made perfect; and the Holy Ghost was with me, and said, "Behold me as I stand in the Heavens"—and I looked and saw the forms of men in different attitudes—and there were lights in the sky to which the children of darkness gave other names than what they really were—for they were the lights of the Saviour's hands, stretched forth from east to west, even as they were extended on the cross on Calvary for the redemption of sinners. And I wondered greatly at these miracles, and prayed to be informed of a certainty of the meaning thereof—and shortly afterwards, while laboring in the field, I discovered drops of blood on the corn as though it were dew from heaven—and I communicated it to many, both white and black, in the neighborhood—and I then found on the leaves in the woods hieroglyphic characters, and numbers, with the forms of men in different attitudes, portrayed in blood, and representing the figures I had seen before in the heavens. And now the Holy Ghost had revealed itself to me, and made plain the miracles it had shown me—For as the blood of Christ had been shed on this earth, and had ascended to heaven for the salvation of sinners, and was now returning to earth again in the form of dew—and as the leaves on the trees bore the impression of the figures I had seen in the heavens, it was plain to me that the Saviour was about to lay down the yoke he had borne for the sins of men, and the great day of judgment was at hand. About this time I told these things to a white man, (Etheldred T. Brantley) on whom it had a wonderful effect—and he ceased from his wickedness, and was attacked immediately with a cutaneous eruption, and blood oozed from the pores of his skin, and after praying and fasting nine days, he was healed, and the Spirit appeared to me again, and said, as the Saviour had been baptised so should we be also—and when the white people would not let us be baptised by the church, we went down into the water together, in the sight of many who reviled us, and were baptised by the Spirit—After this I rejoiced greatly, and gave thanks to God. And on the 12th of May, 1828, I heard a loud noise in the heavens, and the Spirit instantly appeared to me and said the Serpent was loosened, and Christ had laid down the yoke he had borne for the sins of men, and that I should take it on and fight against the Serpent, for the time was fast approaching when the first should be last and the last should be first. Ques. Do you not find yourself mistaken now? Ans. Was not Christ crucified. And by signs in the heavens that it would make known to me when I should commence the great work—and until the first sign appeared, I should conceal it from the knowledge of men— And on the appearance of the sign, (the eclipse of the sun last February) I should arise and prepare myself, and slay my enemies with their own weapons. And immediately on the sign appearing in the heavens, the seal was removed from my lips, and I communicated the great work laid out for me to do, to four in whom I had the greatest confidence, (Henry, Hark, Nelson, and Sam)—it was intended by us to have begun the work of death on the 4th July last—Many were the plans formed and rejected by us, and it affected my mind to such a degree, that I fell sick, and the time passed without our coming to any determination how to commence—Still forming new schemes and rejecting them, when the sign appeared again, which determined me not to wait longer.

Since the commencement of 1830, I had been living with Mr. Joseph Travis, who was to me a kind master, and placed the greatest confidence in me; in fact, I had no cause to complain of his treatment to me. On Saturday evening, the 20th of August, it was agreed between Henry, Hark and myself, to prepare a dinner the next day for the men we expected, and then to concert a plan, as we had not yet determined on any. Hark, on the following morning, brought a pig, and Henry brandy, and being joined by Sam, Nelson, Will and Jack, they prepared in the woods a dinner, where, about three o'clock, I joined them.

Q. Why were you so backward in joining them.

A. The same reason that had caused me not to mix with them for years before.

I saluted them on coming up, and asked Will how came he there, he answered, his life was worth no more than others, and his liberty as dear to him. I asked him if he thought to obtain it? He said he would, or loose his life. This was enough to put him in full confidence. Jack,

I knew, was only a tool in the hands of Hark, it was quickly agreed we should commence at home (Mr. J. Travis') on that night, and until we had armed and equipped ourselves, and gathered sufficient force, neither age nor sex was to be spared, (which was invariably adhered to.) We remained at the feast, until about two hours in the night, when we went to the house and found Austin; they all went to the cider press and drank, except myself. On returning to the house, Hark went to the door with an axe, for the purpose of breaking it open, as we knew we were strong enough to murder the family, if they were awaked by the noise; but reflecting that it might create an alarm in the neighborhood, we determined to enter the house secretly, and murder them whilst sleeping. Hark got a ladder and set it against the chimney, on which I ascended, and hoisting a window, entered and came down stairs, unbarred the door, and removed the guns from their places. It was then observed that I must spill the first blood. On which, armed with a hatchet, and accompanied by Will, I entered my master's chamber, it being dark, I could not give a death blow, the hatchet glanced from his head, he sprang from the bed and called his wife, it was his last work, Will laid him dead, with a blow of his axe, and Mrs. Travis shared the same fate, as she lay in bed. The murder of this family, five in number, was the work of a moment, not one of them awoke; there was a little infant sleeping in a cradle, that was forgotten, until we had left the house and gone some distance, when Henry and Will returned and killed it; we got here, four guns that would shoot, and several old muskets, with a pound or two of powder. We remained some time at the barn, where we paraded; I formed them in a line as soldiers, and after carrying them through all the manoeuvres I was master of, marched them off to Mr. Salathul Francis', about six hundred yards distant. Sam and Will went to the door and knocked. Mr. Francis asked who was there, Sam replied it was him, and he had a letter for him, on which he got up and came to the door; they immediately seized him, and dragging him out a little from the door, he was dispatched by repeated blows on the head; there was no other white person in the family. We started from there for Mrs. Reese's, maintaining the most perfect silence on our march, where finding the door unlocked, we entered, and murdered Mrs. Reese in her bed, while sleeping; her son awoke, but it was only to sleep the sleep of death, he had only time to say who is that, and he was no more. From Mrs. Reese's we went to Mrs. Turner's, a mile distant, which we reached about sunrise, on Monday morning. Henry, Austin, and Sam, went to the still, where, finding Mr. Peebles, Austin shot him, and the rest of us went to the house; as we approached, the family discovered us, and shut the door. Vain hope! Will, with one stroke of his axe, opened it, and we entered and found Mrs. Turner and Mrs. Newsome in the middle of a room, almost frightened to death. Will immediately killed Mrs. Turner, with one blow of his axe. I took Mrs. Newsome by the hand, and with the sword I had when I was apprehended, I struck her several blows over the head, but not being able to kill her, as the sword was dull. Will turning around and discovering it, despatched her also. A general destruction of property and search for money and ammunition, always succeeded the murders. By this time my company amounted to fifteen, and nine men mounted, who started for Mrs. Whitehead's, (the other six were to go through a by way to Mr. Bryant's, and rejoin us at Mrs. Whitehead's,) as we approached the house we discovered Mr. Richard Whitehead standing in the cotton patch, near the lane fence; we called him over into the lane, and Will, the executioner, was near at hand, with his fatal axe, to send him to an untimely grave. As we pushed on to the house, I discovered some one run round the garden, and thinking it was some of the white family, I pursued them, but finding it was a servant girl belonging to the house, I returned to commence the work of death, but they whom I left, had not been idle; all the family were already murdered, but Mrs. Whitehead and her daughter Margaret. As I came round to the door I saw Will pulling Mrs. Whitehead out of the house, and at the step he nearly severed her head from her body, with his broad axe. Miss Margaret, when I discovered her, had concealed herself in the corner, formed by the projection of the cellar cap from the house; on my approach she fled, but was soon overtaken, and after repeated blows with a sword, I killed her by a blow on the head, with a fence rail. By this time, the six who had gone by Mr. Bryant's, rejoined us, and informed me they had done the work of death assigned them. We again divided, part going to Mr. Richard Porter's, and from thence to Nathaniel Francis', the others to Mr. Howell Harris', and Mr. T. Doyles. On my reaching Mr. Porter's, he had escaped with his family. I understood there, that the alarm had already spread, and I immediately returned to bring up those sent to Mr. Doyles, and Mr. Howell Harris'; the party I left going on to Mr. Francis', having told them I would join them in that neighborhood. I met these sent to Mr. Doyles' and Mr. Harris' returning, having met Mr. Doyle on the road and killed him; and learning from some who joined them, that Mr. Harris was from home, I immediately pursued the course taken by the party gone on before; but knowing they would complete the work of death and pillage, at Mr. Francis' before I could get there, I went to Mr. Peter Edwards', expecting to find them there, but they had been here also. I then went to Mr. John T. Barrow's, they had been here and murdered him. I pursued on their track to Capt. Newit Harris', where I found the greater part mounted, and ready to start; the men now amounting to about forty, shouted and hurraed as I rode up, some were in the yard, loading their guns, others drinking. They said Captain Harris and his family had escaped, the property in the house they destroyed, robbing him of money and other valuables. I ordered them to mount and march instantly, this was about nine or ten o'clock, Monday morning. I proceeded to Mr. Levi Waller's, two or three miles distant. I took my station in the rear, and as it 'twas my object to carry terror and devastation wherever we went, I placed fifteen or twenty of the best armed and most to be relied on, in front, who generally approached the houses as fast as their horses could run; this was for two purposes, to prevent their escape and strike terror to the inhabitants—on this account I never got to the houses, after leaving Mrs. Whitehead's, until the murders were committed, except in one case. I sometimes got in sight in time to see the work of death completed, viewed the mangled bodies as they lay, in silent satisfaction, and immediately started in quest of other victims—Having murdered Mrs. Waller and ten children, we started for Mr. William Williams'—having killed him and two little boys that were there; while engaged in this, Mrs. Williams fled and got some distance from the house, but she was pursued, overtaken, and compelled to get up behind one of the company, who brought her back, and after showing her the mangled body of her lifeless husband, she was told to get down and lay by his side, where she was shot dead. I then started for Mr. Jacob Williams, where the family were murdered—Here we found a young man named Drury, who had come on business with Mr. Williams—he was pursued, overtaken and shot. Mrs. Vaughan was the next place we visited—and after murdering the family here, I determined on starting for Jerusalem—Our number amounted now to fifty or sixty, all mounted and armed with guns, axes, swords and clubs—On reaching Mr. James W.

Parker's gate, immediately on the road leading to Jerusalem, and about three miles distant, it was proposed to me to call there, but I objected, as I knew he was gone to Jerusalem, and my object was to reach there as soon as possible; but some of the men having relations at Mr. Parker's it was agreed that they might call and get his people. I remained at the gate on the road, with seven or eight; the others going across the field to the house, about half a mile off. After waiting some time for them, I became impatient, and started to the house for them, and on our return we were met by a party of white men, who had pursued our blood-stained track, and who had fired on those at the gate, and dispersed them, which I knew nothing of, not having been at that time rejoined by any of them—Immediately on discovering the whites, I ordered my men to halt and form, as they appeared to be alarmed—The white men, eighteen in number, approached us in about one hundred yards, when one of them fired, (this was against the positive orders of Captain Alexander P. Peete, who commanded, and who had directed the men to reserve their fire until within thirty paces) And I discovered about half of them retreating, I then ordered my men to fire and rush on them; the few remaining stood their ground until we approached within fifty yards, when they fired and retreated. We pursued and overtook some of them who we thought we left dead; (they were not killed) after pursuing them about two hundred yards, and rising a little hill, I discovered they were met by another party, and had halted, and were re-loading their guns, (this was a small party from Jerusalem who knew the negroes were in the field, and had just tied their horses to await their return to the road, knowing that Mr. Parker and family were in Jerusalem, but knew nothing of the party that had gone in with Captain Peete; on hearing the firing they immediately rushed to the spot and arrived just in time to arrest the progress of these barbarious villains, and save the lives of their friends and fellow citizens.) Thinking that those who retreated first, and the party who fired on us at fifty or sixty yards distant, had all only fallen back to meet others with ammunition. As I saw them re-loading their guns, and more coming up than I saw at first, and several of my bravest men being wounded, the others became panick struck and squandered over the field; the white men pursued and fired on us several times. Hark had his horse shot under him, and I caught another for him as it was running by me; five or six of my men were wounded, but none left on the field; finding myself defeated here I instantly determined to go through a private way, and cross the Nottoway river at the Cypress Bridge, three miles below Jerusalem, and attack that place in the rear, as I expected they would look for me on the other road, and I had a great desire to get there to procure arms and ammunition. After going a short distance in this private way, accompanied by about twenty men, I overtook two or three who told me the others were dispersed in every direction. After trying in vain to collect a sufficient force to proceed to Jerusalem, I determined to return, as I was sure they would make back to their old neighborhood, where they would rejoin me, make new recruits, and come down again. On my way back, I called at Mrs. Thomas's, Mrs. Spencer's, and several other places, the white families having fled, we found no more victims to gratify our thirst for blood, we stopped at Majr. Ridley's quarter for the night, and being joined by four of his men, with the recruits made since my defeat, we mustered now about forty strong. After placing out sentinels, I laid down to sleep, but was quickly roused by a great racket; starting up, I found some mounted, and others in great confusion; one of the sentinels having given the alarm that we were about to be attacked, I ordered some to ride round and reconnoitre, and on their return the others being more alarmed, not knowing who they were, fled in different ways, so that I was reduced to about twenty again; with this I determined to attempt to recruit, and proceed on to rally in the neighborhood, I had left. Dr. Blunt's was the nearest house, which we reached just before day; on riding up the yard, Hark fired a gun. We expected Dr. Blunt and his family were at Maj. Ridley's, as I knew there was a company of men there; the gun was fired to ascertain if any of the family were at home; we were immediately fired upon and retreated, leaving several of my men. I do not know what became of them, as I never saw them afterwards. Pursuing our course back and coming in sight of Captain Harris', where we had been the day before, we discovered a party of white men at the house, on which all deserted me but two, (Jacob and Nat,) we concealed ourselves in the woods until near night, when I sent them in search of Henry, Sam, Nelson, and Hark, and directed them to rally all they could, at the place we had had our dinner the Sunday before, where they would find me, and I accordingly returned there as soon as it was dark and remained until Wednesday evening, when discovering white men riding around the place as though they were looking for some one, and none of my men joining me, I concluded Jacob and Nat had been taken, and compelled to betray me. On this I gave up all hope for the present; and on Thursday night after having supplied myself with provisions from Mr. Travis's, I scratched a hole under a pile of fence rails in a field, where I concealed myself for six weeks, never leaving my hiding place but for a few minutes in the dead of night to get water which was very near; thinking by this time I could venture out, I began to go about in the night and eaves drop the houses in the neighborhood; pursuing this course for about a fortnight and gathering little or no intelligence, afraid of speaking to any human being, and returning every morning to my cave before the dawn of day. I know not how long I might have led this life, if accident had not betrayed me, a dog in the neighborhood passing by my hiding place one night while I was out, was attracted by some meat I had in my cave, and crawled in and stole it, and was coming out just as I returned. A few nights after, two negroes having started to go hunting with the same dog, and passed that way, the dog came again to the place, and having just gone out to walk about, discovered me and barked, on which thinking myself discovered, I spoke to them to beg concealment. On making myself known they fled from me. Knowing then they would betray me, I immediately left my hiding place, and was pursued almost incessantly until I was taken a fortnight afterwards by Mr. Benjamin Phipps, in a little hole I had dug out with my sword, for the purpose of concealment, under the top of a fallen tree. On Mr. Phipps' discovering the place of my concealment, he cocked his gun and aimed at me. I requested him not to shoot and I would give up, upon which he demanded my sword. I delivered it to him, and he brought me to prison. During the time I was pursued, I had many hair breadth escapes, which your time will not permit you to relate. I am here loaded with chains, and willing to suffer the fate that awaits me.

I here proceeded to make some inquiries of him, after assuring him of the certain death that awaited him, and that concealment would only bring destruction on the innocent as well as guilty, of his own color, if he knew of any extensive or concerted plan. His answer was, I do not. When I questioned him as to the insurrection in North Carolina happening about the same time, he denied any knowledge of it; and when I looked him in the face as though I would search his inmost thoughts, he replied, "I see sir, you doubt my word; but can you not think the same ideas, and strange appearances about this time in the heaven's might prompt others, as well as myself, to this undertaking." I now had much conversation with and asked him many questions, having forborne to do so previously, except in the cases noted in parenthesis; but during his statement, I had, unnoticed by him, taken notes as to some particular circumstances, and having the advantage of his statement before me in writing, on the evening of the third day that I had been with him, I began a cross examination, and found his statement corroborated by every circumstance coming within my own knowledge or the confessions of others whom had been either killed or executed, and whom he had not seen nor had any knowledge since 22d of August last, he expressed himself fully satisfied as to the impracticability of his attempt. It has been said he was ignorant and cowardly, and that his object was to murder and rob for the purpose of obtaining money to make his escape. It is notorious, that he was never known to have a dollar in his life; to swear an oath, or drink a drop of spirits. As to his ignorance, he certainly never had the advantages of education, but he can read and write, (it was taught him by his parents,) and for natural intelligence and quickness of apprehension, is surpassed by few men I have ever seen. As to his being a coward, his reason as given for not resisting Mr. Phipps, shews the decision of his character. When he saw Mr. Phipps present his gun, he said he knew it was impossible for him to escape as the woods were full of men; he therefore thought it was better to surrender, and trust to fortune for his escape. He is a complete fanatic, or plays his part most admirably. On other subjects he possesses an uncommon share of intelligence, with a mind capable of attaining any thing; but warped and perverted by the influence of early impressions. He is below the ordinary stature, though strong and active, having the true negro face, every feature of which is strongly marked. I shall not attempt to describe the effect of his narrative, as told and commented on by himself, in the condemned hole of the prison. The calm, deliberate composure with which he spoke of his late deeds and intentions, the expression of his fiend-like face when excited by enthusiasm, still bearing the stains of the blood of helpless innocence about him; clothed with rags and covered with chains; yet daring to raise his manacled hands to heaven, with a spirit soaring above the attributes of man; I looked on him and my blood curdled in my veins.

I will not shock the feelings of humanity, nor wound afresh the bosoms of the disconsolate sufferers in this unparalleled and inhuman massacre, by detailing the deeds of their fiend-like barbarity. There were two or three who were in the power of these wretches, had they known it, and who escaped in the most providential manner. There were two whom they thought they left dead on the field at Mr. Parker's, but who were only stunned by the blows of their guns, as they did not take time to re-load when they charged on them. The escape of a little girl who went to school at Mr. Waller's, and where the children were collecting for that purpose, excited general sympathy. As their teacher had not arrived, they were at play in the yard, and seeing the negroes approach, she ran up on a dirt chimney, (such as are common to log houses,) and remained there unnoticed during the massacre of the eleven that were killed at this place. She remained on her hiding place till just before the arrival of a party, who were in pursuit of the murderers, when she came down and fled to a swamp, where, a mere child as she was, with the horrors of the late scene before her, she lay concealed until the next day, when seeing a party go up to the house, she came up, and on being asked how she escaped, replied with the utmost simplicity, "The Lord helped her." She was taken up behind a gentleman of the party, and returned to the arms of her weeping mother. Miss Whitehead concealed herself between the bed and the mat that supported it, while they murdered her sister in the same room, without discovering her. She was afterwards carried off, and concealed for protection by a slave of the family, who gave evidence against several of them on their trial. Mrs. Nathaniel Francis, while concealed in a closet heard their blows, and the shrieks of the victims of these ruthless savages; they then entered the closet where she was concealed, and went out without discovering her. While in this hiding place, she heard two of her women in a quarrel about the division of her clothes. Mr. John T. Barron, discovering them approaching his house, told his wife to make her escape, and scorning to fly, fell fighting on his own threshold. After firing his rifle, he discharged his gun at them, and then broke it over the villain who first approached him, but he was overpowered, and slain. His bravery, however, saved from the hands of these monsters, his lovely and amiable wife, who will long lament a husband so deserving of her love. As directed by him, she attempted to escape through the garden, when she was caught and held by one of her servant girls, but another coming to her rescue, she fled to the woods, and concealed herself. Few indeed, were those who escaped their work of death. But fortunate for society, the hand of retributive justice has overtaken them; and not one that was known to be concerned has escaped.

The Commonwealth } Charged with making insurrection, and plot-
vs. } ting to take away the lives of divers free white
Nat Turner. } persons, &c. on the 22d of August, 1831.

The court composed of _____, having met for the trial of Nat Turner, the prisoner was brought in and arraigned, and upon his arraignment pleaded *Not guilty;* saying to his counsel, that he did not feel so.

On the part of the Commonwealth, Levi Waller was introduced, who being sworn, deposed as follows: (agreeably to Nat's own Confession.) Col. Trezvant* was then introduced, who being sworn, narrated Nat's Confession to him, as follows: (his Confession as given to Mr. Gray.) The prisoner introduced no evidence, and the case was submitted without argument to the court, who having found him guilty, Jeremiah Cobb, Esq. Chairman, pronounced the sentence of the court, in the following words: "Nat Turner! Stand up. Have you any thing to say why sentence of death should not be pronounced against you?

Ans. I have not, I have made a full confession to Mr. Gray, and I have nothing more to say.

Attend then to the sentence of the Court. You have been arraigned and tried before this court, and convicted of one of the highest crimes in our criminal code. You have been convicted of plotting in cold blood, the indiscriminate destruction of men, of helpless women, and of infant children. The evidence before us leaves not a shadow of doubt, but that your hands were often imbrued in the blood of the innocent; and your own confession tells us that they were stained with the blood of a master; in your own language, "too indulgent." Could I stop here, your crime would be sufficiently aggravated. But the original contriver of a plan, deep and deadly, one that never can be effected, you managed so far to put it into execution, as to deprive us of many of our most valuable citizens; and this was done when they were asleep, and defenceless; under circumstances shocking to humanity. And while upon this part of the subject, I cannot but call your attention to the poor misguided wretches who have gone before you. They are not few in number—

---

*The committing Magistrate.

they were your bosom associates; and the blood of all cries aloud, and calls upon you, as the author of their misfortune. Yes! You forced them unprepared, from Time to Eternity. Borne down by this load of guilt, your only justification is, that you were led away by fanaticism. If this be true, from my soul I pity you; and while you have my sympathies, I am, nevertheless called upon to pass the sentence of the court. The time between this and your execution, will necessarily be very short; and your only hope must be in another world. The judgment of the court is, that you be taken hence to the jail from whence you came, thence to the place of execution, and on Friday next, between the hours of 10 A.M. and 2 P.M. be hung by the neck until you are dead! dead! dead and may the Lord have mercy upon your soul.

A list of persons murdered in the Insurrection, on the 21st and 22d of August, 1831.
Joseph Travers and wife and three children, Mrs. Elizabeth Turner, Hartwell Prebles, Sarah Newsome, Mrs. P. Reese and son William, Trajan Doyle, Henry Bryant and wife and child, and wife's mother, Mrs. Catharine Whitehead, son Richard and four daughters and grandchild, Salathiel Francis, Nathaniel Francis' overseer and two children, John T. Barrow, George Vaughan, Mrs. Levi Waller and ten children, William Williams, wife and two boys, Mrs. Caswell Worrell and child, Mrs. Rebecca Vaughan, Ann Eliza Vaughan, and son Arthur, Mrs. John K. Williams and child, Mrs. Jacob Williams and three children, and Edwin Drury—amounting to fifty-five.

A List of Negroes brought before the Court of Southampton, with their owners' names, and sentence.

Daniel,	Richard Porter,	Convicted.
Moses,	J.T. Barrow,	Do.
Tom,	Caty Whitehead,	Discharged.
Jack and Andrew,	Caty Whitehead,	Con. and transported.
Jacob,	Geo. H. Charlton,	Disch'd without trial.
Isaac,	Ditto,	Convi. and transported.
Jack,	Everett Bryant,	Discharged.
Nathan,	Benj. Blunt's estate,	Convicted.

Nathan, Tom, and Davy, (boys,)	Nathaniel Francis,	Convicted and transported.
Davy,	Elizabeth Turner,	Convicted.
Curtis,	Thomas Ridley,	Do.
Stephen,	Do.	Do.
Hardy and Isham,	Benjamin Edwards,	Convicted and transp'd.
Sam,	Nathaniel Francis,	Convicted.
Hark,	Joseph Travis' estate.	Do.
Moses, (a boy,)	Do.	Do. and transported.
Davy,	Levi Waller,	Convicted.
Nelson,	Jacob Williams,	Do.
Nat,	Edm'd Turner's estate,	Do.
Jack,	Wm. Reese's estate,	Do.
Dred,	Nathaniel Francis,	Do.
Arnold, Artist, (free,)		Discharged.
Sam,	J.W. Parker,	Acquitted.
Ferry and Archer,	J.W. Parker,	Disch'd without trial.
Jim,	William Vaughan,	Acquitted.
Bob,	Temperance Parker,	Do.
Davy,	Joseph Parker,	
Daniel,	Solomon D. Parker,	Disch'd without trial.
Thomas Haithcock, (free,)		Sent on for further trial.
Joe,	John C. Turner,	Convicted.
Lucy,	John T. Barrow,	Do.
Matt,	Thomas Ridley,	Acquitted.
Jim,	Richard Porter,	Do.
Exum Artes, (free,)		Sent on for further trial.
Joe,	Richard P. Briggs.	Disch'd without trial.
Bury Newsome, (free,)		Sent on for further trial.

APPENDIX

Stephen,	James Bell,	Acquitted.
Jim and Isaac,	Samuel Champion,	Convicted and trans'd.
Preston,	Hannah Williamson,	Acquitted.
Frank,	Solomon D. Parker,	Convi'd and transp'd.
Jack and Shadrach,	Nathaniel Simmons,	Acquitted.
Nelson,	Benj. Blunt's estate,	Do.
Sam,	Peter Edwards,	Convicted.
Archer,	Arthur G. Reese,	Acquitted.
Isham Turner,		Sent on for further trial.
Nat Turner,	Putnam Moore, dec'd,	Convicted.

Index

Aaron, Daniel. See *The Structure of American History*
Abolition (Abolitionists), 41, 210, 268, 281, 286–87, 311
Adams, John Quincy, 195, 221
Africa, (African Roots), 40, 42, 59, 164, 196, 215, 225–29, 238–41, 363–66, 368, 370
The Afro-American Experience: A Cultural History Through Emancipation, (Dormon and Jones), 312–16.
Aker, Homer F., and Varza Aker. See *America: Today and Yesterday*
Alinsky, Saul, 297
America, The Glorious Republic (Graff), 352, 401 (n. 9)
America: Today and Yesterday (Aker, Hilton, and Aker) 302, 303, 304, 398 (n. 2)
American Bicentennial, 329, 331, 333, 336
American Children's Library Association, 304
The American Experience: A Study of Themes and Issues in American History, 353–55, 358, 401 (n. 9)
American Heritage, 285
American History (Garraty), 355, 401 (n. 9)
American Negro Slave Revolts. See Aptheker, Herbert
American Place Theatre, New York, 178, 228
American Revolution, 200, 221, 256, 313, 342
American Scholar, 125, 393 (n. 27)
American Spirit: A History of the United States, 352, 356, 401 (n. 9)
America's Heritage, 352, 355, 401 (n. 9)
America's Story, 355, 401 (n. 9)
Les Amis des noirs, 201
Amistad Mutiny, 221
Amistad-I, 128, 231
Ancrum, Calhoun, See *Charleston [S.C.] News & Courier*
Angelou, Maya. See *I Know Why the Caged Bird Sings*
Anthropology, and cultural history, 313–16, 358–62, 363–66
Apocalypticism, 136
Aptheker, Herbert, 36, 116, 118–20, 129, 134, 152–53, 156, 157, 158, 171, 172, 173, 174, 190, 230, 247, 255, 264, 267, 289, 295, 297, 310, 314, 329, 337, 346, 359, 389 (n. 11), 392 (n. 20), 394 (n. 33); *American Negro Slave Revolts*, 151, 200, 257, 268, 271–82, 297, 375–76, 377, 380, 403 (n. 35); and Styron, 230, 346, 392 (n. 20), 394 (n. 33); *Nat Turner's Slave Rebellion*, 271, 272, 278;. as paradigm-maker, 271–84; contributions to sixties debates, 283–84
Assassinations, 1, 105, 193, 293, 325
Atlanta Constitution, 106, 218
Atlantic Monthly, 23, 107, 181

Aubert, Alvin, 229, 242–43, 347 (n. 41)
The Autobiography of Malcolm X, 168, 271

Babo (in Melville's "Benito Cereno"), 366
Babu (in Lowell's "Benito Cereno"), 223, 224, 225, 226, 227, 228, 229, 366, 396 (n. 23)
Baldwin, James, 3, 105, 110, 122–23, 127, 128, 141, 147, 294, 306
Baraka, Amiri (Leroy Jones), 147, 223, 342–43, 400 (n. 2)
Beacon Press, 26, 126, 148, 153, 169–71, 172, 193, 195
Before the Mayflower: A History of the Negro in America, 1619–1962. See Bennett, Lerone, Jr.
"Benito Cereno" (Lowell), 178, 220–29, 243
"Benito Cereno" (Melville), 178, 220–23, 226–28
Bennett, Lerone, Jr.: *Ten Black Writers Respond*, 127, 129, 130–31, 142, 143, 153, 173; *Before the Mayflower*, 284, 285, 286, 287–92, 296, 297, 318, 325, 335, 398 (n. 22)
Bennett, Tony, 25–27, 67, 104, 326, 382, 388 (nn. 15, 19)
Beveridge, Lowell P., Jr., 299–302, 304, 308
Bible, the: in Styron, 74, 75, 84, 86, 90, 97, 98, 100, 109, 111, 125, 133, 143; in Panger, 181, 184, 187, 189; in Bontemps, 198, 202; in Edmonds, 208, 209; in Peters, 213; in Pawley, 215; in Hayden, 238, 240; in Stuckey, 366

Black History, 129–36, 150–52, 153, 157–59, 163–64, 171–73, 173–74, 199–203, 228–29, 233–34, 243–45, 286–87, 293–97, 300–301, 303–5, 324, 329, 332, 346, 357, 358–62, 368–72, 373, 374, 375–76, 381–82; Franklin, 250–52, 254; Stampp, 256, 258, 260–62, 263; David Brion Davis, 264; Elkins, 266–67, 269; Stuckey, 269, 363–66; Aptheker, 271, 273–84; L. Bennett, 287–92; Dormon and Jones, 312–16; Blassingame, 317–22; Genovese, 322, 338–42, 343–44; Levine, 322–24; Tragle, 325–29; Harding, 330, 333–38, 342–43; Cruse, 393–94 (n. 30)
Black History and the Historical Profession (Meier and Rudwick), 263, 284, 337, 338, 350, 397 (n. 4), 398 (nn. 9, 11, 12, 13, 17), 400 (n. 5)
Black History for Beginners, 357, 401 (n. 13)
Black Nationalism, 232–33, 331, 393–94 (n. 30)
Black Panthers, 221, 331
Black Power (Black Nationalism), 3, 14, 37, 127, 165, 173, 232–33, 325, 351, 393–94 (n. 30)
Black Preachers (Black Religion), 2, 12, 34, 109, 111, 124, 132–34, 140, 143, 164–65, 183, 186–87, 196, 198, 252, 254, 260, 262, 277, 311, 313–15, 322, 323–24, 331, 334–37, 339–40, 342, 355, 360, 363–66. *See also* Turner, Nat; Harding, Vincent
Black Studies, 170, 312, 332
Black Thunder. See Bontemps, Arna
Black World, 27, 128
Blair, John F. (publisher), 179

INDEX 433

Blassingame, John, 313, 316, 317–22, 324, 329, 337, 360, 362, 363, 369, 399 (n. 17)
Blau, Herbert, 172, 394 (n. 44)
Bond, Julian, 234
Bondmaster Series, 89
Bontemps, Arna, 24, 36, 40, 164, 209, 221, 247, 257, 355, 365–66, 367, 368, 373, 375; *Black Thunder*, 33–34, 43, 120, 170, 177, 192–205, 211, 212, 214, 230, 243, 251, 271, 364, 377; *The Story of the Negro*, 304–5, 306
Book-of-the-Month-Club (*BOMC News*), 1, 26, 38, 54, 67, 68–9, 70–71, 72, 73, 76, 372, 390 (nn. 21, 22)
Boston Globe, 153, 168–71, 394 (nn. 41, 42, 47)
Bracey, John, 271, 272
Bradley, David, 331, 366–72, 375, 377, 380, 381
Brantley, Ethelred T., 133–34
Brooks, Gwendolyn, 231, 243
Brown, John, 108, 115, 175, 219, 322, 343
Brown, Rap, 3, 108, 127
Brown, Richard H., 21, 387–88 (n. 13)
Brown, Sterling, 24, 33, 163, 231, 234, 237–38, 243, 362; "Remembering Nat Turner," 177, 230, 234–37, 243
Brown vs. Board of Education of Topeka, Ks, 35, 255
Brown, William Wells, 43, 131, 388 (n. 4)
Buchwald, Art, 112
Butterfield, Roger, 284, 285, 286–87, 292, 295, 347, 398 (n. 21)

Calendar of Virginia State Papers, 200, 203, 395 (n. 14)
Calhoun, John C., 256, 269, 290
Calverton, V. F., 271
Carby, Hazel V., 366–67, 402 (n. 26)
Carmichael, Stokely, 3, 108, 125, 127
Carroll, Joseph C., 271, 397 (n. 8)
Carver, George Washington, 351
Casciato, Arthur: and James West, 44, 389 (n. 5), 392 (n. 1)
Casebooks, 307–8, 399 (nn. 9, 10)
Cash, W. J., 362
Center for Afro-American Studies, UCLA, 333
Chappell, Fred, 35, 158, 247, 328
Charleston [S.C.] News & Courier, 109, 392 (n. 10)
Chestnut, Mary, 219
Chicago Defender, 55
Chicago Sun-Times, 124, 393 (n. 25)
Chicago Tribune Book World, 27, 347
Childress, Alice. See *A Hero Ain't Nothin' but a Sandwich*
Chowan Valley, Va., 23, 49
Chronicles of Negro Protest: A Background Book for Young People, 306–7, 399 (n. 6)
Civil Rights Movement, 15, 35, 73, 105, 108, 111, 118, 150, 216, 221, 234, 272, 287, 293, 312–13, 331, 342–43, 351
Civil War, 48, 52, 158, 159, 221, 253, 281, 362
Clarke, John H., 3, 127, 128, 129–30, 136, 147, 148, 157, 170, 171, 387 (n. 6)
Claud, Percy, 49, 328
Cleaver, Eldridge, 3, 89, 127, 331
Cobb, Jeremiah, 79, 82–85, 87, 97, 112, 138

Cocke, John Hartwell, 361
Coffin, Joshua, 131
Columbia University, 102, 105, 106, 127, 271, 286, 308
The Communist, 274
The Confessions of Nat Turner (Gray), 9, 10, 11, 24, 34, 36, 44, 55, 77–78, 86, 96, 110, 118, 190–91, 193–94, 203, 207, 209, 210, 212, 218, 222, 238, 239, 240, 241, 242, 256, 260, 269, 307, 308, 314, 317, 321, 325, 327, 334, 337, 357, 362, 376, 387 (n. 8); white writer, 10, 23, 55; black preacher-prisoner, 12; as historical document, 24, 25, 34, 42–43, 110, 130–32, 153, 159–60, 174, 292; Styron and, 49–50, 74, 75, 76, 77, 78, 94–95, 113–14, 134, 154, 156, 169, 327–28; Panger and, 183, 185, 187, 189, 190, 204; Aptheker and, 278, 280; Appendix, 407–29
The Confessions of Nat Turner (Styron): reception and controversy, 3–15, 22, 24, 27, 36, 47, 48–49, 101–2, 106–75 passim, 193, 307, 345–50, 382–85; pre-publication and superintendence, 3, 26, 38, 53–54, 55–64, 64–67; author's note, 5, 75–76, 78, 326; as history, 9–10, 31, 50–51, 52–53, 73–74, 75–76, 114–16, 127–36, 321, 324, 326–27, 329; as psychological-spiritual discourse, 9–12, 31, 49–50, 73, 74–75, 80–82, 84–85, 88–89, 90–93, 95–100, 113, 117, 142–47; film contract, 14, 387 (n. 10); as fiction, 17, 33, 78–80, 87, 94–95, 118–19; readerships, 45–47, 67–72, 87–88; and Panger, 180, 184, 187–89, 190–91; and Bontemps, 203–4; and Lowell, 222, 228; and Robert Hayden, 241–42;

and Bradley, 367–68, 371–72; and Sherley Anne Williams, 375–76, 377, 380–81
Contingencies of Value (Smith), 69–70, 390 (n. 20)
Cooke, Michael, 125, 393 (n. 26)
Cowley, Malcolm, 103
The Crisis, 234–35, 396 (n. 31)
Crisis in Black and White (Silberman), 292–97, 398 (n. 23)
Cross-Section: A Collection of New American Writing (Seaver), 209–10
Crowe, Eyre, 353
The Crucible (Miller), 171–72
Cruse, Harold, 147, 166, 393–94 (n. 30)
Cultural History, 30–37, 59, 123–24, 131–34, 140, 164, 171–76, 189–90, 200–202, 225–27, 259–62, 269–70, 282, 296, 312–14, 317–18, 323, 339–40, 353–55, 360–61, 363–65, 377–38, 402 (n. 25)
Cultural Work, 203–4, 206, 219, 229, 230, 234, 243–44, 249–50, 263–64, 283–84, 296–97, 299–301, 302–3, 307–8, 310, 312–14, 328–29, 332–33, 335, 349–50, 351–52, 362, 371–72, 375, 376, 380, 381, 384–86, 390 (n. 16)
Culture, 2, 3, 8, 16, 20–24, 25–26, 29, 30, 35–36, 140, 164, 259–61, 312–14, 323–24, 355, 385–86. *See also* Cultural History; Cultural Work; History and Literature.

DAB (Dictionary of American Biography), 40–41, 42, 54, 78, 388 (n. 3)
Daedalus (magazine), 263, 398 (n. 10)
Davis, Angela, 376, 380, 403 (n. 35)

Davis, David Brion, 125, 263, 264, 267, 269, 270, 272, 284, 317
Davis, Jefferson, 256, 290, 309
Davis, Ossie, 14, 148–50, 180, 209
Dee, Ruby, 14
Delaney, Lloyd, 180
Delano, Amasa, Capt.: *Narrative of Voyages and Travels*, 220, 221, 222, 396 (n. 24); dramatic characterizations of, 222–28
Delany, Martin, 117, 309, 395 (n. 2)
Dennis, Denise. See *Black History for Beginners*
Des Moines Register, 382–83, 403 (n. 40)
Diddie, Dumps, and Tot, 109
Dismal Swamp, Va., 52, 54, 177, 210, 340
Dixon, Thomas, 149
Docudrama, 219
Dominican Republic, 135, 161, 221, 340
Dormon, James H., See *The Afro-American Experience*
Douglass, Frederick, 86, 163, 206, 269, 309, 353, 354, 357
Douglass, H. Ford, 163
Dred: A Tale of the Dismal Swamp (Stowe), 177, 248, 355, 394 (n. 2)
Drewry, William S. See *The Southampton Slave Revolt*
Duberman, Martin, 34, 148–49, 150–52, 221, 348, 355, 381; *In White America*, 178, 216–19, 247, 333, 396 (n. 22)
Du Bois, W. E. B., 43, 254, 264, 296, 304
Duff, John B. See *The Nat Turner Rebellion*

Ebony (magazine), 27, 107, 127, 128, 287, 306
Edmonds, Randolph. See *Six Plays for a Negro Theatre*
Elkins, Stanley, 36, 123, 134, 147, 255, 272, 274, 282, 297, 309, 314, 316, 321, 337, 344, 354, 361; *Slavery: A Problem in American Institutional and Intellectual Life*, 50, 124, 254, 262, 264–71, 283, 284, 285, 289, 294–95, 398 (n. 14)
Ellison, Ralph, 3, 5, 6–7, 9, 15, 16, 17–19, 20, 22, 23, 39, 43, 209, 296, 352, 384
Encyclopedia Britannica, 49, 356–57, 401 (n. 11)
Encyclopedia of Southern Culture, 362, 401 (n. 18)
English Institute, 366–67, 382
Erikson, Erik, 51
Esquire (magazine), 45, 68, 372, 389 (n. 9), 402 (n. 30)

Facts, Historical, 130, 131, 133, 134, 153, 204, 273–74, 326–29
Fadiman, Clifton, 38, 68
Falconhurst Series, 89
Family: in slave society, 40, 59–60, 118–19, 132, 296, 339, 369–70
Fanon, Frantz, 159
Farmer, Ruth, 384
Faulkner, William, 18, 108, 139, 141, 248
Fitzgerald, Frances, 39, 299, 301, 303–4, 350–53, 388 (n. 1)
Foley, Barbara, 368, 402 (n. 28)
Folklore, 18, 23, 43, 164, 314, 322–24, 334, 363–64, 370
Foner, Eric, 270, 308, 399 (n. 10)
Fortune (magazine), 285

Franklin, John Hope, 36, 114, 124, 125, 126, 170, 247, 248–54, 255, 257, 264, 271, 272, 283, 284, 285, 297, 304, 308, 311, 313, 317, 337, 347, 393 (n. 25), 397 (n. 2)
Frazier, E. Franklin, 252, 261, 316
Free blacks, 90–91, 135
Freedomways (magazine), 127, 128, 147, 148, 152, 172, 173, 180, 299, 301, 348, 393 (nn. 30, 31)

Gaither, Frances, 177, 395 (n. 4)
Garnet, Henry Highland, 163, 269, 309, 369
Garraty, John. See *American History*
Garrison, William L., 41, 286, 288, 310, 342, 362. See also *The Liberator*
Garvey, Marcus, 15, 111, 163
Gayle, Addison, Jr., 231
Genovese, Eugene, 13, 89, 152, 157–63, 164, 165, 166–68, 171–76 passim, 270, 311, 316, 322, 324, 325, 329, 330, 337, 338–42, 343, 348, 363, 391 (n. 29), 394 (n. 40), 399 (n. 19), 400 (n. 6)
Giovanni, Nikki, 232, 233, 234
Goffman, Erving, 20, 318, 387 (n. 11)
Gone with the Wind (Mitchell), 14, 50, 58, 103, 104, 302
Gray, Thomas R., 23, 36, 110, 142, 327, 376. See also *The Confessions of Nat Turner* (Gray)

Hackett-Fischer, David, 360
Hairston, Loyle, 128, 136, 139, 142, 143, 180–81
Haiti, 135, 338. *See also* L'Ouverture, Toussaint
Haley, Alex, 168, 271, 332, 333, 376

Hamilton, Charles V., 127, 131, 136
Hamilton, James G. deR., 42, 78, 271
Harding, Vincent, 128, 238, 264, 269, 311, 329, 340, 342, 344, 346, 363, 394 (n. 39), 400 (nn. 3, 4); *Ten Black Writers Respond*, 130–34, 135–36, 139, 142, 143, 150, 152, 157, 162, 163–66, 167, 168, 175, 176, 178; *The Other American Revolution*, 330, 332–36; *There is a River*, 335–38, 343, 349
Harper's (magazine), 45–46, 47, 49, 53, 54, 55–64, 66, 67, 73, 100, 113, 349, 388 (n. 2), 390 (nn. 15, 16)
Hayden, Robert E., 24, 34, 85, 164, 185, 229, 230, 231, 238–42, 243, 244, 307, 396 (nn. 27, 36)
Hayden, Tom, 117–18
Haydn, Hiram, 112
Hernton, Calvin, 89, 162
A Hero Ain't Nothin' but a Sandwich (Childress), 374–75, 380, 402 (n. 32)
Hero and Heroism, 2, 14–15, 26, 64, 86, 103, 145, 149–51, 187, 256, 277, 305, 315, 346
Higginson, Thomas W., 131, 132, 154, 181, 218, 219
Highway Historical Markers, 44–45, 94, 237
Hilton, Eugene. See *America: Today and Yesterday*
Historical Fiction, 2–3, 4–9, 10–11, 16–20 passim, 22–23, 24–25, 33–37, 58, 118, 129–32, 137, 141–42, 150, 154, 156, 171–72, 176, 199, 204–5, 348–50, 366–67, 368, 375–76, 380–81
Historicism (Theories of History), 4–5, 8, 18–19, 51, 75–76, 117–20, 135, 153, 157, 200–201, 248, 250, 256, 263, 269, 276, 283–84, 311,

323, 335, 339, 362, 370–71, 379, 385–86
History (Research and Writing), 5, 10, 17–18, 23–24, 27–28, 45, 48, 118, 130–31, 135, 172–76, 195, 209, 218–19, 220, 241, 254, 280, 288, 292, 318–22, 326–27, 354, 361
History and Literature, 4–9, 11, 12, 16, 18–19, 20, 22, 25–26, 29–30, 31, 35, 53, 73–74, 75–76, 107, 113, 115–16, 129, 137–42, 153, 154, 171–72, 199–204, 214–15, 217–19, 241, 244–45, 273, 276, 286–87, 295–96, 302, 315, 332, 337, 348, 364, 366–67, 376–77
Hofstadter, Richard. See *The Structure of American History*
Hogan, William, 108–9, 126
Holocaust, 100, 265, 266
Homosexuality, 12, 62, 88–91, 132, 133, 146
Howells Medal, 101
Hughes, Langston, 209, 231
Hutchins, John K., 102

Identity, Personal, 2, 116–17, 259–60, 296, 321
Ideology, 42, 129–30, 148–51, 153, 155–56, 157–58, 160, 162–63, 163–64, 170–71, 171–76, 189, 203–4, 209, 210, 214–15, 216, 219, 228–29, 230–33, 234–35, 238, 243, 256, 263, 265, 272–74, 286, 293, 300–301, 302–3, 307–8, 314, 323–24, 333–34, 336, 342, 351–52, 362, 365–66, 369, 372, 377–78, 380, 381–82, 385–86
I Know Why the Caged Bird Sings (Angelou), 373, 375, 380, 402 (n. 31)
Illustrations, 55, 60, 215, 286, 290–91, 306, 321, 351, 353, 357, 383, 396 (n. 23)
Imagination (intuition), 4, 5, 7, 19, 47, 48, 76, 113, 114, 117, 121, 137, 175, 180, 199, 219, 229, 237, 238, 349, 366–67, 376, 380
Imitation, 222
Institute of the Black World, 333, 335
Integration, 162, 165–66, 381–82, 386
Intermediary, White, 120–22, 163, 231
Invisible Man (Ellison), 1, 15
In White America. See Duberman, Martin
Iowa, University of, 215, 353
"I Spit on the Pulitzer" (G. Wilson), 104–6

Jackson, Jesse, 331
Jackson, Luther P., 254
Jacobs, William Jay, 355–56
Jakes, John, 72
James, C. L. R., 264, 341–42
James, G. P. R., 24, 177, 394–95 (n. 2)
Jameson, Frederic, 29, 104, 248, 331, 384, 388 (n. 18), 400 (n. 1)
Jefferson, Thomas, 195, 220, 221
Jerusalem (Courtland), Va., 41, 44, 54, 64, 90, 94, 208, 236, 290, 314, 337
Joan of Arc, 108
Johnson, Charles S., 289, 362
Johnson, Eastman, 353
Johnson, Lyndon, 123, 218
Johnson, F. Roy, 321, 399 (n. 18)
Johnson Publishing Co., 128, 285
Johnston, Mary, 24, 177, 395 (n. 3)
Jones, Robert R., 312–16
Jordan, June Meyer. *See* Meyer, June

Jordan, Winthrop, 125, 201, 270, 395 (n. 17)
Journal of American History, 362, 381, 402 (nn. 20, 24), 403 (n. 38)
Journal of Negro History, 43, 107, 272, 285
Journal of Popular Culture, 107

Kaiser, Ernest, 128, 131, 134, 138, 147, 176, 177
Katz, William, 306
Kauffmann, Stanley, 32
Kenyon Review, 107, 402 (n. 18)
Killens, John O., 128, 130, 131, 136, 137, 139–41, 176
Kilson, Martin, 344, 400–401 (n. 7)
King, Martin L., Jr., 1, 105, 128, 193, 287, 306, 325, 331, 333, 335, 342–43
Kirk, Grayson, 102, 105, 106
Knopf, A. A., 249, 285
Kozol, Jonathan, 122

Lane, Ann, 268, 398 (n. 15)
Language: Styron's fictional, 58–59, 69, 76, 78, 95, 111–12, 133, 138–43; Panger's fictional, 182, 185; Bontemps's fictional, 202–3; Lowell's dramatic-poetic, 222; black poets', 232, 243; Sterling Brown's poetic, 237; Robert Hayden's poetic, 238; Aptheker's historical, 273, 282; Lerone Bennett's historical, 288, 290; Bontemps's historical, 304–5; Morison's historical, 309; Dormon and Jones's historical, 315; Levine's historical, 323; Tragle's historical, 328; Harding's sermonic-historical, 336–37; Styron's non-fictional reflective, 348–49; Stuckey's historical, 364; Bradley's fictional-historical, 369–70; Childress's fictional, 374; S. A. Williams's fictional, 376–77
Lester, Julius, 264, 399 (n. 8)
Levine, Lawrence, 316–17, 322–24, 329, 399–400 (n. 20)
Levitt, Saul, 205
Lewis, David Levering, 362, 381–82, 386, 402 (nn. 20, 24), 403 (nn. 38, 44)
Lewis, R. W. B., 22, 114
Liberal, White, 31, 114, 116, 166, 195
The Liberator, 135, 210, 281, 286, 288, 310. *See also* Garrison, William L.
Library, Public, 40, 43, 44, 76
Lie Down in Darkness (Styron), 55, 68, 101, 109
Life (magazine), 64–67, 68, 73, 100, 210
Lincoln, C. Eric, 306–7
The Little Confederate, 109
Long, Elizabeth, 71–72, 390 (n. 23)
Longfellow, Henry W., 233
The Long March (Styron), 68
Louisiana State University, 338, 343
L'Ouverture, Toussaint, 135, 159, 161, 201, 202, 211, 213, 221, 289, 322, 338, 343, 354
Lovejoy, Elijah P., 286–87
Lowell, Robert, 34, 216, 219–29, 366, 377, 396 (nn. 23, 25)
Lowenfels, Walter, 231–33, 396 (n. 28)
Lukács, Georg, 8, 154, 156
Luther, Martin, 51, 113

MacDowell Award, 383
MacLeish, Archibald, 214
McKay, Claude, 231
McKissick, Floyd, 127

INDEX 439

Madgic, Robert F., See *The American Experience*
Mailer, Norman, 34, 67, 209, 210
Malcolm X, 125, 164, 331, 335. See also *The Autobiography of Malcolm X*
Malone, Dumas, 42
Marxism, 157, 271, 272–75, 277. *See also* Lukács, Georg
Massachusetts Review, 128, 156, 326
Mays, Benjamin, 252
Meier, August. See *Black History and the Historical Profession*
Melville, Herman, 34, 115, 178, 220–29, 248, 355, 366, 377
Merleau-Ponty, Maurice, 129
Meyer, Eric, 383–84
Meyer, June (Jordan), 120–23, 125, 170, 216, 231, 392 (n. 21), 396 (n. 29)
Miller, Arthur, 171–72, 205, 209
Miller, Jonathan, 228–29
Mink, L. O., 72–73, 390 (n. 24)
Minneapolis Star, 108, 392 (n. 8)
Mitchell, Margaret. See *Gone with the Wind*
Mitchell, Peter. See *The Nat Turner Rebellion*
Monroe, James, Gov., 201
Morgan, Edmund, 316, 317
Morgan, James C., 358, 401 (n. 14)
Morgan State College, 206, 209
Morison, Samuel E., 308–10, 321, 399 (n. 11)
Morrison, Toni, 382
Moynihan Report, 119, 261, 354
Mullin, Gerald, 316, 317, 325, 364, 399 (n. 16), 402 (n. 23)
Murray, Albert, 3, 123–24, 126, 170
Muzzey, David, 39
Myrdal, Gunnar, 293

Myth, 6, 14, 15, 19, 48, 175, 233–34, 302, 370

Napoleon, 135
Narrative of Voyages and Travels. See Delano, Amasa, Capt.
Nat, stereotype, 319–21
The Nation, 107, 116–20, 120–22, 147, 152–57, 172, 272, 392 (nn. 18, 19, 20, 21)
National Negro Convention, 288, 369
Nat Turner (Foner), 308, 399 (n. 10)
The Nat Turner Rebellion (Duff and Mitchell), P. M., 307–8, 312, 315, 399 (n. 9)
Negro Digest, 128, 242, 287
Negro History Bulletin, 154, 394 (n. 34)
Negro History Week, 43, 124, 332
Negro Intercollegiate Drama Association, 206
Negro Little Theatre Movement, 206
Negro World, 163
New American Library, 26, 53, 67, 69, 72
New Historicism, 366, 402 (n. 25)
New Leader, 2, 123–24, 393 (n. 24)
New Literary History, 366, 388 (n. 23), 402 (n. 25)
New Masses, 272
New Orleans, 3, 6, 19, 43, 97. *See also* Southern Historical Association
Newport News, 23
New Republic, 114–16, 157, 387 (n. 4)
Newsweek, 2, 122–23, 218
New Testament, 97, 98, 100, 125, 143. *See also* Bible, the
New York Amsterdam News, 27, 53–55, 104–6, 169, 389 (n. 13), 392 (n. 6)

New Yorker, 125, 299
New York Herald Tribune, 231
New York: Past and Present, 301
New York Review of Books, 50, 67, 72, 89, 107, 121, 147, 152, 156–68, 170, 172, 322, 340, 348, 389 (n. 11), 391 (n. 29), 392–93 (n. 22), 394 (nn. 39, 40)
New York Story, 301
New York Times, 2, 67, 69, 102, 106, 110–14, 147, 148–52, 170, 171, 218, 231, 362, 382, 387 (n. 5), 390 (n. 19), 392 (nn. 12, 14), 394 (n. 32), 402 (n. 19), 403 (n. 39)
Novick, Peter, 249, 284, 397 (n. 3)

Oates, Stephen B., 324, 329, 400 (n. 25)
O'Connell, Shaun, 116–18, 392 (n. 18)
The Old Glory. *See* Lowell, Robert
Old Testament, 64, 97, 133, 143, 208. *See also* Bible, the
Olmsted, Frederick L., 44, 262, 264, 355, 389 (n. 5)
Olsen, James E., 316, 399 (n. 14)
Onstott, Kyle, 89
Our Blood and Tears: Black Freedom Fighters (R. Wilson), 356
Owens, Leslie, 316, 337
Oxford History of the American People. *See* Morison, Samuel E.

Panger, Daniel, 24, 34, 179–92, 195, 204, 205, 210, 215, 243, 395 (nn. 7, 8, 10, 11)
Parker, Roy, Jr., 48–49, 110, 389 (n. 10), 392 (n. 11)
Partisan Review, 194, 395 (n. 13)
Paternalism, 159, 258–59
Pawley, Thomas, 178, 205, 215, 221, 395 (n. 5)

Per Se (magazine), 53, 389 (n. 12)
Peters, Paul, 24, 34, 177, 205, 209–15, 221, 257, 395 (n. 4)
Phillips, Ulrich B., 35, 130, 249, 250, 251, 255, 263, 264, 278, 289, 303, 321, 337
Phylon (magazine), 246, 400 (n. 7)
Playboy (magazine), 107, 112, 392 (n. 13)
Plimpton, George, 112–14, 325, 392 (nn. 13, 14)
Politics, Cultural, 2–3, 7, 72–74, 110–12, 286–87, 295–97, 302–3, 307–8, 334–36, 351–57, 362, 372, 380–82, 384–86
Poussaint, Alvin, 128, 142–47, 198–99, 325
Powledge, Fred, 306, 399 (n. 5)
Prosser, Gabriel, 33, 194, 199, 200, 202, 203, 221, 237, 251, 256, 257, 267, 268, 289, 295, 300, 304, 305, 322, 339, 340, 342, 354, 357, 360, 364, 365, 366, 395 (nn. 14, 15, 16). *See also* Bontemps, Arna: *Black Thunder*
Psychology, 142–47, 156–57, 175
Publisher's Weekly, 2, 68, 387 (n. 1)
Pulitzer Prize, 1, 14, 34, 67, 88, 101–6, 120, 169
Putnam's (magazine), 178

Quarles, Benjamin, 105, 125–26, 264

Racism, 2, 15, 17–19, 105, 113, 120–26, 138, 146, 149, 264, 293, 296, 346–47, 381–82
Radway, Janice, 70–71, 390 (nn. 21, 22)
Rage, Black, 92, 121–22, 143–44, 147–48, 160, 172–74, 184, 289, 319–20, 337, 341, 373, 374

Rahv, Philip, 121–22, 392–93 (n. 22)
Raines, Howell, 362, 402 (n. 19)
Raleigh [N.C.] News & Observer, 48–49, 389 (n. 10), 392 (n. 11)
Random House, 1, 45, 54, 67, 68, 112, 117
Rape, 11, 59–60, 91–92, 160–61, 190, 201, 278
Ratner, Marc, 33, 388 (n. 22)
Rawick, George, 253, 316, 397 (n. 6)
Readers, 16, 38–39, 43, 47, 53–54, 55, 64–65, 67–72, 76–77, 87–88, 102–4, 154, 163–64, 166, 249, 255, 284–85, 286, 287, 297, 306, 307, 332, 343, 349–50, 362, 372, 381, 383–84. *See also* Reading Formations
Reader's Digest, 285, 287
Reading Formations, 21, 25–27, 28–29, 30, 32–33, 54–55, 67–100 passim, 101–7, 171–76, 214–15, 230–33, 263, 271, 307–8, 317, 324–25, 331–32, 335, 343, 348, 352–53, 356–57, 382–86. *See also* Readers
Rebellion in Newark, 117–18
The Red Cock Crows (Gaither), 177, 395 (n. 4)
Redding, J. Saunders, 44, 125, 126
Reed, Ishmael, 367
Religion, 2, 51–52, 85, 97, 99–100, 132–34, 143, 164–65, 183–85, 194, 219, 254, 305, 311, 313, 323, 335–37, 339–40, 360, 364, 374, 377; *See also* Bible, the
Reviews and Book Reviewing, 106–76 passim
Revolt: Insurrection and Revolution, 2, 40–41, 75, 135, 143–44, 156, 158, 196, 228, 257–58, 273, 276, 286, 292, 314, 318, 369
Richmond, Va., 188, 195, 197, 201, 278, 292, 327

Ridley, Thomas, Major, 44–45, 90, 94, 119, 153, 327
Robinson, Ophelia, 34, 229, 233–34, 243, 396 (n. 30)
Rodman, Selden, 231
Rose, Peter I., 324–25, 400 (n. 22)
Roxbury, Conn., 45
Rubin, Joan Shelley, 70, 72, 390 (n. 21)
Rudwick, Elliot. See *Black History and the Historical Profession*

Sambo, 134, 140, 147, 250, 265–67, 270, 294, 319–20, 354
San Francisco Chronicle, 108–9, 114, 392 (nn. 9, 15)
Saturday Review, 147, 170, 231, 232
Science and Society, 272
Scott, Walter, Sir, 8
Scottsboro Boys, 193
Seaver, Edwin, 209, 395 (n. 4), 396 (n. 21)
Set this House on Fire (Styron), 68
Sex, 2, 12, 52, 61–62, 89, 92, 113, 123, 124, 146, 155, 161, 165, 199, 201, 222, 372, 378, 383–85
Sex and Racism in America (Hernton) 89, 162
Sexual repression, 52, 113, 125, 190
Shaap, Dick, 114
Sharpe, Sam, 341, 344
Sheed, Wilfred, 2, 110–12, 121, 392 (n. 12)
Sherman, John K., 108, 392 (n. 8)
Shugg, Roger, W., 249
Silberman, Charles, 284, 285–86, 292–97, 306, 398 (n. 23)
Simpson, Louis, 231
Singal, Daniel, 362, 401–2 (n. 18)
Singer, Isaac B., 102
Six Plays for a Negro Theatre: "Nat

Six Plays for a Negro Theatre (cont.)
  Turner" Edmonds, 24, 33, 34, 177, 178, 205, 206–9, 210, 215, 243, 396 (n. 20)
Slave Narratives, 248, 317–20; *See also* Douglass, Frederick
Slavery, 2, 13–14, 43–44, 50–51, 59, 76, 82–83, 115, 130, 135, 136, 150, 152, 156–58, 255–63, 302–3, 309, 317–22, 339–42
Smith, Barbara Herrnstein, 25, 27–29, 69–70, 72, 79, 326, 388 (n. 17), 390 (n. 20)
Social Studies, 125, 393 (n. 28)
Sokolov, R. A., 122, 387 (n. 2), 390 (n. 14), 393 (n. 23)
Sophie's Choice (Styron), 344
The Souls of Black Folk (Du Bois), 304
Southern Christian Leadership Conference (SCLC), 336
Southern Historical Association (SHA), 1–23, 39, 68, 73, 97, 244, 376, 384; *See* "The Uses of History in Fiction"
Southern Literary Journal, 20–22, 387 (n. 7)
Southampton County, Va., 45–52, 207–9, 210, 235–37
Southampton Slave Revolt, 10–11, 34, 40–45 passim, 52–53, 54, 64–66, 75–76, 94–96, 115, 119, 136, 182–92, 207–9, 210–14, 215, 218–19, 236, 252–53, 256–58, 266–67, 275–81, 286, 290–92, 295, 300, 304–5, 307–8, 310, 311, 315–16, 320–21, 325, 326–29, 336–37, 339, 373, 397 (n. 8), 400–401 (n. 7)
Stair, Gabin, 167–70, 394 (n. 42)
Stamberg, Susan, 383–84
Stampp, Kenneth, 36, 247, 254–64, 271, 283, 284, 285, 289, 290, 294–95, 297, 313, 316, 321, 329, 355, 357, 397 (nn. 7, 8), 398 (n. 19)
Starobin, Robert, 264, 364
Stowe, Harriet Beecher, 34, 177, 248, 355, 394 (n. 2)
The Structure of American History (Hofstadter, Miller, and Aaron), 308–9, 310–12, 321, 399 (n. 12)
Stuckey, Sterling, 269, 271, 328, 358, 363–66, 369, 400 (n. 5), 402 (n. 22)
Stuckey, William F., 102–4, 392 (n. 2)
Styron, William, 1–19, 21, 22; his "meditation on history," 7, 31–99 passim; ten black writers criticism of, 126–47; and counter-arguments to ten black writers, 147–76; and comparisons with other writers, 178, 179, 180, 181, 184, 185, 186, 187–91, 192, 193, 195, 199, 201, 203, 204, 210, 215, 216, 222; black poets and, 230, 235, 237, 241–42; historians and, 246–47, 249, 258, 264, 307, 321, 324, 325, 326–28, 329; recent responses to, 331, 334, 340, 343, 355, 357, 358, 367–68, 372, 375, 376, 377, 381, 382–85; recent statements by, 344–50
Sunday Edition, National Public Radio, 383–85

Tannenbaum, Frank, 50, 118, 134, 264, 389 (n. 11)
Taylor, Councill S., 335
Taylor, Robert, 168–71, 175, 394 (n. 41)
Taylor, William R., 22
Teacher's Guide to American Negro History (Katz), 306
Ten Black Writers Respond (Clarke), 3, 9, 26, 32, 36, 120, 126–47, 148–

INDEX **443**

52, 153, 156, 157–76, 264, 335, 346–48, 387 (n. 6)
Textbooks, History, 39–40, 299–301, 302–4, 306–8, 308–12, 312–16, 331, 350–57, 388 (n. 1), 401 (nn. 9, 10, 12, 13)
Thelwell, Mike, 128, 131, 134–35, 136–37, 138, 140–42, 147, 150, 152, 155, 156, 157, 158, 160, 167, 173, 174, 325
There Is a River, 335–38, 343, 349
Third Reich, 52, 79–80, 100, 159, 265, 266, 294
"This Quiet Dust" (Styron), 45–53, 58–59, 73–74, 90, 175, 344–50, 358, 388 (n. 2)
Thompson, Iowa, School Board, 382–83, 403 (nn. 40, 41)
Time (magazine), 2, 122, 218
Tolson, Melvin, 231
Tompkins, Jane, 204, 243, 395–96 (n. 18), 397 (n. 45)
Toomer, Jean, 231
Tragle, Henry I., 10, 34, 49, 325–29, 337, 348, 387 (n. 9), 400 (n. 23)
Trilling, Lionel, 386, 403 (n. 43)
Turner, Nat: as literary character, 1, 2, 5, 9, 11, 12, 21, 22, 23, 24–25, 27, 29, 38, 46–47, 54, 55–63, 64–67, 73–74, 74–100, 177–79, 179–92, 203–5, 205–15, 218–19, 230, 233–45, 248, 369, 373, 374, 375, 385–86, 387 (n. 6), 393 (n. 29); as historical figure, 2, 3, 9, 10, 13, 14, 23–24, 26, 29, 30–37, 38–45, 48–49, 50–53, 64, 73–74, 101, 104–76 passim, 193–94, 247, 249, 252–54, 256–63 passim, 265–71, 272–82, 283, 286, 290–92, 295, 300, 303, 304–5, 307–8, 310–11, 314–16, 317–22, 322–24, 325, 326–29, 334, 336–37, 339–42, 345–49, 354–57, 358–61, 365, 382–84, 385–86, 387 (n. 8), 388 (n. 2), 397 (n. 8), 398 (n. 18), 399 (nn. 9, 10), 400 (n. 23); as religious fanatic, 13, 40, 51–52, 77–78, 108, 113, 132–33, 241, 256, 290, 314–15, 322, 323–24, 337
Twain, Mark, 77, 139, 377
Twentieth Century Fox, 14, 210

Uncle Remus, 296, 319
Uncle Tom, 145, 319
Underground Railroad, 367, 368, 369, 377
"The Uses of History in Fiction," 1–19, 20, 387 (n. 7). *See also* Southern Historical Association; *Southern Literary Journal*

Vesey, Denmark, 191–92, 193, 252, 257, 267, 268, 289, 295, 300, 304, 305, 310, 323, 339, 340, 342, 357, 365, 369
Vietnam War, 37, 331
Village Voice, 148
Virginia, 39, 80, 83, 158, 164, 253, 279, 355
Visions, 12, 40, 60, 185–86, 194, 207, 239–40, 256, 314

Walker, Alice, 125, 126, 382
Walker, David, 135, 252, 269, 309, 336–37, 343, 357, 365
Walker, Margaret, 164, 367
Ward, Samuel Ringgold, 164
Warner, Samuel, 131, 378 (n. 5)
Warren, Robert Penn, 1, 5–6, 7, 8, 16, 17, 26–27, 68, 123, 388 (n. 16)
Washington, Booker T., 206, 309
Washington, George, 200, 251, 280, 302

Washington Post, 106, 114
Wesley, Charles H., 254, 264
West, James L. W., III, 44, 344
White, Hayden, 244, 248, 397 (n. 47)
White, Poppy Cannon, 104
White, Robert, 55, 60
In White America. *See* Duberman, Martin
Whitehead, Margaret: as literary character, 10–11, 12, 43, 82, 86–87, 90, 92, 93, 95–96, 97, 98–99, 117, 138, 146, 155, 161–62, 164–65, 168, 187, 190, 315; as historical figure, 12, 49, 73, 79, 96, 155, 321, 328
Wilberforce University, 169
Williams, George Washington, 43, 234, 274, 388–89 (n. 4)
Williams, John A., 128, 135, 137–39, 176
Williams, Sherley A., 331, 367, 375–81, 385, 402 (n. 33), 403 (n. 34)
Wilson, Gertrude, 104–6
Wilson, Ruth, 356, 401 (n. 10)
Winks, Robin, 353, 401 (n. 9)
Wise, Gene, 248, 397 (n. 1)

Wish, Harvey, 271, 399 (n. 8)
Wood, Peter H., 316, 317, 399 (n. 16)
Woodson, Carter G., 43, 254, 264, 389 (n. 4)
Woodward, C. Vann, 1, 2, 4–5, 8, 14, 15, 16, 17, 18, 20, 114–16, 118, 123, 125, 157, 244, 303, 317, 326, 387 (n. 4), 390 (n. 25)
Woodward, William E., 302–3, 398 (n. 3)
The Worker, 107
Wright, Jay, 117, 230
Wright, Richard, 40, 194, 197, 296
Writers and Readers Documentary Comic Books, 357, 401 (n. 13)
Wyatt-Brown, Bertram, 358–62, 363, 366, 401 (n. 15)

Yale Alumni Magazine, 114, 390–91 (n. 25), 392 (n. 16)
Yale Review, 107, 125, 393 (n. 26)
Yerby, Frank, 58, 72

Zinn, Howard, 335